Business Challenging Business Ethics:
New Instruments for Coping with Diversity
in International Business

The 12th Annual EBEN Conference

Edited by
JACEK SÓJKA
Adam Mickiewicz University, Poznan, Poland

and

JOHAN WEMPE
Erasmus University, Rotterdam, The Netherlands,
KPMG, Ethics & Integrity Consulting, Amstelveen, The Netherlands

Reprinted from *Journal of Business Ethics*, Volume 27, Nos. 1–2 (September 2000)

Kluwer Academic Publishers
Dordrecht / Boston / London

Table of Contents

A C.I.P. Catalogue record for this book is available from the Library of Congress.

ISBN 0-7923-6586-0

Published by Kluwer Academic Publishers,
P.O. Box 17, 3300 AA Dordrecht, The Netherlands.

Sold and distributed in the U.S.A. and Canada
by Kluwer Academic Publishers,
101 Philip Drive, Norwell, MA 02061, U.S.A.

In all other countries, sold and distributed
by Kluwer Academic Publishers,
P.O. Box 322, 3300 AH Dordrecht, The Netherlands.

Printed on acid-free paper

Printed in the Netherlands.

Business Challenging Business Ethics: New Instruments for Coping with Diversity in International Business

The 12th EBEN Annual Conference was held in Amsterdam from the 1st to the 3rd of September 1999. It was organised by the European Institute for Business Ethics (EIBE) and the Nijenrode University. The conference facilities of the Grand Hotel, the old city hall located in the centre of Amsterdam, proved to be a perfect venue for the main event and for other social activities.

The purpose of this conference was to bring to the attention of business people and business ethicists the fact that today's business has been frequently challenged by different interest groups, academic circles, consumer organisations and media regarding its ethical performance. How business responds to this demanding task was the subject of many plenary sessions and concurrent workshops which gave to their participants a unique opportunity to witness the exchange of views among the representatives of business, academia, public sector and NGOs. What is worth mentioning in this connection is the very high proportion of non-academics registered at the conference which was in full harmony with the original ideals of European Business Ethics Network (EBEN) and in itself an important achievement of EBEN's 12th Annual Conference.

Since its foundation in 1987, the European Business Ethics Network – as a non-profit association of business people, public sector managers and academics – has been dedicated to promoting research relating to business ethics and value-based management, organising conferences and encouraging the establishment of national or regional networks. The presentations and discussions which took place during the 12th EBEN Annual Conference were yet another realisation of EBEN's mission. The Amsterdam Conference was also an opportunity to held a General Assembly of EBEN members.

This issue of "Journal of Business Ethics" offers a selection of papers presented at the conference. The range of topics reflects the challenge posed by the complicated nature of international business. The papers not only pose questions and analyse possible types of business response to growing expectations that it should become more aware of its new, global responsibilities, but also gave many hope raising examples of the new policies, methods and instruments which business has already started to use.

The articles in this issue can be arranged in three following groups:

(1) The pressure on management and the response of companies – with contributions by Henk J.L. van Luijk, John Rosthorn, Bryan W. Husted and David B. Allen, André Nijhof, Olaf Fisscher and Jan Kees Looise, Laura J. Spence and José Félix Lozano, Reggy Hooghiemstra, Robert van Es and Tiemo L. Meijlink, and Eberhard Schnebel.

(2) Coping with cultural diversity – with contributions by Gael McDonald, Chris J. Moon and Peter Woolliams, Mari Meel and Maxim Saat, and Warren French and Alexander Weiss.

(3) Overcoming companies' self-interest – with contributions by Peter Koslowski, Rodger Spiller, John Kaler, José Félix Lozano, Alejo José G. Sison, Yves Fassin, and Wesley Cragg.

Jacek Sójka
Johan Wempe

In Search of Instruments.
Business and Ethics Halfway

Henk J. L. van Luijk

ABSTRACT. Business ethics has gradually acquired a stable status, both as an academic discipline and as a practice. Stakeholdership is recognised as a guiding concept, business has widely accepted that it has a license to operate to win from society at large, and operational instruments such as codes of ethics and forms of ethical auditing and accounting take shape more and more. Yet lacunae remain. Three are mentioned explicitly. Business ethics has to improve its relations with business law, the concept of competition deserves much more ethical attention than it has received up to now, and the shifting relations between the market, governmental agencies and civil society require the elaboration of an institutional business ethics.

KEY WORDS: business law, codes of ethics, competition, ethical auditing and accounting, institutional business ethics, stakeholdership

Introduction

What happened, that today we are not really surprised seeing top executives publicly discuss issues of ethics in business? Ten or fifteen years

Henk van Luijk is emeritus professor of business ethics. In 1984 he was appointed at Nyenrode University, Breukelen, The Netherlands as the first full professor of business ethics in Europe. From 1987 to 1997 he was chairman of EBEN, the European Business Ethics Network. From 1994 to 2000 he served as academic director of EIBE, the European Institute of Business Ethics at Nyenrode University. He is the author of five books and co-editor of five others. He published over one hundred chapters and articles in his field, among others in Journal of Business Ethics, Business Ethics Quarterly, Business Ethics. A European Review, *and in Dutch journals.*

ago this would have been a rather remarkable event. Have business leaders, all of a sudden, seen the light? Have business ethicists finally found the golden key to the board room? No, what we are watching is not the happy end of a fairy tale. It is an episode in a chain of strenuous efforts to place "ethics" or "corporate responsibility" on the business agenda. An episode, for there is more needed, and more to come. Or, to put it in the form of a thesis: for ethics to be firmly rooted in daily business practices, a public discussion is needed, but, on top of that, well-designed *instruments* are needed, to make ethical intentions operational in real-life business relations. Constructive *criticisms* are needed, to keep all parties alert. And genuine *commitments* are needed, to avoid gallery play and opportunism, be it of an academic or of a business nature. I include the thesis of the triple need of instruments, criticisms and commitments in the simple title of my contribution: *In search of instruments. Business and ethics halfway*, for criticisms and commitments too can be seen as a kind of instruments. To defend the thesis I first look back to how we got to where we are today. I then count our blessings, to follow up with remarks about what is still lacking and how we could fill the gaps. In due course it will become clear also who I mean when I say "we". For the time being, let "we" stand for *us*, as we are present here, whatever our background and functions.

In brief retrospect

Two developments have greatly contributed to the present state of affairs with regard to ethics in business. First: "Responsibility", and more specifically "Social Responsibility", has become a major theme in the social discourse of present-day Western societies. And second: business ethics as an academic discipline has matured to such an extent that it is now able to provide a vocabulary and a set of instruments with which we can not only discuss ethics in business in an articulated way but also work on it effectively. I elaborate both developments.

"Responsibility" is seen today as a central concept *and* a major requirement, in society at large, and in business relations more specifically. For several reasons. In society at large, because a shift has taken place, from clearly located public authorities as sources of moral guidelines to individuals and groups designing their own concepts of life and action. Political, moral and religious authorities have seen their directive power largely evaporating without people becoming moral orphans. Call it secularisation, call it individualisation, call it emancipation, but don't call it moral degeneration. For never before in this outgoing century have moral questions attracted so much attention, and required so much mental and social energy. Out of sheer necessity, to a large extent. Moral and political leadership is withering away, science and technology confront us with totally new decisions to be taken, and globalisation, understood as ever increasing interdependencies on a global scale, links us with parties and powers that we are hardly able to influence but that do have a serious impact on our realm of action. In this situation, firmly determining where we stand and who we want to be is not a luxury but a question of survival. People increasingly recognise that they have to assume responsibility for their own life and functioning, and for the future of at least the next two or three generations, and they expect others to do the same. For this to become part and parcel of one's mental setup, education is needed, together with a degree of economic stability, if not prosperity. But where these conditions are more or less fulfilled, as in the Western world today, no one is entitled anymore to refuse his or her social responsibility, be he or she a politician, a public administrator, a teacher, a craftsman, or a business person. Or a business organisation, for that sake.

If we now blow up this picture, and look more closely at the business world, a very striking development becomes visible. Since three or four decades already, we are accustomed to the fact that business, or the market, has acquired a dominant position, compared to the other two basic institutions of our social fabric, government and civil society. Really striking, however, is the change that only recently has taken place in the *colour* of that dominance. In the late seventies and early eighties, business, especially big business, was glaringly coloured by isolation, arrogance, and social disinterest. Today, the market is two or three times more powerful than it was twenty years ago. Yet, arrogance and isolation have largely be replaced, maybe not by modesty and deep social involvements, but at least by the sober recognition that business "has a licence to operate to win from society at large", to use the wordings of the Anglo/Dutch Shell company. And this licence will only be awarded as long as a corporation is prepared to take its share in the total social responsibility that keeps our social fabric running. In their best-selling book: *The Commanding Heights* Yergin and Stanislaw (1998) have formulated five critical tests that together define what it means for the market to take its share in the total social responsibility. First: Does the market deliver growth, higher standards of living, better quality services, and jobs? Second: Is the economic success distributed fairly? Third: Is the new global economy capable of upholding the national identity especially of less powerful nations? Four: Is it capable and willing to ensure the environment? And five: Can it cope with demographic developments, the globally increasing numbers, differently spread, of both youngsters and elderly people? For market activities, being confronted with these tests largely suffices to discourage any arrogance.

Or, to put it in one more way: studying this state of affairs I recently found three books on my desk with strikingly similar titles, all published in the last one to three years. In an arbitrary order: Will Hutton: *The Stakeholding Society* (1999), Michael Power: *The Audit Society* (1997), and Avishai Margalit: *The Decent Society* (1996). The three books have one message in common: Corporate *decency* today means taking into account the rights and interests of your *stake-holders*, and being prepared to subject corporate behaviour to an open *auditing* process. This may sound like an idealistic principle. But it is also a very realistic social requirement. And that is new in business.

To count our blessings

Some of us will be inclined to count this shift toward responsibility as already a part of our blessings, and rightly so. For the standing public requirement itself is an incitement to an active participation of the market in the shaping of our common future. But for this participation to be effective, instruments are needed, well suited to transform social expectations into practical operations and institutions. Here the second development that I mentioned earlier comes to the fore: the maturing of business ethics as an academic discipline. And here, so it seems, we have indeed some blessings to count.

During the last fifteen to twenty years people active in the field of business ethics have worked hard to develop a vocabulary and a set of instruments as an enhancement of social consciousness and moral competence in business. Their contributions are of both a conceptual and an operational nature. By way of example I elaborate two central concepts and the impact they have on the development of operational devices.

The first concept is the already mentioned notion of *stakeholders*. In a sense it is *the* core concept of business ethics, if not of ethics in general. For behaving morally, taking a moral point of view, comes down to taking into account the rights and interests of all parties concerned, parties that nowadays are commonly designed as *stakeholders*. In fact, the debate on corporate social responsibility has as its point of departure the very question: Who are the stakeholders of the corporation? Which individuals and groups can legitimately claim that their rights and interests are taken into account in the decision processes of a company or branch? The answer has a bearing on very concrete issues: Are human rights in Burma to be considered a Western businessman's burden? Should the

prospects of future generations also in the twenty second century be included in the business decisions of today?

But does business ethics answer these questions? Not really, but fundamentally yes. Not really, through the provision, that is, of one definite and final list of stakeholders: employees yes, applicants no; people asking for political asylum yes, asking for economic asylum no; vertebrate animals yes, non-vertebrate no – such a list. This is as ridiculous as it sounds.

Fortunately, in two ways business ethics contributes to finding a more substantial answer. First: by indicating that stakeholder theories vary in range: the *narrow* variant, not often defended anymore, that includes only shareholders and shareholders value; the *medium-range* variant, frequently defended, that includes all categories that take a share in the economic risks, so shareholders, employees and suppliers; and the *open* variant, now increasingly defended outside and inside business, that includes all parties directly or indirectly affected by the transactions of the company. The second contribution is the insight that it is not the *list* that matters most, but the *justification* of a list under given circumstances. And this justification should not be based on political or social preferences of the company board, but on well-argued statements about whom the corporation is prepared to consider as its stakeholders, and to what extent, statements that subsequently are submitted to public criticism in an open debate.

Earlier I indicated that business ethics in its maturing form not only makes *conceptual* tools available, but also an increasing number of *operational* instruments. We should think here of devices like corporate codes, auditing and accounting procedures, and training sessions meant to enhance the moral competence of people in business. This whole conference is intended to share and discuss experiences with precisely these kinds of instruments, in the assumption that this is what business is looking for. In fact, it is what business is saying itself. In the very first years of its existence, EBEN, the European Business Ethics Network, had an Advisory Council composed of senior executives from all over Europe. One of them was an elder

Italian CEO who, contrary to his national character, was not a very talkative person. In the highly academic discussions about the nature and prospects of business ethics, his contribution often consisted in just one disturbing question: "But, gentlemen, what are your saleable goods?" It took the network years to come up with a saleable answer. Sir Geoffrey Chandler, former director of Shell International and initiator, in 1976, of the first Statement of General Business Principles of the Shell Company, recently pleaded urgently to standardize the measuring and reporting of non-financial issues in business as a whole. This would make comparisons possible, and development – or the lack of it – visible. But there is a risk involved too in standardization. Experience teaches that the efforts an organisation makes to list for itself its stakeholders and to define its pattern of responsibilities are extremely valuable in order to raise the corporate consciousness and commitment. Externally imposed standardization could easily block this process. So again there appears a tension between the conceptual and the operational contributions of business ethics.

Something similar occurs with regard to a second recently developed central concept, a pair of concepts this time. In a seminal article on *Managing for Organizational Integrity*, published in 1994, Lynn Sharp Paine distinguishes two ethical strategies: a *compliance* strategy and an *integrity* strategy. The distinction has been broadly adopted as standing for managing by rules and managing by self-regulation based on shared convictions respectively. As an operational consequence on the level of codes of conduct, a distinction is then made between *limiting* codes and *aspirational* codes, which strikes many as a perfectly sensible distinction. Yet a serious risk is implied here. For reflection *and* experience teach us that rules can be *imposed*, externally or internally, but can also be *accepted* voluntarily, in which case they are not felt as limiting anymore. And self-regulation can stay confined *inside the organisation*, once the members have reached shared convictions about how to behave. But it can also be the result of a critical exchange with *outside stakeholders* about legitimate expectations and deeply cherished values. This being the case,

the nature of codes, and the ways they can be applied, or the sequences in auditing procedures become obviously more complicated. To that extent, the blessing turns into a blessing in disguise. Sometimes it even may remind us of the remark Winston Churchill made when he was unexpectedly defeated in the first post-war elections in Britain. His wife called it a blessing in disguise, but Churchill responded that then the blessing was "quite effectively disguised".

In the relation between business and business ethics important progress has been made, concepts are clarified, valuable instruments are designed or under construction. There are quite some blessings to count. But the present search for instruments risks to yield adverse effects when, in order to make them user-friendly, the instruments are cut off from basic notions that, by definition, first complicate things before clarifying them at a deeper level.

Lacunae and prospects

Things even get worse, I am afraid, when we notice that, on the deeper but also on the instrumental level, some serious lacunae are to be found, – the third and shortest part of my contribution, as I announced earlier. I restrict myself to three lacunae.

The first is mainly of an instrumental nature, the fact namely that in theory as well as in practice connections with the realm of *law*, and specifically of *business law*, are virtually non-existent. The brand-new *Encyclopedic Dictionary of Business Ethics* (1997) lacks an article on law or business law. It only recommends an ethical code for lawyers. Business ethicists fiercely defend their proper domain against any legal invasion, out of fear maybe to loose their job, or out of misplaced self-confidence that they can handle the social control of corporate behavior all by themselves. None of the two is correct. Business ethics and business law have to cooperate where control, compliance and enforcement is required, but also where sensitivity is needed in order to know what deserves explicit legal regulation and what can better be left to the moral forces of decency, commitment, and responsibility. Covenants, codes and mission statements are powerful moral devices. But it helps sometimes when they also prove to be legally relevant, and can be successfully referred to in court. And inversely, obedience to the law is greatly supported when an organisation makes it into one of its basic moral principles. There is no valid reason why the two domains should be kept so frenetically separated as they have been up to now.

The second lacuna is predominantly of a conceptual nature. What I have in mind here is the still more surprising fact that business ethics as an academic discipline up till now has not seriously studied the issue of *competition*. Competition is the motor of market transactions, but is it morally acceptable? If morality, also market morality, is about respecting the rights and interests of other parties, allowing them the same space for action we require for ourselves, how can this be combined with the attempt to outstrip them in every possible respect under the motto that winner takes all? And if there is a morally acceptable form of competitiveness, on what moral principles is it based, and where does it end? Moral science is deadly silent in these questions.

The last lacuna I want to mention is neither of an instrumental nor of a conceptual nature. It is even more serious, for it is *institutional*. With eyes wide shut business ethics is witnessing the institutional revolution that takes place at this very turning of the century. The basic institutions of our social fabric, government, the market and civil society, are profoundly rearranging their mutual relations, power, and functions. New configurations emerge, public/private partnerships, creative alliances between governmental agencies and market parties, between market players and NGO's, promising but ephemeral often, attempts to find new solutions for incompletely defined problems. Political scientists are studying these institutional ground swells, some professionals of administrative sciences are. Hardly any business ethicist is. And yet, if there is one domain that needs to be redefined in order to determine the range of corporate responsibilities today, it is the domain where the market, civil society and the government meet and clash

and recommence. At the end of the day, ethics in business depends not primarily on individual and collective moral competence, nor on a positive corporate moral climate, a well-balanced code or an open auditing system. It depends on the courage and commitment of all social players to take part in the design of a new and flexible social blueprint that enables all parties to stand the fivefold test of Yergin and Stanislaw I mentioned earlier: to deliver higher standards of living, and jobs; to distribute welfare fairly; to uphold national identities; to protect the environment; and to cope with demographic developments.

I started with a thesis about a triple need, of instruments, criticisms and commitments. Instruments we discussed extensively, commitments were supposed all the way long. But what about criticisms? Allow me a last remark in this respect. I hesitate to voice it, for I know that it is inconsistent, contradictory, ungrateful and unfair. So I will keep it short. What every now and then I miss among parties involved in the issue of ethics in business is a serious fight. Sincerely trying to understand what is going on in business, to do justice to demands and requirements that live there, determined to keep the flag of dialogue waving, we, ethicists, risk to come too close to our sparring partners, where a critical distance suits us better. On our business card it should say: "To be of any use, we take it that objections are allowed and reproaches tolerated". And than see what happens. What *could* happen is that we succeed in constructing a kind of *quarrel platform*. I agree, it is an inconsistent and ungrateful suggestion. Maybe that is what makes it so exciting.

References

Hutton, W.: 1999, *The Stakeholding Society. Writings on Politics and Economics*. Edited by David Goldblatt (Polity Press).

Luijk, H. van: 1999, 'Business Ethics in Europe: A Tale of Two Efforts', in R. Frederick (ed.), *A Companion to Business Ethics* (Blackwell, Cambridge MA/Oxford), pp. 643–658.

Margalit, A.: 1996, *The Decent Society* (Harvard University Press, Cambridge MA).

Power, M.: 1997, *The Audit Society. Rituals of Verification* (Oxford University Press).

Sharp Paine, L: 1994, 'Managing for Organizational Integrity', *Harvard Business Review* (March–April), 106–117.

Sharp Paine L.: 1997, *Leadership, Ethics, and Organizational Integrity. A Strategic Perspective* (Irwin, Chicago).

Werhane, P. H. and R. Edward Freeman (eds.): 1997, *The Blackwell Encyclopedic Dictionary of Business Ethics* (Blackwell Business).

Yergin, D. and J. Stanislaw: 1998, *The Commanding Heights. The Battle between Government and the Marketplace that is Remaking the Modern World* (Simon and Schuster, New York).

Michelangelostraat 62,
NL 1077 CG Amsterdam,
The Netherlands.

Business Ethics Auditing
– More Than a
Stakeholder's Toy

John Rosthorn

ABSTRACT. The explosion of interest in responsible corporate citizenship since 1995 has reminded many of the earlier rapid development of interest in environmental management issues. Active stakeholders and lobby groups have successfully exerted pressures on management for improved corporate behaviour. The paper looks at some recent initiatives and draws conclusions about the imprecise terminologies in use. It moves on to consider tools to better manage business risk exposures within the corporation. The example of the "Business Ethics Strategic Survey" is described, together with the attendant benefits it can deliver to company chairmen, Audit Committees and investment fund managers.

KEY WORDS: business ethics, business risk, conduct risk management, corporate social responsibility, ethics, ethics auditing, licences to operate, risk management, social accountability, social audits, social reporting

Introduction

In applications of Darwin's generally troublesome theory, sales, marketing and senior managers generally are wont to look fearsomely at "the competition". It is as if their future well-being was wholly dependent on what "the competi-

John Rosthorn had a 30 year main stream business career working with two eminent transnational corporations. In 1991 he led the formation of the consultancy partnership LaMP which has a focus on business ethics and conduct in international business. The consultancy was based first in Sri Lanka where the partners then lived. His major consultancy assignments have been undertaken with Asian and European multinationals. His ethics educational and auditing products are licenced to European multinational corporations.

tion" might do to them; or vice versa. Survival of the fittest.

No responsible manager would argue against giving some thought to the competition, and taking a realistic account of the competitor's capabilities. Procter & Gamble and Levers have been doing this for most of the century, sometimes gaining a little, sometimes losing a little. And those corporations are still functioning well enough to have books (Decker, 1999) written about them and their campaigns.

The more serious survival issue for top managers and investors is not the "competition", but the enemies within the corporation. It was Nick Leeson who sank Barings Bank with fraudulent and misplaced trades. It was Shell managers in Nigeria who caused immense difficulties for the Shell corporation by their blindness toward basic human rights and misplaced loyalties. In the case of British Biotech where the market capitalisation fell by 90% in just a few months, it was about the integrity of its top management team that the deepest concerns existed. Survival issues for the business managers, but not out of jungle law.

A big issues thus for company chairmen, top managers and investment fund managers in the very late 1990's are their need to protect businesses against risk exposures which can arise from inside the company, and the requirement to be able to do so in a resource effective manner.

In addition, the corporate ratings of social and environmental performance which had in the 1960's and 1970's appeared to be almost irrelevant to the then top managers, have come to take on a greater influence by the 1990's. The narrowly environmental voice came to touch a fine chord with the consumer public. As it grew

John Rosthorn

in breadth, that environmental voice became more social responsibility aware, and in recent times has sought to inquire into the conduct of managers and even of government. 1990's managers find themselves unable to proceed to whence they wish, nor in the managerial style they might have wished. The stakeholders outside the company are also more used to flexing their lobbying muscles successfully in order to constrain corporate activities.

The Amnesty International (AI) work in the field of human rights is commendable. The AI human rights code (Amnesty International, 1998), together with AI's solid reputation acquired over years, already makes it much more difficult for companies to invest, for example, in Myanmar. The AI position will also make it hard for those businesses which have just a symbolic or toehold presence in Myanmar to continue in that mode of corporate operation. Green Peace can mount a substantial and professional media presence to argue an environmental case against the business. So good a presentation was it when they took up the Brent Spar oil platform disposal discussion with Shell, they scored a technical win, even when perhaps they ought not to have done so on environmental grounds.

With expertise and funds at their disposition, the stakeholder groups are free to define their own research within their own agendas and their own terms of reference. Societal groups plainly have their own conceptual frameworks and measure them in their own way (Enderle, 1998). By using results of either high or dubious robustness, such groups are then free to make their findings available to whatever common interest groups they choose. They make good use of the media to communicate audit conclusions which, in general, may seem to be hostile to the corporate sector (Whawell, 1998). Increasingly web sites provide audit data at the corporate level – Corporate Watch, 21 March 1999 'Monsanto Tactics Condemned' (www.corpwatch.org/).

The interventionist stakeholder groups are conducting and reporting on audits of their carefully selected measures of corporate responsibility. Pearce et al wrote "the 'overarching' principle is improved social performance" (Pearce, Raynard and Zadek, 1996).

Yet confusion prevails

Is their work in sustainable development, or is it in corporate social responsibility, or ethical auditing, or ethical accounting, or ethical book-keeping, or social auditing or SA8000 audits, or social reporting, or ethics reports, or social accountability, or sustainable business development, or corporate accountability, or reputation assurance, or public interest accountability? (see Figure 1).

To consider some of the more frequently used terms – The Social Accountability 8000 (Social Accountability, 1997) audits represent an interesting recent advance. Social Accountability 8000 (SA8000), based loosely on BS5750/ISO9000 thinking, is an attempt to create an international standard for human rights in the industrial context. The need for progress in human rights management is evident from the reported abuses notably, but not only, in the garment and footwear trades. SA8000 deals with management systems, child labour, forced labour, disciplinary procedures, rights to collective bargaining and association, working hours and compensation.

Other examples of externally driven audits of company performance include the Corporate Profiles (*The Times*, 1997, 1998, 1999) of FTSE 100 London-listed companies published weekly on Mondays during 1997–1999. The Corporate Profiles range through ten business monitors, and significantly one of them is "Ethical Expression" (see Figure 2), provided by the "Integrity Works" (IW) ethics consultancy against measures devised by IW. John Drummond at IW reports that the publication of audit data generates both management interest and management stress.

The financial investment community does not stand idly on the sideline either. Sustained by a rapid growth in "ethical investments" (U.K. £2.2 bn under management in June 1998; +47% on June 1997), the players in the industry have developed their own individualistic audit screens as an aid both to investment selection and to marketing of the fund (Figure 3).

Taking a more radical stance and encouraging direct consumer action is EC Magazine of the Ethical Consumer Research Association (ECRA), Manchester, England. EC Magazine

Terminological Confusions

CORPORATE SOCIAL RESPONSIBILITY - understanding and acting upon stakeholder and wider interests in order to deliver obligations to society (after British Telecommunications)

ETHICAL ACCOUNTING - the process through which the company takes up a dialogue with major stakeholders to report on past activities with a view to shaping future ones

ETHICAL AUDITING - regular, complete and documented measurements of compliance with the company's published policies & procedures

ETHICAL BOOK-KEEPING - systematic, reliable maintaining of accessible records for corporate activities which reflect on its conduct and behaviour

REPUTATION ASSURANCE - A number of common global principles for the business environment assembled to provide quantitative and trend information

SOCIAL ACCOUNTABILITY 8000 - An international standard for human rights in the industrial setting

SOCIAL REPORTING - Non financial data covering staff issues, community economic developments, voluntarism and environmental performance (after Vancouver City Savings Credit Union)

SUSTAINABLE DEVELOPMENT - environmental impact measurement, improvements, monitoring and reporting

Figure 1.

runs campaigns in which product groups are subject to comparative analyses mainly for their impact on the environment and animals. In so doing it produces "best buy" recommendations, and promotes other forms of direct consumer action, such as letter writing. In 1989 ECRA conceived the descriptor "irresponsible marketing", and since then have employed editorial pressure against oppressive regimes, animal tests and environmentally unfriendly building methods. Since then ECRA have developed and maintained a 15 point screen of "environmental", "animal", "people" and "other" criteria by which companies are judged (ECRA, 1998).

In spite of confusion in the terms applicable to corporate activity auditing, a rich variety of experts is bringing audit results into the public domain with little or no involvement of the business managers.

Managers are free to benefit from the audit process

Ethics reports have been defined as "a snapshot of a process taking place at various levels within a company and between its stakeholders." (Kaptein and Wempe, 1998). In 1995, The Body Shop undertook their first Social Audit reaching out to ten stakeholder groups. The Body Shop places great value on stakeholder consultations, external verification and continuous improvement. Continuous improvement extended to the audit itself which, by 1997, had become the "Values Report". For The Body Shop, the audits were not only part of stakeholder engagement, they were also part of adding value to the business – more than a stakeholder toy.

Another example of the shared internal and external approach is that of The Co-operative Bank's "Partnership report" (Co-operative Bank, 1998). In this work the bank identifies seven

CORPORATE PROFILE: *Associated British Food*s

(as published in 'The Times' of London, March 29 1999)

OUR VERDICT

Ethical Expression...2/10
Fat-cat quotient......10/10
Financial record.......7/10
Share performance..5/10
Attitude to staff.........6/10
Strength of brands....6/10
Innovation...............4/10
Annual Report.........4/10
City star rating.........4/10
Future prospects.....4/10
Total....................52/100

Ethical Expression is evaluated by Integrity Works.
The Fat-cat quotient is provided by Crisp Consulting.

Figure 2.

stakeholder groups and three areas of assessment, Delivering Value, Social Responsibility and Ecological Sustainability. The "Partnership report" was itself the subject on an independent, external audit as part of audit verification.

British Telecommunications (BT) also see benefits to the business arising from the corporate responsibility. BT find such responsibility to be justifiable on three grounds, that it is morally right, that it wishes to put something back into the society in which it operates, and finally that it is good for the business (Grimshaw, 1997). More than a stakeholder's toy.

These reporting initiatives are characterised by, amongst other things, great variations in reporting methods and content. U.S.-based Coalition for Environmentally Responsible Economies (CERES) is this year attempting to grapple with that very diversity thorough its Global Reporting Initiative (GRI) to crystallise the independent reporting styles that have grown up around the world. GRI will aim for a form of "triple bottom line" by covering economic returns to shareholders, social responsibility and environmental protection. The initial drafts were presented on 1–2 March 1999, and after taking feedback and doing field tests, CERES hope to deliver a final GRI standard in AD2000.

Audit Screens Used by 'Ethical' Investors

- *environmental record*

- *human rights stance*

- *functioning under oppressive regimes*

- *military contracts*

- *nuclear power*

- *tobacco and habit forming drugs*

- *alcoholic beverages*

- *gambling*

- *pornography, prostitution*

- *animal rights/animal testing, intensive farming*

- *consistent with pharmaceuticals and baby milk substitutes marketing codes*

- *banks with large third world debts*

Figure 3.

Yet as John Elkington wrote ". . . there is no such things as a 'standard' social report, because the nature of each report depends on the range of stakeholders for whom it is intended. . . ." (Elkington, 1997).

Therefore the confusion in the terms applicable to auditing seems unlikely to disappear; nevertheless businesses can, and some do, benefit from the variety of external and internal assessments of management activity.

More than a stakeholder's toy

Some soundly managed commercial organisations have taken and used business ethics auditing opportunities. Though they could have left the field to the stakeholders, non-governmental organisations (NGO's) and lobby groups, some have chosen to engage the stakeholders and to find consequential business benefits.

Without prejudice to the benefits from either

externally led or externally engaged audits, there is an additional auditing opportunity close to the management locus in the company's internal audit function. In the British corporate governance context, this business function will generally work under the direction of the Audit Committee and led by the Chief Internal Auditor.

In work which offers some encouragement to internal auditors done in Australia, Zaid showed that of a sample of 15 internal auditors, 25% of them reported giving "high" importance to accommodating changes in social values and expectations into professional and legal auditing standards (Zaid, 1997). Perhaps against initial expectations, internal auditors can contribute much to the improvement process in business management. In line with expectations, they already contribute much to the control of business risk. Professional interest in codes of business conduct is also exemplified by the survey of CEO's views of internal controls as a means to monitor and control standards of business conduct (U.K. Institute of Internal Auditors – U.K., 1995).

Knowing that the corporate social responsibility caravan is on the move, but not waiting for the sandstorm of definitions to clear, the internal auditing function has much at its fingertips already. Neither would it need to wait on successors to the Cadbury and Hampel committees on corporate governance to redefine the scope of internal controls. The auditor knows that the long-term health of the business depends on the management of business risk, the preservation of the de facto and de jure licences to operate, and on the improved understanding of key success factors. Thus Figure 4 makes clear that the risk exposure arising from unethical conduct within the business is in triple jeopardy.

Nowadays stock market quoted companies in U.S.A., Europe and U.K. generally have Mission Statements, Values Statements, and Statements of Business Principles or Business Ethics Codes. The company chief internal auditor is well placed to write into the company's annual audit programme the plan to audit business conduct. He/she is well placed to handle the audit on the bases of the Statements of Business Principles and

John Rosthorn

Business Conduct/Ethics Audit Risk Assessment

*RISK
FACTORS -*

INHERENT	CONTROL	DETECTION	<u>AUDIT</u>
RISK	RISK	RISK	<u>RISK</u>

*RISK
RATINGS -*

high	x	low to high	x	high	=	<u>HIGH</u>

Figure 4.

Business Ethics Codes. This audit is a General Business Ethics Audit (GBEA).

The general business ethics audit

At the time when high level company policy documents such as its business ethics code were being prepared, little thought was given to subsequent internal auditing of compliance with the policies. Figure 5 illustrates the sort of control objective that is hard to test. As corporate experience in business ethics audit cycle grows, the auditors will be allowed to contribute more substantially to the preparation of subsequent generations of business ethics policies and codes of business conduct.

Not all control objectives are difficult hard to audit. Nevertheless some interpretative business skills are required to turn the company policy statement into a useful business ethics audit control question. When it is done, opportunities to set out tracking and benchmark performance measures may be set out. Examples are given in Figure 6.

The auditor works with a diagonal slice through the levels of management in the business. In the present de-layered management world, the representative, but not quota, sample of managers is drawn from just three levels – top, middle and junior management. The major functions of the business e.g. marketing, operations, logistics, human resources, financial – should likewise be represented in the interview sample. Where the

Difficult-to-Audit Control Ethics Code Objectives

"have regard for matters of conscience of others"
UK business management institution

*"should conduct himself with consideration towards all with whom
he comes into contact"*
Far Eastern Code of Professional Ethics

"to avoid sharp practice"
Asian business

*"company policy requires employees to observe high standards of
business and personal ethics"*
US based multi-national corporation

"comply with the spirit as well as the letter of each policy"
UK based multi-national corporation

Figure 5.

Audit Control Objectives and Business Improvement Planning

Code of Ethics Chapter - Equal Opportunities

Control Objective
"... promotion should be made on the basis of a person's ability & potential..."

Control Question
**'How well are women and minority groups
(identify local relevant groups and fill in A, B etc below)
represented in junior, middle and senior management positions?'**

		Test Groups	
		(junior/middle/senior-delete)	
	women	minority A (name)	minority B (name)
Rates - % **Trends - annual change** **Benchmarks %** **Targets - next year %** **3 year %**			

Figure 6.

business has distinct strategic business units, these too should be represented in the interview sample. Hence GBEA employs a three dimensional sample frame. In good GBEA's, between 10 and 15 interviews are completed, in discussions which last 60–90 minutes. Some thoughtful editing of the control questions by the internal auditor proves to be helpful when very junior staff are being interviewed.

Experience of GBEA's in Europe and Asia show that the auditor is able to identify the nature of business risk. The more experienced business ethics auditor, working together with informed managers, may be able to quantify the size of that exposure. The risk analysis leads into a consideration of the business processes which have given rise to the risk exposure. To be able to do this through the chapter headings (see Figure 7) which make up the company's business

ethics policy document is found to be helpful when drawing up the GBEA report to management.

The GBEA report to management is almost certain to make some suggestions about needed improvements to key processes which impact on conduct within the business. In so doing, the business ethics auditor is protecting the existing licences to operate from which the company benefits.

A goal of the business ethics auditor is to set out supportable conclusions and recommended improvement plans. To achieve this the auditor is, in effect, making the sum of the "apples" of "conflicts of interest" to the "oranges" of "sexual harassment", both in compliance's and in negative compliance's (= violations). When the goal is achieved, the auditor in the GBEA report to management provides a cocktail which has

Content Analyses for
Codes of Business Ethics

CHAPTER HEADINGS	NGO Model	Far East Professional	US Oil Major	US MNC	UK MNC
Core values	/	/	/	/	/
Relationships					
employees	/	/	/	/	/
customers	/	/	/	/	/
suppliers	/	/	/		
competitors	/	/	/		/
shareholders	/		/		
community	/		/		
government		/	/		/
Safety	/	/		/	/
Environment	/	/	/	/	/
Conflicts of interest			/	/	/
Gifts & Entertainment		/	/	/	/
Insider trading			/		
Confidential information		/	/	/	/
Political contributions				/	/
Rules & regulations	/		/	/	/
competition law			/	/	/
pricing	/	/		/	/
Accounting standards				/	/
Equal opportunities	/		/	/	/
Sexual harassment	/		/	/	/
Substance abuse					
Software piracy	/				
World trade	/				
Individual conscience		/			

Figure 7.

practical significance and value to the senior executives in both the shape of risk exposures, of the identification of the more important "key issues", and with "recommended actions".

The business ethics auditor looks for formal management responses to the audit report, and summarises them for the Audit Committee. A responsive internal audit function also seeks feedback from management on the GBEA process and its value to management. As with internal financial audits, there would be benefit in having the GBEA process externally verified from time to time.

When successfully done, GBEA is thus much more than a stakeholder's toy: it is an instrument for better management of the profitable business survival issue.

Precision instruments for the top management

GBEA is a powerful, albeit blunt, tool for shifting management awareness and performance. It is good, and probably more agreeable than some stakeholder-driven audits which are done on terms defined by the stakeholder.

The rather more precise instrument devised to support Chairmen, Audit Committees and fund managers is the Business Ethics Strategic Survey (BESS). The fund manager may be looking to commit a major tranche (up to 5%) of his risk funds under management to a small management team led by the CEO. In his diligent approach to the investment, the fund manager will have

Extract from the Business Ethics Strategic Survey (BESS)

Answer
Mark 'Yes', 'No'
or 'Cannot Answer'

Control Questions: For the future of the company in ethical terms -

a   **is an independent audit of business conduct done annually?**   --------

b   **is there a written, approved business ethics plan for the present financial year?**   --------

Auditors Notes   *(at a high level in the business e.g. the board, there should be hard evidence of the approval of a written commitment to stated business conduct objectives, accountabilities, their monitoring and achievement alongside visible milestones. The clear dissemination of the plan well into the management pyramid will be evident. The plan will identify where the business presently is, and where it intends to be at due date)*

c   **is there a strategy for the further development of good ethical conduct in the business?**   --------

Auditors Notes   *(with good data to hand to describe the present state of business conduct, management will be well aware of the key ethical business risks to which they are over-exposed. In general, we may say that employees, customers, governmental relations and near-money assets may be business threatening risks in need of sound management.*

For the present year through the ethics plan, and for future years through the ethics strategy, we expect to see how management will handle these risks. The directions in which management might take the business could read, for example -
i   ethics code, code updates, monitoring and data collection, education and training
ii   ethics auditing, business risk analysis, improvement planning and monitoring
iii   organisation development, ethics committees, ombudsman, 'hot-lines', field counsellors
iv   company operations, 'due diligence', joint ventures, acquisitions, divestments, SHE, closures
v   products and services, R&D, NPD, A&P, government department liaisons, the regulatory interface; etc)

Figure 8.

learned much about the market, the technology and the competitors. But the fund manager may well be uninformed about the integrity of the CEO, and to the ethical robustness of the business. BESS provides the fund manager with access to information of this sort. BESS is updatable at a sensible frequency, longitudinally and latitudinally comparable. BESS is immediately communicative to the CEO about the fund manager's expectations for the manner in which the business will be conducted and the required ethical robustness of the CEO's strategies.

In the same way, the Chairman or the Audit Committee may use BESS to communicate and measure their expectations regarding the manner in which the business will be managed and how managers will conduct themselves and the business strategies.

BESS features a short battery of audit type questions for the CEO, and designed to lead to the discovery of management information, documentation, attitudes and, to some extent, actual behaviour. For a specimen control question, and the related notes for the internal auditor, see Figure 8.

Best BESS practice includes the release of the full questionnaire and supporting notes to the CEO seven to ten days ahead of the audit. The CEO is encouraged to assemble papers the CEO considers to be relevant. The BESS questions are put in private by preferably one, or sometimes two auditors. The CEO is free to have a relevant manager to contribute to the CEO's answers. The verbatim answers remain confidential to the BESS audit meeting participants.

The outputs from BESS include a numerical report, a seven axis performance display (see Figure 9), and a short written commentary iden-

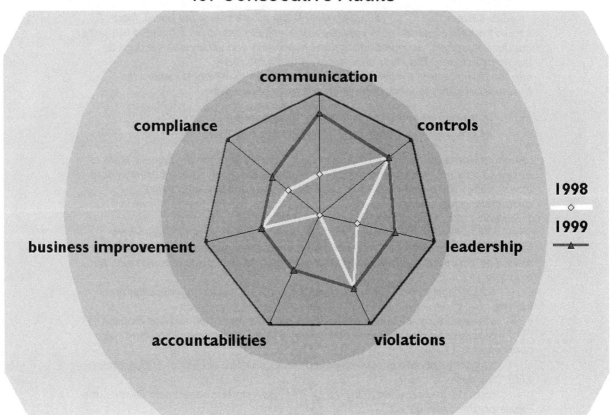

Figure 9.

tifying to points for improvement. In time, there will be a facility for making inter-BESS audit comparisons, either down the stream of time (longitudinal) or across similar businesses (latitudinal). As with internal financial audits, there is benefit in having the BESS process externally verified from time to time.

Conclusions

In summary, there are commendable developments in social accountability auditing – regardless of what nomenclatures are assigned to them. Though being driven externally in the first place, these developments have their own features and benefits. Through time, some of the good developments have begun to appeal to managers with responsibility for community relations, public relations, advertising, marketing, regulatory affairs and corporate planning.

Those caring for corporate governance and internal audit are able to respond to other business improvement opportunities within the company. Notwithstanding the proper views of the stakeholders, the management must manage. From the perspective view of a qualified internal auditor, and based on the company's current ethical policies and procedures, business risk may be mitigated, licences to operate be protected and continuous improvement to business processes sought. GBEA highlights non-compliance with existing ethical policies, and prioritises business improvement opportunities. GBEA recommendations prove to be positive actions aimed at the further protection of the company's licences to operate.

The more surgically precise BESS looks incisively to the integrity of the CEO and to the ethical robustness of the CEO's business strategies.

GBEA is an instrument for the benefit of the entire management team. BESS benefits company operations and its top management in particular. There is no requirement for GBEA and BESS information to enter the public domain. When implemented, the stakeholders will see the resulting difference.

Whilst it may remain only that, business ethics auditing can mean more than improving social performance, be more than a stakeholder's toy. Business ethics auditing thus described is a systematic attempt to describe, analyse and evaluate appropriate aspects of behaviour within the corporation (Kaptein, 1998) as it seeks to improve the company's profitable survival.

References

Amnesty International: 1998, *Human Rights Guidelines for Companies*.

Co-operative Bank: 1998, *The Partnership Report*.

Council on Economic Priorities Accreditation Agency (CEPAA) New York, U.S.A.: 1997, *Social Accountability 8000*.

Decker, C.: 1999, *P&G 99* (Harper Collins).

ECRA: 1998, *An Introduction to the Ethical Consumer Magazine*.

Elkington, J. and F. van Dijk: 1997, *Socially Challenged*.

Enderle, G. and L. A. Tavis: 1998, 'A Balanced Concept of the Firm and the Measurement of Its Long-term Planning and Performance', *Journal of Business Ethics* **17**, 1129–1144.

Grimshaw, Howard and Willmott: 1997, *The Responsible Organisation* (The Future Foundation, as commissioned by British Telecommunications plc.).

Institute of Internal Auditors:1995, *Survey of Chief Executive Officers*.

Kaptein, M.: 1998, *Ethics Management – Auditing and Developing the Ethical Content of Organisations* (Kluwer Academic Publishers).

Kaptein, M. and J. Wempe: 1998, 'The Ethics Report: A Means of Sharing Responsibility', *Business Ethics* **7**(3).

Pearce, Raynard and Zadek: 1996, *Social Auditing for Small Organisations* (New Economic Foundation).

The Times (of London): 1997, 1998, 1999, *Corporate Profiles*.

Whawell, P.: 1998, 'The Ethics of Pressure Groups', *Business Ethics* **7**(3).

Zaid, O. A.: 1997, 'Could Auditing Standards be Based on Society's Values?', *Journal of Business Ethics* **16**, 1185–1200.

The Logistics & Marketing Partnership,
Lavinia Court, 12 East Castle St.,
Bridgnorth, Salop, WV16 4AL,
U.K.
E-mail: lamp@clara.co.uk

Is It Ethical to Use Ethics as Strategy?

Bryan W. Husted
David B. Allen

ABSTRACT. Increasingly research in the field of business and society suggests that ethics and corporate social responsibility can be profitable. Yet this work raises a troubling question: Is it ethical to use ethics and social responsibility in a strategic way? Is it possible to be ethical or socially responsible for the wrong reason? In this article, we define a strategy concept in order to situate the different approaches to the strategic use of ethics and social responsibility found in the current literature. We then analyze the ethics of such approaches using both utilitarianism and deontology and end by defining limits to the strategic use of ethics.

KEY WORDS: corporate citizenship, ethics, social responsibility, strategy

Increasingly research in the field of business and society suggests that ethics and corporate social responsibility can be profitable. Several authors have argued that social responsibility and performance are positively related to business performance (Waddock and Graves, 1997; Hosmer, 1994; Cochran and Wood, 1984). Burke and Logsdon (1996) go further to suggest specific conditions under which corporate social responsibility may be a strategic investment by the firm

Bryan W. Husted is a professor of management at the Instituto Tecnológico y de Estudios Superiores de Monterrey in Mexico and Alumni Association Chair of Business Ethics at the Instituto de Empresa in Madrid. His current research interests include corporate social strategy and cross-cultural business ethics.
David B. Allen is a professor of strategic management and associate dean for research at the Instituto de Empresa. His current research deals with corporate social strategy and the theory of the firm.

to create competitive advantage. Husted and Allen (1998), in a presentation at the Academy of Management, have even begun speaking of "corporate social strategy." Yet this work raises a troubling question: Is it ethical to use ethics and social responsibility in a strategic way? Is it possible to be ethical or socially responsible for the wrong reason?

In this paper, we define a strategy concept in order to situate the different approaches to the strategic use of ethics and social responsibility found in the current literature. We then analyze the ethics of such approaches and end by defining the limits of using ethics strategically.

Toward a working definition of strategy

If the literature is using ethics and corporate social responsibility strategically, we are faced with the task of clarifying what we mean by strategy. Strategy, according to military science, is an unambiguous term. Strategy is the science and art of winning at war. Winning at war, it has long been believed, requires planning. "Strategy," wrote von Clausewitz (1982, p. 4), "makes the plans for the separate campaigns and regulates the combats to be fought in each." Similar military definitions of strategy date as far back as Sun Tzu's *The Art of War* and the Greek writings on the institution of the strategos (Cummings, 1993).

Early definitions of corporate strategy from the 1960's focused on making plans to compete successfully in business. Two classic definitions were those of Chandler (1962) and Harvard Business School's "Business Policy and Strategy" Program (Andrews, 1967). According to

Chandler (1962, p. 13), "Strategy is the determination of the long-run goals and objectives of an enterprise, and the adoption of a course of action and the allocation of the resources necessary for carrying out these goals." Andrews (1967, p. 14) wrote, "Strategy is the pattern of objectives, purposes or goals and the major policies and plans for achieving these goals. . . ." Both definitions incorporate the four principal elements of what has come to be known as the "design" school (Mintzberg, 1990): strategy is long-term, requires setting specific goals, development of a plan, and commitment of resources. All these elements are found in the definitions of corporate and business strategy provided by Ansoff (1985); Bower et al. (1995); Grant (1995); Hax and Majluf (1996), as well as in most strategic management textbooks used in universities in the United States and Europe.

In this paper, strategy refers to the plans and actions taken to achieve competitive advantage and superior performance. Yet this is not enough. The plans and action taken must also lead to the creation of unique resources and capabilities (Peteraf, 1993) that leverage organizational routines (Nelson and Winter, 1982) and that are the source of *sustainable* competitive advantage and superior performance.

Our definition incorporates elements of both the design school approach to strategy and the resource-based view, providing a much fuller approach to strategy behaviors. Defining strategy in this way focuses us on the contribution of the design school in emphasizing the role of social responsibility and ethics in understanding strategic behavior. The Harvard Business School model has always included among its four key elements of strategy formulation "corporate social responsibility." This concept, with its roots in Puritan, New England philosophy (Bercovitch, 1986) runs through much of the 20th century management literature, in works as diverse as Taylor's *The Principles of Management* (1911) and Chester Barnard's *The Function of the Executive* (1938) as well as the standard strategic management college texts referred to earlier.

We argue that the lesser weight given to social responsibility in strategic management research in the 1980's and 1990's was a consequence of the difficulties faced in doing research on the core concept of the discipline: competitive advantage. Fortunately, the re-emergence of more socially-oriented research through the resource-based view provide a framework for linking current strategy research with the social orientation of the pioneers of strategic management.

However, it would be a mistake to argue that the resource-based view is simply a sophisticated update of the design school. While the design school focused on plans (deliberate or intended strategy), the resource-based view takes a more "neutral" approach to the strategic process. As we indicated above, this is understandable given that the emergence of the resource-based view coincides with strategic management's incorporation of theories and concepts from the social and natural sciences in an effort to explain the less rational (or, at least, less transparent) elements of strategic behavior within business firms while at the same time insisting on more rigorous research paradigms. However, this "value-neutral" approach creates difficulties when we wish to ascribe to actors ethical positions which inevitably rest on intentions.

Thus, while we recognize that the social science research activity in strategic management during the last decade has brought us a broader view of management and organizational behavior, this has meant that the discipline has lost some of its prescriptive focus. A further step in the development of the discipline would be to incorporate the consensus that is emerging in contemporary cognitive science on human (organizational) intentions and the plans (actions) undertaken to fulfill those intentions (Dennett, 1987), providing us a grounding for the strategic behavior we seek to judge when we talk about ethics.

We are aware that not all researchers share this cognitive approach and that much of contemporary philosophy and culture theory has treated intentions and plans (master narratives) with great skepticism (Lyotard, 1984). The principle argument against the design school and planning (Mintzberg, 1984, 1994) resides in the difficulties we find in demonstrating causal links between stated intentions (and the plans developed to fulfill them) and the patterns of behavior shown by individuals and organizations. To put the question in terms of contemporary philosophy of language, philosophers as different in their approaches as Richard Rorty, Michel Foucault and even John Searle have spent much of their formidable intellects on pondering why we find it so difficult to sort out the "intentions" of ordinary "linguistic representations" (Rorty, 1979; Foucault, 1972; Searle, 1996).

Until recently, however, the strategic management literature rarely asked about problems of representation and social behavior. Immersed in sorting out "what is strategy?" (Hamel and Prahalad, 1994; Porter, 1996), the stated intentions, goals and plans of managers and organizations have rarely been examined. On the one hand, in the business press, in management texts, and even in the cases we teach in business schools, top managers are judged by their ability to meet stated objectives, while on the other hand, strategy research has preferred to concern itself with more tractable issues. Even the exciting research on organizational sense-making has chosen to bracket the difficult issues of intention and focus on the dynamics of the sense-making process itself.

However, ethics demands that we concern ourselves with intentions, and intentions require that we consider the plans we make to fulfill our intentions. This paper is about the representation of intentions and plans in the pursuit of gaining strategic advantage via socially responsible and ethical behavior. We do not claim to provide a recipe for deciding how to evaluate the ethical status of intentions and plans. However, we do explore what we believe are two essential elements in strategic management. We ask first what it means to understand strategic behavior in a more complete framework that includes social responsibility and ethics. And we seek the grounds of dialogue in the field of business ethics by which managers can move forward on their intentions and create plans that fulfill their objectives in meeting their social responsibilities and ethical commitments to their stakeholders.

Current ethics-based and social strategies

Ethics-based and social strategies embrace a large number of approaches that relate the firm to its social environment. Hosmer (1987, p. 3) explains that ethical problems in management "represent a conflict between an organization's economic performance (measured by revenues, costs, and profits) and its social performance (stated in terms of obligations to person both within and outside the organization)." He defines ethics in terms of social obligations or responsibilities. However, technically, ethics tends to focus on personal choice; social responsibility is about meeting generally agreed public expectations of firm behavior. From the point of view of corporate social responsibility, a socially responsible firm (and its members) would behave ethically as part of being socially responsible. In utilitarian philosophy, the concept of the greatest good for the greatest number tends to conflate ethics and social responsibility, but this need not always be the case. The terms are not used here in a precise way to distinguish between two different approaches, but rather as a way to describe a certain kind of strategy, which has not yet received a generally accepted name.

In the management literature, ethics and social responsibility have been linked to corporate "objectives" in various ways. As we indicated earlier, social responsibility and ethics (including personal values) have been an element of management discourse from its inception. In this section, we shall briefly review some of the efforts by management researchers to understand the role of corporate responsibility and ethics in the firm and the research streams that have been developed.

Corporate social responsibility and responsiveness

In the 1950's, business leaders began to debate widely the social and ethical responsibilities of corporate enterprise. Not only in the strategic management literature, but also in the social sciences (Riesman et al., 1950), part of the scholarly effort in the United States was directed to understanding more fully the implications of the triumph of U.S. corporations following World War II. In this context, the corporate social responsiveness literature emerged as a reaction to the corporate social responsibility literature, which was seen as failing to provide managers with tools for managing social responsibility (Frederick, 1994). Corporate social responsibility only spoke of what obligations corporations should fulfill in order to improve their social environment, rather than how they should respond.

Corporate social responsiveness was concerned with the ability of the firm to "respond to social pressures" (Frederick, 1994, p. 154) in an apparently antagonistic environment with the "firm" on one side and the "stakeholders" on the other. Corporate social responsiveness can be understood as a way of protecting the firm's strategy from the social issues affecting the firm.

Corporate citizenship

The concept of corporate citizenship is closely related to corporate social responsibility and responsiveness. These latter concepts emerged from the sociological literatures, while the concept of citizenship came from the political science literature. It tends to focus not only on the legal responsibilities of the corporation, but also on those actions that aim "to enhance the quality of community life through active, participative, organized involvement" (Tichy, McGill and St. Clair, 1997, p. 3). It goes beyond mere philanthropy to actual projects undertaken by the firm and its employees. Instead of the somewhat reactive approach of corporate social responsiveness, citizenship calls upon the firm to engage its social environment proactively. Although its aim is not strategic in intention, corporate citizenship may have positive consequences for the financial performance of the firm.

Stakeholder strategies

Proponents of stakeholder management have characterized the firm as a set of identifiable interest groups to whom management has

responsibilities; activities undertaken by the firm vis-à-vis stakeholders are seen as reflecting values and ethical principles. Stakeholder management treats strategy in at least three different ways: it speaks of the concept of enterprise strategy (Schendel and Hofer, 1979; Freeman and Gilbert, 1988), outlines generic strategies for managing stakeholders (Freeman, 1984; Savage, Nix, Whitehead and Blair, 1991), and finally deals with specific stakeholder strategies (Freeman, 1984). Let us examine each of these in turn.

Freeman (1984, p. 91) explains enterprise strategy in this way: "Enterprise level strategy does not necessitate a particular set of values, nor does it require that a corporation be 'socially responsive' in a certain way. It does examine the need, however, for an explicit and intentional attempt to answer the question 'what do we stand for.'" Enterprise strategy thus serves to set strategic direction for the firm. In the words of Judge and Krishnan (1994, p. 168): "[E]nterprise strategy represents the firm's approach to managing stakeholders." According to Freeman and Gilbert (1988, p. 71), the test for the presence of an enterprise strategy is "a commitment to a set of purposes or values and ethical principles." They then identify seven different kinds of enterprise strategy that reflect different economic and/or ethical priorities. For example, the unrestricted stakeholder enterprise strategy holds that the firm exists to maximize the interests of all stakeholders, while the Rawlsian enterprise strategy seeks to protect the interests of the least advantaged stakeholder.

Stakeholder management contemplates a second kind of strategy in its discussion of generic strategies. These generic strategies are based on Porter's (1980) competitive strategy analysis, which examines the potential for threat or cooperation with suppliers, customers, and competitors. According to Porter (1980), industry attractiveness is determined by five forces that shape industry structure: bargaining power of buyers, bargaining power of sellers, threat of new entrants, threat of substitutes, and rivalry among competitors. Savage, Nix, Whitehead and Blair (1991), based on prior work by Freeman (1984), delineate four generic strategies for managing the firm's stakeholders based on all the stakeholders' potential for threat or cooperation with the firm. The four generic strategies are: collaborate, involve, defend, and monitor. More recently, Polonsky (1997) adds the stakeholder's ability to influence others to act as a third dimension necessary for the identification of generic strategies.

Finally, the literature discusses what may be called specific strategies for stakeholders. These strategies consist of "a statement of purpose and an action plan for each stakeholder . . . identified at the business and corporate level" (Freeman, 1984, p. 115). Freeman (1984) clearly states that we need to incorporate stakeholders into strategic management by thinking about stakeholders, developing a plan of action for each and allocating resources for those plans.

Ethics strategy

Frederick (1986, p. 137) writes of an "ethics strategy whose purpose would be to enhance and improve a company's ability to cope with ethical problems and issues. Central to this strategy is an understanding of the dominant values of the company's culture. Those values will determine how successful an ethics strategy will prove to be." The purpose of this strategy is to align the firm's culture with the core values of society. The ethics strategy of Frederick is very similar to the enterprise strategy of Freeman in that it provides guiding principles based explicitly on ethical criteria. But this is not the same as strategy. The ethics strategy does not require the investment of resources, is not related to financial performance, and does not involve a plan. These principles may guide the formulation of the plan and help set strategic direction, but ethics cannot be a strategy without those additional elements. Finally, if all that is involved is implementing socially-accepted ethical principles, all firms will have the same or similar "ethics strategies" and no competitive advantage will exist. Thus ethics strategies a la Frederick are not really strategic in nature.

Strategic philanthropy

Philanthropy is strategic when it is designed to create value for the firm (Burke and Logsdon, 1996). One special kind of strategic philanthropy is cause-related marketing, which is "organized around the marketing objectives of increasing product sales or enhancing corporate identity" (File and Prince, 1998, p. 1530). Cause-related marketing justifies support of nonprofit organizations by linking such support to corporate benefits (Varadarajan and Menon, 1988). One area of philanthropy sometimes associated with cause-related marketing is corporate sponsorships. In 1996, U.S. corporations donated over $2 billion to non-profit events such as classical music concerts, art exhibitions, golf tournaments, and literacy campaigns (Mullen, 1997). There is a fine line between such philanthropy and publicity for the firm.

Corporate social strategy

Husted and Allen (1998, p. 9) have been developing the concept of corporate social strategy, which they define as "the firm's plan to allocate resources in order to achieve long-term social objectives and create a competitive advantage." Some foundations and consulting firms are using the concept to draw attention to the opportunities that firms have to create value added for the firm through its social and environmental programs (Fundación Empresa y Sociedad, 1997).

Analysis

Now let us examine some of the criticisms that have been leveled against such social and ethics-based strategies that go to the ethics of such strategies. We will first look at utilitarian criticisms and then examine a deontological critique.

Utilitarianism requires us to evaluate the ethics of an ethics strategy in terms of its consequences. Although utilitarian philosophers disagree over the correct standard (whether we should maximize average or total happiness), those consequences which maximize happiness are considered to be ethical (Smart and Williams, 1973). At least five objections may be made to the use of ethics or corporate social responsibility as strategy because of its unfavorable consequences.

First, ethics may be used to create a competitive advantage by imposing the ethical conventions of one firm on an industry. In effect, business ethics creates a monopoly for those firms already in compliance with respect to those that are not, similar to the kinds of monopolies created by professional licensing requirements (Abbott, 1983). Although nothing prevents a firm from complying with specific ethics standards, the firm that already complies with those standards has a cost advantage and thus a short-term competitive advantage with respect to firms that do not comply. An example is that of Chrysler, which urged Congress to adopt higher fuel efficiency requirements for cars in the United States. Since it was already in compliance, it was further along the learning curve than its chief competitor, General Motors, which had lower costs because it did not comply with the same standards. By establishing the same standards for all competitors, the new policy created a real competitive advantage for Chrysler and other car manufacturers already in compliance (Shaffer, 1995). Similar to the argument of Wood (1986) regarding the strategic uses of public policy in the food and drug industries during the Progressive era in the United States, strategies to impose ethical standards may be used without regard to whether they are really helping or hurting society. Ethics strategies may thus be described as anti-competitive practices, which restrain other firms from competing effectively in the marketplace.

However, ethics-based and social strategies are not limited to the construction of ephemeral entry barriers that benefit one firm in detriment of a larger, stronger rival. Though industry ethics codes may acquire a semi-mandatory nature, social and ethics strategies are not focused on minimum standards of conduct, but on a consummate performance that goes beyond minimums. No firm is prevented from finding a unique niche within the panoply of social projects that are available to business. In fact,

social strategies require firms to carefully think about their own unique capabilities to craft strategies that will enable them to make unique contributions. Ethics and social strategies are kinds of differentiation strategies (in the terminology of Porter (1980)), and thus require each firm to look upon its particular situation. In a sense, each ethics or social strategy should create a kind of mini-monopoly for every firm, but each firm needs to do the difficult work of finding its own way in developing projects that take advantage of its core competencies.

A second objection raised against social and ethics-based strategies is that business is ill-equipped to solve social problems. Few firms have the expertise necessary to attack such problems as poverty, illiteracy or AIDS. Like the proverbial elephant in a china shop, many firms are insensitive to social realities (Peel, 1998) and make a muddle of their excursions into the task of helping remedy social ills.

The response to this concern lies, as Logsdon and Burke (1996) argue, in the recognition that a firm is more likely to create value from social projects that are highly central to its mission and objectives than from projects that are not central to its mission and objectives. If a firm is involved in a project that is central to its mission, then it is more likely to have the knowledge necessary to solve a particular problem. We argue that firms that do not have a strategic perspective are more likely to become involved in problems that are not central to their objectives − where they have neither the expertise to make significant contributions nor the commitment to work through problems should they arise. Non-strategic approaches are thus more likely to fail to achieve any real improvement with respect to a given social problem.

A third difficulty is that ethics strategies may subvert ordinary democratic processes. Nobel laureate Milton Friedman (1962, pp. 133–134) asks pointedly:

> If businessmen do have a social responsibility other than making maximum profits for stockholders, how are they to know what it is? Can self-selected private individuals decide what the social interest is? Can they decide how great a burden they are

justified in placing on themselves or their stock-holders to serve that social interest? Is it tolerable that these public functions of taxation, expenditure, and control be exercised by the people who happen at the moment to be in charge of particular enterprises, chosen for those posts by strictly private groups?

As companies become involved in social problems, they begin to make decisions that may not be in the best interests of society as a whole. Only freely elected representatives should be involved in decisions that affect the public interest. For example, in many countries corporate philanthropy is tax deductible. Instead of directing resources to areas that will most benefit the public good through government, tax-deductible philanthropy allows the firm to decide where to direct those resources in terms of its own interests.

Yet the involvement of firms in social projects does not leave the government without means to influence the direction of private investments to serve the public interest. Fiscal policy can still be used to motivate corporate social investments in areas that are particularly important to a nation – drug abuse, racism, poverty, support for the arts, etc. Elected leaders can provide the signals for the kinds of social investments to be made by firms and let firms work with competitive NGOs to achieve their social goals. The U.S. experiment with tax breaks for business development in enterprise zones in inner cities is an example of how government can provide positive incentives for specific kinds of social investments made by the private sector.

A fourth question revolves around the strategic nature of ethics and corporate social responsibility. Given the fact that these strategies must produce value for the firm, corporations tend to be conservative and direct funds toward popular and politically correct causes. Controversial causes do not receive support. Estimates are that 80% of corporate philanthropy is directed toward "safe issues" (Peel, 1998). For example, AIDS has been long neglected by government, science, and business because of its relationship to the, for some, politically unpopular topic of homosexuality (Shilts, 1995).

This concern assumes that supporting contro-versial causes is a necessary objective of social and ethics-based strategies. We would argue that the utilitarian should be concerned with the net increase in strategic social projects, rather than the distribution of causes. It may well be that companies, already somewhat conservative in their choice of social projects, may be even more inclined to choose safe projects if strategic social strategy were to be widespread. On the other hand, social strategy will probably cause an increase in the total number of social projects. It is quite likely that the total number of "unpopular" social projects will increase, even though the average number of such projects per firm would decrease. Thus, the strategic orientation satisfies the utilitarian requirement that seeks to maximize total happiness (Smart and Williams, 1973).

Finally, and possibly the mirror image of the last issue, those firms that are willing to risk support for unpopular or controversial causes risk becoming involved in issues that may be highly distasteful to some sector of the public. For example, Adolph Coors used Coors Brewery to pursue his personal, unorthodox, conservative agenda. It may be better, some may argue, to have companies meet the statutory minimum ethical standards, and let people as individuals decide what is best for them.

However, pursuing "unpopular" causes may provide both utilitarian social benefits as well as profit to the firm. Moreover, there may even be a positive relationship between the two.

One way to look at this surprising result is to consider the utilitarian benefits of social strategy in conjunction with action theory (Argyris, 1993). The commitment to social involvement (social responsibility) in a democracy implies action. *Intentional* social strategies permit firms (and firm members) to extend and focus the already considerable impact they have on the communities to which they belong.

Moreover, those firms that pursue social strategies directly linked to their product offerings and customer base, are actively pursuing the creation of competitive advantage and additional value-added for the customers. As a result, effective social strategy enables competitive success that in turn enables social action.

In such cases, the separation between social strategy and business strategy tends to disappear. For social scientists such as Argyris, Lewin and Drucker, the contemporary firm can best be understood as a purposeful social institution that responds as fully as possible to the needs of its stakeholders, increasing, in utilitarian terms, the total good created for those stakeholders. Of course, this good (or value-added) may not be understood as such by the *entire* society. In fact, the social-value added pursued may even raise controversy. The value-added, however, must be measured in function of the relevant stakeholders (shareholders, employees, customers) who find themselves happier.

Both action theory and stakeholder theory remind us that we must measure the greatest good in function of the importance given by those who consider themselves directly affected. This helps us to understand phenomena such as Benetton. While offending some, Benetton defends its social practices, apparently satisfying those stakeholders essential to the company's profitability and continued survival. If all firms were to pursue social strategies under this dictum, we could then sum the value added of all firms' social strategies with the expected result that we would achieve a new kind of competitive behavior in which the total "social value added" is greatly increased. It is possible that there may be more cases of negative "social value-added," but given that the vast majority of firms look for value-added projects that present low risk, our hypothesis would be that the more firms view social strategy as a positive contribution to overall corporate strategy, the more social value-added we are likely to create.

As regards the argument that social issues should be the domain of individuals rather than firms, it is difficult to see the difference between support by an individual for a cause (radical or otherwise) and support by a corporation. Some may object that the latter case involves the use of stockholder funds, but in cases of publicly traded companies, it is unlikely, though not impossible, that funds would be diverted to a radical cause. In addition, the strategic focus should increase social projects of all kinds, increasing the likelihood that some of these projects will be greeted with approval by certain people, while others are greeted with disapproval. A true utilitarian analysis would measure the benefits of "agreeable" projects as well as the disadvantages of the "disagreeable" projects.

Deontological ethics is concerned with a different kind of problem that may plague ethics and social strategies – the issue of motives. Doing the right thing for the wrong reason is still morally objectionable. Kant (1964) argues forcefully that good actions that arise out of self-interest or immediate inclination are not morally praiseworthy. Only those actions done from the motive of duty are morally laudable. Corporate intentions with respect to social projects are questionable at best, and outright self-interested at worst. By its nature, a strategy seeks to increase value for the firm by the creation of competitive advantages. If an action does not intend to create value for the firm, it is not strategic. By definition strategy requires actions in the interest of the firm. Thus, an ethics strategy would by definition be incompatible with the condition of moral motives required by Kant to evaluate the moral praiseworthiness of a particular action.

Certainly, the firm has a duty to maximize earnings for its owners. It also has duties to other stakeholders such as its customers, suppliers, creditors, the community, and the natural environment (Freeman, 1984). These duties are often opposing and thus provide the crux of ethical dilemmas for managers (Hosmer, 1987). Ethics strategies and social strategies seek to reconcile these opposing duties, in order to create an inclination (in the words of Kant) to do good. To the extent that such motives are not founded on duty, although complying with duty, such motives lack moral content. This is not to say that they are immoral or unethical, only that they are not morally praiseworthy from a Kantian perspective. Such a limitation may be one that social strategies will have to accept.

Nevertheless, ethics and social strategies may very well be an expression of a desire to comply with duties owed to owners as well as to other stakeholders. Thus the problem of good deeds, but questionable motives is not inherent in ethics-based and social strategies. The strategic orientation only reminds those managers with desires to be socially responsible (or the desire to pursue social actions of their choosing) of their duties to owners. The problem of the moral acceptability of corporate social projects depends upon the motives of the actors behind the social project, not upon the nature of social strategy itself. However, we should remember that we only tend to judge the motives of those who offend rather than those who please; nor do most stakeholders have the information necessary to make reasoned judgments regarding the motives of those who propose social projects. In general, the stakeholders are constrained by limited time and information to either accepting or rejecting the social projects (and strategies) of business firms.

Finally, there is concern about what happens when a particular ethics strategy no longer provides the company with a competitive advantage. A firm that is committed to social projects as a question of duty will continue to support them, regardless of the consequences for its competitive advantage. Those corporations that participate in social projects for reasons of competitive advantage may decide not to continue support. Still, the difficult position of the business manager is that he or she owes duties to both owners and other stakeholders. If a particular social strategy loses its competitive advantage, an ethical response to those duties may be to change the social strategy and develop new strategies that do comply with the obligations of duty to owners and other stakeholders.

Conclusion

In this paper, we have defined the nature of strategy and examined whether the nature of such social and ethical-based corporate strategies is, in fact, ethical. From a utilitarian perspective a number of objections were answered. Although ethics can create a monopoly position for a given firm, it does not prevent any other firm from developing the same kind of monopoly with respect to a given social project. Complaints about the inability of firms to effectively solve most social problems may, in fact, be tempered by the strategic nature of social projects that will

limit firm involvement to areas where it does have competencies. Although managers may not be publicly elected officials, governments will still have the means to direct private action in the public interest. Certainly, a strategic focus may increase the likelihood of conservative social projects, but the overall number of social projects, including more controversial ones, should increase. Finally, the possibility of distasteful projects may increase, but overall social projects will also increase, outweighing the damaging effects of a few extreme social projects.

The deontological approach questions the motives of ethics-based and social strategy as inherently self-interested and not based on a sense of duty. Yet social strategy emerges from a sense of the conflicting duties that managers owe to both asset owners as well as other stakeholders. Social strategy is only a tool to comply with conflicting duties and is not itself a motivation. The motives of actors will still have to be judged independently of the strategy in order to determine the moral acceptability of a given strategy.

Social and ethics-based strategies provide new and exciting opportunities to reconceptualize the role of the firm in society. Certainly, such strategies are not without pitfalls, but they have the potential of increasing overall social welfare. The motives behind such strategies are often mixed, but no particular set of motives can be attributed to the strategic focus other than a concern to take into account the impact of a program on the firm. As with any instrument, social strategy can be used in ways consonant with the demands of ethics. It is in this spirit that we urge business people to look at social strategies as a legitimate and ethical option for their firms.

References

Abbott, A.: 1983, 'Professional Ethics', *American Journal of Sociology* **88**(5), 855–885.

Andrews, K.: 1967, *A Concept of Corporate Strategy* (Irwin, Homewood, IL).

Ansoff, I.: 1965, *Corporate Strategy* (McGraw Hill, New York).

Barnard, C.: 1938, *The Functions of the Executive* (Harvard University Press, Cambridge, MA).

Bercovitch, S.: 1986, *The Puritan Origins of the American Self* (Yale University Press, New Haven, CT).

Bower, J. L., C. A. Bartlett, H. Uyterhoeven and R. Walton: 1995, *Business Policy: Managing Strategic Processes*, 8th edition (Richard D. Irwin, Chicago, IL).

Burke, L. and J. Logsdon: 1996, 'How Corporate Social Responsibility Pays Off', *Long Range Planning* **29**, 495–502.

Chandler, A.: 1962, *Strategy and Structure: Chapters in the History of American Industrial Enterprise* (MIT Press, Cambridge, MA).

Cochran, P. L. and R. A. Wood: 1984, 'Corporate Social Responsibility and Financial Performance', *Academy of Management Journal* **27**, 42–56.

Cummings, S.: 1993, 'Brief Case: The First Strategists', *Long Range Planning* **18**, 133–135.

Dennett, D. C.: 1989, *The Intentional Stance* (M.I.T. Press, Cambridge, MA).

File, K. M. and R. A. Prince: 1998, 'Cause Related Marketing and Corporate Philanthropy in the Privately Held Enterprise', *Journal of Business Ethics* **17**, 1529–1539.

Foucault, M.: 1972, *The Archaeology of Knowledge* (trans. A. M. Sheridan Smith) (Pantheon, New York, NY).

Frederick, W. C.: 1986, 'Toward CSR$_3$: Why Ethical Analysis is Indispensable and Unavoidable in Corporate Affairs', *California Management Review* **28**, 126–141.

Frederick, W. C.: 1994, 'From CSR$_1$ to CSR$_2$: The Maturing of Business-and-society Thought', *Business & Society* **33**, 150–164.

Freeman, R. E.: 1984, *Strategic Management: A Stakeholder Approach* (Pitman, Boston, MA).

Freeman, R. E. and D. R. Gilbert, Jr.: 1988, *Corporate Strategy and the Search for Ethics* (Prentice Hall, Englewood Cliffs, NJ).

Friedman, M.: 1962, *Capitalism and Freedom* (University of Chicago Press, Chicago, IL).

Fundación Empresa y Sociedad: 1997, *La Estrategia Social de la Empresa: Un Enfoque de Valor* (Fundación Empresa y Sociedad, Madrid).

Grant, R.: 1993, *Contemporary Strategy Analysis* (Blackwell, London).

Hax, A. C. and N. S. Majluf: 1996, *The Strategy Concept and Process: A Pragmatic Approach*, 2nd ed. (Prentice Hall, Upper Saddle River, NJ).

Hosmer, L. T.: 1987, *The Ethics of Management* (Irwin, Homewood, IL).

Husted, B. W. and D. B. Allen: 1998, 'Corporate Social Strategy: Toward a Strategic Approach to Social Issues in Management', paper presented at the Academy of Management meetings, San Diego, California.

Judge, Jr., W. Q. and H. Krishnan: 1994, 'An Empirical Investigation of the Scope of a Firm's Enterprise Strategy', *Business & Society* **33**, 167–190.

Kant, I.: 1964, *Groundwork of the Metaphysic of Morals* (Harper & Row, New York, NY).

Lyotard, J.-F.: 1984, *The Postmodern Condition: A Report on Knowledge* (University of Minnesota Press, Minneapolis, MN).

Mullen, J.: 1997, 'Performance-based Corporate Philanthropy: How "Giving Smart" Can Further Corporate Goals', *Public Relations Quarterly* **42**(2), 42–48.

Nelson, R and S. Winter: 1982, *An Evolutionary Theory of Economic Change* (Harvard University Press, Cambridge, MA).

Papdakis, V. M., S. Lioukas and D. Chambers: 1998, 'Strategic Decision-making Processes: The Role of Management and Context', *Strategic Management Journal* **19,** 115–147.

Peel, M.: 1998, 'Mind Your Business', *Financial Times* (Supplement on Responsible Business), May 20, 26–27.

Peteraf, M. A.: 1993, 'The Cornerstones of Competitive Advantage: A Resource-based View', *Strategic Management Journal* **14**, 179–191.

Polonsky, M. J.: 1997, 'Broadening the Stakeholder Strategy Mix', in J. Weber and K. Rehbein (eds.), *Proceedings of the Eighth Annual Conference of the International Association for Business and Society*, pp. 377–382.

Porter, M. E.: 1980, *Competitive Strategy: Techniques for Analyzing Industries and Competitors* (Free Press, New York, NY).

Prahalad, C. K. and G. Hamel: 1990, 'The Core Competence of the Corporation', *Harvard Business Review* **68** (May/June), 79–91.

Riesman, D., N. Glazer and R. Denny: 1950, *The Lonely Crowd: A Study of the Changing American Character* (Yale University Press, New Haven, CT).

Rorty, R.: 1979, *Philosophy and the Mirror of Nature* (Princeton University Press, Princeton, NJ).

Savage, G. T., T. W. Nix, C. J. Whitehead and J. D. Blair: 1991, 'Strategies for Assessing and Managing Organizational Stakeholders', *The Executive* **5**, 61–75.

Schendel, D. and C. Hofer: 1979, 'Introduction', in D. Schendel and C. Hofer (eds.), *Strategic Management: A New View of Business Policy and Planning* (Little Brown, Boston, MA), pp. 1–12.

Searle, J. R.: 1996, *The Construction of Social Reality* (Free Press, New York, NY).

Shaffer, B.: 1992, 'Regulation, Competition and Strategy: The Case of Automotive Fuel Economy Standards', in J. Post (ed.), *Research in Corporate Social Performance and Policy* **13**, 191–218 (JAI Press, Greenwich, CT).

Shilts, R.: 1995, *And the Band Played On: Politics, People and the AIDS Epidemic* (Penguin Books, New York, NY).

Smart, J. J. C. and B. Williams: 1973, *Utilitarianism: For & Against* (Cambridge University Press, Cambridge, UK).

Taylor, F. A.: 1911, *The Principles of Management* (W.W. Norton & Co., Inc., New York, NY).

Tichy, N. M., A. R. McGill and L. St. Clair: 1997, *Corporate Global Citizenship: Doing Business in the Public Eye* (The New Lexington Press, San Francisco, CA).

Varadarajan, P. R. and A. Menon: 1988, 'Cause Related Marketing: A Coalignment of Marketing Strategy and Corporate Philanthropy', *Journal of Marketing* **52**, 58–74.

Von Clausewitz, K.: 1982, *On War* (Penguin, London).

Waddock, S. and S. B. Graves: 1997, 'The Corporate Social Performance-financial Performance Link', *Strategic Management Journal* **18**, 303–319.

Wood, D. J.: 1986, *Strategic Uses of Public Policy: Business and Government in the Progressive Era* (Pitman Publishing Co., Boston, MA).

Bryan W. Husted
ITESM/EGADE,
Sucursal de Correos "J",
64849 Monterrey, N.L.,
Mexico
E-mail: bhusted@egade.sistema.itesm.mx

David B. Allen
Instituto de Empresa,
María de Molina, 12,
Madrid, Spain
E-mail: David.Allen@ie.ucm.es

Coercion, Guidance and Mercifulness: The Different Influences of Ethics Programs on Decision-Making

André Nijhof
Olaf Fisscher
Jan Kees Looise

ABSTRACT. The development of an ethics program is a method frequently used for organising responsible behaviour within organisations. For such a program, certain preconditions have to be created in the structure, culture and strategy. In this organisational context, managers have to take their decisions in a responsible way. This process of decision-making, embedded in an ethics program, is the main focus of this article. Ethics programs often influence decision-making in a *formal* way; certain norms and types of behaviour are formalised and controlled within the organisation. Subsequently, individual managers have to infer the meaning of responsible behaviour from the demands laid down in the ethics program. Such a formal ethics program has some important advantages but the dangers of such an approach are often ignored. This article discusses both the advantages and disadvantages of a formal ethics program and adds two alternative ways of stimulating responsible behaviour in the organisation. In a *monological* approach the reflections of the decision makers on their own values are central in differentiating between right and wrong.

In a *dialogical* approach, the communications between decision makers and other stakeholders involved are the foundations for determining a responsible solution. Because each approach is appropriate for certain issues, a well-chosen combination is justified. Such an ethics program should be strict on certain issues but leave room for reflection and interaction on other issues.

KEY WORDS: code of conduct, ethical decision-making, ethics program, indoctrination of employees, resistance

André Nijhof is an Assistant Professor at the University of Twente and is also working at the management consultancy firm Q-Consult. He has completed a Ph.D. on moral responsibilities in processes of organisational change.
Olaf Fisscher is Professor of Quality Management and Business Ethics at the University of Twente in the Netherlands. His area of research encompasses organisational values, quality management and management of technology and innovation.
Jan Kees Looise is Professor of Human Resource Management at the University of Twente. His main research interests are the connections between Human Resource Management and industrial relations, innovation management and employee participation.

Introduction

The process of developing an ethics program is a well-discussed topic in the literature on business ethics (see for example Paine, 1994; Weaver, Trevino and Cochran, 1999). During the process there is, in most cases, an intensive debate between different stakeholders. In this way, a code of conduct is formulated that includes ethical guidelines that are supported by most stakeholders (Hummels, 1998). To enable external monitoring these ethical guidelines are often formulated in strict and measurable terms. Through various monitoring and reward systems, the organisation ensures that individual managers act in congruence with these ethical guidelines.

Such an approach can be characterised as a formal approach to moral decisions; the organisation gives formal guidelines to distinguish between responsible and irresponsible behaviour. *These guidelines might be set through dialogue with all stakeholders, but in terms of decision-making by individual managers this way of stimulating respon-*

Journal of Business Ethics **27**: 33–42, 2000.
© 2000 *Kluwer Academic Publishers. Printed in the Netherlands.*

sible behaviour is not dialogical in nature. Managers have to infer the meaning of right and wrong from the official organisational norms laid down in a code of conduct.

In this article we do *not* examine the process of developing a corporate ethics program. Instead, this article focuses on the different approaches of ethics programs for influencing responsible decision-making in daily operations, hence the application of ethics programs (Figure 1). To an individual manager who has to make a decision concerning an immediate moral dilemma, the content of an ethics program is fixed. It is part of the organisational context within which they have to take their decisions.

From the viewpoint of the individual manager, ethics programs can enforce conformity to strict organisational rules and responsibilities. This is referred to as a formal approach to ethics programs. Alongside a formal approach, two other approaches to ethics programs can be identified; a monological and a dialogical approach. This article discusses the advantages and disadvantages of these different forms of ethics programs and the way they influence individual decision-making.

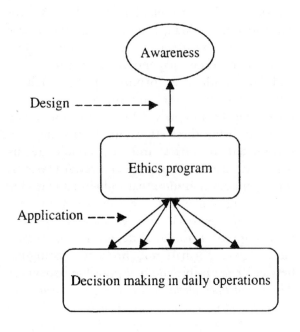

Figure 1. Focus of the research project.

Formal approach: coercing compliance to organisational rules

When an ethics program is started because of external pressures, the organisation has to clarify what it stands for. Therefore, well-defined and measurable rules are written down in a code of conduct. Such a code of conduct clearly states what employees should do to act in a responsible way. It also makes clear what external parties can expect from the company. In order to guarantee these expectations, compliance to the organisational rules needs to be enforced. Measurement and assessment systems in an organisation constitute a control system to ensure compliancy.

This form of an ethics program should be seen as a top-down one. Not because the process that led to the code of conduct is necessarily top down; this might have been done in a bottom-up, top-down or a combined way (Dunbar and Ahlstrom, 1995). The labelling as a top-down ethics program reflects the actions *after* the code of conduct is formulated. The essential point of such an ethics program is that formal rules are established to distinguish between right and wrong. When employees are making decisions these formal rules make clear what they ought to do. In the process of decision-making, as well as when responding to people who question the outcomes of this process, managers will refer to rules and principles. In fact such a formal approach implies a deductive way of decision-making.

Evaluation of a formal approach

A formal approach to ethics programs has some well-known advantages such as clear guidelines for decision-making and a clear statement on what the organisation stands for. Alongside these advantages a formal approach has also some more dubious aspects, especially, natural resistance to coercion, the indoctrination of employees and the possibility of moral inversion. These disadvantages are clarified separately below. First, the advantages and disadvantages of a formal approach are summarised in Table I.

Case I: Social rules at a chemical multinational

There are many examples of formal approaches to ethics programs. All rules in a code of conduct that pose strict guidelines such as "asking for, paying or expecting a bribe is unacceptable" or "creating equal opportunities for employees" are examples of a formal approach. In one of the case studies we performed there were also clear examples of a formal approach in the social rules. This was in a business unit of a large multinational in the chemical industry. The social rules applied to every organisational change in the company that has severe consequences for the employees. The rights and duties of both the company and of the employees were stated in the social rules. An example is: "the company strives to find an appropriate function, by preference within the concern, for every employee who loses his present function due to an organisational change." During the case study a part of the business unit was reorganised. As a consequence 12 of the 20 employees who worked in that department were no longer needed. The managers involved in this change process had clear guidelines in the social rules as to how to deal with the consequences. On the one hand this led to easy decision-making because all discussions, both by managers and by the employees who lost their jobs, could be concluded by referring to the social rules. On the other hand, the employees stated that the managers had no compassion, were strict rule-followers and that there was a large "gap" between managers and production employees.

TABLE I

Main advantages and disadvantages of the formal approach

Amenities	Disadvantages
• Clear guidance for decision-making	• Resistance to coercion
• Fulfilment is measurable	• Indoctrination of employees
• States what the organisation stands for	• Danger of moral inversion

Resistance to coercion

In a formal approach to ethics programs certain rules are written down. Through monitoring and assessment systems the compliance to these rules is coerced. Because of this coercion it is a natural reaction to resist to a certain extent (Beer, 1988). This resistance can only be overcome when compliance with certain norms is felt from within.

This resistance can arise with both decision makers and those influenced by the decision. Many ethics programs are directed at training decision makers to ensure that they act in accordance with the organisational rules. But even when decision makers are convinced that the decisions are responsible it does not automatically follow that others will share that opinion. With a formal approach the consideration of "what's the right thing to do" is based on the norms of the organisation, while the other people involved

judge the decision on the basis of their own values. This will lead to negative reactions when the values of the others do not overlap with the organisational norms.

Resistance to coercive organisational norms is encouraged because a formal approach does not appeal to any feeling of care or compassion. We observed in several case studies that notions of care could be swept away, or omitted completely, by fixed procedures based on an ethics of justice. Because procedures are fixed in a managerial environment there is a distinction between those who design the rules and those who have to carry them out. This results in the disappearance of a feeling of compassion that is essential for notions of care (Gilligan, 1982; Jagger, 1995). One of the preconditions for positive reactions from others involved is that they have to be convinced that decision makers actually care for them. It will be hard to convince others of this with only an abstract reference to organisational norms.

Indoctrination of employees

Formal ethics programs are based on the assumption that an organisation should provide the norms and values needed to distinguish between right and wrong. From a change perspective, in a formal approach to ethics programs, the traditional way of dealing with ethical issues is unfrozen, moved through several training and communication sessions and re-frozen on the basis of the organisational way of dealing with ethical issues. In this process the personal values of the employees are replaced by the organisational norms that come out of the ethics program. People in organisations are indoctrinated with external values which, in itself from a normative perspective, can be criticised (Boje and Winsor, 1993; Willmott, 1993).

The indoctrination of employees can partly be overcome by formulating a code of conduct in a bottom up way. Through dialogue within an organisation all employees have the opportunity to influence and co-determine the organisational norms. In this way, employees set the organisational norms that are then written down in a code of conduct. This does not halt the indoctrination of employees but, at least, the employees are indoctrinated by values that are a compromise or, in the ideal situation, a consensus of the views of all employees.

Danger of moral inversion

The emphasis on fixed ethical rules removes the necessity for employees to ethically reflect on their behaviour. Executives, a study group, or bottom-up discussions within the organisation, have already determined what's right and what's wrong. This uncritical belief in the strength and moral superiority of the organisation can easily lead to processes of "group-think". Janis (1982) states that group-think is most likely to occur when members of a group have the illusion of being invulnerable, have a strong tendency to support dominant beliefs of the group and feel obliged to suppress personal doubts to maintain unanimous consensus. In organisations, group-think can result in moral inversion, through which something evil has been convincingly redefined as something good. This implies that people can engage in acts judged as irresponsible by almost all outsiders, while believing that what they are doing is not only correct but, in fact, good (Adams and Balfour, 1998). To illustrate the meaning of moral inversion a quotation out of the BBC documentary "States of terror" (1993) is very apt. This documentary was about Silke Maier Witt who was a member of the Red Army Faction (RAF). At the time of the interview she was in prison because of her role as an accessory to the kidnapping and murder of a rich German industrialist, Hanns Martin Schleyer.

* Didn't you feel any compassion?

"I think, when you're in a situation like that, you can't dare to feel too much compassion. Because you might not be able to keep on doing it, I think, now. (. . .) I do not think I'm a brutal person or neither the other ones. It was not that we were eager to do it but we felt compelled to do it because of what we wanted."

* Not brutal? This helpless man, pleading for his life was shot and dumped in the back of a car and thrown on the roadside. Not brutal?

"Of course, it was brutal, but I, at that time, I did not let these thoughts affect me. It was awful enough that you really wanted to be like that, to be able to kill somebody. And at the same time we thought that we were trying to make the world a more humane world."

This example clearly shows that within the RAF people believed that they were actually doing the right thing, although almost all outsiders perceived it as brutal and inhuman. In this sense, the members of the RAF felt some kind of a moral superiority because they knew what they had to do, despite all the criticism from the outside world.

It is not our intention to compare an ordinary organisation with a terrorist group like the RAF. Yet the processes of group-think that took place within the RAF can occur within any ordinary organisation. Moral inversion, maybe in a less dramatic form, is a real danger for every group with strict goals and formal guidelines that state what is the right thing to do. Because of the culture and structure of organisations it is hard to eliminate the danger of moral inversion. The example of the RAF shows that in order to maintain their belief in the cause of the RAF they could not let thoughts of their brutality or feelings of compassion affect them. Perhaps the danger of moral inversion can be overcome by not too easily ignoring pangs of conscience and feelings of discomfort. The other approaches to an ethics program include consideration of these kinds of thoughts and feelings.

Different forums for distinguishing between right and wrong

Our criticism of formal ethics programs should not be seen as a plea to maintain the status quo. We do not claim that the traditional way of dealing with ethical questions is perfect because many organisational structures leave little opportunity for ethical reflection. However, there are alternative approaches for stimulating responsible behaviour in organisations. These different approaches are based on various forums for distinguishing between right and wrong.

Decision makers can turn to three different forums to determine what type of moral responsibilities they have: their own values, the norms of the organisation, and the values of other people involved. These norms and values overlap to some extent so that all forums share some moral responsibilities. Other responsibilities are only acknowledged by one or two forums (see Figure 2). This means that even when, according to one forum, all moral responsibilities have been taken into account, other forums might still have criticisms because a further moral responsibility has been ignored.

Based on the distinctions presented in several forums at least four types of "ideal" approaches can be identified to distinguish between right and wrong:

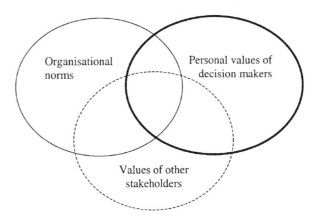

Figure 2. Different sources of ethical norms and values.

1. *Amoral approach*: People with an amoral approach disregard all moral responsibilities when making decisions. Because of its amoral nature it would be totally inappropriate to base an ethics program on an amoral approach.
2. *Formal approach*: With a formal approach moral responsibilities are taken into account insofar as they follow from organisational norms. It tries to set strict norms from which decision makers can infer the right way of acting. The ethics programs discussed earlier are based on this approach.
3. *Monological approach*: In a monological approach moral responsibilities are acknowledged by reference to one's own conscience (the personal values of the decision makers). A monological approach to an ethics program is directed at encouraging decision makers to reflect on their own ethical values. In the following section ethics programs based on a monological approach are discussed in more detail.
4. *Dialogical approach*: In a dialogical approach moral responsibilities are based on the values of both the decision makers and those of the other people involved. This approach is directed at stimulating decision makers to begin a dialogue in order to produce a solution acceptable to all parties involved.

Monological approach

The first alternative builds on the assumption that people can, and should, determine for themselves what is right and wrong. An ethics program that takes this assumption as a starting point should be designed to enable and encourage employees to reflect on their own values in taking decisions. This is reffered to as a monological approach for determining ethical behaviour.

The advantages and disadvantages of a monological approach are listed in Table II. For the managerial decision-making process, a monological approach implies that managers reflect on the situation, on relevant values, on alternative choices, and on behaviour. So it is reasonable to characterise the decision-making process as a reflective one.

Dialogical approach

A second alternative to formal ethics programs is based on the assumption that qualifications such as responsible or irresponsible can only be achieved through communication. Feminist ethics (Gilligan, 1995) and discourse ethics (Steinmann and Löhr, 1996) especially focus on dialogue between the people involved.[1] Ethics programs that aim to stimulate dialogue should create opportunities for communication before decisions are made and carried through. This is referred to as the dialogical approach for determining what is responsible.

The advantages and disadvantages of a dialogical approach are listed in Table III. When strict norms are prescribed in an ethics program, or when these norms are set in a stakeholder debate, it is possible that notions of care are swept away. When a dialogical approach is chosen for decision-making an appeal is made to the relationship between people and the influence of decisions on others. An ethics program that stimulates dialogue should not only find room, but also even create a challenge, to communicate with all people involved. This form of responsible decision-making really can be characterised as interactive.

TABLE II
Main advantages and disadvantages of the monological approach

Advantages	Disadvantages
• Focuses on argument and reflection • Leaves room to act upon specific circumstances	• Performance is difficult to measure • Still a one-sided approach • Possibly leads to differences in behaviour

Case II: Ethics program in a Dutch bank

In the Netherlands there are approximately five large banks in the financial market. One of these banks has built upon a monological approach in order to stimulate responsible behaviour. Through intense discussions in the organisation and the use of a questionnaire, four values were determined that are central to the organisation; "functionality", "durability in relationships", "integrity in acting" and "commitment to the community". These values do not inherently state what is the right thing to do. Their importance lies in stimulating reflection in order to include moral considerations in decision-making. All managers, from every part of the bank, have had discussion sessions where they learned from each other how to work with these values. Discussions on ethical dilemmas with colleagues before a decision was made were encouraged. One of the reasons that this bank chose a monological approach was that the bank consists of autonomous units and so the headquarters is not able to impose strict rules on the management of these units.

TABLE III
Main advantages and disadvantages of the dialogical approach

Advantages	Disadvantages
• Values and opinions of all parties involved are included • Seeks inclusive solutions • Also attention given to the social dynamic side of ethical issues	• Monitoring report based on process and not on outcomes • Danger of relativism • Leads to differences in behaviour, albeit accepted by the parties involved

---

Case III: Novo Nordisk's decision about investment in China[2]

In 1992 Novo Nordisk, a pharmaceutical company with 15,000 employees and headquarters in Denmark, considered starting a joint venture in China. This joint venture would produce medicines for the Chinese market, including insulin for diabetes. From one side this option looked very promising because of the huge market potential. On the other hand the company sensed that starting a joint venture would be a very delicate matter. Reports on the possible partners had produced a lot of rumors and evidence on issues such as child labor, severe consequences for employees who got injured and lack of freedom of association. Instead of turning to regulations and organizational norms Novo Nordisk started a broad dialogue about this option. Representatives of the government, customers, employees in China and in Denmark, and Human Rights groups joined in discussions on what to do. In the end, all parties agreed that a joint venture was desirable provided that the company could enforce improvements in labor conditions and environmental performance. The fact that the joint venture would increase production of life-saving insulin played an important role in the discussion. Because of the importance of these situational factors, preconditions for investing in a developing country were not laid down in a code of conduct. When a new investment decision arises the company and the stakeholders expect to discuss if there are sufficient possibilities and enough trust to improve the social conditions.

Combining the different approaches

The different approaches for distinguishing between right and wrong all have some advantages but also some disadvantages. A combination of the different approaches is potentially attractive because it might include the advantages of one approach while abrogating its disadvantages. However, combining the different approaches is problematic. Not only because this is more complex than a single approach, but also because the approaches are contradictory when applied to the same issue. A formal approach is essentially based on rights ethics, while a monological approach is based on an ethic of justice and a dialogical approach on an ethic of care. These distinct ethical foundations lead to different ways of thinking and different ways of solving ethical dilemmas (Gilligan, 1982; Hekman, 1995). An overview of aspects of the different approaches is given in Table IV (see also Kaptein, 1998).

Due to the differences in the ethical foundations of the distinct approaches it is very difficult, if not impossible, to combine the approaches on an *individual* issue. In our view, this problem can best be resolved by considering the approaches on an issue-by-issue basis. In other words, for certain issues a formal approach may be the most appropriate, while for other issues a monological or a dialogical approach is more appropriate. For example in the Camisea project,[3] Shell will be, for many reasons, very strict on the unacceptability of paying, or asking for, bribes. For this issue a formal approach is best. However, when considering the issue of acquiring accept-

TABLE IV
Aspects of the different approaches of ethics programs

	Formal	Monological	Dialogical
1. Determining moral responsibilities	Through deducing them from a code of conduct	Through reflection on ones own values	Through dialogue with the others involved
2. Solving ethical dilemmas aims to:	Chose the alternative that complies with the code	Chose the right alternative	Find a solution that fulfils all responsibilities
3. Ethical foundation	Rights ethic	Ethic of justice	Ethic of care
4. Core of an ethics program	Stimulating compliancy	Stimulating reflection	Stimulating dialogue
5. Core of a code of conduct	Explicate strict and measurable norms in a code	Indicate fields of attention to be solved through reflection	Indicate fields of attention to be solved through dialogue
6. Core of monitoring systems	Checking compliance with organisational norms	Charting reflection in decision-making	Charting dialogue and registering degree of consensus
7. Typical mediums	– Code of conduct	– Ethics Officer – Asking for a second opinion	Several dialogue forms such as: – Project teams – Moral deliberation
8. Typical examples	– Declaration of human rights – Dismissal as a consequence of bribes	– Responsible care program in the chemical industry	– RU-486 decision at Schering – Shell's Camisea project

able returns on investment a monological approach might be best since it links to the reflection of managers within Shell. For the issues of the effects on the rainforest and the harming of local inhabitants a dialogical way might be chosen, to an extent because it leads to less resistance to the final outcomes.

Conclusion

Much has been written about the need to develop a code of conduct through a debate with all stakeholders. This article defends the position that ethical reflection on ones own values and a dialogue with related people should be included in actual decision-making on daily operations. A stakeholder debate to develop a code of conduct is undoubtedly valuable, but it should

not replace the need for reflection and dialogue when concrete dilemmas have to be solved. Especially when an ethics program is based on strict organisational norms, set during a stakeholder debate or otherwise, this danger of replacing ethical reflection and dialogue in actual decision-making is present.

Organisations that want to stimulate responsible behaviour can choose between ethics programs based on a formal, a monological or a dialogical approach for distinguishing between responsible and irresponsible behaviour. In this *context*[4] of ethics programs, related to the different approaches, the decision-making process by management may be characterised as deductive, reflective or interactive. Which decision-making *process* is to be preferred depends more-or-less on the *content* of the issue. All of the approaches have certain advantages and disadvantages. The view that a formal approach is always to be preferred seems to be misplaced, because of the associated disadvantages like resistance to coercion, the indoctrination of employees and the danger of moral inversion. For certain issues an organisation may indeed want to ensure that certain kinds of behaviour never occur. Examples could be the prevention of bribery or child labor. For other issues a monological, possibly combined with a dialogical, approach might be more appropriate for organising ethics. Especially for issues where specific circumstances have to be considered, an ethics program can usefully take a monological and/or dialogical approach. These approaches stimulate reflection by all employees about questions of right and wrong and leave space for listening to other stakeholders both within and outside the organisation.

In this paper several examples have been given covering all three approaches to ethics programs. It should be noted that it has been much easier to come up with examples of a formal approach then with examples of a monological or a dialogical approach. Maybe combining approaches, and in particular using the dialogical approach, is too demanding.

Further examples would be very valuable for evaluating the theoretical distinctions between, and practical applications of, the different approaches.

The emphasis in this article on codes of conduct disregards the linkages with the other parts of a more comprehensive ethics program. A code of conduct is no more than a piece of paper unless people are stimulated to act in line with the code. For an ethics program to be influential it is crucial that the code of conduct is implemented by adapting all parts of the normal way of doing business (Chen, Sawyer and Williams, 1997; McDonald and Nijhof, 1999; Morgan, 1993). In particular, support of managers, job design, information systems, employee selection, training of employees and reward systems are critical areas in this respect.

Notes

[1] Both discourse ethics and feminist ethics call for dialogue in the actual decision-making process. However, the foundation for the dialogue is different. In discourse ethics a rational way of reasoning is prescribed to determine "the best argument". In feminist ethics the dialogue is focussed on being receptive to the needs of other related people in order to determine inclusive solutions.
[2] More information about the activities and performance of Novo Nordisk in China can be found on their webpage at: www.novo.dk/social_report_1998/china.
[3] A description of the Camisea project is available in the second ethical report of Shell (1999). Additional information is available at: www.camisea.com/english/index.htm.
[4] For the distinction between context, process and content, see Pettigrew and Whipp (1991).

Literature

Adams, G. B. and D. L. Balfour: 1998, *Unmasking Administrative Evil* (Sage Publications, Thousand Oaks).

Beer, M.: 1988, 'The Critical Path for Change; Keys to Success and Failure in Six Companies', in R. H. Kilmann and T. J. Covin (eds.), *Corporate Transformation* (Jossey-Bass, San Francisco), pp. 17–45.

Boje, D. M. and R. D. Winsor: 1993, 'The Resurrection of Taylorism: Total Quality Management's Hidden Agenda', *Journal of Organisational Change* 6(4), 57–70.

Brighley, S.: 1995, 'Business Ethics in Context; Researching with Case Studies', *Journal of Business Ethics* 14, 219–226.

Chen, A. Y. S., R. B. Sawyer and P. F. Williams: 1997, 'Reinforcing Ethical Decision-Making throug Corporate Culture', *Journal of Business Ethics* 167, 855–865.

Dunbar, R. L. M. and D. Ahlstrom: 1995, 'Seeking the Institutional Balance of Power; Avoiding the Power of a Balanced View', *Academy of Management Review* 20(1), 171–192.

Gilligan, C.: 1982, In a Different Voice (Harvard University Press, Cambridge, Mass.).

Gilligan, C.: 1995, 'Moral Orientation and Moral Development, Oorspronkelijk verschenen in 1987', in Virginia Held (ed.), *Justice and Care: Essential*

Readings in Feminist Ethics (Westview Press of HaperCollins Publishers, Colorado), pp. 31–46.

Hekman, S.: 1995, *Moral Voices, Moral Selves; Carol Gilligan and Feminist Moral Theory* (Blackwell Publishers, Oxford).

Hummels, H.: 1998, 'Organizing Ethics: A Stakeholder Debate', *Journal of Business Ethics* **17**, 1403–1419.

Jagger, A. M.: 1995, 'Caring as a Feminist Practice of Moral Reason', in Virginia Held (ed.), *Justice and Care: Essential readings in Feminist Ethics* (Westview Press of HaperCollins Publishers, Colorado), pp. 179–202.

Janis, I.: 1982, *Groupthink*, 2nd edn. (Houghton-Mofflin, Boston).

Kaptein, M.: 1998, *Ethics Management* (Kluwer Academic Publishers, Dordrecht).

McDonald, G. and A. Nijhof: 1998, 'Collective Responsibility; A Framework for Developing an Ethical Climate in Organisations', *Working Paper*, Accepted for publication in Leadership and Organisational Development Journal, MCB Publishers.

Morgan, R. B.: 1993, 'Self- and Co-Worker Perceptions of Ethics and Their Relationships to Leadership and Salary', *Academy of Management Journal* **36**(1), 200–214.

Nijhof, A. and O. Fisscher: 1997, 'Dealing with Ethical Dilemma's in Organizational Change Processes', *International Journal of Value Based Management* **10** (Kluwer Academic Publishers), 173–192.

Nijhof, A.: 1999, *Met zorg besluiten, een studie naar morele afwegingen van leidinggevenden bij organisatieveranderingen* (Samsom publishers, University of Twente, Enschede).

Paine, L. S.: 1994, 'Managing for Organizational Integrity', *Harvard Business Review* (March–April), 106–117.

Pettigrew, A. and R. Whipp: 1991, *Managing Change for Competitive Success* (Blackwell Publishers, Oxford).

Steinmann, H. and A. Löhr: 1996, 'A Republican Concept of Corporate Ethics', in S. Urban (ed.), *Europe's Challenges; Economic Efficiency and Social Solidarity* (Gabler, Wiesbaden), pp. 21–61.

Weaver, G. R., L. K. Trevino and P. L. Cochran: 1999, 'Corporate Ethics Programs as Control Systems; Influences of Executive Commitment and Environmental Factors', *Academy of Management Journal* **42**(1), 41–57.

Willmott, H.: 1993, 'Strength is Ignorance; Slavery is Freedom: Managing Culture in Modern Organizations', *Journal of Management Studies* **30**(4), 515–552.

University of Twente,
Faculty of Technology and Management,
P.O. Box 217,
7500 AE Enschede,
The Netherlands,
E-mail: a.h.j.nijhof@sms.utwente.nl
o.a.m.fisscher@sms.utwente.nl
j.c.looise@sms.utwente.nl

Communicating about Ethics with Small Firms: Experiences from the U.K. and Spain

Laura J. Spence
José Félix Lozano

ABSTRACT. This article introduces the important issue of communicating with small firms about ethical issues. Evidence from two research projects from the U.K. and Spain are used to indicate some of the important issues and how small firms may differ from large firms in this area. The importance of informal mechanisms such as the influence of friends, family and employees are highlighted, and the likely ineffectiveness of formal tools such as Codes and Social and Ethical Standards suggested. Further resarch in the area of small firms and ethics is essential.

KEY WORDS: communication, ethics, small firms, social responsibility, Spain, United Kingdom

Introduction

Communicating about ethics between academics and business is not easy at the best of times. How we communicate and discuss values and generate voluntary commitment to specific rules or ways of behaving is a challenging task. Differences of terminology and the extent of attention to practice rather than reported or desired behaviour are particularly pertinent and can create barriers to proper discussion. Where the businesses concerned are small, which we can define as having fewer than 50 employees, additional problems can be anticipated. On the one hand the personal proximity and the limited number of employees are factors that facilitate communication and the growth of trust. Conversely, however, the lack of formal processes to implement dialogue and the restricted resources, together with the lack of definition of roles and tasks, highlight the potentially problematic nature of small firm communication about ethics compared to their larger counterparts.

The relevance of small firms to the social and economic environment is too significant to be disregarded. In the U.K. in 1998, for example, small firms, defined as those having fewer than 50 employees accounted for 99.1% of private businesses, 44.7% of employment and 38% of turnover (Department of Trade and Industry, 1999). The focus by most business ethicists on large firms is in fact entirely inappropriate in a country in which of "3.7 million enterprises only 25 thousand were medium sized (50 to 249 employees) and less than 7 thousand were large (250 or more employees)" (figures refer to the U.K. in 1998; Department of Trade and Industry, 1999). Furthermore, these statistics relating to small firms are similar across the European Union (ENSR, 1997).

The particular strains on the small firm owner-manager require careful consideration of how best to reach them and enable discussions about ethics. In this paper two streams of research on ethics in small firms in the U.K. (in particular Slough) and Spain (in particular Valencia) are brought together to help add some empirical evidence to the debate on ethics in small firms

Laura J. Spence is a Lecturer and Researcher in Business Ethics at Brunel University, England. She has published in the areas of Comparative Business Ethics, Human Resource Management and Ethics and Ethics in Small Firms. Dr. Spence has been an Executive member of the European Business Ethics Network since 1998.
José Félix Lozano is a Philosophy graduate, with further studies at Erlangen-Nürnberg University (Germany). He is Assistant Director of the ÉTNOR Foundation (Ética de los Negocios y las organizaciones). He is Assistant Lecturer of Business Ethics and Professional Deontology at Valencia Polytechnic University.

Journal of Business Ethics **27**: 43–53, 2000.
© 2000 *Kluwer Academic Publishers. Printed in the Netherlands.*

and demonstrate the need for further research in the area. The studies were not planned together in advance of their completion and hence unfortunately lack full comparability. Nevertheless, both offer an empirically based, primarily qualitative picture of the small firm. The lack of fully comparative research in business ethics needs addressing urgently.

In the U.K. small firms are characterised by being; independent and owner-managed, stretched by multi-tasking, limited by cash flow and "fire fighting", built on personal relationships, mistrustful of bureaucracy and controlled by informal mechanisms (Spence, 1999). These factors mean that small firms are different in nature, not just size, from large firms (Holliday, 1995, p. 2).

In Spain a similar picture of the small firm emerges with the additional perspective that the majority of the firms are founded by individuals who are self-made people, most of whom generally lack adequate professional training and/or a high level of post-secondary education (Palafox et al., 1995).[1] These factors have a tendency to precipitate mistrust and perpetuate an often unfounded fear of change and innovation. Liberal Arts education and up-to-date management training are still the most important areas of general studies which need to be incorporated into the Spanish business environment.

It has been argued elsewhere,[2] that the systems of management in small and medium sized enterprises (SMEs) tend to be of an authoritarian-paternalist nature: Authoritarian in the sense that the basic functions – marketing, sales, development of products, production, accounting, finance, etc. – are monopolised by a limited number of people whose approach to these areas are based in their own personal experiences, standards, and judgement. This is a logical consequence of the nature of the small business and is consistent with the definition for Small Business developed by Baumback (1988), quoted by Vyakarnam et al. (1997): "actively managed by the owner(s); highly personalised; largely local in its area of operation; and largely dependent on internal sources of capital to finance growth".

The system of management in SMEs in Spain tends to be paternalist in the sense that these managers are accustomed to – in executing many of their tasks – relying on people with no actual decision-making responsibility, but who are more often than not held responsible for merely submitting alternatives and rewarded for their support for the manager's decisions.

There has been some very limited research on ethics within small firms in Europe.[3] Examples are that by Vyakarnam (1995), Vyakarnam et al. (1997), Quinn (1997) and Pons et al. (1998). In these examples, talk about "ethics" was quite explicit and introduced as a literal topic of discussion. The work by Vyakarnam used focus groups to investigate what ethical dilemmas small firm owner-managers felt they had encountered. Hence the defining of ethics was left to the individual. Quinn's work involved a postal questionnaire to small business owner-managers who were members of religious, business or community groups, indicating a possible commitment to a non-hedonistic concern for others. Again, the reference to "ethics" was explicit in the survey. The paper by Pons et al. (1998) focused on participation issues in small firms and the dignity of employees.

As the corpus of research on ethics in small firms begins to build momentum, it is timely to consider how best we might communicate about ethics with small firms. It is with this in mind that the following questions are posed for consideration and debate:

1. What terminology are small firms comfortable with in relation to "ethics"?
2. Which stakeholders have the biggest influence on small firms in relation to ethical issues?
3. Can standard tools of ethical communication such as missions statements, codes of conduct, social and ethical accounting, be meaningfully translated for use in small firms?

The indications from the Spanish and U.K. research presented here may have practical implications for those hoping to engage with small firms on ethical issues, but can also inform future research practices in investigating small firm ethics in Europe.

Methodology of the research projects

There were two stages to the U.K. research study drawn on in the discussions here.[4] The first stage was qualitative research in the form of face-to-face interviews. The second stage was quantitative research with a telephone survey of 100 small businesses nation-wide in the U.K.

Twenty small firm owner-managers in the U.K. have been interviewed with a view to improving understanding of the ethical issues that are particularly relevant to the small firm. The qualitative methodology uses a semi-structured interview to explore the motivations, priorities and business practices of the owner-managers of the firms. The firms in the sample were of mixed industrial sectors, based in a county in the south east of England. They were characterised by being independent, owner-managed and with fewer than 50 employees. Access was achieved by letters sent to 40 small firms in the area (randomly chosen from a business directory) and follow up telephone calls to make appointments.

Sector differences can be highly significant in small firm research (see Curran and Blackburn, 1994, pp. 55–61). The purpose of this study is exploratory and a wide base across the range of different sector types was felt to be most illuminating in the first instance to help identify any similarities in small firms across the sectors. Nevertheless, half of the sample is drawn from manufacturing sectors, and half from service sectors in order to allow preliminary sector differences to emerge.

The second stage of the U.K. research was a telephone survey, which was written on the basis of the findings and discussions in the face-to-face interviews. In order to avoid preconceptions and socially desired responses, the survey was worded in such a way that practices and priorities were discussed which might lead to the mention of ethical issues but would not impose such frameworks on the respondent.

The Spanish perspective in this paper is based on the research work promoted and coordinated by the ETNOR Foundation (Ética de los Negocios y las organizaciones) and supported by the Generalitat Valenciana (Valencian Regional Government), whose original title was "El perfil Ètico de la Cultura Empresarial Valenciana (Ethics Profile of Business Culture in the Valencian Community)" (Conill et al., 2000), where some of the questions posed for this paper have been broadly discussed. The main research objective was to analyse the locus and the role that ethics play in the Valencian Community. The research aim was to do a diagnostic about the level of ethics in the Valencian firms.

The basic objective of the research was undertaken by means of studying the following specific objectives:

1. The role of ethics: importance, compatibility and applicability to the business sphere.
2. Definition of what is fair or morally right.
3. Bases for the foundation or legitimisation of moral decisions.
4. Moral dilemmas and perception of their social extension.
5. The role of ethics in certain business conduct; attitudes as regards sexual discrimination and respect for the environment.
6. The role of the external customer (customer service) and the internal customer (training) in the Valencian business world.

The valid response rate was 17.5% (175 Questionnaires). This can be considered high for the customary levels in a postal survey which in this case could appear even more difficult – if possible – bearing in mind the subject and the difficulty in gaining access to the segment studied, among the most inaccessible to any social research (Curran and Blackburn, 1994, pp. 67–71).

In this project, the research was not specifically focused on small firms. 46% of the firms that participate in the research have less than 50 employees, 17% have between 50 and 100 workers, and only 34% of the firms have more than 100 workers.

In addition to this research, experience from running seminars and workshops with managers and owners from the Valencian Community informs the discussion presented here.

How can we talk about ethics?

The U.K. project which was undertaken was done on the basis that the word "ethics" should only be introduced into the dialogue with business owners where they brought it in first. Ethics is held to be the understanding of right and wrong in practice by the owner-managers. The research project thus focused on "priority and practice" as a working title and guide for questioning. This avoided the need for complicated discussions defining ethics or asking participants how they would define ethics. It also, rather instrumentally, was considered to be an aide to access, keeping the perception of the study as practical rather than what might be perceived to be somewhat esoteric by owner-managers.

Nevertheless, owner-managers did bring "ethics" into the discussions in the face-to-face interviews. Some illustrative quotations of this are as follows. It should be stressed that the interviewer had not used the word "ethics" prior to these comments from the respondents. Related words which indicate moral judgement have been highlighted in italics.

One respondent who owned a management consultancy talked fervently about the need for openness and trust in the client relationship.

Respondent: "We have never done just one piece of work for them (our clients). Part of it is getting repeat business so that they *trust* us, and they know we understand them.

Interviewer: How important is that *trust* in your client relationship?

Respondent: Absolutely, it is absolute in both ways because *trust* is also part of business, and I link it with *ethics*. There are times when we say we can't do a job – it doesn't happen very often – but it is very important that all clients *trust* us, it is very important that the people we work with within an organisation not only that they *trust* us but interestingly enough that we *trust* them and that we feel that they are not involved in us doing something that we wouldn't *believe* in as to how a company should run.

We have not had to test that out very much but it is an *inner faith* that it is important that we don't go in there to *screw people for the sake of it*. It is important that our clients *trust* us and that we are very *open* with them."

An owner-manager of a mechanical engineering firm talked about a "code of ethical practice" between competitors.

Respondent: "They are not competitors, they have got their customers and we have got our customers and if any of their customers are *unhappy* they are quite welcome to come – you just don't go around poaching.

Interviewer: Why wouldn't you poach?

Respondent: It is *unethical* to do things like that. If people want you to do the work you will get the work. . . .

Interviewer: Do unto others, type of thing?

Respondent: Yes. There is a bit of a *code of practice* at the end of the day. . . . You ring other companies up and say: "Have you got any overloads?" or "Are you a bit quiet this week?" maybe. People respond because they are dealing with somebody that they *would try and help* out if they can."

The owner of a marketing firm introduced religious based references to ethics.

Respondent: "Hopefully the company encourages *Christian work ethics* in those employees, and therefore in their families. . . . It is what I said before about *not ripping your customers off*. I don't *believe* in it, it is *not right*. We are not here primarily to *rob* a lot of people of their money. We are here to provide a service to people who need what we provide. We are not here to dream up some product and go and sell it to people who *don't need it*. Don't *believe* in that. That's not how I personally work and that, by its definition, goes down through the company. That's why, when people say: "What do you do?" I say: "We make what people want us to make". We don't dream up a product and then go and market it to people who *don't need it*. Very important to me."

The owner-manager of an antiques shop describes her "supplier" relationships as follows:

> Interviewer: "Do you take into account the circumstances of the person you are buying from?
>
> Respondent: Yes, unfortunately, but you *shouldn't*.
>
> Interviewer: How does that work?
>
> Respondent: Particularly if it is some old boy or some old girl that comes in . . . I find I end up offering them more because you *feel so awful*. It is a case of *ethics* and I think it is quite a difficult one to balance. I was saying to someone the other day it is between where's the line between making a reasonably good profit and getting to the point that you are *cheating* someone. Only you can make that decision. They can make it but they might not have the knowledge to base it on. Most people are beginning to know, they have got an idea. In fact a lot of people have got a very inflated idea over what something is worth and that's very *embarrassing*. Trying to talk down their grandmother's credenza that nobody would really want and needs an awful lot of restoration or whatever that they want a massive price for and all they keep saying is: 'It's old, it is old'! That is always difficult to subtly back out like: 'This won't sell', 'We don't really want it', 'You want too much money' and not be *unkind*. You want to be quite *nice*."

Talking about the employee relationship, one respondent, who had recently taken over an interior design firm, stressed the need for openness and honesty with employees.

> Respondent: "We came in and started thinking: 'We have got twelve staff, OK, fine' and you suddenly realise how *badly they have been treated* in the past when you start looking into it. We have reinstated company contributions towards pensions, we instated health care, put the mileage up to a sensible rate, send them birthday cards and generally make sure they are *fine* and you worry that it is not only the fact that

you thought it was just your house on the line and your own future, it is actually theirs as well and that's a *big responsibility* when you are making decisions. . . . I think *honesty is the best policy* in life. If they can see that you work longer hours than they do and you have no real different standard of living and we don't at the moment."

The quotations presented here are just a few examples, but they are not atypical from the U.K. study. They suggest that while small firm owner-managers are able to use the term "ethics" their references to ethics are embedded in other qualifying terms. Words which resonated with the U.K. small firm owner-managers in this sample include the following groups:

- *Quality of communication*: Open, Honesty
- *Quality of relationship with other people*: Trust, Responsibility, Help out, Rip people off, "Screw people", Rob people, Unkind, Badly treated, Cheating.
- *Moral philosophy*: (Christian work) ethics, Should do/not do, Code of practice, Unethical/Ethical.
- *Emotional responses and how I feel*: Believe in, Inner Faith, Unhappy, Dreadful, Pleasure, Embarrassing, Feel awful.

Comparing this to the Spanish research, the very concept of ethics remains unclear to most Spanish small business owners. One important factor that increases this confusion is the education system. Since the mid-1970s, in elementary education there have been two courses, which you choose between: either ethics or religion. This has the influence that many people understand ethics to be opposite to, and incompatible with, religion.

It has been found that in Spanish business, the concept of ethics is especially confused and "dangerous". The researchers of the Ethical Profile project said:

> The Discussion and Interview Groups, previous to the questionnaire, had shown that this was a hard and evasive field of analysis with widespread reticence which blocked participation of those interviewed; it was therefore necessary to use gentle or "mellowed" formulations in the questions included in the Questionnaire. (Conill et al., 2000)

48 *Laura J. Spence and Jose Félix Lozano*

Normally there is a tendency to identify the ethics question with "good" or "bad" (totally good or totally bad), and this is determined by the point of view of the individual. Often the owner-manager understands ethics is a personal and subjective question.

> As regards *convictions*, the dictates of one's own conscience are still decisive, with no need for subjecting these to intersubjective criteria. *Ethics* are recognised, but as something *subjective*. (Conill et al., 2000)

The owner-managers don't like to speak about ethics, and are more comfortable with words like justice, responsibility, or respect when the reality of ethics *is* responsibility, *is* good behaviour, and *is*, most naturally, honesty.

Hence, responding to the findings of the U.K. study presented above, comfort with terms like responsibility, duty, doing the right thing, conscience and priorities are very relevant to the Spanish case. One more concept could be added which is very important and in the ETNOR seminars is often expressed. It is the concept of "business values". Whereas the concept of moral values is used often, and perhaps too loosely, it remains to be clearly defined. Although people understand the concept of values in the Christian tradition, these values fail to be critically analysed nor ranked in preferential order.

From the Spanish perspective we would argue that it is not appropriate to ask directly about one's own company's ethics, for who will identify or accept the fact that their company behaves unethically? Although the word ethics is used as a red flag to discredit other people or companies, it is argued that it is much more useful to employ terms such as values, responsibility, compromise, and trust than use the word "ethics".

It is encouraging to recognise the use of moral language in the everyday speak and thoughts of small business owners in both Spain and the U.K. As a researcher of business ethics it is important to acknowledge the breadth of ways in which

owner-mangers talk about ethics. While traditional terms from moral philosophy may be ways in which ethics is verbalised, personal emotional responses, talk of the quality of relationships with others with whom the business comes into contact, and the quality of communications themselves are also relevant. Investigation of the understood meaning of the terms identified in the studies is needed in future research.

Who can influence and communicate with small firms on ethical issues?

It was found in the U.K. research that the most important social issue for small firm owner-managers in theory and practice is the health and welfare of their employees (see Spence, 2000a). Other important social issues were being a good role model, supporting local business and community, giving to charity and caring for the environment.

From the point of view of lobby groups, consumers and policy makers who might want to influence attention to social issues, information about how owner-managers might alter their degree of attention is crucial. In the telephone survey the U.K. respondents were asked what factors might influence them to pay more or less attention to social issues. The results on the table below show that employees are the most likely to influence business owners to increase their social actions. Attention should also be drawn to the fact that high results were recorded for responses which claimed that the factors mentioned would not influence business owners at all – they are an independent group who follow their own instincts. Factors which might influence business owners to be less socially responsive were felt to be when they experienced strong competition, or if they were to become a larger firm. Some small business owners perceive large firms as being less socially aware than themselves.

Factors likely to influence owner-managers to respond to social issues

Factors or groups	Likely to influence to be more socially active	No influence	Likely to influence to be less socially active	Don't know/ no answer	Total
Employees	62	27	2	9	100
Law	61	28	1	10	100
Customers	56	32	3	9	100
Family and friends	43	49	1	7	100
Being a larger firm	42	40	11	7	100
Strong competition	29	37	25	9	100
Industry norms	26	60	6	8	100
Early mentor	22	44	7	27	100
Trade association	19	64	2	15	100
Suppliers	14	73	6	7	100
Religion	12	80	2	6	100
Bank or financiers	10	75	6	9	100

N = 100.

A manufacturer illustrated the influence which employees could have on his decision-making with the following comment:

> Respondent: "It is not a question of me going there and saying 'I want you to do this'. I never talk to them like that and I treat them with respect in the same way that I would expect anybody to treat me. . . . We are all here together. I have made it plain that I am quite happy for them to say 'Why don't we do this . . . ?' It is my decision eventually but I am always happy to talk about it."

Small firm owner-managers may not see themselves as ethical or moral guardians with a major contribution to make to society. However, when questioned they have responded in this study with evidence that they do have a social role. They feel a responsibility to their employees and often offer them social and welfare protection beyond the law. They often have community and social links which they do not necessarily associate with "business" activities, but are involved with as citizens. Some of them admit to bringing their spiritual and religious beliefs to the workplace with them and using them as moral guidelines. Customers could also play a role in influencing owner-managers in relation to social issues, although suppliers would be less likely to be able to change the behaviour of small firm owner-managers.

From the Spanish project, after experience with owners who participated in the work-shops and seminars facilitated by the ETNOR Foundation, it emerged that some of them were influenced negatively by the competitive environment in which they operated. For example, they made unethical decisions due to high competitiveness of their business environment, decisions that they never really wanted nor intended to make.

> The company thus comes forward as *"a matter for two"*, i.e., owners-directors and employees. At most, customers come timidly forward in third position. *The business is therefore not conceived as a social institution*, where all the groups of people involved and affected have something to say, to a greater or lesser extent. (Conill et al., 2000)

Influence from the industry in which the Spanish small business operates is also low. The level of participation in trade associations are low in the Valencian Community, normally the owner is an individualist and when participating in associations is only making a financial contribution rather than a participatory one. That means that co-operation and communication between firms from the same sector are not integral; if this communication were effective and intense, it would serve in helping to avoid many cases of corruption and unethical behaviour.

The most common Valencian entrepreneur is individualistic and trusts in their capacity and personal effort. When they should make a decision they normally turn to friends and family for advice or to technical or professional consultants such as lawyers or engineers.

> The acceptance of these situations – the widerspread between what is perceived as being immoral and at the same time is recognised as being commonplace – is one of the factors which favour bad practice, damage social life and form a culture medium for corruption. This has given even greater impetus to the social-business disintegration of the Valencian Community, traditionally affected by a lack of association-bonding and integration. And in any event these factors produce widespread demoralisation, above all from the point where the company has an increasingly important role in *social leadership*. (Conill et al., 2000)

To summarise, we can say that the most influential entity in small businesses in Spain are family, friends, the law, the consumer, and in some cases trade associations. The relationship between these entities are generally more competitive than co-operative; confrontations, are the normal way to drive these relationships, rather than the exception.

The Spanish-U.K. comparison illustrates the potential cultural differences in influencing small firms. While friends and family may be important influences in both cases in relation to attention to social and ethical issues, there are differences between the national groups. The law also has a role to play and policy makers should keep this in mind, even though business often lobby against regulation. The role of the employees seems to be more significant in the U.K. than Spain. Perhaps the lesson to be learned from the evidence presented here is that no single approach is likely to be successful in influencing small firm responses to social and ethical issues. A combination of approaches is most likely to lead to more ethically aware behaviour.

Tools of ethics

Tools of ethics such as formal codes of practice, the adoption of standards and mission statements were not evident in almost all the firms in the U.K. study. One example of a formal mission statement was found. The company that had a mission statement, was a marketing firm, and the statement was intended for external display and marketing rather than internal use.

Consideration of the characteristics of small firms may, however throw some light on the potential difficulty of using ethics tools in small firms. The opportunity for dialogue and management without the imposition of formal and bureaucratic controls can lead to the mistrust of bureaucracy and reliance on informal control mechanisms.

There is an interesting conundrum here which highlights the danger of the standard thinking on best practice procedures, particularly in potentially grey areas such as quality, the environment and ethics. All of these factors have associated International Standards which "best practice" would suggest should be followed for the guarantee of good practice in a firm, whatever the size. Examples of these are respectively: Quality, ISO9000; Environment, ISO14001; Social and Ethical Accountability; SA8000. Despite pressure by large firm customers for their suppliers to be accredited in such standards, they often signify a major investment of time, finances and energy for the small firm, none of which are likely to be in ready supply (Frentz et al., 1993). Even where, for example, a quality standard such as BS5750 has been adopted, Holliday (1995, pp. 170–171) has found evidence that the firm's compliance is disingenuous, what she calls "mock bureaucratic", and that everything returns to normal *ad hoc* practices as soon as the quality inspectors leave.

Externally dictated procedures sometimes run contrary to the needs of the small firm, where informal methods of control are preferred (North et al., 1998, p. 157). In a postal survey of 600 small and medium sized firms in Devon and Cornwall, Hutchinson and Chaston (1994) found that little more than a quarter were even *aware* of the well established British environmental management system BS7750. They argue that this lack of awareness is due to a lack of relevant resources and time constraints of small firms (p. 17). These constraints are likely to apply to many issues which are not seen as being of immediate urgency in the small firm. What is more, the need for such bureaucratic controls where systems and practices may not be lost in layers of hierarchy as they might in large firms is questionable. Some go as far as to say "There is no evidence to suggest that informal quality management based upon the personal involvement of business owners and employees with detailed knowledge of customer requirements is in any way inferior to more formal systems" (Chittenden et al., 1998, p. 85).

Social and ethical accounting standards and codes of practice may be inappropriate in the small firm where acceptable standards of behaviour can be clearly conveyed by the readily accessible example, and guidance, of the leadership. Small firms in the U.K. are, we can surmise, no more likely genuinely to take up standard, formalised controls for ethics than they have been enthusiastic for quality or environment standards. Ironically, it is this lack of inclination to embrace bureaucratic controls that can give the small firm the flexibility and responsiveness to demand which may afford them competitive advantage over larger, more cumbersome and formalised competitors.

From the Spanish perspective a workshop about management values for managers and owners of small businesses has been held. One of the principal objectives was to clarify if this management system was appropriate for small business. Most people considered that ethics in small businesses are applicable and very important. In fact, they think that although ethics itself is not formally institutionalised in business, it is omnipresent. But it is important to say that ethics in general are normally personal ethics, values that reflect the ideas and morals of the proprietor.

There is much scepticism about codes of ethics and the like. The participants in the workshop confirmed that it is possible and even very positive to develop and adopt a code of ethics, but they considered it not to be essential to develop such documents that depict the overall business values of the enterprise. They said that: "more than a mere written code, it was important that people knew and believed in the ethical and moral integrity of the business". Conill et al. (2000) said that:

> Businessmen and executives state that it "is no easy task" to bring *moral dynamism* into business practice, but they also confess that they have not bothered themselves over much about the matter, or made any special investment in creating the ideal mediation work to accomplish this business innovation. They prefer routine. As tends to be said: better the devil you know than the devil you don't know! They are in fact *frightened of ethical innovation*, distrusting its profitability and even its feasibility. They do not really believe that ethics will contribute anything substantial to social progress through the moral renovation of the life of companies. This is the reason for the lack of interest in institutionalising ethics in the life of companies, even though some refer to the need for "ethical codes ". It seems, once more, a symptom of not wishing to assume its "complexity", of rejecting this for all it entails in social commitment, and at most, a matter of putting up with an "institutionalising prescription" known as an ethical code.

Referring back to the sections on communicating about ethics with small firms and influences on ethics, more appropriate "tools" of ethics for small firms are likely to be consideration of how individual owner-managers feel about the work they do and themselves, sector acceptable standards, and how stakeholders feel about their relationships with the firm. The influencing of employees, family and friends through the media and education about acceptable business practices, may also have an important role to play.

Conclusions

The research presented here is intended to offer the basis for discussion and further research on ethics in small firms. The fact that small firms are different in nature from large firms, and their important role in the economy and society, means that ethics in the small firm requires special attention. Business ethics researchers would be well advised to take care in the terminology they adopt when attempting to access information about ethics issues in the small firm.

The indications are that the language of ethics as moral philosophy, while not totally alien to small firms is not readily part of their business discourse. However, the importance of the nature of relationships with stakeholders, and very personal, sometimes emotional, responses to business life do incorporate ethical elements. Certainly small firm owner-managers may have very firm personal convictions and these include ethical perspectives which, because of their position, can influence the activities of the firm as a whole.

Small firm owner-managers in the U.K. particularly are most likely to be influenced to pay more attention to social and ethical issues by their employees. This indicates the close knit nature of many small firm internal relations. In both Spain and the U.K., the law is also a strong influence on ethics, and policy makers would do well to recognise this and not necessarily rely on self-regulation. Customers and family and friends also have an important influence on small firm behaviour.

Education and training have a significant role to play. We agree with the conclusion of the research project *An ethical profile of business culture in the Valencian Community*, when they say: "Not many so far, but a few indeed are already well aware of the need to change the mentality of economic agents through their professional training, through the introduction of subjects in statutory training of the corresponding mid-level and higher level studies". What is needed, then is a culture shift on reasonable expectations of business as responsible actors in society.

This paper opens up more questions than it answers. Further research is critically important to help us understand the way small firm owner-managers think and act in their businesses in relation to ethics.

Notes

[1] In this research it was discovered that only 3% of the entrepreneurs have a five year University degree, 4.5% have a three year University degree, 4.4% have a 2nd level of professional raining, 4.2% have a 1st level of professional training, 11.7% have secondary education (upto 18), 23% have an elementary secondary education (upto 16), 43% have only primary education (upto 14); and 6.3% are illiterate.

[2] Cf. P. Pons et al., 1998. We accept the standard definition of small and medium sized enterprises as those businesses that have under 250 workers, although it should be recognised that in the Valencian environment there are few companies that exceed this number of workers (18.2%) and the majority are those with under 100 workers (64.1%); therefore companies with 150 workers are effectively "large companies". Cf. J. María Gil Suay (1995) ETNOR Documents.

[3] For a fuller account of the literature on "small business ethics", see Spence, 1999.

[4] The U.K. research reported upon here was funded by Kingston University, U.K. and the Institute of Business Ethics in London. The complete findings are in Spence (2000b).

References

Baumback, C.: 1988, *How to Organize and Operate a Small Business*, 8th ed. (Prenctice Hall, Englewood Cliffs).

Chittenden, F., S. Jack, J. Bower and E. Crabtree: 1998, 'Small Firms and the ISO 9000 Approach to Quality Management', *International Small Business Journal* **17**(1), No. 65, 73–88.

Conill, J. et al.: 2000 *El perfil Ético de la cultura empresarial en la Comunidad Valenciana*. ÉTNOR – Economía 3.

Curran, J. and R. Blackburn: 1994, *Small Firms and Local Economic Networks: The Death of the Local Economy?* (Paul Chapman, London).

Department of Trade and Industry: 1999, *Small and Medium Enterprise (SME) Statistics for the U.K., 1998*. Statistical Press Release P/99/662, 5 August 1999.

ENSR (European Network for SME Research): 1997, *The European Observatory for SMEs*. Fifth Annual Report (EIM Small Business Research Consultancy, Zoetermeer).

Frentz, A., J. Nouws and A. Zwaard: 1993,

Milieubeleid en MKB (Economic Institute for the Small and Medium Sized Firm, Zoetermeer).

García-Echevarría, S.: 1994, *Innovación y competitividad en la PYMES*. Instituto de Dirección y Organización de empresa. Working-Papers no. 212. Universidad de Alcalá.

Gil Suay, J. María: 1995, *ETNOR Documents* (Valencia).

Holliday, R.: 1995, *Investigating Small Firms: Nice Work?* (Routledge, London).

Hutchinson, A. and I. Chaston: 1994, 'Environmental Management in Devon and Cornwall's Small and Medium Sized Enterprise Sector', *Business Strategy and the Environment* **3**(1), 15–22.

North, J., R. Blackburn and J. Curran: 1998, *The Quality Business: Quality Issues in Smaller Firms* (Routledge Studies in Small Business, London).

Palafox, J., J. G. Mora and F. Perez: 1995, *Capital Humano, Educación y Empleo* (Fundación BANCAIXA).

Pons, F., E. Belenguer and J. Félix Lozano: 1998, 'The Participation of Workers in the Company', paper presented at the European Business Ethics Network conference on *The Ethics of Participation* (Leuven, Belgium), 9–11 September.

Quinn, J. J.: 1997, 'Personal Ethics and Business Ethics: The Ethical Attitudes of Owner/Managers of Small Business', *Journal of Business Ethics* **16**(2), 119–127.

Spence, L. J.: 1999, 'Does Size Matter? The State of the Art in Small Business Ethics', *Business Ethics: A European Review* (July, 8).

Spence, L. J.: 2000a, 'Towards a Human Centred Organisation: The Case of the Small Firm', paper pesented at the 3rd Conference on Ethics in Contemporary Human Resource Management, Imperical College, London, 7 January.

Spence, L. J.: 2000b, *Practices, Priorities and Ethics in Small Firms* (Institute of Business Ethics, London).

Vyakarnam, S.: 1995, 'Focus Groups: Are They Viable in Ethics Research?', *Business Ethics: A European Review* **4**(1), 24–29.

Vyakarnam, S., A. Bailey, A. Myers and D. Burnett: 1997, 'Towards an Understanding of Ethical Behaviour in Small Firms', *Journal of Business Ethics* **16**(15), 1625–1636.

Laura J. Spence
School of Business and Management,
Brunel University,
Uxbridge, Middlesex, UB8 3PH,
U.K.
E-mail: Laura.Spence@brunel.ac.uk

J. Félix Lozano
ETNOR, Navarro Reverter,
10, 8 46004 Valencia,
Spain
E-mail: jflozano@etnor.org

Corporate Communication and Impression Management – New Perspectives Why Companies Engage in Corporate Social Reporting

Reggy Hooghiemstra

ABSTRACT. This paper addresses the theoretical framework on corporate social reporting. Although that corporate social reporting has been analysed from different perspectives, legitimacy theory currently is the dominating perspective. Authors employing this framework suggest that social and environmental disclosures are responses to both public pressure and increased media attention resulting from major social incidents such as the Exxon Valdez oil spill and the chemical leak in Bhopal (India). More specifically, those authors argue that the increase in social disclosures represent a strategy to alter the public's perception about the legitimacy of the organisation. Therefore, we suggest using corporate communication as an overarching framework to study corporate social reporting in which "corporate image" and "corporate identity" are central.

KEY WORDS: corporate communication, corporate social reporting, impression management, theoretical framework

1. Introduction

Corporate social behaviour has become an important aspect of business society. Not only are the press and society increasingly paying attention to it, the number of companies reporting on their social and environmental achievements has also increased over the years (e.g. Brown and Deegan, 1998; Deegan and Gordon, 1996; Gray et al., 1997; Gray et al., 1996; Zadek et al., 1997).[1]

Apart from business society and the media, academics also increasingly are paying attention to corporate social reporting. This research, however, is mainly descriptive and aimed at the identification of factors that explain why one firm pays more attention to corporate social reporting than another (Hackston and Milne, 1996). Although it seems that firm size, industry type, profitability, and country influence the amount of corporate social reporting (e.g. Adams et al., 1998; Deegan and colleagues, 1996, 1998; Gray et al., 1995, 1996; Guthrie and Parker, 1990; Hackston and Milne, 1996; Neu et al., 1998; Patten, 1991, 1992), the results are characterised by diversity (Belkaoui and Karpik, 1989) and inconsistencies (Ullmann, 1985). According to Ullmann one of the main reasons for these inconsistencies is a lack in a comprehensive theory.

The different theoretical perspectives employed to study corporate social reporting, e.g. agency and legitimacy theories have in common that they all stress that companies engage in corporate social reporting to affect public's perceptions of the company (e.g. Brown and Deegan, 1998; Neu et al., 1998; Zadek et al., 1997). Most clearly such a notion emerge in the studies utilising the legitimacy framework which currently is the dominating perspective (Gray et al., 1995). Authors employing this framework suggest

Reggy Hooghiemstra is a doctoral candidate in international financial accounting at the Erasmus University Rotterdam. In addition, he is a research associate in corporate governance at the University of Groningen.

Journal of Business Ethics **27**: 55–68, 2000.
© 2000 *Kluwer Academic Publishers. Printed in the Netherlands.*

that social and environmental disclosures are responses to both public pressure (Patten, 1991, 1992; Walden and Schwartz, 1998) and increased media attention (Brown and Deegan, 1998; Deegan et al., 1999) resulting from major social incidents such as the Exxon Valdez oil spill and the chemical leak in Bhopal (India). More specifically, these authors argue that the increase in social disclosures "represent a strategy to alter the public's perception about the legitimacy of the organisation" (Deegan et al., 1999, p. 4). Therefore, we suggest using corporate communication as an overarching framework to study corporate social reporting in which "corporate image" and "corporate identity" are central. Following Van Riel (1995, p. 27) the first refers to "the picture people have of a company", whereas corporate identity refers to "all the forms of expression that a company uses to offer insight into its nature", including corporate social reporting.

The remainder of the paper is organised as follows. First, we will briefly pay attention to the legitimacy perspective on corporate social reporting. After having discussed the essentials of corporate communication, we will apply the concepts to Shell/Royal Dutch, and, more specifically, to its reactions after the controversies regarding the Brent Spar. The paper ends with a discussion and suggestions for future research.

2. Legitimacy theory

Of the theoretical frameworks employed to analyse corporate social reporting, viz. decision usefulness studies, economic theory studies, and the social and political economy studies (e.g. Gray et al., 1995, 1996; Hackston and Milne, 1996) the latter is particularly relevant in the context of this paper. Within that category, several theoretical frameworks are used, viz. the political economy, the stakeholder theory, and the legitimacy theory which may be viewed as overlapping perspectives (Gray et al., 1995, 1996). Of these, legitimacy theory is the most widely used framework to explain disclosures with regard to the environmental and social behaviour of organisations (Gray et al., 1995; for

applications see e.g. Adams et al., 1998; Deegan and colleagues, 1996, 1998, 1999; Guthrie and Parker, 1989; Neu et al., 1998; O'Donovan, 1997; Patten, 1991, 1992). Central to legitimacy theory is the concept of a social contract, implying that a company's survival is dependent on the extent that the company operates "within the bounds and norms of [the] society" (Brown and Deegan, 1998, p. 22). However, as the societal bounds and norms may change over time, the organisation continuously has to demonstrate that its actions are legitimate and that it behaved as a good corporate citizen, usually by engaging in corporate social reporting. Therefore, corporate social reporting may primarily be considered as a reaction to factors in the company's environment (Guthrie and Parker, 1989) and notably public pressure (Neu et al., 1998; Patten, 1991; Walden and Schwartz, 1997). Indeed, research by Deegan and colleagues (1996, 1998, 1999) and Patten (1991, 1992) indicate that the amount of environmental and social disclosures is particularly high when the organisation or the industry in which it operates has to face a predicament, e.g. environmental pollution, violation of human rights, prosecution of the company, et cetera. Companies' responses to such public pressure and/or negative media attention, involving increasing the amount of – mainly self-laudatory – disclosures, is aimed at reducing the "exposure of the company to the social and political environment" (Patten, 1992, p. 472).[2] Following Lindblom (1994; quoted in Gray et al., 1996) companies can adopt four possible strategies to respond to such public pressure, viz.: (1) inform stakeholders about the intentions of the company to enhance its social performance, (2) try to influence stakeholders' perceptions concerning certain (negative) events, but without changing actual behaviour, (3) distract attention away from the legitimacy threatening event by emphasising more positive actions which not necessarily have to be related, and (4) try to influence external or stakeholders' expectations about its behaviour.

3. The corporate communication concept

3.1. *Introduction; from legitimacy theory to corporate communication*

As emerge from the preceding discussion it seems that corporate social reporting is aimed at influencing people's perceptions about the company. To do so management is willing to report "good news" but reluctant to disclose "bad news", implying that social and environmental disclosures are to a large extent self-laudatory (Deegan and colleagues, 1996, 1998, 1999; Hackston and Milne, 1996). According to legitimacy theory corporate social reporting is aimed at providing information that legitimises company's behaviour by intending to influence stakeholders' and eventually society's perceptions about the company (e.g. O'Donovan, 1997; Neu et al., 1998) in such a way that the company is regarded a "good corporate citizen" and its actions justify its continued existence (Guthrie and Parker, 1989). In this respect then, corporate social reporting is "a public relations vehicle" aimed at influencing people's perceptions. Part of this proposition can be substantiated by Elkington's (1997, p. 171) comment that "a large part of companies engaging in corporate social reporting view their reports as public relations vehicles, designed to offer reassurance and to help with "feel-good" image building", an argument that was also made by Gray et al. (1993). This is when corporate communication comes into play and to which we turn our attention now.

3.2. *Corporate communication defined*

Corporate communication is a relatively new field of interest within marketing research. Van Riel (1995, p. 26) defines corporate communication as "an instrument of management by means of which all consciously used forms of internal and external communication are harmonised as effectively and efficiently as possible, so as to create a favourable basis for relationships with groups upon which the company is dependent". Others, e.g. Argenti (1994) and Gray and Balmer (1998) employ similar definitions of corporate communication. The closely related concepts of "corporate identity" and "corporate image" (Argenti, 1994; Van Riel, 1995) are central to corporate communication and are covered below.

3.3. *Corporate identity*

Birkigt and Stadler (1986) as quoted in Van Riel (1995, p. 30) describe corporate identity as "the strategically planned and operationally applied internal and external self-presentation and behaviour of a company". Albert and Whetten (1985) employ a similar definition as they see corporate identity as what organisational members believe to be the organisation's central, enduring, and distinctive character, which filters and moulds an organisation's interpretation of and action on an issue (Dutton and Dukerich, 1991). So, essentially, corporate identity refers to the way the organisation presents itself to an audience. Following Birkigt and Stadler (1986, as cited in Van Riel, 1995) this self-presentation of companies may be developed in three ways, namely: behaviour, communication, and symbolism. According to them a company's behaviour is the most effective medium to create or to harm a corporate identity. After all, target groups will judge the company by its actions although it is acknowledged that providing information on the actions is also important (Deegan et al., 1999). Hence, it is also possible to emphasise particular aspects of company behaviour by means of communication and/or symbols. Concerning communication both Birkigt and Stadler (1986) and Van Riel (1995) comment that it is the most flexible medium and that it can be used tactically, so that it may "help to manage an organisation's relationship with relevant publics through the shaping of external perceptions – by echoing, enlisting and harmonising with other discourses" (Neu et al., 1998, p. 266).

Others, e.g. Elsbach (1994), Meyer and Rowan (1977), and Pfeffer (1981) also point to the importance of communication and symbolism as self-presentational devices. More specifically, Pfeffer proposed that an important function of management is a symbolic one. By providing explanations, rationalisations, and legitimation for the organisational activities (Pfeffer, 1981; Elsbach, 1994), management wants to create an image that the organisation's activities are legitimate (Dowling and Pfeffer, 1975; Neu et al., 1998). It has been argued that language (and symbolism) may be used as responses to legitimacy threats (e.g. Carter and Dukerich, 1998; Elsbach, 1994; Elsbach and Sutton, 1992). These authors seem to support Dowling and Pfeffer's notion that "[t]he organisation can attempt through communication, to alter the definition of social legitimacy so that it conforms to the organisation's present practices, output and values [or] . . . the organisation can attempt, again through communication, to become identified with symbols, values, or institutions which have a strong base of social legitimacy" (1975, p. 127). For example, Elsbach and Sutton (1992) illustrate how an environmental protest organisation like Earth First! – which typically applies violence if necessary, and as a consequence continuously has to face legitimacy threats after committing an illegitimate action – can use the negative publicity to its advantage by first decoupling from the action ("it was committed by individuals, which were no Earth First! members"), then justifying the actions ("they were necessary to save the life of the planet"; thereby also shifting attention from means to ends), and finally using enhancements and entitlements (which emphasise the good intentions of the actions, respectively the successful outcomes which otherwise could not have been achieved) in order to arouse sympathy, which in turn secures the organisational legitimacy.

In a way corporate social reporting may also be viewed as such a self-presentational device. As previous research revealed, social disclosures are mainly self-laudatory (e.g. Deegan and colleagues, 1996, 1998; Neu et al., 1998) which indicates that the use of enhancements and entitlements is common here. The main goal of these disclosures is to show that the company is legitimate (Elsbach and Sutton, 1992), i.e. that organisational actions and the values of relevant publics are congruent (e.g. Dowling and Pfeffer, 1975; Meyer and Rowan, 1977; Neu et al.,

1998). In addition, it also may be intended to inspire confidence among the company's external target groups and acknowledging their vital role in order to secure their contribution to the organisation (Van Riel, 1995).

3.4. *Corporate image/reputation*

This brings us to corporate image which Van Riel (1995, p. 23) (following Dowling, 1986) defines as "a set of meanings by which an object is known and through which people describe, remember and relate to it. That is the result of the interaction of a person's beliefs, ideas, feelings and impressions about an object". Dutton and Dukerich (1991) in a similar way define an organisation's image as the way organisational members believe others see the organisation. Hence, corporate image involves other people's perceptions of the organisation (e.g. Argenti, 1994; Gray and Balmer, 1998), which is the result of information transmitted via mass media and through interpersonal communication (Dowling, 1986). Therefore, it is suggested that a company's image or reputation depends on "what people *think* is true and *feel* is important" (Zadek et al., 1997, p. 29; italics in original).[3]

Many authors have stressed the importance of images or reputations for firms (e.g. Carter and Dukerich, 1998; Dowling, 1986; Fombrun, 1996) and the individuals connected therewith (e.g. Dutton et al., 1994). From Fombrun (1996) it is apparent that firms with good reputations can among other things charge premium prices, enhance their access to capital markets, attract investors more easily, and have better credit ratings, which usually imply lower interest rates. Hence, reputation can form a competitive advantage for firms. It seems that a firm's reputation is affected by, among others, the quality of management, company's financial soundness and its demonstration of social concerns. In addition, it has also been proposed that narratives may contribute to the building of a company's reputation (Vendelø, 1998). Therefore, we assume that firms can try to influence their reputation by engaging in corporate social reporting. One way of doing this is the use of impression management techniques described below.

3.5. *Relationship between corporate identity and corporate image*

It is clear that there is a relationship between image and identity (e.g. Argenti, 1994; Birkigt and Stadler, 1986; Dutton and Dukerich, 1991; Van Riel, 1995). Birkigt and Stadler (1986) note that the image of a company is a projection of its identity, an argument that is supported by Van Riel (1995). Basically, these authors argue that the way organisations present themselves to an audience (corporate identity) may influence the audience's perceptions of the organisation (corporate image). However, this relationship does not confine itself to a one-way interaction. Several authors stress that the way the audience perceives the organisation also influences the organisation's self-presentation (e.g. Dutton and Dukerich, 1991; Elsbach and Kramer, 1996; Gray and Balmer, 1998; Morsing, 1999), mainly because "the media play a significant role in affecting organisational identity by influencing members' perception of how non-members perceive the organisation [. . .] (Dutton and Dukerich, 1991; Dutton, Dukerich, and Harquail, 1994)" (Morsing, 1999, p. 118). In support of this view, Dutton and Dukerich (1991) show how organisations typically react to image threats. The early response will according to them be in line with the organisation's identity and may include for example the use of denials; a result Elsbach and Kramer (1996) also found in their study of reactions of university administrators to *Business Week*'s ranking of universities. The response, however, aggravates the problems with the image. As a consequence organisations will adapt its strategy and use more pronounced and assertive image management strategy, e.g. "seeking (communication) partners which eventually may modify the organisation's future identity or make certain features of the identity more or less salient" (Dutton and Dukerich, 1991, p. 520).

3.6. *Reputation/image, industry, and mass media*

So far we basically proposed that companies use corporate social reporting as a corporate communication instrument. The main aim of the use of corporate communication instruments is to influence people's perceptions of the company. That is, it is aimed at influencing corporate images or reputations. Reputations or images, however, are to a certain extent beyond the organisation's control as they are also based on affiliations (Vendelø, 1998), implying that a company's reputation depends on the industry in which it operates and the narratives in the mass media about that company. Indeed, some of the previous studies on corporate social reporting seem to support this notion. Blacconiere and Patten's (1994) study supports the first claim, as it shows that although other chemical companies were not involved in the Union Carbide chemical leak in Bhopal, they also experienced a decrease in share prices, maybe because they were associated with the leak. In another study, Patten and Nance (1998) found that the disaster with the Exxon Valdez in Alaska provided "good news" for the oil sector in that gasoline and oil prices subsequently rose. Their results indicate that the oil industry's reaction (in terms of share prices) in general was positive, although "firms with operations in Alaska had a less positive reaction than firms with no such operation" (Patten and Nance, 1998, p. 411). These results suggest the presence of such an affiliation relationship. This is also confirmed by Patten's (1992) and Deegan et al.'s (1999) study in which they showed that companies operating in an industry that experienced a major social incident, responded to it by increasing their coverage of environmental issues in annual reports. Notably these disclosures were to a large extent aimed at showing the legitimacy of their ongoing operations (Deegan et al., 1999; Patten, 1992).

Concerning the narratives in the mass media, there is evidence (e.g. Adler and Milne, 1997; Deegan and colleagues, 1998, 1999; O'Donovan, 1997) that firms respond to it by increasing the amount of social and environmental disclosures in their annual reports. These studies, and especially those of Brown and Deegan (1998) and Deegan et al. (1999), employed the (media) agenda-setting theory. The underlying assumption of this framework is that the media is able to "change the public's perception about the importance of particular issues" (Deegan et al., 1999, p. 11). In addition, these authors propose that "as a result of extensive media coverage [. . .] the *perceived* legitimacy of the specific corporations involved, as well as the corporations operating in that industry" may be threatened (Deegan et al., 1999, p. 3; italics added). Other studies (Dutton and Dukerich, 1991; Elsbach and Sutton, 1992) also showed that the media is able to influence public's perceptions with regard to corporate images/reputations. Indeed, O'Donovan (1997) interviewed senior executives of three large Australian companies who confirmed that the media is able to shape society's expectations and that social and environmental disclosures are used to correct "misperceptions held or presented by the media". Therefore it is not surprising that management will use the annual report in an attempt to counteract the effects of the negative media coverage following a major social incident which, according to the media agenda setting theory, will influence public perceptions relating to the issue (Brown and Deegan, 1998). In a similar way, Duimering and Safayeni (1998, p. 63) propose that "organisations compensate for negative information by attempting to construct images that overemphasise the positive aspects of their activities and by attempting to manage and control the flow of organisational information received by these constituents". Indeed, Brown and Deegan (1998) confirmed this in their study of Australian corporations, although *not* for the oil and gas industry.

4. Impression management

4.1. *Definition*

As indicated before, organisations can try to influence people's perceptions of the company by using self-presentational devices. Self-presentation or impression management is a field of study

within social psychology and is concerned with studying how individuals present themselves to others in order to be perceived favourably by others. Schlenker defines impression management as "the conscious or unconscious attempt to control images that are projected in real or imagined social interactions" (1980, p. 6; see also e.g. Rosenfeld et al. (1995) and Tedeschi and Riess (1981)).

Impression management can take many forms, both verbally as well as non-verbally (e.g. facial expression, dress, et cetera). Although people are not always aware of the impression they convey, a certain strategic behaviour can be assumed. According to Schlenker and Weigold (1992, pp. 134–135) impression management is influenced by people's agenda's, i.e. their overt or covert interpersonal goals and their plans to achieve these goals. Impression management, though essentially being a "theory" of the individual, has been applied extensively to organisations for example to explain the reactions of firms facing legitimacy threats (Elsbach, 1994; Elsbach and Kramer, 1996; Elsbach and Sutton, 1992) and to account for directors' self-serving way of explaining changes in firms' performance in the annual reports (e.g. Aerts, 1994; Staw et al., 1983).

In the context of corporate social reporting, impression management may be important considering two aspects (which have been addressed earlier in the paper). First, corporate social reporting as a form of impression management can contribute to firms' reputations. Second, especially firms faced with a predicament, can, by using impression management, effectively handle legitimacy threats that in turn could affect both reputation and stock price. Below some relevant impression management techniques are covered.

4.2. *Impression management strategies*

In the literature on impression management many possible strategies and typologies thereof are presented (e.g. Rosenfeld et al., 1995; Schlenker, 1980). For the purpose of this paper, however, the distinction between acquisitive (or proactive) and protective (or reactive) strategies is suitable.

The most interesting acquisitive tactic is that of acclaiming. This form of impression management is mainly used in the case of a successful or desired outcome and are, according to Schlenker (1980, p. 163), "designed to explain a desirable event in a way that maximises their desirable implications for the actor". The tactics of acclaiming, comprising of "enhancements" and "entitlements", are adopted particularly when circumstances appear to deprive the actor of credit for desirable events (Schlenker, 1980, pp. 163ff.). Entitlements is a tactic that maximises the actor's responsibility for the event and is used when that responsibility is either ambiguous or unclear (Schlenker, 1980). In the case of enhancements the responsibility question is beyond doubt, so the actor will try to maximise the desirability of the event itself (Schlenker, 1980).

These two acclaiming tactics have exact opposites: viz. excuses and apologies, the so-called accounting tactics (Schlenker, 1980), that originally have been proposed by Scott and Lyman (1968); see also Table I below.

Accounting tactics are, according to Schlenker (1980) a form of remedial tactics aimed at offering the audience, real or imagined, an explanation of or an apology for a predicament that can place the actor and the event in a different perspective. By doing so, Schlenker proceeds, the actor attempts to minimise the negative repercussions of the predicaments. In the case of excuses the actor tries to deny responsibility for an action he admits is wrong. The "best" excuses

are in general those which attribute failure to external, uncontrollable, or unintentional causes and offer the actor effective protection (Schlenker and Weigold, 1992). As is the case with many other forms of impression management, excuses are effective only if and so far as they provide a believable explanation for the problem. As a consequence, the excuses offered by people "fit the facts" to a large extent (Schlenker, 1980). In the case of justifications the person accepts responsibility but denies that the act was bad or wrong, in order to reduce the negativeness of the consequences. Scott and Lyman (1968) and more recently Tedeschi and Riess (1981) presented more detailed typologies of these two accounts to which we would like to refer the interested reader. Another remedial tactic is the use of apologies in which the actor admits blameworthiness for an undesirable event, but at the same time he attempts to convince the audience that the undesirable event should not be considered a fair representation of what the actor is "really like" as a person (Schlenker, 1980). The use of an apology in an annual report is, however, not very likely. According to Giacalone (1988) it is often not the best strategy for the failing manager to use, because an apology explicitly admits failure, leaving the leader at the mercy of observers. The use of accounts seems better: inasmuch as an individual's accounts usually involve the denial of responsibility, the leader's audience will be less likely to make a dispositional attribution, because the leader's intent to commit the questionable act is directly denied by the use of the account (Giacalone, 1988, p. 196).

5. The Shell/Royal Dutch case

In 1995 Shell experienced a lot of negative publicity after it announced its decision to sink the Brent Spar in the Atlantic Ocean. Environmental protection groups, especially Greenpeace, started a public offence, i.e. an "anti-Shell campaign", in order to prevent this, which received a considerable amount of media coverage in both the United Kingdom as well as in the Netherlands. The initiatives of Greenpeace were successful in influencing public opinion: not only was Shell

TABLE I
Acclaiming versus accounting tactics (based on Tedeschi and Riess, 1981)

	Positive, acclaiming	Negative, accounting
Addresses responsibility	Entitlements	Excuses
Addresses consequences	Enhancements	Justifications

confronted with a boycott (to which many customers responded) in, e.g. The Netherlands, Germany and the United Kingdom (and as a consequence Shell experienced a drop in sales), but also the politicians outside the United Kingdom put question marks with Shell's decision, though being formally and governmentally approved.

In order to counter these effects, and possibly to try to influence people's perceptions, Shell responded somewhat stubbornly (but in conformity to their identity; see Dutton and Dukerich, 1990): they remained that the sinking of the Brent Spar was the best solution, and tried to substantiate this by placing adds in national newspapers in which they referred to independent research, and they said that Greenpeace made false accusations (for which Greenpeace afterwards made apologies). Typically, Shell in its initial reactions and even after its "climbdown" stressed that it had followed the rules, as may be clear from the following quotation from *The Financial Times* (21 June 1995):

> Shell's decision to abandon its plans for the Brent Spar is a deeply humiliating climbdown for a company which prides itself on its high environmental standards and thoroughness.
>
> Mr Chris Fay, the chairman of Shell UK, normally an ebullient man, looked downcast and dismayed last night as he broke the news in the glare of television lights. But even in defeat, Shell found it difficult to accept that it had made a catastrophic misjudgement. Deep-sea disposal was still the option favoured by years of independent study, Mr Fay insisted, and everything had been done exactly according to the book.

These reactions, however, had no effect on public opinion, except that it worsened Shell's image. By communicating this way Shell, unintentionally, confirmed people's (including at that time media's) perceptions that Shell was a powerful company which did what it wanted and hardly reckons with its social responsibilities.[4] Further "evidence" for this negative image was provided some months later regarding Shell's role in Nigeria and especially with concern to the Ogonis. In addition, also the images of other oil companies were affected negatively by these

controversies, as research by Shell indicated (*The Financial Times*, 19 September 1995), confirming the existence of an affiliation relationship.

Having learned from this experience and its negative consequences (drop in share prices and sales), Shell decided to initiate a debate with some of its stakeholders. Not only were several researchers, environmental interest groups, and other experts invited to bring up possible, alternative solutions, but Shell also changed its communication style from "buffering" to "bridging" (Van Riel and Van den Bosch, 1997),[5] showing their vulnerable position to society (Kaptein and Wempe, 1998) and thereby somewhat changing their identity, i.e. way of presenting themselves. Representatives from several stakeholder groups, e.g. employees, Greenpeace, Pax Christi, et cetera, were also invited to discuss with the management board on a kind of a code of best practice. This led to the (revision of the) statement of business principles which was published in 1997. Furthermore, in order to communicate to the community on its achievements with respect to its social responsibilities, Shell published an ethical report in 1998: "Profits and principles: Does there have to be a choice?" that in 1999 was followed by "People, planet, and profits – An act of commitment". In these reports Shell made use of the impression management techniques described earlier. Some examples from the 1998 report are provided below.

> Shell companies have invested in the development of biomass (plant matter) and solar energy for the past 20 years. We have tree plantation interests in Argentina, Chile [. . .]. We have played a lead part in the development of sustainable forestry standards and the use of wood as a clean source of renewable energy (entitlement).

> Shell South Africa continues to fund and promote a wide range of community projects in the country. Its work has been publicly recognised and was most recently shortlisted for the Worldaware Award for Sustainable Development in 1997. It won the Lawrie Group Award for Social Progress in 1997 [. . .]. The judges said with its [. . .] project and ongoing educational services, Shell has been a long-standing contributor to South African education, both during and after apartheid (enhancement).

The execution in 1995 of Ken Saro-Wiwa and eight other Ogonis shocked and saddened as of us. Before Mr Saro-Wira's arrest we said that while we did not necessarily agree with all of his views, he had the right to voice his opinions. After his arrest we said he said be treated fairly in prison and should be given the necessary medical attention. We did not seek to influence his trial, but after the verdict the Chairman of the Group's Committee of Managing Directors sent a letter to the Nigerian head of state urging him to grant clemency for all those sentenced. [. . .] We are the only major company operating in the country to call publicly, and repeatedly, for humane treatment, a fair trial for the detainees and clemency for those found guilty (excuse).

Brent Spar, the redundant storage and loading buoy which was the centre of controversy over plans for its deep-sea disposal in 1995, will be used to build a quay extension near Stavanger in Norway, if the plans meets official approval. The original plans, which were given statutory and governmental approval, were opposed when the time came to carry them out. Protesters felt that the sea should not be used as a dumping ground and were concerned that other oil installations would be disposed of in the same way if the sinking of the Spar went ahead. Many false allegations were made but these were difficult to rebut in the highly-charged atmosphere of confrontation that prevailed at the time. [. . .] In the face of such public opinion against its plans, Shell UK halted the disposal and the Spar was towed to a mooring . . . while its final fate was decided. Test by an independent Norwegian foundation . . . disproved claims by Greenpeace that the Spar was a "toxic timebomb". Greenpeace later apologised (justification).

Although not formally tested it may be expected that the use of entitlements and enhancements will be more prominent than the use of excuses and justifications. Not only would this be in conformity with the earlier findings of, e.g. Deegan and colleagues (1996, 1998, 1999) that corporate social reporting is mainly self-laudatory, moreover such a strategy would contribute to (re)build the image of a socially and environmentally aware company (Grolin, 1998; Neale, 1997; *The Financial Times*, 20 June 1995). Indeed, it was much easier to find examples of

the acclaiming tactics than the accounting tactics in the 1998 Shell report.

These changes in communication are a clear indication of Shell's response to a changing business environment:

Business is starting to talk about a move away from a "trust me" world of the past where people trusted business (and government) to do the best for society, to a "tell me" and increasingly "show me" world, where business has to demonstrate that it is indeed doing the best it can do for the broader society (The Shell Report 1998).

In addition, Shell acknowledged in that report that in the past communication was not as open as it should be. By inserting so-called "Tell Shell"-cards, readers were given the opportunity to express their ideas on dilemmas such as shareholder value versus social investment, doing business with a developing country where corruption and bribery are commonplace, the way of communicating by multinationals, et cetera. Furthermore, to stimulate openness Shell posted these views on the Internet and some of them – including critical ones – in "The Shell Report 1999".

These initiatives also contributed to the improvement of their image as indicated by Elkington in Shell's "Profits and Principles"-report. In addition in the Netherlands, Shell was rewarded the Yearly Communications Price in 1996, because "the company publicly faced the communicative consequences of the Brent Spar fiasco and responded to it by taking a drastic U-turn in its communication policy" (*Het Financieele Dagblad*, 2 June 1996). Finally, Shell seems to be committed to this new communication strategy: it launched a Corporate Reputation Campaign in the beginning of 1999. With this new campaign Shell also acknowledged the importance of a favourable reputation. To create or sustain a favourable reputation the campaign will concentrate on three issues, which are: "What Shell does (the business performance and quality of that performance), How Shell does it (its culture, approach and values), and How it is seen to do it (social accountability" ("Enhancing our reputation" in Shell World, December 1998 on www.shell.com). Furthermore, as part of the campaign, Shell launched "Profits and Principles"-advertisements which deal with eight different dilemmas. In addition, as part of this campaign and to stimulate a dialogue people are requested to offer their views regarding Shell's position on each of these dilemmas. To stimulate openness, the views are presented on the Internet at www.shell.com/explore. This commitment to more openness and accountability is clearly expressed by Mr. Moody-Stuart, the Group Chairman of Shell/Royal Dutch, at the launch of the Web-site:

> While much of our attention this year is going into making the business more profitable, this is not an excuse to neglect our longer-term responsibilities. That would have been very easy, but also very wrong. We are making a real commitment to sustainable development and we want to talk about what that means in practice. [. . .] We don't claim to have all the answers on how multinationals should behave in terms of human rights and environmental stewardship. But we have learned from our consultations and from hard experience that we won't achieve our business goals unless we are listening to and learning from the full range of our stakeholders in society. [. . .] This new campaign is about widening the reach of that engagement and developing the dialogue to take in all aspects of sustainable development, the economic as well as environmental and social. That is why advertising has a role to play – to bring our issues into the open and invite comment ("Shell steps up dialogue with stakeholders" on media.shell.com).

6. Discussion

From the preceding discussion on the application of corporate communication to corporate social reporting it is clear that there are commonalties and differences with the current framework. The most obvious commonality is that both the corporate communication as well as, e.g. the legitimacy perspective view corporate social reporting as a means to influence people's perceptions. Whereas under the current framework corporate social reporting is aimed at providing information to legitimise company's actions, corporate social reporting from a corporate communication perspective is aimed at protecting or enhancing its image or reputation. Moreover, from the corporate communication perspective it also can be argued that corporate social reporting can contribute in creating a competitive advantage: creating a positive image may imply that people are to a greater extent prepared to do business with the company and buy its products.

The application of the corporate communication concepts to Shell's handling of the Brent Spar shows that Shell's early responses, placing an emphasis on rationality and compliance to regulations, were not very successful. Indeed, this way of responding seemed to worsen Shell's image (and that of the whole oil sector too): media coverage of Shell in Germany, the Netherlands, and the United Kingdom was very negative as research of Oegema et al. (1998) has indicated. However, this way of communicating or self-presentation ("buffering") was in conformity with its identity (Dutton and Dukerich, 1991) and seems "natural" to large companies that possess an important resource (Meznar and Nigh, 1995). Having learned from its experiences and because "a company's reputation can be its most valuable asset, but when it is damaged it becomes the albatross around the corporate neck" ("Projecting the values" in Shell World, April 1999 on media.shell.com), Shell not only changed its communication strategy to "bridging" but, in addition, placed a large emphasis on ethical standards. In doing so, Shell changed its identity, indicating that business is not a question of "profits *or* principles" but that both are important. This "new" image of a company that highly values principles and strives at more openness and transparency became apparent through several initiatives, e.g. a stakeholder dialogue on its business principles and the publication of a value reports since 1998. Although Shell's intentions may be pure, it also seems that these initiatives were in fact aimed at influencing people's thoughts about Shell and its place in society and, hence, its reputation.

Concerning the possibilities for future research the "Shell-case" could be very interesting: especially studies whether, and if so, to what extent the publication of its ethical report has contributed to create a more positive image may be very useful. Such research may validate the application of corporate communication to corporate social reporting. Furthermore, "The Shell Report" as well as other corporate social reports can be used to study which are the impression management techniques organisations typically use, whether the acclaiming tactics are more prominently used than the accounting tactics, and also which of these are, given the circumstances, most appropriate from the audience's perspective.

Acknowledgements

Earlier versions of the paper have been presented at the 22nd European Accounting Association Congress in Bordeaux (July 1999) and at the12th European Business Ethics Network Congress in Amsterdam (September 1999). The author would like to acknowledge the helpful comments made by Muel Kaptein, Jacek Sojka, Leo van der Tas, Johan Wempe, and the participants at the two workshops.

Notes

[1] Following Gray et al. (1996, p. 3) corporate social reporting may be defined as ". . . the process of communicating the social and environmental effects of organisations economic actions to particular interest groups within society and to society at large. As such, it involves extending the accountability of organisations (particularly companies), beyond the traditional role of providing a financial account to the owners of capital, in particular, shareholders". Usually it involves reporting on the following areas: the environment, human rights, animal protection, employees' interests, and ethical standards (Gray et al., 1995, 1996).

[2] Research in different countries show that social and environmental disclosures in annual reports are biased: companies stress positive achievements, but hardly pay attention to negative news (Deegan and colleagues, 1996, 1998; Guthrie and Parker, 1990; Neu et al., 1998). Such a self-serving bias is also present in the explanations of improvements or deterioration of companies' results in the CEO's Letter to the Shareholder. Research by, e.g. Aerts (1994) and Staw et al. (1983) show that managers claim responsibility for successes, but are less prepared to accept responsibility for failures (i.e. deterioration of performance).

[3] The distinction between "corporate image" and "corporate reputation" is not very clear. Authors use them interchangeably without any clear difference of meaning. Definitions of reputation are neither very helpful as they are very broad. E.g. Fombrun (1996) describes corporate reputations as perceptions of a company held by people inside and outside a company, which is the outcome of a competitive process in which firms signal their key characteristics to constituents to maximise their social status. Maybe the only difference relates to time: while image refers to more momentarily perceptions a reputation refers to more enduring, stable characteristics (e.g. Gray and Balmer, 1998; Rindova, 1997).

[4] Research of major Dutch, English and German newspapers in the first month of the Brent Spar controversy shows that in the media Shell was evaluated very negative, while Greenpeace was evaluated positively (Oegema et al., 1998). Despite the large amount of negative publicity, Shell only dropped two places – from 3rd to 5th – in *The Financial Times' Survey of Europe's Most Respected Companies*. A possible explanation for this slight decrease may be that the survey was conducted "too soon after the Brent Spar fiasco" or "that businessmen take a longer view than the media when judging companies' reputations" (*The Financial Times*, 19 September 1995). In 1996 Shell was even considered, in the same survey, as one of the best companies dealing with environmental and ethical issues suggesting that "companies can ride out short-term reverses or blemishes to their reputation" (*The Financial Times*, 18 September 1996).

[5] Meznar and Nigh (1995, pp. 976–977) describe "buffering" and "bridging" as follow. "Buffering is aimed at protecting the organisation from the external environment. It implies that a firm is trying either to insulate itself from external interference or to actively influence its environment through such means as contributions to political action committees, lobbying, and advocacy advertising. By buffering, a firm either resists environmental change or tries to control it. [. . .] Bridging, on the other hand, occurs as firms seek to adapt organisational activities so that they conform with external expectations. It implies that the firm actively tries to meet and exceed regulatory requirements in its industry or that it attempts to quickly identify changing social expectations in order to promote organisational conformance to those expectations. In bridging, firms promote internal adaptation to changing external circumstances".

References

Adams, C. A., W. Hill and C. B. Roberts: 1998, 'Corporate Social Reporting Practices in Western Europe: Legitimating Corporate Behaviour?', *British Accounting Review* 30(1), 1–21.

Adler, R. W. and M. J. Milne: 1997, 'Media Exposure, Company Size, Industry, and Social Disclosure Practice', Paper presented at the Fifth Interdisciplinary perspectives on accounting conference, Manchester.

Aerts, W.: 1994, 'On the Use of Accounting Logic as an Explanatory Category in Narrative Accounting Disclosures', *Accounting, Organisations, and Society* 19(4/5), 337–353.

Albert, S. and D. A. Whetten: 1985, 'Organisational Identity', in L. L. Cummings and B. M. Staw (eds.), *Research in Organisational Behaviour*, volume 7 (JAI Press, Greenwich CT).

Argenti, P. A.: 1994, *Corporate Communication* (Irwin, New York).

Belkaoui, A and P. G. Karpik: 1989, 'Determinants of the Corporate Decision to Disclose Social Information', *Accounting, Auditing, and Accountability Journal* 2(1), 36–50.

Blacconiere, W. G. and D. M. Patten: 1994, 'Environmental Disclosures, Regulatory Costs and Changes in Firm Value', *Journal of Accounting and Economics* 18(3), 357–377.

Birkigt, K. and M. M. Stadler: 1986, *Corporate Identity – Grundlagen, Funktionen, Fallbeispiele* (Verlag Moderne Industrie, Landsberg am Lech).

Brown, N. and C. Deegan: 1998, 'The Public Disclosure of Environmental Performance Information – A Dual Test of Media Agenda Setting Theory and Legitimacy Theory', *Accounting and Business Research* 29(1), 21–41.

Carter, S. M. and J. M. Dukerich: 1998, 'Corporate Responses to cChanges in Reputation', *Corporate Reputation Review* 1(3), 250–270.

Deegan, C. and B. Gordon: 1996, 'A Study of the Environmental Disclosure Practices of Australian Corporations', *Accounting and Business Research* 26(3), 187–199.

Deegan, C. and M. Rankin: 1996, 'Do Australian Companies Report Environmental News Objectively? An Analysis of Environmental Disclosures by Firms Prosecuted Successfully by the Environmental Protection Authority', *Accounting, Auditing, and Accountability Journal* 9(2), 50–67.

Deegan, C., M. Rankin and P. Voght: 1999, 'Firms' Disclosure Reactions to Major Social Incidents: Australian Evidence', Paper presented at the 22nd European Accounting Association Congress, Bordeaux.

Dowling, G. R.: 1986, 'Managing Your Corporate Image', *Industrial Marketing Management* 15, 109–115.

Dowling, J. and J. R. Pfeffer: 1975, 'Organisational Legitimacy: Societal Values and Organisational Behaviour', *Pacific Sociological Review* 18(1), 122–136.

Duimering, P. R. and F. Safayeni: 1998, 'The Role of Language and Formal Structure in the Construction and Maintenance of Organisational Images', *International Studies of Management and Organisation* 28(3), 57–85.

Dutton, J. E. and J. M. Dukerich: 1991, 'Keeping and Eye on the Mirror: Image and Identity in Organisational Adaptation', *Academy of Management Journal* 34(3), 517–554.

Dutton, J. E., J. M. Dukerich and C. V. Harquail: 1994, 'Organisational Images and Member Identification', *Administrative Science Quarterly* 39(2), 239–263.

Elkington, J.: 1997, *Cannibals with Forks – The Triple Bottom-line* (Capstone, Oxford).

Elsbach, K. D.: 1994, 'Managing Organisational Legitimacy in the California Cattle Industry: The cConstruction and Effectiveness of Verbal Accounts', *Administrative Science Quarterly* 39(1), 57–88.

Elsbach, K. D. and R. M. Kramer: 1996, 'Members' Responses to Organisational Identity Threats: Encountering and Countering the Business Week Rankings', *Administrative Science Quarterly* 41(3), 442–476.

Elsbach, K. D. and R. I. Sutton: 1992, 'Acquiring Organisational Legitimacy Through Illegitimate Actions), A Marriage of Institutional and Impression Management Theories', *Academy of Management Journal* 35(4), 699–738.

Fombrun, C.: 1996, *Reputation: Realising Value from the Corporate Image* (Harvard Business School Press, Boston).

Giacalone, R. A.: 1988, 'The Effect of Administrative Accounts and Gender on the Perception of Leadership', *Group and Organisation Studies* 13(2), 195–207.

Gray, E. R. and J. M. T. Balmer: 1998, 'Managing Corporate Image and Corporate Reputation', *Long Range Planning* 31(5), 695–702.

Gray, R., K. J. Bebbington and D. Walters: 1993, *Accounting for the Environment* (Chapman, London).

Gray, R., R. Kouhy and S. Lavers: 1995, 'Corporate Social and Environmental Reporting: A Review of the Literature and a Longitudinal Study of UK Disclosure', *Accounting, Auditing, and Accountability Journal* **8**(2), 47–77.

Gray, R., D. Owen and C. Adams: 1996, *Accounting and Accountability – Changes and Challenges in Corporate Social and Environmental Reporting* (Prentice Hall, London).

Grolin, J.: 1998, 'Corporate Legitimacy in Risk Society: The Case of Brent Spar', *Business Strategy and the Environment* **7**(4), 213–222.

Guthrie, J. and L. D. Parker: 1989, 'Corporate Social Reporting: A Rebuttal of Legitimacy Theory', *Accounting and Business Research* **19**(76), 343–352.

Hackston, D. and M. J. Milne: 1996, 'Some Determinants of Social and Environmental Disclosures in New Zealand Companies', *Accounting, Auditing, and Accountability Journal* **9**(1), 77–108.

Jones, E. E.: 1990, *Interpersonal Perception* (Freeman, New York).

Kaptein, M. and J. Wempe: 1998, 'The Ethics Report: A Means of Sharing Responsibility', *Business Ethics: A European Review* **7**(3), 131–139.

Lindblom, C. K.: 1994, 'The Implications of Organisational Legitimacy for Corporate Social Performance and Disclosure', Paper presented at the Critical perspectives on accounting conference, New York.

Meyer, J. and B. Rowan: 1977, 'Institutional Organisations: Formal Structure as Myth and Ceremony', *American Journal of Sociology* **83**(2), 340–363.

Meznar, M. B. and D. Nigh: 1995, 'Buffer or Bridge? Environmental and Organisational Determinants of Public Affairs Activities in American Firms', *Academy of Management Journal* **38**(4), 975–996.

Morsing, M.: 1999, 'The Media Boomerang: The Media's Role in Changing Identity by Changing Image', *Corporate Reputation Review* **2**(2), 116–135.

Neale, A.: 1997, 'Organisational Learning in Contested Environments: Lessons from Brent Spar', *Business Strategy and the Environment* **6**(2), 93–103.

Neu, D., H. Warsame and K. Pedwell: 1998, 'Managing Public Impressions: Environmental Disclosures in Annual Reports', *Accounting, Organisations, and Society* **23**(3), 265–282.

O'Donovan, G.: 1997, 'Legitimacy Theory and Corporate Environmental Disclosure: Some Case Study Evidence', Paper presented at 1997 Accounting Association of Australia and New Zealand Annual Conference, Hobart.

Oegema, D., M. de Haan and B. van Leur: 1998, 'Shell en de Publiciteit over de Brent Spar', in V. M. G. Damoiseaux and A. A. van Ruler (eds.), *Effectiviteit in Communicatiemanagement* (Samson, Deventer).

Patten, D. M.: 1991, 'Exposure, Legitimacy, and Social Disclosure', *Journal of Accounting and Public Policy* **10**(4), 297–308.

Patten, D. M.: 1992, 'Intra-industry Environmental Disclosures in Response to the Alaskan Oil Spill: A Note on Legitimacy Theory', *Accounting, Organisations, and Society* **17**(5), 471–475.

Patten, D. M. and J. R. Nance: 1998, 'Regulatory Effects in a Good News Environment: The Intra-industry Reaction to the Alaskan Oil Spill', *Journal of Accounting and Public Policy* **17**(4/5), 409–429.

Pfeffer, J. R.: 1981, 'Management as Symbolic Action: The Creation and Maintenance of Organisational Paradigm', in L. L. Cummings and B. M. Staw (eds.), *Research in Organisational Behaviour*, volume 3 (JAI Press, Greenwich, CT).

Riel, C. B. M. van: 1995, *Corporate Communication* (Prentice Hall, New York).

Riel, C. B. M. van and F. A. J. van den Bosch: 1997, 'Increasing Effectiveness of Managing Strategic Issues Affecting a Firm's Reputation', *Corporate Reputation Review* **1**(1/2), 135–140.

Rindova, V. P.: 1997, 'The Image Cascade and the Formation of Corporate Reputations', *Corporate Reputation Review* **1**(1/2), 188–194.

Rosenfeld, P., R. A. Giacalone and C. A. Riordan: 1995, *Impression Management in Organisations* (Routledge, London).

Schlenker, B. R.: 1980, *Impression Management: The Self-concept, Social Identity, and Interpersonal Relations* (Brooks/Cole Publishing Company, Montery).

Schlenker, B. R. and M. F. Weigold: 1992, 'Interpersonal Processes Involving Impression Regulation and Management', *Annual Review of Psychology* **43**, 133–168.

Scott, M. B. and S. M. Lyman: 1968, 'Accounts', *American Sociological Review* **33**(1), 46–62.

Staw, B. M., P. I. McKechnie and S. M. Puffer: 1983, 'The Justification of Organisational Performance', *Administrative Science Quarterly* **28**(4), 582–600.

Tedeschi, J. T. and M. Riess: 1981, 'Verbal Strategies in Impression Management', in C. Antaki (ed.), *The Psychology of Everyday Explanations of Social Behaviour* (Academic Press, London).

Ullmann, A. E.: 1985, 'Data in Search of a Theory: A Critical Examination of the Relationship's among Social Performance, Social Disclosure and Economic Performance of US Firms', *Academy of Management Review* **10**(3), 540–557.

Vendelø, M. T.: 1998, 'Narrating Corporate

Reputation: Becoming Legitimate Through Storytelling', *International Studies of Management and Organisation* **28**(3), 120–137.

Walden, W. D. and B. N. Schwartz: 1997, 'Environmental Disclosures and Public Policy Pressure', *Journal of Accounting and Public Policy* **16**(2), 125–154.

Zadek, S., P. Pruzan and P. Evans: 1997, *Building Corporate Accountability – Emerging Practices in Social and Ethical Accounting, Auditing and Reporting* (Earthscan, London).

Erasmus University Rotterdam,
Faculty of Business Administration,
Financial Management Department, Room F4-31,
P.O. Box 1738,
3000 DR ROTTERDAM,
The Netherlands
E-mail: R.Hooghiemstra@fbk.eur.nl

The Dialogical Turn of Public Relation Ethics

Robert van Es
Tiemo L. Meijlink

ABSTRACT. The ethics of Public Relations is changing: the pragmatical approach is giving way to the dialogical approach. Pragmatical PR Ethics concentrates on issues and cases and hardly has a conceptual core. Dialogical PR Ethics concentrates on procedures and structures and uses symmetric communication as its core concept. Both approaches of PR ethics have their strong and weak points. A meta-ethical framework is presented to combine both approaches.

Three examples of the dialogical turn in the practice of PR in the 1990-ties:

1. Premature and idealistic deals with a paper factory in Katmandu caused sales problems for The Body Shop in the early nineties. The product did not belong in its line of business and after more than two years sales were still unacceptably low. Meanwhile the factory, solely depending on The Body Shop, grew out to be a social-economical pilar of Katmandu. Careful dialogue and cooperative research provided a win–win-solution for both companies in 1994.
2. The Association for Professional Communication in the Netherlands awarded the Dutch Shell a price for communication. The company was praised for its willingness to change its strategic communication in 1996. This was shown by Shell's turn to start listening to important public groups and to start a dialogue on the social

responsibility of corporations, also in effect of the Brent Spar affair. Groups of stakeholders were invited to join the discussion on parts of a new business code, which resulted in the adaption of human rights as a leading principle.
3. Unilever vision on responsible entrepeneuring was presented in 1997 by the President of the Board of Directors M. Tabaksblat. "Unilever considers it of great importance to carry on a dialogue with consumers and public organisations on important social issues, like the application of biotechnological methods in the production of food and sustainable methods of production. Also the dialogue with co-workers of a different cultural background for Unilever is an important aspect of responsible entrepeneurial behaviour."

Introduction

Public Relations is the classical term for the organisational function to maintain relations with internal and external groups of people on whose support the organisation depends. In the early 80's the new expressions "coporate communications" and "communication management" emerged. Little by little the classical term PR is loosing ground: "maintaining relations" is giving way to "strategic communication". In this process PR ethics is included.

In PR ethics two approaches can be distinguished: the pragmatical and the dialogical approach. The first one is known since the 1960-ties as the standard approach of ethics in PR textbooks. The second one is relatively new and emerged at the end of the 1980-ties. This article focuses on two questions. What are the strong and weak points of the two basic ethical

Robert van Es is Assistent Professor in Organizational Philosophy at the University of Amsterdam, and Consultant in Organizational Culture and Ethics.
Tiemo L. Meijlink is Lecturer in Communication Ethics at the Hanzecollege of Groningen, and Trainer in Moral Competence.

Journal of Business Ethics **27**: 69–77, 2000.
© 2000 *Kluwer Academic Publishers. Printed in the Netherlands.*

approaches to public relations? This question is
dealt with in the first three chapters. The fourth
chapter offers an answer to the second question:
In what meta-ethical framework can both
approaches be combined? In the closing fifth
chapter the pragmatical and the dialogical
approach are specified in this meta-ethical framework.

1. Pragmatical PR ethics

The usual approach of PR ethics finds its justification in professional practice. Everyday cases
are the starting point for moral analysis. As such
the usual approach of PR ethics can be characterized as pragmatical or situational (Leeper,
1996; Martinson, 1998). This is no surprise: PR
itself arose in a culture of pragmatism, in which
norms were derived from professional behaviour.
The well-known textbook on PR ethics by
Philip Seib and Kathy Fitzpatrick (1995) is a
good example of the pragmatical approach.

For Seib and Fitzpatrick the profession of the
PR practitioner is under stress. The profession
suffers from a negative image, while at the same
time it performs an important social function:
fostering mutual understanding between different
social groups and contributing to societal stability.
To handle this stress the profession has to be practised on an ethical basis. The PR practitioner
often acts as an advisor to the customer. How
does Seib and Fitzpatrick's PR ethics work? From
cases in PR ethics questions are generated.
Answers must be found by applying the principles and rules present in professional codes. Of
course, in actual situations of moral choice there
are shades of grey. PR ethics depends to a high
degree on the personal values of the professional.
Therefore, personal values carry more weight
than organisational values. In their explanation
Seib and Fitzpatrick deal with two moral
theories: deontology and teleology. They also
present different models for making moral decisions. However, these instruments are mentioned
in passing; theories nor models are applied
explicitly.

Seib and Fitzpatrick give special attention to
the norm of truth. They use a broad spectrum

of definitions of truth, locating "absolute truth"
at the one end and at the other end the cavalier
"tell truth when it happens to be convenient and
don't be afraid to embellish it along the way".
Against this spectrum they list a series of standard
questions regarding puffery, plagiarism, disinfor-
mation and correcting errors. Finally, they
conclude that "truth is a precious commodity
and should be cherished as such. To take a
cavalier approach is to undermine the integrity
and credibility of the profession" (1995, p. 66).
In telling the truth facts are important, but at the
same time perception, interpretation and opinion
all have their influence on "truth". At the end
of the book the authors return to the societal
function of PR. They again state that in our
communicative society the pervasiness and influence of PR neccesitate that it be practised ethically (1995, p. 117).

2. Dialogical PR ethics

Simultaneously with the pragmatical approach
the dialogical approach was developed. James
Grunig (1984 and 1989) distinguishes oneway
and two-way streams of information between
organisations and their relevant communication
groups. When only these groups are expected to
change, the process of communication is asymmetric. This is the case in asymmetric communication like propaganda and advertising. When
both the relevant groups and the organization
are expected to change during the interaction
process, communication is symmetric. For
Grunig PR is essentially symmetric communication. Information does not only runs from
organizations to their relevant groups, but these
groups also supply the organisation with information on what they aspire and what their interests are. This opens up loopes of feedback.
Grunig characterizes such interaction with the
term reciprocity: in exchanging ideas and points
of view the parties are willing to acknowledge
and respect one another, and they are willing to
change their perception of the other. As a result
of such interaction an organisation might change
its policy.

The idea of reciprocity was taken up by Ron

Pearson (1989a en 1989b), who gives the term dialogue a central place in his PR ethics. For him, an organizational communication process is in fact a reciprocal, dialogical process. In order to maintain a minimal balance between the communicating parties, the communication proces must comply to several rules. They can be clustered under three headings. Parties must reach agreement on procedures: the start, duration and closing of a communication process on a topic. Parties must agree on the agenda: the freedom to put relevant items on the agenda and to discuss them in full, and parties must agree on the media: the selection of media that will be used during the communication process.

The dialogical approach to PR is elaborated by Jon White and Laura Mazur in their study on communications management (1993). For them strategic communication is a central concern for management. Presentation, image and reputation are relevant topics to consider, but the real function of PR should be to create and maintain a dialogue with all the relevant corporate audiences. For White and Mazur ethics is integrated in PR. Internal policy must be tuned to ongoing external developments. Such developments are shifting product responsibilities, the rise of ethical consumers and of ethical investigating, changing concepts of fairness and responsibility in human resources management, the growth of codes of ethics in several branches, and the growth of transnational environmental regulations. In this view public relations ethics means fostering consistent longterm relationships with different corporate audiences by using dialogue.

3. Pragmatical and dialogical PR ethics compared

The pragmatical approach of PR ethics operates on the level of professional ethics. The focus is on the professionalism of the PR practitioner. Seib and Fitzpatrick acknowledge the importance of the rules and regulations of the professional codes, but at the same time they stress the decisiveness of the personal values of the PR practitioner. They only mention the interaction between the level of personal values and profes-

sional norms. Although Fitzpatrick later (1996) shows awareness of the importance of the management level, the idea of PR as an organisational function is missing in Seib and Fitzpatrick (1995). They don't link their moral theory with the recent attention in business ethics for organisational integrity (Sharpe Paine, 1994). However, PR as an organisational task can be an important element in integrity programs and ethical management. For this, one must concentrate on company values and standards. Pragmatical PR ethics just concentrates on issues. The pragmatical approach offers us information on all sorts of professional questions and supplies us with a carefully balanced appraisal of practical issues. What is missing in the pragmatical approach of Seib and Fitzpatrick is a conceptual or methodological main line. The norm of truth is elaborated in detail, but not integrated with other elements. The approach does not offer a vision on the practice of PR. The statement of Seib and Fitzpatrick that PR aims at the "promotion of mutual understanding and peaceful coexistence" lacks enforcement.

The presence of a conceptual main line is exactly what distinguishes the dialogical from the pragmatical approach. The central concept in dialogical PR ethics is Grunig's two way symmetric communication, specified with the terms reciprocity and dialogue. A normative vision on PR is the starting point for elaborating PR ethics. The centre of gravity is not the practice of the PR practitioner, but the sum total of relationships between organisations and their communication groups or audiences. As such the dialogical approach takes an organisational-ethical perspective. The way the process of communication runs, is crucial for the moral assessment of that process. An important criterium is the degree of participation of all relevant groups or audiences. Pearson concentrates on procedural rules and conditions to guide and to judge processes of communication. White and Mazur distinguish different sorts of communication processes and stress the importance of the management perspective.

The major objection against the dialogical approach to PR ethics is the presupposed idealism (Meijlink, 1997). Part of the field of

PR has an asymmetric character. For example activities like the management of events, the preparing of campaigns and the writing of effective texts, are not in itself forms of symmetric communication. Do they not really belong to PR? Or must we qualify them as a-moral? Grunig would answer the second question affirmativly (Grunig and White, 1992, p. 40). Others are inclined to locate the two-way symmetric model on the one side of a PR continuum, while one-way asymmetric communication occupies the other side (Van der Meiden et al., 1994, p. 138; Oltshoorn, 1997, p. 119). The idea of a continuum may be an acceptabel solution for empirical and pragmatical reasons. From a moral point of view this "solution" is too easy. What we need first is an extension of the conceptual framework.This brings us to our second question: In what meta-ethical framework can both approaches be combined?

4. A meta-ethical framework for practical ethics

Developing a meta-ethical framework for PR ethics means looking for a framework that handles the basic concepts of practical ethics. The meta-ethical framework we have in mind distinguisehes two models. The first is a search model to map moral problems. In this model the central questions are: In which field is the problem located?; What responsibilites are important in that field?; In what way are these responsibilities linked? This is the model of discovery. The second model primarily has a crticial function. The findings of the first model are now entering a critical process of consideration and selection. Searching for best reasons is at the heart of the model of justification.

Of course, in looking for answers to moral questions we oscillate between both mental models. We try and formulate answers and immedeately ask ourselves what the justification of that answer could be. But in making the final decision and especially in the public account-ability of that decision, we are expected to present a firm distinction between the moral discovery of the moral problem, and the justifica-

tion of the decision made. Therefore, two mental models must be distinguished in handling practical ethics.

I. *The model of discovery*

In everyday professional practice there are no clearcut simple moral questions. Instead there is a mix of three fields of ethics, each operating on another level. Each field has a specific focus on morality in a broad sense: not only in terms of moral norms or moral concerns (Van Es et al., 1995), but, as also in terms of moral responsibility.

The first field is Personal Ethics: the reflection on morality as it develops in your own life, not only as introspection, but also in interaction with significant others, especially the ones you love. Introspection tells us where we are on our path of life, where we came from, what our plans are and why we have these plans. We are responsible for leading our own life and render ourself account in the "forum internum". Of course, we are not alone. Our moral considerations are influenced by our relations with family and friends, and the projected commentary of heroes and other inspirators. This social forum is a basis testcase for taking moral responsibility. Therefore, moral responsibility in personal ethcis concentrates on responsibility for self (character, identity) and responsibility for significant others (family, friends).

The second field is Professional Ethics: the reflection on morality as it develops in the organisation (the place of work) or in the profession (the sort of work). The place of work implicates a position in the organization, and the moral, vertical responsibilities that go with it, in relation to co-workers and superiors. The sort of work implicates a professional attitude in doing one's job, and the moral, horizontal responsibilities that go with it in relation with colleagues inside and outside the organization. Both forms of responsibility are illustrated in Figure 1. Vertical and horizontal responsibilities sometimes coincide, sometimes collide. A strict seperation of horizontal and vertical responsibilities (Van der Meiden et al., 1994) easily leads to the idea of

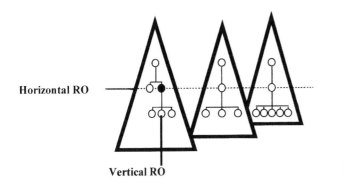

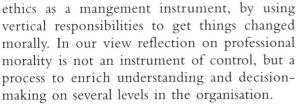

Figure 1. Vertical and horizontal role obligations in professional ethics.

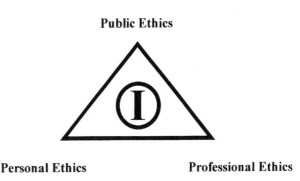

Figure 2. Three fields of ethics in the model of moral discovery.

ethics as a mangement instrument, by using vertical responsibilities to get things changed morally. In our view reflection on professional morality is not an instrument of control, but a process to enrich understanding and decision-making on several levels in the organisation.

The third field is Public Ethics: the reflection on morality as it develops in public debates. Public debates on morality are found in the media: daily's, weekly's, journals, news- and discussion programs on radio and television, and several sites on internet. Important contributors with their own debating showrooms are, of course, the houses of parliament, the local councils, and special governmental committees and study groups, but also non-governmental organizations in the realm of critical consuming, human rights and the environment. Public debates have two functions: bringing important but underexposed topics to the publics attention, and preparing a compromise on a topic that already has been discussed in full. Moral responsibility in public ethics concentrates on social-political responsibility (societal justice and care) and environmental responsibility (common good, ecological interests).

Personal ethics not simply equals subjective ethics. To a high degree personal ethics is the result of the interaction with parents, siblings, teachers and peers. Public ethics is not simply objective ethics. Public ethics is always bound to culture, time and political space. Of course, the three fields of ethics interact, and we are confronted with a mix of the three fields in everyday

moral practice. As Figure 2 shows, every "I" has to handle a mix of the three fields of ethics in everyday moral practice.

II. *The mental model of justification*

Once a practice is morally clarified, other topics gain importance: the relevant moral considerations, the possible choices, the fitting plans of action, the moral judgements. This means entering the mental model of moral justification. The most famous of these mental models is the so called method of reflective equilibrium. First elaborated by John Rawls (1971), this method has been developed by several ethicists, recently by Van den Burg (1998) and Van Willigenburg (1998). The method of wide reflective equilibrium primarily is a method of justification, used in tackling practical moral problems.

Wide reflective equilibrium is an attempt to bring coherence between different moral considerations. Deontological and teleological principles must come together with intuitions and other factors. The function of a wide reflective equilibrium model is to bring the different considerations in a well-balanced thinking process, aiming at an optimal decision on the moral question.

Heeger et al. (1991) distinguished three elements in their wide reflective equilibrium model: morally relevant facts, intuitions and principles. Morally relevant facts are facts that justifiably bear moral weight in a particular situation. They have a self-reliant epistemic function in moral thinking. Acknowledging the role of relevant facts in ethical decision making means accepting an epistemology of particularism and contextualism. This is necessary because a generalist epistemology cannot sufficiently take account of facts that are morally relevant in one situation and morally irrelevant in another. Context analysis is an important method in practical ethics because of the connectedness of morality with time, place and tradition (Van Es et al., 1995, p. 122). Intuitions can be defined as a way of understanding moral situations without mediation of general moral principles of theories. It is a kind of moral experience in direct relation to particular situations. Van Willigenburg speaks of intuitions as a particularist idea of rationality in seeing the overall pattern of a moral situation. Principles are more or less stringent, durable moral requirements and play a fundamental role in many systems of moral belief. One can distinguish principles on a deontological basis and principles on a teleological basis, for example in rule utilitarianism. They differ in their measure of concreteness: we use principles as more or less general prima facie duties, and also as rules.

Van der Burg (1998) adds a fourth element to the wide reflective equilibrium process: ideals. Ideals can promote critical imput. Ideals are values rather than direct action guides like principles or rules. An ideal is both grounded in reality and oriented towards the future. Ideals are vague and cannot be grasped completely in words, nor can they be realised completely. That enables them to play a critical role in the reflection on the first three elements.

All together this leads us to four elements in a model of reflective equilibrium. An appropriate representation of this model can be found in the loopfigures of system dynamics (Senge, 1990), see Figure 3. A casedescription first supplies us with information on an event or a situation. After moral clarification we have an inventory of the relevant facts (1) in their contexts and we use our intuitions (2) for scanning any more relevant notions. In this oscillation between intuitions and relevant facts we try to denominate the moral principles that are involved (3), and the values

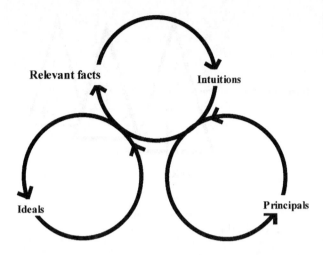

Figure 3. The model of moral justification.

that are relevant in the form of ideals (4). Finally, we turn back critically to facts, intuitions and principles, and in so doing process through the loops again.

When is a satisfying outcome reached? Of course, there must be an equilibrium of moral considerationss, but when do we call an equilibrium satisfying or even justified? The model of reflective equilibrium consists of loops of interaction. In that process several questions are posed: To what extent do these considerations support or exclude each other? Can we integrate them? Do some considerations fit the situation at hand better than others? By posing such questions and scanning the possible answers a "balance of thought" arises between relevant facts, intuitions, principals and ideals. When exactly the point of equilibrium is reached, is an open question. In most cases that point is an agreement of the parties involved. Parties will come to that agreement after a dialogue, a discussion, or even after conditional negotiations (Van Es, 1996).

The model of discovery offers an inventory system: the different fields of ethics and their moral responsibilities are mapped. The model of justification has a criticial function. Critical questions are asked with regard to the responsibilities of the first model. These questions will have the effect of a selection process. Some responsibilities will appear to be of less weight and influence, while others will be confirmed as important or even decisive. Together these two models make up a fitting meta-ethical framework for practical ethics, including PR ethics.

5. The dialogical turn of PR ethics

The two approaches of PR ethics offer certain advantages and perspectives that deserve to be combined in a more integrated approach. Both the inventory quality of the discovery model and the critical selection quality of the justification model are helpfull to elaborate such an approach.

In the model of discovery the pragmatical approach of Seib and Fitzpatrick can be situated on the levels of personal and professional ethics. The approach stresses the personal values of the PR practitioner and the informal and formal codes in PR. In elaborating the norm of truth they touch, for a moment, the level of public ethics, but their elaboration is determined by practical questions of the PR profession. The dialogical approach of White and Mazur can be situated on the levels of professional and public ethics. The moral concerns are reciprocity, participation, care, and the common good. The dialogical approach also facilitates strategic communication on the professional level, but harldy touches personal ethics. Both approaches are complementary as can be illuminated by placing them in the first model (see Figure 4).

Each approach only covers part of the model and is in need of a widening of perspective. Ethics in professional practice is not only about classical professional ethics, it is also about personal ethics and public ethics. All three fields of ethics must be handled coherently. To develop a fully balanced PR ethics we must have coherent theories of morality that cover all fields of the discovery model; in that way an integrated approach to PR ethics can be developed.

In the justification model the responsibilities in the pragmatical and the dialogical approach will find a suitable place, but now in a critical way. For instance, in the continuum model of PR it is not possible to ask the normative critical question to what extend Grunig's two way symmetrical view should be the standard for all fields of PR. This is possible in the justification model. In the same way responsibilities specified in the model of discovery can be brought in a process of critical interaction by placing them in the model of justification (see Figure 5).

The moral concerns in the pragmatical approach will find a place under the viewpoints Morally relevant facts, Intuitions, and Principles. One could rewrite situational PR ethics in the form of a critical process of interaction between these three considerations. The fourth consideration, Ideals, is missing in the situational approach. The dialogical approach is strong in the viewpoints Principles and Values. Pearson directs the dialogical approach into a set of rules

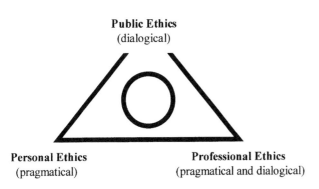

Public Ethics
(dialogical)

Personal Ethics
(pragmatical)

Professional Ethics
(pragmatical and dialogical)

Figure 4. Both approaches in the model of moral discovery.

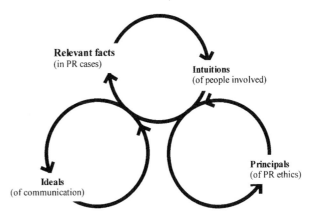

Relevant facts
(in PR cases)

Intuitions
(of people involved)

Ideals
(of communication)

Principals
(of PR ethics)

Figure 5. Both approaches in the model of justification.

and procedures for conditional communication, and thus concentrates on principles. Others prefer to see dialogue as an ideal in which the values participation and reciprocity have their place. Criticism of PR is often driven by the same values. Reciprocity, openess and fairness are ideals of public communication, that causes criticists to accuse PR of window dressing. Such ideals will find their due place in the dialogical approach.

The justification model puts the perspectives of both approaches of PR in a critical tension. This is to the advantage of PR ethics because the meta-ethical framework considers not only the actual PR practice, but also the wider moral values, ideals and principles that are relevant to the practice of PR.

The statements at the beginning of this article reminded us of the growing concern companies have with their external relations. The Body Shop took its responsibility for a small firm in Katmandu, that was totally depending on the multinational. Shell learned from the Brent Spar affair and their Africa-experiences to start a dialogue with their stakeholders. And Unilever publicly declared the importance of dialogue with consumers, public organisations and co-workers. This concern stimulated PR ethics, as we developed it here. Larger organisations are developing their policy more and more in close dialogue with a broad set of stakeholders. The meta-ethical framework for practical ethics outlined here, offers an appropriate context for the further development of that communication practice.

Literature

Fitzpatrick, K. R.: 1996, 'The Role of Public Relations in the Institutialization of Ethics', *Public Relations Review* 22(3), 249–258.

Grunig, J. E.: 1989. 'Symmetrical Presuppositions as a Framework for Public Relations Theory', in H. Botan and V. Hazleton (eds.), *Public Relations Theory* (Hillsdale).

Grunig, J. E. and T. Hunt: 1984, *Managing Public Relations* (Holt, Rinehart and Winston).

Grunig, J. E. and J. White: 1992. 'The Effect of Worldviews on Public Relations Theory and Practice', in J. E. Grunig (ed.), *Excellence in Public Relations and Communication Management* (Hillsdale).

Leeper, R. V.: 1996, 'Moral Objectivity, Jurgen Habermas's Discourse Ethics, and Public Relations', *Public Relations Review* 22(2), 133–150.

Martinson, D. L.: 1998 'Public Relations Practitioners Must Not Confuse Considerations of the Situation with "Situation Ethics", *Public Relations Quarterly* (winter), 39–43.

Meijlink, T. L.: 1997. 'Ethiek van Public Relations', in J. Groenendijk, G. Hazekamp and J. Mastenbroek (eds.), *Public Relations. Beleid, organisatie en uitvoering* (Samsom).

Oltshoorn, A.: 1997, *Cultuur en communicatie* (Bohn Stafleu van Gorcum).

Pearson, R.: 1989a. 'Beyond Ethical Relativism in Public Relations: Coordination, Rules and the Idea of Communicative Symmetry', in J. E. Grunig and L. A. Grunig (eds.), *Public Relations Research Annual* (Hillsdale).

Pearson, R.: 1989b. 'Business Ethics as Communication Ethics: Public Relations Practice and the Idea of Dialogue', in H. Botan and V. Hazleton (eds.), *Public Relations Theory* (Hillsdale).

Rawls, J.: 1971, *A Theory of Justice* (Harvard Colllege).

Seib, P. and K. Fitzpatrick: 1995, *Public Relations Ethics* (Orlando Florida).

Senge, P.: 1990, *The Fifth Discipline. The Art and Practice of the Learning Organization* (Currency Doubleday).

Sharpe Payne, L.: 1994, 'Managing for Organizational Integrity', *Harvard Business Review* (March/April), 106–117.

Tabaksblat, M.: 1997, 'Dialoog binnen de samenleving. Unilevers visie op verantwoord ondernemen', Paper on the Veer Association Symposium, October 17.

Van der Burg, W.: 1998. 'Ideals and Ideal Theory: The Problem of Methodological Conservatism', in W. van der Burg and T. van Willigenburg (eds.), *Reflective Equilibrium. Essays in Honour of Robert Heeger* (Kluwer Academic).

Van der Meiden, A. and G. Fauconnier: 1994, *Public Relations. Profiel en professie* (Wolters Noordhoff).

Van Es, R.: 1996, *Negotiating Ethics. On Ethics in Negotiation and Negotiating in Ethics* (Eburon, Delft).

Van Es, R. and T. L. Meijlink: 1995, *Ethiek en Professie* (Kok, Kampen).

Van Willigenburg, T.: 1998, 'Morally Relevant Facts. Particularism and Intuitionist Rationality', in W. van der Burg and T. van Willigenburg (eds.),

Reflective Equilibrium. Essays in Honour of Robert Heeger (Kluwer Academic).

Van Willigenburg, T. and F. R. Heeger: 1991, 'Rechtfertigung moralischer Urteile: Ein Netzmodell', *Zeitschrift fur Evangelische Ethik* **35**, 88–95.

White, J. and L. Mazur: 1995, *Strategic Communications Management. Making Public Relations Work* (Addison-Wesley).

Robert van Es
Universiteit van Amsterdam,
Faculteit der Maatschappij en
Gedragswetenschappen,
Oudezijds Achterburgwal 237,
1021 DL Amsterdam

Tiemo L. Meijlink
Hanzehogeschool Groningen

Values in Decision-Making Processes: Systematic Structures of J. Habermas and N. Luhmann for the Appreciation of Responsibility in Leadership

Eberhard Schnebel

ABSTRACT. "Ethical Leadership" in modern multicultural corporations is first the consideration of different personal and cultural value systems in decision-making processes. Second, it is the assignment of responsibility either to individual or organisational causalities. The task of this study is to set the stage for a distinction between rational entities and the arbitrary preferences of individuals in economic decision making processes.

Defining rational aspects of behaviour in economics will lead to the formal structures of organisational systems, which are independent of concrete but varying "values". Luhmann's "Theory of systems of communication" describes the internal dynamic forces of economic communication processes in terms of formal structures. On the other hand Habermas' "Theory of discourse" integrates the previous relationship between individual subjectivity and rational behaviour. Habermas gives an indication of how to separate subjective values and meaning from rational arguments in rational communication processes. The translation of these theoretical structures into practical applications for decision making processes and decision taking acts links the ethical, or value-oriented, context precisely to both individual and organisational areas of responsibility.

E. Schnebel is currently employed at the corporate planing division of Württembergerische Hypothekenbank AG and is working as scientist in business ethics. From 1992 to 1995 he was a member of the Interdisciplinary Ethics Institute of the University of Munich and obtained the doctoral degree (Ph.D.) in May 1995 with the topic: "Description of specific references between economy and ethical behaviour in management".

KEY WORDS: business ethics, communication, discourse, ethics, Habermas, implicit contracts, Luhmann, multicultural organisations, organisation, values

Introduction

Following Max Webers understanding of moral behaviour in economics, as well as the tradition of Christian professional ethics, cultural values and personal responsibility shape the orientation of work ethics of top management. Primary personal space and freedom (Freiräume) determine the ethical impacts of managerial decisions and, furthermore, their limitation by rules and regulations. This forms the background to the kind of decisions managers make.

The task of this study is to demonstrate the need for the development of two aspects within the managerial structures of companies in order to work successfully with multinational and multicultural employees. The first aspect is the need to distinguish between rational entities and arbitrary preferences of individuals inside the management. The second aspect is more organisational and addresses the equal integration of various cultural values. Effectively, this study takes up the notion of defining formal structures of rational behaviour in economics, considering various kinds of cultural specifics in international business.[1]

1. Ethics, values and the cultural context in organisations

1.1. *Association of soft rules and values in decision-making processes*

Ethics in decision-making processes is a unique interface for understanding the interrelationship between personal space and freedom and organisational guidelines. Ethics works as "soft rules" for combining the "corporate culture" with personal responsibility. The specific characteristics of these ethics are determined in the form of values. These values give individuals indications in detail on how to act and decide. They are a useful vehicle for identifying and pronouncing the soft rules of a company and in this sense they are part of the corporate culture. Values are an indicator of the kind of responsibility adopted by the employees of a corporation (Figure 1).

In this sense the term "values" contains everything that can define, influence or shape the style of management and business execution of a corporation. But values differ according to the cultural background of employees. The focus on management values can entail multiple interpretations, especially in multinational organisations. In such multicultural, international settings, management has yet to ensure the mutual fit of employees even when issues might appear to be simple or common sense.[2]

A spectrum of values, from individual personal responsibility in business all the way to "values" embedded in organisational structures, generate the ethical evaluation. They structure implicit

meanings as soft rules in the space between explicit meanings of organisational conditions and the individual responsibility of personal evaluation (Figure 2). Particular values interfere with organisational conditions in the same way as with explicit meanings of economical, technical and moral aspects.

1.2. *Management framework and cultural distinctions*

Values that correspond to leadership relate to current management frameworks, to demands on teams for optimised cooperation and to individual preferences. Roughness in the marketplace, open policy towards employees, recklessness against competitors, targeting market segments, the supported style of leadership – all these characteristics can be part of an organisation's executive management value system. Values are the key factors in identifying the motivating aspects of decisions after the decision-making processes in business.

The "values" which a person is committed to are deeply rooted in his or her social and the socio-cultural background. By the same token, "values" used in a corporation are either related to the tradition of the company or to a person's individual and social history. Each aspect has its own cultural tradition and can differ in crucial points. Each aspect can be traced within different civilisations and social strata.

The integration of cultural distinctions and boundaries inside a corporation requires open leadership tools, in order to avoid conflicts and stimulate people through incentives. It is necessary for the organisational design to take into

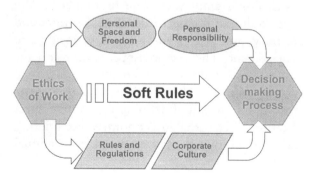

Figure 1. Framework of ethics in decision making process.

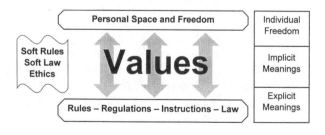

Figure 2. Values as soft rules in decision-making processes.

consideration the existing cultural differences of values. Current management tools can determine the formal structure of day to day cooperation (code of conduct, audit, goals and objectives, strategic planning and controlling, jurisdictional structures, career steps, revenue generation, divisional management). But these tools must be connected with clear value management in order to support the "entrepreneurial success" of a team – which is the framework for measuring the quality of teamwork in a corporation.

Within various cultures, different emphasis is placed on either individual personality or leadership instruments within organisational structures. In Germany, for example, most corporations require a high degree of "personal leadership" with large elbowroom and individual variations. Especially "tolerance against and integration of differing individual values" is ensured more by individual culture of managers and personal education rather than by clear proclaimed organisational structures.[3]

1.3. *Corporate culture and interactions between individuals*

Each employee, in his or her day to day work, experiences corporate values as transmitted by the leadership of a corporation and represented by the "corporate culture". The notion of "corporate culture" (Unternehmenskultur) summarises how the personalities of managers (Persönlichkeit) contribute to and form organisational settings.[4] In fact, corporate culture is the framework in which managers can assess their own behaviour within the cultural context of their firm. It is the clue for identifying the "soft rules" of a company. In this sense, the ethical behaviour of management is a blend of individual character as well as of corporate culture and of the organisational set-up, which structures an appropriate business workflow. Corporate culture is an instrument which supports the management of office communication, business execution and manager-employee relationships. This formal description of the relation between individual values and organisational principles describes the boundaries of organisational value management.

Its primary task is to define precisely the dynamics of communication and interaction between particular individuals and between individuals and the company.

In most fast growing organisations, however, the elements of individual personality and corresponding leadership instruments are usually lacking. Often there is a deficit of established corporate culture because of the different cultural traditions of individuals. Also modern management tools are occupied with quantitative assessment of individual values according to the company's short-term success. They don't ensure the integration of different individual value systems within the entire organisation nor do they help to communicate corporate values to the individual.

In order to discuss the values of a corporation honestly and frankly, we need criteria for describing which values used in organisations are related to objective, formal and rational aspects and which are related to unique individual preferences. This question creates a deeper understanding of how decisions in corporations are taken and how to influence and control decision taking in future. Two aspects are fundamental:

1. How can we communicate if we belong to different cultural and individual value sets?
2. Which rational systems are relevant to, and independent of, different individual values and preferences?

Defining the formal structures of organisational systems which are independent of concrete, but varying, "values" is the primary task of rational reasoning.[5] The first step therefor, is to brake down the motivating aspects of decisions into formal aspects and into communication of subjective meaning and arbitrary preferences. With these distinctions we can appraise objectively the contribution of "values" concerning their usefulness in economic organisations (Figure 3).

2. Arguments in the system of rational reason: Luhmann's "Theory of systems"

Niklas Luhmann's "Theory of systems of communication" describes the previous relationship

82 Eberhard Schnebel

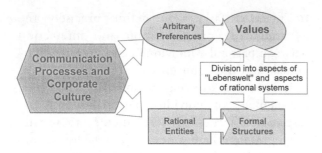

Figure 3. "Pragmatic" split into rational and arbitrary aspects.

between individual subjectivity and rational behaviour in terms of formal structures and rational systems. Luhmann gives an indication on how to divide subjective meaning from rational argument in communication processes. This indication clarifies the sort of possible differentiation and how disagreements must be handled. If social communication is a combination of formal internal structures and individual preferences, every event of communication has formal aspects, which are structured rationally (and therefore void of individual choice). Furthermore, it contains aspects of meaning which are related to subjective or individual values (Figure 4).

Rational structures are formed in "subsystems" with a "leading difference" (Leitdifferenz) and a "medium" to carry out the communication.[6] As a result of his analysis, we can distinguish between rules of rational common behaviour and individual features. Rational common behaviour

in economics draws its understanding out of the "subsystem" economy with its "leading difference" of paying money and keeping money. The economic thinking and acting in his rational relationship only belongs to this distinction. Issues with other meaning belong to other subsystems or belong to individual preferences. The subsystem itself is influenced by its environment, which in turn influences the value of goods in the economic system. The transaction itself is neutral and supports any values. The process of evaluation itself is part of communication about individual and cultural preferences. Thus the subsystem demonstrates that it is not the transaction of money as such that is value based, but rather its goal, for the attainment of which the transaction is used (Figure 5).

Luhmann defines transcultural elements of the systemic context to create objective economic measurements. This is the "payment" as a sheer communication act, independent from the amount or the partner. The medium of this communication act is "money" in the abstract sense, not as currency or as a kind of real value. This shapes a formal system to separate objective organisational or economical requirements from subjective values or principles, which define their effectiveness. With Luhmann we can distinguish between an objective context and subjective values. We see the rational components of communication like "payment" in the economic system, "power" in the political system, or "rights" in the legal system. But he gives no regard for the assessment of different subjective values communicated inside of these systems, for instance, the subjective company values and the

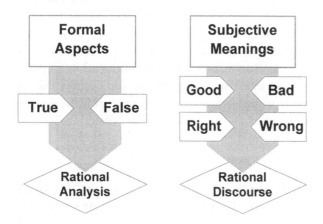

Figure 4. Categories of value-assessment in the system of rational reason.

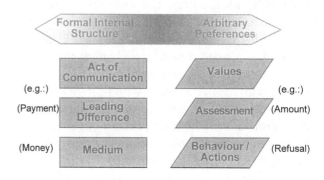

Figure 5. Distinction into formal aspects and subjective meaning in the system of Luhmann.

subjective individual values or the style of obtaining power and the practise of power.

"Corruption" for example, in this definition, is a subjective value with which companies or societies define the preferred style of economic communication. But it has no consequences on the formal structure of the economic or political system. Each participant of the communication process called "corruption" is carrying out a "true" economic or political act of communication. The problem would be to define the surrounding of this communication act in order to determine if this communication is "good or bad", "right or wrong". Corruption is not assessable in terms of rational objective structures because it is not a character of the economic communication system but a value of the environment of that system.

The "Theory of Systems" of Niklas Luhmann helps to differentiate between rational components of communication in the subsystem of economics and other subsystems and cultural or subjective specifications of companies. He offers a tool for designing rational components of organisational structures and their specifications based on cultural values.

3. Structured processes of communication: Jürgen Habermas and the "Principles of Discourse"

Jürgen Habermas, in his formal "Principles of Discourse", makes the distinction between rationality and subjectivity within the argument process, in as much as it is involved in a rationally structured process of communication. The rational elements of arguments can only be related to the process of communication, not to aspects of meaning and values. His principles form a tool for designing rational structures inside communication processes. Inside these communication processes individual values are articulated as meaning. Meaning, in terms of this discourse, is always subjective.

Habermas' principles of discourse are:[7]

1. Everyone must have the same chance to take part and to act in the discourse.

2. Everyone should be able to pronounce his or her values and have them critiqued.
3. Everyone must speak honestly and authentically.
4. All participants must have equal chances to articulate their values and critics, to order, to resist, to permit and to forbid, to account and to call to account.

This method leads to a point were all participants could decide whether their individual choices match their private opinions or is related to rational common principles. This creates rational arguments for structuring communication processes effectively and becoming goal-oriented in situations where individual values or cultural differences make the agreement processes more difficult.

Translated into the economic requirements of management, the methods of Habermas improve a company's capability for employing the values determined by management and the values related to formal structures and rational arguments. According to Habermas, each and every opinion is just an individual opinion, just as the values, rules and instructions of the head of a company are only opinions. Only the process of discourse and agreement can be structured rationally and this would provide a chance for management to create an effective structure of communication. Therefor discourse principles provide a technique for structuring agreement processes and agreement acts. This enables those who manage to deal with value-based conflicts and differences of opinion. In this type of communication process management can identify their values as their style of leadership. Or they can demand on rational economic causalities to optimise management structures.

Procedures based on rational discourse principles create insights into individual preferences as well as into their relation to the systems of formal structures. It integrates the complexities of the "Lebenswelt" where it is impossible to bridge the gap between implicit and explicit meanings. It is not the meaning of the messages that are structured and defined, but rather the way their meaning is communicated. The analysis of the relation between individual values and rational communication forms the basis for the integration of economic theories into the practical processes and tasks of decision-making.

Habermas' approach of formal principles of discourse offers a technical approach for the effective communication of different subjective ideas and values. Habermas defines discursive conditions for relating various subjective value systems and for creating comprehension. The introduction of discursive "rules" into an organisation creates understanding and verifiability for people's values. In this framework, management tools based on individual values can be evaluated in respect to a company's priority ethical and economic perspectives. The values enclosed in the corporate culture and in the goals of the company become transparent. Key values needed for organisational success develop into explicit factors; e.g. organisational structures, rules, instructions and contracts.

4. Luhmann and Habermas: a model for the explanation of values in economic organisations

4.1. *Rational basis in business communication*

Both Luhmann and Habermas are closely related to the approach of Kant: They divide human thinking and behaviour into rational components and individual values. As a result, on the one hand, Luhmann postulates a rational system of economic communication through the medium of monetary exchange. On the other hand Habermas describes a rational process of discursive communication. Each system presents as its subject equally weighted individual preferences and values but also concrete rules and frameworks for communication and evaluation.

For Luhmann, rational social communication is only possible in terms of such formal structures. Individual preferences are optional and exchangeable. Habermas also attributes rationality only to the process of communication, not to the meaning involved. He even denies the existence of general values. With this methodology, the

discoursive communication of cultural traditions together with strict economic communication – reduced to its formal economic elements – become one of the top attributes of the modern international business system. This includes the separation between rational and non-rational aspects of behaviour and constitutes the foundation for the communication and integration of differing cultural traditions in one "managerial culture".

On the basis of these structures, we can recognise in detail the divergences originating through subjective and, consequently, arbitrary distinctions. We are able to assess the intrinsic values of an organisation and the motivational incentives it gives to its managers. Furthermore, these two systems allow us to make an evaluation of the systematic ethical impacts of an organisation: Do they correspond with the goal values of the organisation?

These results complement corresponding aspects of economic theories, e.g. the "game theory", "transaction-cost economics" and the "constitutional economics", by modelling rules and targets for individual incentives based on values. The methods also open a view into the economic theories themselves. They allow for the assessment of specific cultural aspects of these theories and of aspects belonging to their rational elements (Figure 6). Analytical ethics will investigate the relation between "Lebenswelt" and the inherent systems and laws of communication: How does communication between the several levels and areas happen? In what respect are the acting people responsible? The economists, however, can show the inherent economic laws and the specification of economic communication. They get insights into the inherent values of the economical theories.

4.2. *Three categories of values*

The implementation of these theoretical structures creates, in principal, three levels of values relevant in companies. This opens employee consciousness towards the space and freedom required for taking ethical and moral responsibility. In organisational structures therefor we

**Luhmann's
"Theory of Systems"**
(Link between formal structures
and complex systems of values)

**Habermas's
"Theory of Discourse"**
(Link between "Systemparadigm"
and "Lebensweltparadigm")

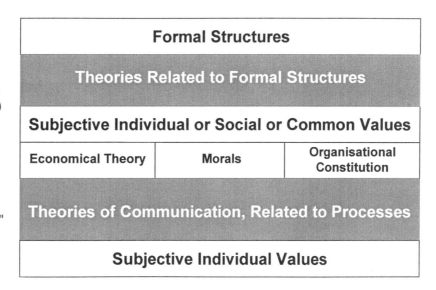

Figure 6. Determination of systematic levels of rationality and values.

recognise the difference between objective and value based elements. We can separate arguments that are related to formal economic facts and to the specific corporate style of a business. Subsequently, we can assess to what extent leadership tools contain specific ideas of values in addition to objective economic or systemic aspects which support both individual and company goals. The three categories are:

1. *Objective economic principles* related to rational systems (e.g.: to be profitability oriented, to fulfil established jurisdictional rules, to respect the power of the political system). With Luhmann we are focused on the core meaning of these principles, independent from subjective meaning.
2. *Subjective company characteristics* and values related to the corporate culture and tradition (e.g.: leadership style, product quality, product style, the favoured kind of teamwork, organisational structures). They are made to empower the managerial organisation and in order to compete with other companies.
3. *Individual values and arbitrary preferences*, respectively. "Team values" or values related to social groups inside the company (if they are not part of organisational specifications) are also assigned to this level. With

Habermas we are focussed on process of communication and not on meaning of specific values or preferences of individuals.

4.3. *Areas for operating with values in organisations*

International companies have many possibilities to determine and communicate their objective and subjective principles. If these elements in a company are transparent and well known (and therefor explicit) the employees will adjust themselves to the demands of their jobs. On this basis, management is able to design and implement leadership tools for considering various cultural distinctions of individual personality. It can assess the role of individual personality in decision-making processes and integrate individual responsibility more effectively. It can measure the output of the employees' contracts in relation to the corporate culture. Moreover, it can control precisely the development of the corporate culture with organisational and managerial tools. This gives a new insight into the objective quality of the employees' work and the quality of the managerial structure. At the same time the systematic integration of discourse into communication processes integrates implicit meaning. The result is a realm of open communication acts and also a deeper understanding of implicit meaning.

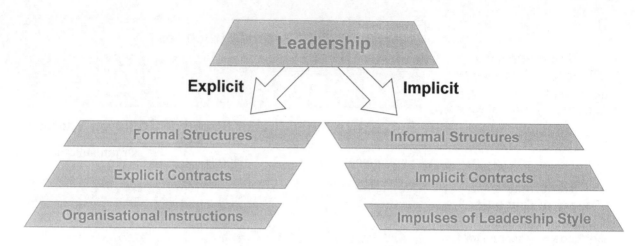

Figure 7.   Possible areas for the management of explicit and implicit meaning.

Management, in terms of informal structures and impulses of style, develops into a second pillar even in multicultural organisations (Figure 7).

For the communication of corporate culture, for example, management can substitute the so far informal structures for focused value training and a code of conduct concentrating on the central aspects of cultural value shift. Ethical responsibility of leadership in an international company ranges from value-definition, value-communication, and managing agreement processes up to value based conflict handling. This will be the basis for settling, systematically and in a timely manner, upcoming conflicts due to contradicting value-patterns and disagreements among the values of the organisations.

5. Conclusion

"Ethical Leadership" in modern multicultural organisations incorporates the dimensions of integration and responsibility. This is firstly the integration of people with different personal and cultural value systems in decision-making processes and, second, the assignment of responsibility either to individual or organisational causalities.

Niklas Luhmann's reduction of rational communication to basic terms (e.g. payment, power, law) opens a wide range of subjective interpretation of the other elements. He presents the meaning inherent in communication as moti-

vating elements in economy and society related to the subjective values of individuals or organisations. In addition, Habermas defines rational aspects only in terms of communication. His "Principles of Discourse" are a possible objective basis for rational intersubjective communication.

These two rational systems – although they are contradictory – empower the personal responsibility needed to create transparent organisational structures as well as to overcome the restrictions given by institutions, organisations and the economic system. The differentiation of motivating elements into objective principles, subjective company values and individual values creates a basis for the evaluation and communication of the subjective aspects inherent in the theories of modern leadership (game theory, transaction-cost economics and constitutional economics). The distinction between subjective and objective values, and between individual personality and organisational structures, enables the design of leadership tools and of agreement processes. The communication of corporate values becomes effective, structured, clear and understandable. It forms agreements and contracts for allocating and motivating employees in a more explicit manner.

Notes

[1] Actually, reason in decision-making processes could be divided in three elements: rational entities, arbi-

trary preferences and passions (Frank, 1988). To get a comprehensive idea of the term "values", I subsume passions or emotions into the area of arbitrary preferences.

[2] Several problems of this area are discussed as aspects of: 1. Freedom as opportunity to pursue and to achieve what is valued (Amartya Sen, 1992). 2. Implicit rules and contracts dealing with asymmetric information and opportunism (Williamson, 1979, 1985; Kay, 1993). 3. Asymmetric information between "principal" and "agent" and the resulting "moral hazard" and "adverse selection" which will give rise to transaction costs (Akerlof, 1970).

[3] This was a result of an inquiry inside of MANAG made in the years 1993 and 1994 (Schnebel, 1997).

[4] For the term of "corporate culture" as a medium by which organisational practices are understood and transmitted see Collier (1997, p. 32).

[5] Schnebel (1996, pp. 63–76).

[6] In the area of economics there are mainly four "Subsystems" relevant (Luhmann, 1984):

1. Die Wirtschaft mit der Leitdifferenz von Geldzahlungen und Nichtzahlungen (Medium: Geld).
2. Das Recht mit der Leitdifferenz von Recht und Unrecht (Medium: Recht).
3. Die Politik mit der Leitdifferenz von Innehaben und Nichtinnehaben von Machtpositionen (Medium: Macht).
4. Die Wissenschaft mit der Leitdifferenz von Wahrheit und Nichtwahrheit (Medium: Fakten).
5. Die Moral mit der Leitdifferenz von gut und schlecht (Luhmann, 1989).

[7] Habermas' principles of discourse are:

1. Alle Teilnehmer müssen die gleichen Chancen haben, im Diskurs zu agieren.
2. Alle Teilnehmer müssen ihre Vormeinungen thematisieren können und kritisiert werden können.
3. Im Diskurs müssen alle Teilnehmer gleichermaßen "repräsentative Sprechakte", die ihre innere Wahrhaftigkeit transparent machen, verwenden können.
4. Im Diskurs müssen alle Teilnehmer die gleiche Chance haben, zu befehlen, sich zu widersetzen, zu erlauben und zu verbieten, Rechenschaft abzulegen und zu verlangen (vollständige Reziprozität zur Gleichverteilung der Chancen) (Habermas, 1984, pp. 177f).

Literature

Akerlof, G. A.: 1970, 'The Market of "Lemons": Qualitative Uncertainty and the Market Mechanism', *Quarterly Journal of Economics* **84**, 488–500.

Alchian, A. and H. Demsetz: 1972, 'Production, Information Costs and Economic Organisation', *American Economic Review* **62**, 777–795.

Binmore, K.: 1992, *Fun and Games: A Text on Game Theory* (Lexington/Toronto).

Buchanan, J. M.: 1975, *The Limits of Liberty, Between Anarchy and Leviathan* (Chicago).

Buchanan, J. M. and G. Tullock: 1982, *The Calculus of Consent. Logical Foundations of Costitutional Democracy* (Ann Arbor).

Coase, R. H.: 1937, 'The Nature of the Firm', *Economica* **4**, 386–405.

Collier, Jane: 1998, 'Theorising the Ethical Organisation', *Business Ethics Quarterly* **8**(4), 621–654.

Frank, R. H.: 1988, *Passions within Reason. The Strategic Role of Emotions* (New York/London).

Habermas, Jürgen: 1981, *Theorie des kommunikativen Handelns* (Frankfurt a.M.).

Habermas, Jürgen: 1984, *Vorstudien und Ergänzungen zu einer Theorie des kommunikativen Handelns* (Frankfurt a.M.).

Habermas, Jürgen: 1993, 'Anerkennungskämpfe im demokratischen Rechtsstaat', in Charles Taylor (ed.), *Multikulturalismus und die Politik der Anerkennung* (Frankfurt a.M.), pp. 187–196.

Habermas, Jürgen: 1997, 'Vom Kampf der Glaubensmächte', in *Vom sinnlichen Einruck zum symbolischen Ausdruck* (Frankfurt a.M.), pp. 41–58.

Homann, Karl: 1994, 'Ethik und Ökonomik. Zur Theoriestrategie der Wirtschaftsethik', in K. Homann (ed.), *Schriften des Vereins für Socialpolitik*, Band 228/I (Berlin), pp. 9–30.

Kay, J.: 1993, *Foundations of Corporate Success* (Oxford University Press, Oxford).

Kreps, D. M.: 1990, *Game Theory and Economic Modelling* (Oxford).

Kreps, D. M.: 1997, 'Intrinsic Motivation and Extrinsic Incentives', *American Economic Review* **87**(2), pp. 359–364.

Luhmann, Niklas: 1984, *Soziale Systeme. Grundriß einer allgemeinen Theorie* (Frankfurt a.M.).

Luhmann, Niklas: 1988, *Die Wirtschaft der Gesellschaft* (Frankfurt a.M.).

Luhmann, Niklas: 1989, *Gesellschaftsstruktur und SemantikStudien zur Wissenssoziologie der modernen Gesellschaft*, Band 3 (Frankfurt a.M.).

Luhmann, Niklas: 1990, *Paradigm Lost: über die Ethische Reflexion der Moral* (Frankfurt a.M.).

Luhmann, Niklas: 1993, 'Wirtschaftsethik – als Ethik?', in Josef Wieland (ed.), *Wirtschaftsethik und Theorie der Gesellschaft* (Frankfurt a.M.), pp. 134–147.

Schnebel, Eberhard: 1995, *Ethos des Managements in Gestalt der Unternehmenskultur. Ethische Dimensionen von Managementstrukturen als Problem christlicher Berufsethik* (Egelsbach).

Schnebel, Eberhard: 1996, 'Wissen im Management – Wissen als Intuition'; in Nikolaus Knoepffler (ed.), *Wie entsteht Wissen?* (München), pp. 71–90.

Schnebel, Eberhard: 1997, *Management – Werte – Organisation. Ethische Aufgaben im Management der Industrie* (Wiesbaden).

Sen, Amartya: 1992, *Inequality Reexamined* (Oxford).

Sen, Amartya: 1993, 'Markets and Freedoms: Achievements and Limitations of the Market Mechanism in Promoting Individual Freedom', *Oxford Economic Papers* **45**, 519–541.

Simon, H: 1957, *Models of Man. Social and Rational* (New York).

Weber, Max: 1920, 'Die protestantische Ethik und der Geist des Kapitalismus (1904–1905)', in *Gesammelte Aufsätze zur Religionssoziologie*, Band I (Tübingen), pp. 17–206.

Willliamson, O. E.: 1979, *The Economic Institution of Capitalism* (New York).

Willliamson, O. E.: 1985, 'Transaction Cost Economics: The Governance of Contractual Relations', *Journal of Law and Economics* **12**(2), 233–261.

Reutlinger Straße 63,
70597 Stuttgart
E-mail: schnebel@t-online.de

Cross-Cultural Methodological Issues in Ethical Research

Gael McDonald

ABSTRACT. Despite the fundamental and administrative difficulties associated with cross-cultural research the rewards are significant and, given an increasing trend toward globalisation, the move away from singular location studies to more comparative research is to be encouraged. In order to facilitate this research process it is imperative, however, that considerable attention is given to the methodological issues that can beset cross-cultural research, specifically as these issues relate to the primary domain or discipline of investigation, which in this instance is research on business ethics. Utilising the experience of a four country comparative study of both Asian and Western cultures in the field of business ethics, the following presents a discussion of methodological concerns under the three broad areas of operationalising culture, operationalising business ethics, and data interpretation.

KEY WORDS: business ethics, cross-cultural research, equivalence, methodological issues

Introduction

The primary concern of comparative research is to distinguish between culturally specific and universal behaviours. Rather than denying universality, pure comparative research studies contrast cultures with a search for both similarities and differences. However, cross-cultural studies are beset by comparability problems in the measurement of concepts, and a dysfunctional consequence of the concern for these methodological issues (for example, Easterby-Smith and Danusia, 1999; Sin, Cheung and Lee, 1999; Mezias et al., 1999; Small et al., 1999a; Small et al., 1999b; Samiee and Athanassiou, 1998; Teagarden and Von Glinow, 1995; Ember and

Ross, 1991; Tamer and Das, 1997; Ronen, 1986; Adler, 1983, 1991; Adler, 1982; Berrien, 1967; Hudson et al., 1959) is the plethora of published criticism which has only served to deter many researchers from comparative research (Lincoln and Kalleberg, 1990, p. 49). Specifically, the overriding methodological issue in cross-cultural research is one of equivalence in variable identification, operational definitions, instrument design, sample selection, sample treatment, and analysis. In other words, are the meanings of key concepts defined equivalently and has the research been designed such that the samples, instrumentation, administration, analysis, and interpretation are equivalent with reference to the cultures in the study (Adler, 1983, p. 30).

In order to discuss the issues associated with cross-cultural research, experience is drawn from an extensive four country cross-cultural comparison study of ethical attitudes and cognitive processes of managers ($n = 4044$) in the Asia Pacific region. The countries utilised were New Zealand, Malaysia, Hong Kong and Canada and the respondents were drawn from two groups; (1) graduate MBA students who are in full-time employment but attending a part-time postgraduate business degree programme, (2) general business respondents who were drawn from business associations with Pacific Rim referents.

The problems experienced in cross-cultural ethical research need to be examined both in a general discussion of comparative research and, specifically, in relation to issues of ethical studies. These methodological concerns and potential research limitations are addressed under the three broad areas of operationalising culture, operationalising business ethics, and data interpretation, and are discussed with relevance to this

Journal of Business Ethics **27**: 89–104, 2000.
© 2000 *Kluwer Academic Publishers. Printed in the Netherlands.*

cross-cultural business ethics project. Where relevant, procedural recommendations will be provided for overcoming these research concerns.

Operationalising culture

Defining culture has often proved difficult and so, too, has operationalising the concept for the benefit of research analysis, particularly when researchers have attempted to go further than the purely descriptive selection of locations. For those with a specific interest in cultural dimension research Triandis (1982–1983) provides a typology of culture that is useful in providing an operational definition of culture. His variables of cultural variation provide an appropriate structure within which cross-cultural differences can be explained. While there are several typologies of this sort available that are helpful in discerning structural elements of culture, it is important that the dimensions isolated are those of immediate relevance to the construct(s) under investigation. For example, differences in time dimensions, while informative, are probably of less explanatory value than collective/individualistic or power distance dimensions in explaining differences in ethicality across cultures. Researchers are, therefore, encouraged to compile their own dimensions relevant to the construct they are measuring. In a 15 year review of cross-cultural research specifically in regard to management control systems, Harrison and McKinnon (1999) observed that not only was there a tendency to treat culture simplistically as a limited set of aggregate dimensions, but there was an assumption of a uniformity and universality of those dimensions. Harrison and McKinnon also noted an excessive reliance on the value dimension in the conceptualisation of culture, failure to consider the totality of the cultural domain, and a tendency not to consider the intensity of cultural norms and values across nations.

Nationality as a surrogate for culture

A common methodological dilemma in cross-cultural ethical research that significantly affects the sampling plan is the issue of using nationality as a surrogate for culture. Upon reviewing comparative management studies, the most common research approach is to make national rather than cultural comparisons. However, these comparative results are most often presented as cultural and consequently reported differences attributed to culture are really due to national characteristics or situational exigencies (Kelly et al., 1987, p. 28). For valid conclusions to be generated from cross-cultural research, researchers need to differentiate whether influential effects are cultural and which are situational or national. Concerning this issue Bhagat and McQuaid (1982) have commented:

> Culture has often served simply as a synonym for nation without further conceptual grounding. In effect, national differences found in the characteristics of organisations or their members have been interpreted as cultural differences (Bhagat and McQuaid, 1982, p. 653).

Although often defined in terms of similar variables, a nation, that is, people inhabiting a country under the same government, may contain several cultures, and a culture may be present in many nations (Ronen, 1986, p. 44). For example, consider the circumstance of a given culture being divided into several nations as in African states and more recently East European states. Alternatively, prior to disintegration of the former Soviet Union, several cultures existed within one nation. In the Asia Pacific region Malaysia is comprised of Malay, Indian and Chinese sub-cultures. In New Zealand, Maori, Pacific Island, and Pakeha (those of European descent) dominate an array of cultural sub-groups and, Melbourne in Australia is reported to be the second largest Greek population outside of Athens.

Within the ethical research study, particularly in relation to a country location like Malaysia, it is evident that interpretative use of nation as a surrogate for culture is methodologically incorrect, although the inherent difficulties of isolating national and cultural differences must be acknowledged. Further attention needs to be directed to this issue. To overcome this problem Kelly and Worthley (1981) and Kelly et al. (1987)

developed a research design that attempted to isolate the influence of culture, utilising a three group study of (1) individuals in a given culture, for example, Chinese managers; (2) ethnic Americans with that cultural heritage, for example, Chinese-American managers; and (3) local Americans with that cultural heritage, for example, Caucasian-Americans. The two groups of American managers have all been exposed to the same economic, political, legal and educational systems but not the same ethnic culture, therefore, any commonality detected is due to national differences. The Chinese-American managers and the Chinese managers (from Hong Kong) share an intergenerationally-transmitted culture but do not share similar national experiences because they live in different countries. If cultural influence is stronger than national influence, one would then predict that Chinese-American managers would be more like the Chinese managers from Hong Kong than the Caucasian-American managers. In this design, culture can be effectively and methodologically isolated from other national and societal influences.

To summarise, "nation" could be defined as people inhabiting one country under the same leadership and administration, whereas "culture" refers to the shared beliefs and symbols of a group of individuals. Adler (1983, p. 40) has observed "in most of the comparative management studies, national boundaries are implicitly accepted as operational definitions of culturally distinct units". However, clearly the existence of subcultures within a national boundary is often so pronounced that care needs to be taken in the overt generalisation of country for culture.

Cultural homogeneity

Given the generality of many cross-cultural ethical studies, it appears that researchers are not making the distinction that domestic populations are multi-cultural but are resting on the assumption that the populations are culturally homogeneous. The current research study attempted to overcome this limitation by evoking the assumption that domestic populations are multi-cultural.

In cross-cultural ethical research, data gathering should be specific enough to be able, at a later date, to isolate within reason, not only sub-cultural referents but also respondents which approximate the dominant characteristics of the domestic culture, that is, local managers as opposed to those with alternative ethnic or country origins. Intra-country contrasts can then be undertaken to determine the strength of culturally specific assumptions and observations. Specific sampling difficulties do exist for research involving ethnic sub-groups and include: defining ethnicity, obtaining relevant population denominations, determining the most appropriate sampling and recruitment strategies, achieving meaningful sample sizes and assessing the representativeness of recruited samples (Small et al., 1999a). In addition to individuals of similar origin but with ethnic diversity, the presence of foreign nationals (that is, those living and working for extended periods in countries that are not their native origin) also must be taken into consideration. It would appear imperative, particularly in specific geographic regions which experience considerable population movement, for example, Europe, North America and Asia, that cultures need to be considered as multi-cultural and not homogeneous.

Culture as an independent, dependent or residual variable

A critical problem in using the concept of culture is the perceptual variability of perceiving culture as a causal, intervening, or residual variable. This perceptual process is largely dependent on the research question under investigation and the analytical methods used. The mediating influence of culture on individually based determinants of behaviour is well recognised although, in a special Fall 1983 issue of the Journal of International Business Studies, Negandhi (1983), the guest editor, observed "judging from the review of recent literature and 36 papers submitted for consideration . . . one can clearly see that cross-cultural management scholars continue to use cultural variables as residual elements". More commonly, culture has been specified as a moderating variable although, it has been advo-cated that researchers should not only specify which element of culture moderates the rela-tionship but also demonstrate the existence of variation in that element across two or more societies. In the current study, culture was clas-sified, among other things, as an independent variable that impacts on ethical attitudes. Where multiple variables are used in regression analysis it is somewhat tempting, although not entirely appropriate because of its nominal nature, to use culture as a residual variable in an effort to "mop up" remaining accountability. It has been advo-cated that nominal variables can be incorporated into regression analyses through the use of "dummies", while non-linear and non-additive relationships can be handled through transfor-mation of variables or through the introduction of product terms (Kim and Kohout, 1975, p. 321). Where culture has been used as an inde-pendent variable it is, consequently, important that further cultural distinctions are made, that is, clear distinction needs to be made regarding whether the dominant culture, sub-culture or origin culture is being utilised in the research model.

Culturally specific or universal phenomenon

In pure comparative studies researchers must not assume that the behaviour of people is either wholly culture specific or wholly universal. The results of comparative management studies should reveal the extent to which the particular behav-iour being studied depends on cultural factors. Jaccard and Wan (1986, p. 123) have, however, asserted that decision-making is a basic phe-nomenon that occurs across cultures. With this phenomenon classified as universal, considerable effort, both etic and emic, has been directed at determining potential differences in the processes and decision outcomes. It could, therefore, be suggested that while ethical decision making per se (the exposure and consideration of ethical dilemmas) is universal across all cultures, the circumstances which activate this process (the antecedents that are considered sufficiently unethical, the cognitive processes utilised and the

cognitive frameworks employed) are both uni-versal and different as is evident by the model evaluations across all four locations.

The issue of universality is also applicable to decision outcomes where the level of agreement or disagreement expressed regarding an ethical scenario could naturally be culturally specific. What prompts an individual to consider an issue to be an ethical dilemma in one culture could, due to value divergence, not be considered an ethical issue in another culture. Alternatively, similarities in decision-making responses could belie culturally specific differences in the actual cognitive processes used in deriving the decision outcome. It is, therefore, important that inves-tigative comparisons of cultural universals and differences use emically defined etic constructs to make cross-cultural comparisons and that these constructs are equivalent between two or more cultures (Jaccard and Wan, 1986).

Masking cultural bias

A problem in ethical studies common to all research is objectivity and concern about what personal values the researcher might bring to the research. Wilson (1993) has pointed out that in ethical research it is imperative that the researcher is both independent and objective, however, he or she will nevertheless have their own set of values and ethics which may colour analysis. Originating from the Hawthorne experiments, there is a wealth of evidence concerning the experimenter effects on test responses (Masling, 1960). In an applied form, experimenter effects are seen when the researcher, in some manner or form, creates a bias in the data collected or where the researcher may have inadvertently commu-nicated his/her preferred research outcomes. To avoid this effect, the current research was fre-quently referred to as a study of managerial values, not ethical attitudes, in the cover letter.

Not only experimental effects but also the cultural origin of the researcher can impact on cross-cultural research. In designing and con-ducting cross-cultural ethical research an issue of concern is the cultural identity of the researcher. More recently, the influence of the researcher has been noted in regard to Hofstede's (1980) cross-cultural work. Westwood (1992, p. 42) has commented that Hofstede's questionnaire was developed by a team of Europeans and may reflect their culturally-informed interpretation of what is culturally relevant and significant. Hofstede is well aware of this problem and has reflected that theories about organisations and organisational behaviour cannot be considered as culture-free. He has noted that theorists and researchers are subject to cultural "mental programming" of their assumptions. Value systems, and the perceptions and interpretations they make of the world cannot avoid being shaped by this cultural conditioning. Therefore, any theory or research interpretation is marked by the culture in which, and for which, it is constructed (Westwood, 1992, p. 41).

Cultural bias is undoubtedly more problematic in pure experimental designs, qualitative research and with the use of interviewing as a data gathering technique. In these circumstances research data is filtered through a researcher's perceptual process and, where additional interpretation and reconstruction of research data is required as in interview analysis, then the opportunity for the cultural bias of the researcher becomes evident. It could, therefore, be assumed that cultural bias effects have a lesser influence in mail administered questionnaires and pure quantitative research.

Although most pronounced in the data gathering, interpretation and analysis, a more subtle consideration of researcher effect needs to be considered in the conceptualisation phase of the research design, and cultural awareness by the researcher is imperative. In general, it has been suggested that when several researchers collaborate in the instrumentation, data gathering, and analysis, there is less likelihood that a culture biased framework will be artificially imposed on the project (Brislin et al., 1973, p. 6). Concerning the current study, the researcher was cognisant of this potential limitation and utilised a Chinese colleague for the validation of research assumptions and conclusions. Having lived in North America, and having been acculturated to Asia after over a decade in the region, the researcher has, where possible, utilised the

knowledge base of local academics and managers in the development, pre-testing, administration, and interpretation of the research project. Despite this background, extreme care and cultural sensitivity continually need to be exhibited by cross-cultural researchers in the selection of appropriate research methodology, and extensive pre-testing of research instruments is imperative.

Operationalising business ethics

When considering ethical research a paradigm shift is often necessary. Researchers are required to loosen their perceptual hold on ethics as associated with philosophy rather than social science, and to consider the use of social scientific tools in the development of experimental approaches. Several researchers have promoted the study of business ethics from a social scientific perspective and considerable attention is being given to methodological and analytical issues in business ethics research (for example, Langholm and Lunde, 1977; Kahn, 1990; Randall and Gibson, 1990; Trevino, 1992; Robertson, 1993; and Crane, 1999). Undoubtedly, one of the major difficulties to overcome in ethical research, and initially in relation to this study, is the selection of an appropriate research methodology. The difficulty centres on the methodological techniques required to study a low base rate phenomenon, and particularly the problem of eliciting honest, and not purely socially acceptable, responses relevant to unethical business behaviour.

> The measurement of attitudes toward deviant behaviour is compounded by a host of factors. In many instances the researcher finds it difficult or even impossible to measure attitudes and participation – for one can scarcely hope to obtain honest answers from respondents who may by definition be dishonest (Pitt and Nel, 1988, p. 32).

The research difficulty of operationalising a concept like business ethics is not unique and is frequently encountered in the behavioural sciences, particularly when interviews or attitude surveys are used to investigate psychological constructs (for example, democracy, brotherhood etc), and where respondents are asked to make judgements on abstract concepts. These concepts are difficult to assess because of the varying perceptions people have of what these concepts actually mean (Laczniak et al., 1981). In addition, in ethical research ethical theories are frequently normative and consequentially difficult to operationalise.

It should be remembered that the intention of ethical research is not to determine *what is* ethical or unethical but to assess – how the characteristics of issues influence ethical beliefs, how individuals think and devise what is ethical and unethical, and how variables, either culturally, organisationally or personally influence ethical perceptions (Trevino, 1992). The direct questioning of respondents in ethical research is not common for the obvious reason that overt questioning of opinions would undoubtedly produce unreliable and biased results. Apart from the concern of respondents providing a socially acceptable response for each question, respondents are also likely to resort to their own, private situational example, or set of circumstances, relating to each issue. In doing so we run the risk of imposing our own culturally based etic without concern for the emic underlying the response. Each question would, therefore, be subject to personal interpretation with little or no consistency across circumstances (Ferrell et al., 1983). It is, therefore, important in ethical research to "anchor" respondents etic perceptions relevant to the construct(s) under study and, for this reason, specific ethical issues in the form of vignettes (Alexander and Becker, 1978) are frequently selected to provide emically sound structure. However, business ethics covers a wide spectrum of business issues under the general term of "ethics", for example, bribery, employee theft, discriminatory personnel policies and conflicts of interest. Naturally, not all issues can be realistically examined at one time and, when selecting the ethical issues to be investigated, consideration also needs to be given to the variety of problems that could be presented under these issues.

A variety of alternative methodologies are available and should be explored, such as: (1) predesigned value instruments e.g., England Personal Value Survey (England, 1967), Rokech Value Survey (Rokech, 1973), Hogan Survey of Ethical Attitudes (Hogan, 1972), Social Attitudes Questionnaire (Aldag and Jackson, 1984), Multidimensional Ethical Scale (Hansen, 1992), Ethical Judgement Measurements (Van Hoose and Paradise, 1979; Skipper and Hyman, 1993); (2) in-basket exercises (Gill, 1979); (3) role playing; (4) interview and focus groups; and (5) situational vignettes (Moon and Woolliams, 1999).

Whatever data capturing methodology is employed a significant problem in cross-national research is posed by language differences. Variations in language exert a considerable concern for comparative research designs as substantive differences between countries become confounded with measurement incongruencies (Lincoln and Kalleberg, 1990; Temple, 1997). Different cultural and linguistic backgrounds lead to different ways of perceiving the world. Unless the linguistic backgrounds are similar, or can be calibrated, people who speak different languages will not perceive the world in the same way (Adler, 1983). Ryan et al. (1999) have attempted to overcome with the use of multiple groups covariance structure analysis the linguistic difficulties in their study utilising 4 scales in 4 countries. Cultural and linguistic influences were considered by assessing equivalence across two pairs of countries having the same language but different cultures, and across countries differing in culture and language. With the concern of non-equivalences as sources of measurement error, this highlights the necessity to accurately translate measurement instruments from one language to another. The common process involves translation and back translation (Davis et al., 1981) although errors that creep into this process can naturally create further measurement problems. Where interviews are used as the data collection methodology, a number of strategies for improving interview quality have been proposed such as careful selection and comprehensive training of interviewers, standardising interviewing techniques, close supervision, re-interviewing of selected participants and timely feedback to interviewers regarding performance (Small et al., 1999b) It should be noted that while linguistic errors can be minimised through a standardised questionnaire, this does not account for possible conceptual errors such as concept or score equivalence that could arise through the interpretation process.

Interestingly, when bilingual subjects are observed using their two languages, the results may differ depending on differences in the two cultures associated with the languages. It has been found that bilingual subjects showed results closer to those of monolinguals of the second language group when the bilinguals were tested in their second language as compared to the first (Yang, 1979; Yang and Bond, 1980). Yang and Bond (1980) found that for Chinese students there was a tendency for them to respond in a more "Chinese" way when the questionnaire was printed in English than when printed in Chinese. Reporting on contradictory findings on bilingual response patterns and the influence of contextual factors in cueing subjects to the appropriate direction for their responses when responding in English, Yang and Bond (1980, p. 423) cautioned that the contextual cueing effect could raise doubts about the validity of measures collected in a host country from foreign nationals living in that country. It is suggested that if contextual cueing was in effect, presumably these subjects would respond in a direction closer to that of their hosts, thus playing down the actual differences between the two cultures.

Data interpretation and analysis

A variety of statistical methods are available to cross-cultural ethical researchers. Prior to the 1960's the principal tool used in cross-cultural data analysis was bivariate correlation although it has been noted that such a simplistic technique could often lead to spurious relationships between variables (Ronen, 1986, p. 51). Several statistical methods have been recommended by cross-cultural researchers. Berrien (1970) described correlational methods designed to elicit the meaning of concepts in the cultures under study and simultaneously maintain an emic-etic distinction. Brislin et al. (1973) has suggested intercorrelating specific questions with the identical indicators found in each culture within the

study. The researcher is then able to determine whether the specific questions are eliciting functionally equivalent responses in each of the cultures (one needs to initially identify these identical indicators). Hudson et al. (1959) suggested a similar analysis and recommended that cross-cultural data analysis be done on an item-by-item basis so as to gain further insight into the meaning of summary scores on several items.

Specifically in relation to business ethics research, the analytical problems have centred on: non-existent multivariate analyses, the prevalence of non-parametric statistics due to small sample sizes, and tenuous analytical comparisons, that is, small firms in one study with large firms in another study (Vyakarnam, 1995, p. 24). Given the complexity of the analytical task, cross-cultural research today favours multiple regression and multivariate techniques with alternative use being made of factor analysis, cluster analysis, componential analysis and multi-dimensional scaling (Ronen, 1986, p. 51).

Independent variable scaling

The importance of "equivalence" in cross-cultural ethical research cannot be overstated. Naturally, equivalence extends from conceptual concerns of linguistic consistencies in the data capturing methodology to the practicalities of score equivalence. Score or metric equivalence exists when all cultures adhere to a common quantitative measure. Prior research has, however, indicated potential problems. As an apparent consequence of Asian collectivism and Western individualism, it has been found that there is a tendency for Japanese respondents to give average or non-committal answers while Anglo-American respondents are more prone to take an extreme stand on issues (Dore, 1973, p. 232). In effect, the "psychological mid-point" on the scale may differ across cultures. If this is a true phenomenon, this problem can be partially avoided through the use of both equal interval scales and expanding the number of response options, notably from five to seven response codes.

Score or metric equivalence is achieved more easily through the use of known and recognised interval measures. Garland (1990) investigated whether labelling the scale points, that is, unlabelled, labelled or numbered, affects the way the scales are used and found no differences in the ratings that were obtained with each form but with a preference for a labelled form of semantic scale for surveying diverse audiences. In the current study, both numeric and label measures were used (for example, strongly agree) in order to facilitate cross-cultural score equivalences. Angelmar and Pras (1978) have shown how adjectives used to define response scale alternatives can be developed in different languages to achieve metrically equivalent scale values and homogeneity of meaning. Scaling is an important aspect of instrument development and, in cross-cultural research, Barry (1969) found that a five point scale, as used in this research, was more sensitive than a four point scale. Garland (1990) has also supported the use of five point scales suggesting that these tend to be more easily understood by respondents than scoring systems using more points.

Where semantic scaling is used, consideration also needs to be given to the probability of a response set bias (that is, central tendency error) and the variance in this bias across different country locations. Investigating this phenomenon, Si and Cullen (1998) noted that differences were found in central tendency between Asian and Western respondents. Using scales with even numbered response categories decreased the central tendencies of the Asian (Chinese, Japanese and Hong Kong) respondents.

In regard to vignette methodology (which is commonly used in ethical research) as a consequence of response bias, a limited number of ethical vignettes and variation in the response methodology is recommended. It should be remembered that the closed-ended nature of vignettes with attached semantic scales greatly facilitates empirical analysis but, in doing so, loses insight into the likely responses. Alternatively, free response formats are not common (Randall and Gibson, 1990, p. 266).

Dependent variable determination

In many empirical studies of business ethics the dependent variable is frequently depicted as the sum of ethical attitudes responses. Within the study fourteen ethical scenarios solicited ethical attitudes. Yielding interval data, it could be assumed that despite covering specific issues such as whistleblowing and bribery, the fourteen measures may be considered jointly since they are expected to be related to the major area of concern, that of ethics. Closer examination of the data does, however, suggest that the use of an aggregate, or total scenario score, may be inappropriate for the reason that scores display varying degrees of consistency in their responses. Following a correlational analysis on the scores for the total sample, low correlations between the various questions were recorded illustrating that an individual who agreed strongly with one unethical practice might disagree strongly with another. Acceptance of unethical behaviour in one situation cannot be used as an indication of likely agreement to unethical behaviour in another situation, nor can it be taken as a measure of complete agreement to unethical behaviour. Thus, an individual should not be labelled "unethical" in a general sense; each circumstance would need to be examined separately. When examining ethical issues studies by Krugman and Ferrell (1981) and Ferrell and Weaver (1978), Becker and Fritzsche (1987) and Fritzsche (1988) also found a differential response affect across issues. As a partial explanation, Reidenbach and Robin (1988) have suggested that individuals may not use clearly defined normative ethical philosophies in evaluating ethics but appear to organise and use the evaluative criteria differently from situation to situation.

To minimise the likely analytical profusion that could result from analysing each situational scenario as a separate entity, an alternative method of analysis was experimented with. A factor analysis was undertaken for each country research location and, from the factors observed, the factor that generated the greatest similarity was isolated. The combined scores for the restricted number of scenarios contained in the relevant factor were used as the dependent variable in regression analysis. The cognitive frameworks, individual and situational factors were used as independent variables and the total samples were delineated according to the research hypotheses.

Researchers are cautioned on the form of aggregation used, which in pure organisational studies may be better than with individual data, and the use of aggregate summations in relation to cross-cultural research. Most of the cross-cultural studies in business ethics deal with aggregate individual data. Interestingly, no attempt has been made to follow existing methodological models available in cross-cultural research and to investigate cross-cultural ethics where a single organisation across differing cultures (for example, a multi-national) is the unit of analysis. Realistically, despite commonality in ownership within a multi-national, some differences across regional operations are to be expected and, while it has been admitted this will limit the comparability of the unit of analysis and reduce the sampling to a purposive level, it has also been suggested that even if the organisation is the unit of analysis, the variable "organisation" can transcend classification (Drenth, 1983). So, why not solely utilise the cross-cultural organisational methodology with cluster sampling as was successfully employed by Hofstede (1980)? Primarily it has been argued that it may not be justified to make inferences about relationships between variables at an individual level on the basis of correlational data based upon groups as units (Drenth, 1983). Cross-cultural ethical studies would, therefore, be greatly advanced if, in addition to the more generalised individual sampling across cultures, coincidental sampling within a single multinational organisation with a similar profiling of respondents is suggested.

Focused research with salient individuals could also be used as further evaluative assistance in discerning the true validity of any findings. If cultural norms truly exist at every level of a national system, clearly a more extensive triangulated approach in international comparative ethical research is needed with extensive use of in-depth interviews.

Statistical methods

Although possibly easier to recover from failures in statistical manipulation than, say, unreliable instrumentation (Tamer and Das, 1997), it should be recognised that differing statistical methods can, however, give rise to differing results and consequential errors in interpretation. For example, while apparent differences can occur in the ethical attitudes and antecedents detected through regression analysis, overall similarities might be revealed through alternative statistical methodology.

In the current study through T-Test and ANOVA analysis, several situational and individual factors did not, except in isolated country circumstances, indicate significant relationships with ethical attitudes. However, regression analysis of some of these factors was important enough to impact on total and sub-group regression outcomes.

Contrasting the findings from ANOVA and multiple regression methodology has interesting implications for analysis of ethical data, and the evaluative decision rests on which method is the more appropriate for analytical and interpretative purposes. In the current research, for example, ANOVA analysis compared the mean values of the cognitive frameworks, as reported by respondent managers in four different locations, while multiple regression analysis examined the linear relationship between a dependent, or criterion variable, that is, the responses to the ethical issues and a set of independent or predictor variables, or the cognitive frameworks. Through these alternative methods it has been found that differences clearly exist between what managers *say* are the cognitive frameworks they use and the frameworks that are *actually* employed. Specifically, while most managers profess a lofty concern for duty and justice, in reality, self-interest (the desire to selfishly gain the greatest degree of personal satisfaction) and neutralisation (the use of rationalisations that deny hurt or injury) are more apparent in the ethical decision making process. By virtue of the human cognitions being studied here these differences are to be expected. Many individuals are probably not consciously aware of the parameters of their decision process and, therefore, when asked will state the obvious, socially acceptable response. It is, therefore, important that the subconscious and rarely articulated factors are, in fact, revealed.

Researchers of business ethics should not only carefully select the appropriate methodology for their studies. Care also needs to be taken in interpretation of the findings of empirical research, as an overt dependence on self-reported data and ANOVA analyses (as is common in ethical research) could result in alternative conclusions with stated expectations not necessarily reflecting reality.

Social desirability response bias

Ethical instruments have been subject to criticism because of what is referred to as social desirability response bias, a common problem in the data gathering process where individuals are more inclined to respond in a socially acceptable manner. The pressure for respondents to provide morally correct answers, instead of true answers, is considered stronger in ethics research than in other attitudinal research, and Nyaw and Ng (1994) have suggested that a failure to consider and control for this potential response bias can have an adverse impact on the validity of the research findings. It should be remembered although that there are a number of additional factors which will also impact on validity.[1]

The means by which social response bias might be measured has been incorporated in at least three studies (Fernandes and Randall, 1992; Randall and Fernandes, 1991; and Nyaw and Ng, 1994) through the use of Crowne and Marlowe's (1960) Social Desirability Scale that includes questions such as "I never hesitate to go out of my way to help someone in trouble". In Marlowe's original study, the Social Desirability Scale consisted of 33 items. Where the Social Desirability Scale is being used as a supplementary measure it is, however, unlikely because of length that the full scale would be used and a cut down version, as used by Nyaw and Ng (1994), is recommended. A reliability estimate should be given for this revised version. This was not offered in the Nyaw and Ng study. Selection

of the items for use on the revised scale should also consider cultural differences. For example, when using the scale in Hong Kong, Nyaw and Ng appropriately removed the item "I never make a long trip without checking the safety of my car". Long trips are not possible in such a geographically confined area and where very few members of the population own a motorcar.

In an extensive discussion of social desirability bias in cross-cultural ethics research, Randall et al. (1993) propose four measures for controlling the bias. In addition to the use of pre-tests, pilot tests, and social desirability scales imbedded in research instruments, Randall et al. (1993, p. 185) also suggest a longitudinal research design to "help disentangle the impact of culture values, personal values, and social desirability bias".

Non-response bias

To conclude this section on potential interpretative problems in ethical research, brief mention should be made of the measurement equivalence concern of non-response bias. Research into non-response bias has provided a number of recommendations. For example, Hegarty and Sims (1978 and 1979) utilised a computerised data entry methodology to measure the effects of potential rewards and punishments on students paying kickbacks in simulated business situations. The experimental design consisted of a 3×3 factorial analysis of variance with selected personality and demographic variables as co-variates. Subjects entered decisions into an on-line, time-shared computer programme, allowing experimental control over key variables and an assessment of causal relationships. Consideration could also be given to the use of interactive video for presenting realistic ethical dilemmas and accurate data recording. Response bias can also be addressed by increasing response rates (through the use of such strategies as preliminary notification, rewards, personalisation, the use of real stamp postage, and undertaking follow-ups), and increased sample sizes.

Conclusions

Much insight is to be gained from cross-cultural research. The cumulative efforts of investigators to recognise and systematically deal with the inherent methodological difficulties of applied research, particularly in cross-cultural research, will enable investigators to move from purely descriptive analysis to pursue unique areas of investigation in the international arena.

Independently, both cross-cultural (for example, Adler, 1983) and ethical research (for example, Collier, 1995) have been critically evaluated. The methodological issues identified in these discussions are not insurmountable and already there exists a volume of research experience that has drawn heavily from investigative work in other social sciences. Besides the basic issues of validity, the research designs used in cross-cultural research must be reliable across different settings and cultures, as it is recognised that a fundamental problem in any cross-national research is the isolation of true differences in the phenomena studied from possible variations caused by different methodologies. The solution to the problem is to ensure equivalence in all areas such as sampling procedures, stimulus material (that is, questionnaire, test or task) as well as the mode of quantifying responses (that is, the scale used and procedures of scoring and coding). While identical replication of all aspects of the research methodology in each cultural location is a utopian ideal, in reality, "measure equivalence" across cultures is the essential feature of cross-cultural research. This equivalence exists in five forms – linguistic, conceptual, score, scale and sample equivalence.

In cross-cultural research, ideally, the research questions, concepts, approaches and sampling should be identical and, at the operational level, cultural equivalence rather than literal identicality is more common. Many commentaries have been written on potential measurement error problems encountered by behavioural scientists conducting cross-cultural studies and the requisite dimensions of equivalency, particularly in regard to vocabulary, idiomatic, grammatical, syntactical and score components. These types of non-equivalences are considered to be a source of measurement error

and methodological strategies such as back translation have been devised to minimise their presence (Davis et al., 1981, p. 99). Davis et al. (1981) have stressed that while researchers strive to reduce measurement error, particularly linguistic and conceptual non-equivalences in questionnaire instruments, some degree of fallibility will always be present in survey data. This should, however, not deter researchers from undertaking research of a cross-cultural nature but should encourage them to exert additional effort in investigating appropriate research methodologies that might eliminate many of the problems encountered.

Sampling issues in cross-cultural research relate to the dual concerns of selecting country locations and the intra-country subjects that best reflect the nation's central tendencies. Ideally, the selection of countries for inclusion in the study should be on the basis of theory or a testable hypothesis. The selection is commonly confined to a representative sample of countries or, if research funds permit, the total set of countries within a certain domain (for example, Asia, Western Europe, Latin America). In discussing sampling methodology, Drenth (1983) presents two options: countries are selected by (a) the most similar systems design (that is, countries differ only on the independent variable), or (b) the most different systems design (that is, countries differ as much as possible so as to check the theory under the "unfavourable conditions"). Having selected a country for investigation a representative sample of the population is required. Sekaran (1983) has suggested the use of matched samples. Matched samples are functionally equivalent but not identical across various cultures. Alternatively, where specific research objectives in relation to specific sub-cultural groups are indicated, stratified sampling may be required.

Where the unit of analysis is one organisation (for example, the same multi-national as used by Hofstede, 1980) across all the cultural locations then naturally this standardisation is further enhanced. Regrettably, difficulty in gaining access and the generation of limited sample sizes from one company often lead to the use of additional data collection sample frames. The trade-off is that this often renders tenuous the comparability of the units of analysis and reduces sampling to the purposive level (Drenth, 1983).

In cross-cultural research, possible threats to interpretation can be caused by the interactions between culture and the research variables. The confounding of results by an interaction between the cultural and experimental variables should not be ignored. Rather than shying away from these issues, Brislin et al. (1973) have encouraged researchers to embrace these alternatives in what has been described as the plausible rival hypothesis approach. Pointing out that plausible rival hypotheses can be both substantive (that is, other cultural or variable differences) and methodological (that is, instrument, sampling or administration), Brislin et al. (1973) have commented:

> There is no possible method that will eliminate such rival explanations in a priori or wholesale fashion. Instead, one must approach each singularly and eliminate it by introducing supplementary variations within one or both of the comparison populations (Brislin et al., 1973, p. 16).

Some attempts have been made to isolate and examine these alternative hypotheses. For example, in regard to organisational variables the question has been asked: does organisational culture diminish national culture? Surprisingly, the answer is no. Research indicates that employees and managers do bring their ethicality to the workplace. Hofstede (1980) found striking cultural differences within a single multi-national. In his study, national culture explained 50% of the differences in employees' attitudes and behaviours. National culture explained more of the differences than did professional role, gender or race (Hofstede, 1980).

Laurent (1981) found cultural differences even more pronounced among foreign employees working within the same multi-national organisation than among employees working for organisations in their home location. Observing managers in 10 locations who were working for organisations in their own native lands, and then replicating the research in one multi-national with subsidiaries in each of the 10 locations, Laurent assumed employees working for the

same multi-national would be similar to their domestically employed colleagues. There were, however, significantly greater differences between managers in 10 countries working within the same multi-national corporation than there were between local managers working for the same multi-national corporation. He found employees maintaining and even strengthening their cultural differences. For example, when they work for multi-national corporations Germans become more German. Laurent has replicated the research in two other multi-national corporations with the conclusions that, far from reducing national differences, organisational culture maintains and enhances these differences.

Threats to interpretation caused by interactions between culture and the research variables are to be expected in cross-cultural research. It is, therefore, up to the researcher to fully consider the confounding impact of these variables. Rather than deny their presence, researchers are encouraged to deliberate on their influence and to selectively analyse rival hypotheses that may be of contributory value.

To conclude, despite the inherent difficulties of defining culture, comparative management research aims at identifying those aspects of social behaviour in work settings that are culturally specific and those which are universal. Isolating the influence of culture on the development of ethical attitudes is a difficult problem for comparative international management researchers, as ethical attitudes and behaviour could be attributed to individual differences, situational contingencies, or cultural dimensions. This discussion has examined a number of issues of relevance to cross-cultural research, independent of the sociological or psychological focus of the study, and has addressed the areas of conceptual development, instrument design, pre-testing and administration. Examination of these issues is deemed imperative for appropriate consideration of methodological constraints relevant to the cross-cultural ethical studies.

Note

[1] Social desirability bias is not the only factor that will impact on the validity of the results. Campbell (1959) listed fifteen factors that may jeopardise the validity of obtained data:

1. History
2. Testing
3. Maturation
4. Instrumentation
5. Statistical regression
6. Instability
7. Selection
8. Experimental mortality
9. Selection-maturation or selection-testing interaction
10. Interacting effects of testing
11. Interacting of selection and experimental treatment
12. Reactive effects
13. Multiple treatment interference
14. Irrelevant responsiveness of measures
15. Irrelevant replaceability of treatments.

References

Adler, L. L.: 1982, *Cross-Cultural Research at Issues* (Academic Press, New York).

Adler, N. J.: 1983, 'A Typology of Management Studies Involving Culture', *Journal of International Business Studies* (Fall), 29–47.

Adler, N. J.: 1991, *International Dimensions of Organisational Behaviour*, Second Edition (PAS-Kent Publishing Company, Boston).

Aldag, R. J. and D. W. Jackson: 1984, 'Measurement and Correlates of Social Attitudes', *Journal of Business Ethics* **3**, 143–151.

Alexander, Cheryl S. and H. J. Becker: 1978, 'The Use of Vignettes in Survey Research', *Public Opinion Quarterly*, 93–104.

Angelmar, R. and B. Pras: 1978, 'Verbal Rating Scales for Multinational Research', *European Research* **6**, 62–67.

Barry, M.: 1969, 'Cross-Cultural Research with Matched Pair of Societies', *Journal of Social Psychology* **79**, 25–33.

Becker, H. and D. J. Fritzsche: 1987, 'A Cross-Cultural Comparison of Managers' Attitudes', *Journal of Business Ethics* **6**(4), 289–296.

Berrien, F. K.: 1967, 'Methodological and Related Problems in Cross Cultural Research', *International Journal of Psychology* **75**, 3–9.

Berrien, F. K.: 1970, 'A Super-ego for Cross-Cultural Research', *International Journal of Psychology* **75**, 3–5.

Bhagat, R. S. and S. J. McQuaid: 1982, 'Role of Subjective Culture in Organisations: A Review and Directions for Future Research', *Journal of Applied Psychology Monograph* **67**(5), 653.

Brislin, R., W. J. Loaner and R. M. Thorndike: 1973, *Cross-Cultural Methods* (John Wiley and Sons, New York).

Campbell, D. T. and D. W. Fiske: 1959, 'Convergent and Discriminant Validation by the Multi-trait Multi-method Matrix', *Psychological Bulletin* **52**(2), 81–105.

Collier, J.: 1995, 'Business Ethics Research: Shaping the Agenda', *Business Ethics and European Review* **4**(1), 6–11.

Crane, A.: 1999, 'Are You Ethical? Please Tick Yes or No on Research Ethics in Business', *Journal of Business Ethics* **20** (July), 237–248.

Crowne, D. P. and D. Marlowe: 1960, 'A New Scale of Social Desirability Independent of Psychopathology', *Journal of Consulting Psychology* **24**, 349–354.

Davis, H. L., S. P. Douglas and A. Silk: 1981, 'Measure Unreliability: A Hidden Threat to Cross-National Marketing Research', *Journal of Marketing* **45** (Spring), 98–109.

Dore, R.: 1973, *British Factory – Japanese Factory: The Origins of Diversity in Industrial Relations* (University of California Press, Berkeley). In Lincoln, J. R. and A. L. Kalleberg: 1990, *Culture Control and Commitment: A Study of Work Organisation and Work Attitudes in the United States and Japan* (Cambridge University Press, Cambridge).

Drenth, P. J.: 1983, 'Cross-Cultural Organisational Psychology: Challenges and Limitations', in S. H. Irvine and J. W. Berry (eds.), *Human Assessment and Cultural Factors* (Plenum Press, New York).

Easterby-Smith, M. and M. Danusia: 1999, 'Cross-cultural Collaborative Research: Towards Reflexiity', *Academy of Management Journal* **42** (February), 76–86.

Ember, C. R. and M. H. Ross: 1991, 'Problems of Measurement in Cross-cultural Research', *Behavior Science Research* **25**, 187–217.

England, G. W.: 1967, 'Personal Value Systems of American Managers', *Academy of Management Review* **10**(1), 56–68.

Fernandes, M. F. and D. M. Randall: 1992, 'The

Nature of Social Desirability Response Effects in Ethics Research', *Business Ethics Quarterly* **2**(2), 183–204.

Ferrell, O. C. and K. M. Weaver: 1978, 'Ethical Beliefs of Marketing Managers', *Journal of Marketing* (July), 69–73.

Ferrell, O. C., M. Zey-Ferrell and D. Krugman: 1983, 'A Comparison of Predictors of Ethical and Unethical Behaviour among Corporate and Agency Advertising Managers', *Journal of Macro Marketing* (Spring), 19–27.

Fritzsche, D. J.: 1988, 'An Examination of Marketing Ethics: Role of the Decision Maker. Consequences of the Decision, Management Position and Sex of Respondent', *Journal of Macromarketing* **8** (Winter), 29–39.

Garland, R.: 1990, 'A Comparison of Three Forms of the Semantic Differential', *Marketing Bulletin* **1**, 19–24.

Gill, R. W.: 1979, 'The In-tray (in-basket) Exercise as a Measure of Management Potential', *Journal of Occupational Psychology* **52** (June), 185–197.

Hansen, R. S.: 1992, 'A Multidimensional Scale for Measuring Business Ethics: A Purification and Refinement', *Journal of Business Ethics* **11**, 523–534.

Harrison, G. L. and J. L. McKinnon: 1999, 'Cross-Cultural Research in Management Control Systems Design: A Review of the Current State', *Accounting, Organisations and Society* **24** (July/August), 483–506.

Hegarty, W. H. and H. P. Sims: 1978, 'Some Determinants of Unethical Decision Behaviour: An Experiment', *Journal of Applied Psychology* **63**(4), 451–457.

Hegarty, W. H. and H. P Sims: 1979, 'Organizational Philosophy, Policies, and Objectives Related to Unethical Decision Behaviour: A Laboratory Experiment', *Journal of Applied Psychology* **64**(3), 331–338.

Hofstede, G.: 1980, *Culture's Consequences: International Differences in Work Related Values* (Sage Publishing, Inc., Beverly Hills).

Hogan, R.: 1972, 'Review of the Survey of Values', in O. Buros (ed.), *The Measurement Tea-book*, Seventh Edition (Gryphon Press, Highland Park NJ), pp. 355–356.

Hudson, B., B. Barakat and R. Laforge: 1959, 'Problems and Methods of Cross-Cultural Research', *Journal of Social Issues* **15**, 5–19. In Brislin, R., W. J. Loaner and R. M. Thorndike: 1973, *Cross-Cultural Methods* (John Wiley and Sons, New York).

Jaccard, J. and C. K. Wan: 1986, 'Cross-Cultural Methods for the Study of Behavioral Decision Making', *Journal of Cross-Cultural Psychology* **17**(2), 123–149.

Kahn, W. A.: 1990, 'Toward an Agenda for Business Ethics Research', *Academy of Management Review* **15**(2), 311–328.

Kelly, L. and R. Worthley: '1981, 'The Role of Culture in Comparative Management: A Cross-Cultural Perspective', *Academy of Management Journal* **24**(1), 164–173.

Kelly, L., A. Whatley and R. Worthley: 1987, 'Assessing the Effects of Culture on Managerial Attitudes: A Three Culture Test', *Journal of International Business Studies* (Summer), 17–31.

Kim, Jae-On, and F. J. Kohout: 1975, 'Multiple Regression Analysis: Sub-program Regression', in N. H. Nie, C. Hadlaihull, J. C. Jenkins, K. Steinbrenner and D. H. Bent (eds.), *Statistical Package for the Social Sciences*, Second Edition (McGraw Hill, New York).

Krugman, D. M. and D. C. Ferrell: 1981, 'The Organisational Ethics of Advertising Corporate and Agency Views', *Journal of Advertising* **10**, 21–30.

Laczniak, G. R., R. F. Lusch and W. A. Strong: 1981, 'Ethical Marketing: Perceptions of Economic Goods and Social Problems', *Journal of Macro Marketing* (Spring), 49–57.

Langholm, O. and J. Lunde: 1977, 'Empirical Methods for Business Research', *Review of Social Economy* **35**(2) (October), 133–143.

Laurent, A.: 1981, *Organisation Culture Magnifies Cross-Cultural Differences* (Insead, Fontainebleau, France).

Lincoln, J. R. and A. L. Kalleberg: 1990, *Culture Control and Commitment A Study of Work Organisation and Work Attitudes in the United States and Japan* (Cambridge University Press, Cambridge).

Masling, J.: 1960, 'The Influence of Situational and Interpersonal Variables in Projective Testing', *Psychological Bulletin* **57**, 65–68.

Mezias, S. J., Y. Chen and P. Murphy: 1999, 'Toto, I Don't Think We're in Kansas Anymore. Some Footnotes to Cross Cultural Research', *Journal of Management Inquiry* **8**(3), 323–333.

Moon, C. and P. Woolliams: 1999, 'Managing Cross-Cultural Business Ethics through an Interactive Computer Model', Unpublished Paper. See Moon, C.: 1999, 'Business Challenging Business Ethics. New Instruments for Coping with Diversity in International Business', 12th EBEN Annual

Conference, 1999. Amsterdam, The Netherlands, 1–3 September.

Negandhi, A. R.: 1983, 'Cross-Cultural Management Research: Trend and Future Directions', *Journal of International Business Studies* (Fall), 1–28.

Nyaw, M. and I. Ng: 1994, 'A Comparative Analysis of Ethical Beliefs: A Four Country Study', *Journal of Business Ethics* **13**, 543–555.

Pitt, L. F. and D. Nel: 1988, 'The Wearer's Merit. A Comparison of the Attributes of Suppliers and Buyers to Corruption in Business', *Industrial Marketing and Purchasing* **3**(1), 30–38.

Randall, D. M. and M. F. Fernandes: 1991, 'The Social Desirability Bias in Ethics Research', *Journal of Business Ethics* **10**, 805–817.

Randall, D. M. and A. M. Gibson: 1990, 'Methodology in Business Ethics Research: A Review and Critical Assessment', *Journal of Business Ethics* **9**, 457–472.

Randall, D. M., P. Y. Huo and P. Pawelk: 1993, 'Social Desirability Bias in Cross-Cultural Ethics Research', *The International Journal of Organisational Analysis* **1**(2), 185–202.

Reidenbach, R. E. and D. P. Robin: 1988, 'Some Initial Steps Toward Improving the Measurement of Ethical Evaluations of Marketing Activities', *Journal of Business Ethics* **1**, 877–879.

Robertson, D. C.: 1993, 'Empiricism in Business Ethics: Suggested Research Directions', *Journal of Business Ethics* **12**, 585–600.

Rokech, M.: 1973, *The Nature of Human Value* (The Free Press, New York).

Ronen, S.: 1986, *Comparative and Multinational Management* (John Wiley and Sons, New York).

Ryan, A., D. Chan, R. E. Ployhart and L. A. Slade: 1999, 'Employee Attitude Surveys in a Multinational Organisation: Considering Language and Culture in Assessing Measurement Equivalence', *Personnel Psychology* **52**, 37–58.

Samiee, S. and N. Athanassiou: 1998, 'International Strategy Research: Cross-Cultural Methodological Limitations', *Journal of Business Research* **43** (October), 79–86.

Sekaran, U.: 1983, 'Methodological and Theoretical Issues and Advancements in Cross-Cultural Research', *Journal of International Business Studies* **14**(2), 61–73.

Si, S. X. and J. B. Cullen: 1998, 'Response Categories and Potential Cultural Bias: Effects of an Explicit Middle Point in Cross-Cultural Surveys', *International Journal of Organisational Analysis* **6**(3), 218–230.

Sin, L. Y., G. W. Cheung and R. Lee: 1999,

'Methodology in Cross-Cultural Consumer Research and Critical Assessment', *Journal of International Consumer Marketing* **11**(4), 75–96.

Skipper, R. and R. R. Hyman: 1993, 'On Measuring Ethical Judgments', *Journal of Business Ethics* **12**, 535–545.

Small, R., J. Yelland, J. Lumley and P. L. Rice: 1999a, 'Cross-Cultural Research: Trying to do it Better 1. Issues in Study Design', *Australian and New Zealand Journal of Public Health* **23**(4), 385–389.

Small, R., J. Yelland, J. Lumley, P. L. Rice, V. Cotronei and R. Warren: 1999b, 'Cross-Cultural Research: Trying to Do it Better 2. Enhancing Data Quality', *Australian and New Zealand Journal of Public Health* **23**(4), 390–395.

Tamer, S. and C. A. Das: 1997, 'Methodological Issues in Empirical Cross-Cultural Research: A Survey of the Management Literature and a Framework', *Management International Review* **37**(1), 71–96.

Teagarden, M. B. and M. A. Von Glinow: 1995, 'Toward a Theory of Comparative Management Research', *Academy of Management Journal* **38** (October), 1261–1289.

Temple, B.: 1997, 'Watch Your Tongue: Issues in Translation and Cross-Cultural Research', *Sociology* **31** (August), 607–619.

Trevino, L. K.: 1992, 'Moral Reasoning and Business Ethics: Implications for Research, Education and Management', *Journal of Business Ethics* **11**, 445–449.

Triandis, H.: 1982–1983, 'Dimensions of Cultural Variations as Parameters of Organisational Theories', *International Studies of Management and Organisations* **12**(4), 142–143.

Van Hoose, W. H. and L. V. Paradise: 1979, 'Ethical Judgement Scale', in Q. S. Doromal and P. G. Creamer: 1978, 'An Evaluation of the Ethical Judgement Scale', *Journal of College Student Development* **29**(2) (March), 151–158.

Vyakarnam, S.: 1995, 'Focus Groups: Are They Viable in Ethics Research', *Business Ethics and European Review* **4**(1), 24–29.

Westwood, R. I.: 1992, 'Culture, Cultural Differences, and Organisational Behaviour', in R. I. Westwood (ed.), *Organisational Behaviour South East Asia Perspectives* (Longman Group, Hong Kong).

Wilson, A.: 1993, 'The Role of Research in Business Ethics', The European Business Ethics Network. Sixth Annual Conference. 15–17 September. Norwegian School of Management.

Yang, Kuo-Shu and M. H. Bond: 1980, 'Ethnic

Affirmation by Chinese Bilingual', *Journal of Cross-Cultural Psychology* **11**(4) (December), 411–425.

Yang, K. S.: 1979, 'Social Orientation and Individual Modernity Among Chinese Students in Taiwan', Presented at the First Asian Regional Meeting of the International Association of Cross-Cultural Psychology, Hong Kong, March, in Yang Kuo-Shu and M. H. Bond: 1980, 'Ethnic Affirmation by Chinese Bilingual', *Journal of Cross-Cultural Psychology* **11**(4) (December), 411–425.

UNITEC Institute of Technology,
Private Bag 92 025,
Auckland, New Zealand.
E-mail: gmcdonald@unitec.ac.nz

Managing Cross Cultural Business Ethics

Chris J. Moon
Peter Woolliams

ABSTRACT. The Trompenaars database (1993) updated with Hampden-Turner (1998) has been assembled to help managers structure their cross cultural experiences in order to develop their competence for doing business and managing across the world. The database comprises more than 50,000 cases from over 100 countries and is one of the world's richest sources of social constructs. Woolliams and Trompenaars (1998) review the analysis undertaken by the authors in the last five years to develop the methodological approach underpinning the work. Recently Trompenaars with Hampden-Turner (Trompenaars and Woolliams, 1999) have extended the concepts into a new model on dilemma reconciliation of cultural differences. This paper reviews these latest updates in relation to dilemmas of cross-cultural business ethics. The paper asserts that knowledge in relation to business ethics is culturally specific; and that ethnocentrism is not easy to avoid. Too great an emphasis on rational-analytic conceptions of reality may mean that syntheses, emotion, and intuition, are not adequately developed. This presents implications for doing business and managing across cultures and for resolving ethical dilemmas.

KEY WORDS: business ethics, cross-cultural management, dilemma reconciliation, ethical codes, trans-cultural competence

Chris Moon is Manager, Ethics & Responsible Business Practice Consulting, Arthur Andersen. He is Secretary of EBEN-UK and taught all the MBA Business Ethics classes at The Management School, Imperial College, University of London, for 3 years. He has published over 20 articles and several book chapters concerning Business Ethics; and is a member of The Institute of Social and Ethical AccountAbility and a Fellow of the Royal Society for the encouragement of Arts, Manufactures & Commerce.

Peter Woolliams is Clifford Thames Professor of International Business at the Anglia Business School having been formerly Professor of Management at the East London Business School. He has worked extensively as an academic and practitioner consultant throughout the world with many leading organisations and management gurus. His main interests are comparative management and international business dynamics. He has been visiting research fellow for the Centre for International Business Studies (Amsterdam) 10 years and has worked closely with Dr. Fons Trompenaars and Dr. Charles Hampden-Turner.

1. Introduction

It is becoming clear that the quest for a universal (i.e. global) theory of international ethics is based on a false premise that such a single unifying theory is possible – let alone desirable. The intention of this paper is not to dismiss the valuable insights of such eminent writers on international business ethics as Donaldson (1985, 1989) and De George (1985, 1992). However, the authors of this paper wish to draw on their own research (Woolliams and Moon, 1999) and that of key gurus in the arena of cross-culture, such as Trompenaars (1993) and Trompenaars, Hampden-Turner (1998), to increase the depth of current understanding and to add value to the work of writers in the business ethics field. By being provocative it is hoped that fresh insights can be gleaned. Thus this paper asserts that all ethical codes are subjective because they are interpreted differently by each reader. Any quest for the application of a universal code that fails to take this into account should be abandoned. Of course it may be true that most societies value loyalty, honesty, promise-keeping, privacy, etc. but these values vary considerably in their practical interpretation. Thus the value to managers and business professionals comes from understanding and evaluating the *meaning* they give to any published or evolving codes to thereby determine appropriate personal effective behaviours.

The authors have attempted to achieve this through the development of computer models available on CD-ROM that enable users to undertake self-sufficiency evaluations to explore their "subjectivities". The rationale for this approach is grounded in the research of Trompenaars et al. (1993 and 1998) who, building on the work of earlier researchers on cross culture, have extensively delineated the importance of recognising the different meanings given by people in different cultures to apparently the same things. Trompenaars' well-known model based on seven dimensions of cross culture helps to structure, generalise and explain these differences. They owe their origin from the different meanings given to relationships between people, meanings of their relationships with time and nature (the environment). Research processes, methods and techniques are themselves related to the cultures in which they are used and have been developed. How can we overcome defensive responsiveness to a questionnaire validated in Anglo-Saxon countries for use in the United Arab Emirates? A recent researcher had to jointly swear on the Quaran with the respondent before he would even consider looking at a questionnaire that contained ethical dilemmas (Al-Refaei, 1998).

2. The research

From an initial data set of 50,000, Woolliams and Trompenaars (1998) selected some 40,000 comparative valid cases from 60 countries in order to validate a model for managers from multi-national and international corporations faced with international operations and cultural barriers of communication. Functionally equivalent managers were selected in order to "assail" the integrity of existing research into national and organizational culture. Scenarios were presented that portrayed a dilemma between two principles such as respect for law and loyalty among friends. The 58-item questionnaire was

validated through discussion; structured interviews, oral histories, cognitive mapping, and strategy based consulting, such that idiomatic ambiguities and temporary oddities were ironed out. The rationale behind the forced-choice format was that the respondent reconstructs the meaning of culture through how they perceive they and others around them ought to behave:

> . . . most, although not all respondents, would probably behave in ways of which their culture approved. Where cultural beliefs prove ill suited to the conduct of successful business we might find behaviour deemed "corrupt", "unethical", "illegal". Rules against insider dealing, for example, are particularly difficult to enforce, where competitive advantage lies in better information. There is always a gap between cultural prescriptions and actual conduct. Ours is a description of the former, which leads to approved conduct, not conduct *per se*."
> (Woolliams and Trompenaars, 1998, p. 11)

Although the dilemmas are hypothetical, and abstraction can never replicate reality, all the scenarios were conducted around situations that sought to be common to the experiences of managers in all cultures. "You are getting promoted . . ."; "An employee's dismissal is being discussed . . ."; "You have come from a secret board meeting . . .". Translation problems across cultures were considered by asking translators to consider the wider context of the scenario and to "balance the alternatives". These investigations were undertaken on the full database and for each country. Thus various revisions were made to the questionnaire as a result of experience in Asia, Africa, the Middle East and Eastern Europe.

The validity of the questionnaire was normatively tested in terms of coherence, pragmatism, and correspondence. The reliability of the dimension scales inherent in the questionnaire was constantly revised based on tests using Cronbach's Alpha measure of internal consistency for each combinatorial scale. Administration of the questionnaire was carefully managed to minimise defensive responsiveness by ensuring anonymity, etc; and emphasising the independent basis of the research.

The dilemmas were selected on the basis that

they were shared by all cultures to a varying degree. What is significant is that the attitude and response to the challenge of each dilemma was found to vary significantly between cultures. Of particular relevance to the subject of business ethics, is the group of dilemmas that arises between the seemingly opposing values of universalism and particularism. People everywhere are confronted with choices when considering their obligations to their personal friends and/or society at large. The universalism-particularism dilemma defines how we judge other people's behaviour. Trompenaars asserts in this respect that there are two "pure" yet alternative types of judgement.

- At one extreme we encounter an obligation to adhere to a moral or ethical code which is universally agreed to by the culture in which these codes are accepted. This is adherence to the golden rule and its derivatives ("*do unto others as you would have them do unto you*"). In business as well as society, this translates into rules defining conducts such as equal opportunities, political correctness, etc.
- At the other, we encounter an equally valid type of particular judgement based on obligations to people we know. Here the relationship is dominating and behaviour is determined by this relationship. Any ethical code is deemed secondary to this relationship. Obligations to friends are perceived as more important than obligations to adhere to a code that appears abstract. Behaviour is determined by a thinking process based on: "*I must protect my partner or friend, irrespective of what any abstract ethical rules may say. Otherwise, what are friends for?*"

The above research by Woolliams and Trompenaars includes extensive quantitative analysis of this paradigm as contained in the Trompenaars' database. Scales were constructed to place some 50,000 individuals and groups of individuals along an Universalism-Particularism scale. Extensive database mining sought linkage of this scale to other cross-cultural scales and other variables – such as education, socio-economic grouping, gender, religion, job

function, etc. The most significant variable was confirmed to be nationality. This supports Trompenaars' propositions concerning ecological aspects of cross-culture.

3. The dilemmas

Earlier research (based mainly in the U.S. such as Lewin, 1936), identifies the underlying concept of *universalism* as a feature of modernisation – where the role of the family becomes more fragmented. People live on their own, or as a one-parent family. Work and career places higher demands on individuals and personal life may become secondary. Technology replaces traditional roles. Whereas, *particularism* tends to be a feature of smaller, largely rural communities, or where the terrain so dictates. Here everyone continues to know everyone personally.

The frequently cited incident from Stouffer and Toby (1951), that poses the dilemma of a passenger in a car illustrates this paradigm. The driver has an accident by driving too fast. Does the passenger have an obligation to tell the truth in court or to protect his/her friend? If the friend was a mother, an illicit lover during an assignation, or just an occasional work colleague, the judgement may remain the same i.e. the universalistic requirement is to tell the truth. Or the need to protect his/her friend, or his or her lover to conceal the affair, may mean that aspects of the particular situation are taken into account.

Trompenaars' extensive data on this case reveals statistically highly significant differences between nationalities. Whilst there is always the individual response to consider, there are significant trends that some cultures tend to be more universalistic (Americans and Germans), whereas others are more particularistic (Venezuela and Gulf Countries) (Al-Refaei, 1998). The dilemma is often revealed when multi-national companies try to define a single (best way?) for a system from head office in the home country and try to impose it as the universal system throughout the world. Rules about "Pay for performance" based on individual sales may work well in countries that are individualistic, but in countries which are more communitarian, the idea of differentiating or highlighting the performance of one employee compared to another may be alien – and counter-productive.

Whilst previous research has considered the importance of "culture" in defining an orthogonal set of ethical principles, most has focussed on corporate rather than national culture (Linthicum 1994). Thus, for example, when there is a value congruence between the dominant organisational values and the values of the work force, it is not surprising that a code of ethics for which the organisation can achieve acceptance is based on the underlying value systems of the employees. Customers and other stakeholders may be in second place. However, such codes may overlook the vital role that national culture plays. As Tayeb (1996, p. 85) maintains:

> . . . in unitarian cultures organisations . . . tend to follow a narrow set of goals, have few stakeholders to whom they are accountable, and are less responsive to the needs and interests of their employees and their communities alike. In pluralistic nations organisations cater for the interests of a large number of stakeholders, and are expected to be part of the society at large and take responsibility for its well-being.

Similarly, in more individualistic societies, such as the U.S. and U.K., it is maintained that work and private life are emotionally distinct whereas in some communitarian societies such as Japan the organisation is a source of emotional and material support (i.e. it has a different *meaning*). National culture even appears to correlate with the size of the organisation. The Chinese appear to have a strong preference for small family-owned businesses (as in Taiwan and Hong Kong) whereas SMEs in the U.S. are on average much larger. Such culture-specific factors seem to outweigh intra-cultural ones. Tayeb (1996) recalls a matched-pair study of Indian and English organisations which found that on a number of measures the differences between the two samples were consistent with cultural differences between Indian and English peoples as a whole.

4. Questions of meaning

What concerns the main focus of this paper are questions of *meaning*. The meaning attributed to ethical issues in business and professional life is, therefore, an important point of enquiry – not least of all because Business and Professional Ethics may be misconceived as a type of universalistic code. Acceptable behaviours may be defined on the assumption that there is a universal truth or best way or code of behaviours. Previous debates on ethical issues have tended to ignore these issues i.e. issues deriving from *meaning*. Thus power and dependency issues between individual and business, often ask such questions as to what extent business should support their employees as an alternative to family and church – and the very act of asking this question is itself culturally specific.

As Trompenaars and his co-researchers continually comment, such debates have ignored the fundamental question about the *meaning* of any factor to people or peoples. For example, when translating text to and from English and German the translations seeks to achieve linguistic transparency and equivalence. In many cases confusion results even with "perfect translations" – viz.: at the end of meal, do you "pay the check with a bill (U.S.)" or pay the bill with a cheque (U.K.)? But even linguistics fail to overcome the fundamental problem of *what does it mean?* In marketing its famous Sony Walkman, it is assumed that the product (which is technically identical wherever it is manufactured and sold throughout the globe) has the same *meaning* to customers. However, studies show that Americans perceive it as a product they can use to listen to music *without being disturbed by others*, whereas in China it is perceived as a product they can use to listen to music *without disturbing others*. *Same product, different meaning*. Similarly, "banking" has different meanings to different peoples; Islamic Banking is far different to other European and American Banking.

Writers on ethics rarely point to the "law" as the final arbiter of ethical matters. However, business practitioners may prefer to define and resolve ethics through changes in (company) law; and this is particularly relevant to international business law which has shown some convergence (Carroll and Gannon, 1997). But again, the law has a different purpose because of its different role deriving from its *different meaning* in different parts of the world. Does a red traffic light cause drivers to stop, or pedestrians to not jay walk? (Perhaps yes in Germany, but not so in Taiwan!). Speed cameras are accepted in some countries (for the greater good), but are considered a threat to individual liberties in others. The law, may be regarded as the moral minimum and in terms of providing guidance to managers the law alone may not be enough.

The issue of universal truth is not the only source of differences between cultures. Trompenaars reminds us that these also include:

A. Meanings of rights given to individuals compared to groups (Individualism or Communitarianism)
B. Meanings given to the degree of involvement in relationships (Specific or Diffuse)
C. Meanings given to body language and other non-verbal leakage
D. Meaning given to status (Achieved or Ascribed)
E. Meaning given to time
F. Meaning given to nature

A. *Meaning of rights*

In an INDIVIDUALISTIC culture, the freedom of the individual comes first and serves society. Society is thought to improve because individuals have their freedom to improve and develop. In a COMMUNITARIAN culture, we take care of society even at the cost to individual freedom.

Thus what is the ethical position of Pay for Performance? Individualism versus Communitarianism can impact on business policies such as "pay for performance". Consider a pay scheme devised at the Head Office of a multinational company based in an Individualistic Culture. The scheme would emphasise the individual, differentiate one individual from another, and show some personnel as having achieved high and others low. If this pay scheme is implemented in a Communitarian Culture, the effect of breaking up the group identity may result in disastrous consequences. In such a culture, perhaps the pay/bonus scheme should depend on the overall performance of the whole group or even go to the group member with the greatest need.

B. *Meaning of involvement*

Regardless of how important privacy is, every culture has a private domain they will not even discuss with many other people. Kurt Lewin, a German Psychologist, appraising the Americans, said, "It's wonderful to be in the States because people tend to be so hospitable. They have open personalities, and visitors can easily get into contact". Lewin concluded, "It's because the Americans have a relatively small domain of privacy which is very sealed off – and because it's sealed off, they can have a big public life".

In some cultures (such as American), this domain is very limited – related to just a few areas – and this leads to lots of relationships where privacy is not actually involved. These are therefore SPECIFIC relationships. Specific in this instance means that what is shared is determined one specific situation at a time, without any necessary implications for the overall relationship. Each interaction stands alone in the specific situation of the present moment.

A specific relationship is without any symbolic meaning about the relationships between the individuals' more secret domains of personal privacy. What is private is clearly very different and is separated from what is public. In specific cultures, nothing that applies to relationships in one situation necessarily carries over into the next one. Each event of relationship is its own little drama with its specific roles and costumes.

In a DIFFUSE culture – everything is private. The car is private, the refrigerator is private. In the beginning of any relationship, you protect this privacy. Initially this leads to a no-no relationship. Everything is very polite and deliberately distant and has a "cool" feeling. Don't try to do business at this stage of the relationship! Nobody is available for anything yet other than being polite. For people in diffuse cultures, the intermixture of private and public is a source of comfort, confidence, strength and pride. But a person from a specific culture usually experiences it as a suffocating burden.

Specific cultures separate their tiny private from their large public, and enjoy the accomplishments of highly focused relationships, and further the freedom that comes from being able to break and remake such relationships. These differences create all kinds of confusion and alarm between the two cultures. When a representative of a diffuse culture meets an individual from a specific culture, their domains of privacy collide. A German, Italian or Frenchman may see an Englishman as rude and careless – as someone who is pushy and premature in trying to do business for instance – and as someone who doesn't understand the importance of business agreements and is not very responsible in honouring them! The Englishman may see the German, Italian or Frenchman as snobbish and arrogant – as typically bureaucratic – that is unreasonable, timid and careful as a business partner – and as someone who seems to want "all or nothing" even when the "all" is completely impractical.

C. *Meaning of body language*

Trompenaars also reminds us that some societies easily display emotions, and others withhold the expression of them. All people find ways to release pent-up emotions, but each culture has its own sanctioned way of doing so – some privately and some publicly. Some cultures express their emotions continuously. AFFECTING cultures such as Americans and Europeans, display emotions relatively easily. The Japanese call these "transparent cultures" because they show their emotion about everything – their material possessions, themselves, other people, their ideas, beliefs – everything.

In many other societies, including the Japanese, you may never reveal what you are feeling, thinking or believing. In these NEUTRAL cultures, such public displays may be considered childish, harmful and even rude. These differences in displaying emotions may lead to distrust and hostility between neutral and

affecting cultures. For example, if you were working with a team of Italians and you accidentally insulted them; they may show their displeasure by talking together excitedly in Italian and then walking out of the room. The Italians are an especially affecting culture. In contrast, if you accidentally insulted a group of Indonesians they would probably not walk out. They may feel insulted but probably would not show it. You might not even be aware that you had insulted them but their trust in you would be damaged. You might find your project failing and never understand why – and the more you express your frustration and disappointment, the more rapidly the project fails!

D. *Meaning of status*

In an ACHIEVEMENT orientated culture, you are what you do and have done. The emphasis is on the results you attain and the performance, results and materialistic gains you can exhibit as proof of your achievement. Competition and individual effort enhances status. In an ASCRIBING culture, you are who you are by virtue of your birth and position. Your ascribed status has no reference to ability or innate differences between individuals. Thus, when we introduce ourselves, we are positioning ourselves in terms of status. Some may introduce themselves by firstly describing their job (achievement orientated) others may do so by reference to their family and social position (ascribing).

E. *Meaning of time*

St. Augustine said in effect, "All this about past, present, and future is nonsense because the only thing that exists is the present." But he went on to say "we have three presents, the present of the past, the present of the present and the present of the future." A theme taken up to good effect by Charles Dickens with his ghosts of Christmas – past, present, and future. Thus, the meaning we assign to the present depends on which time sense we relate to predominantly. We have moments where the present is much more affected by the past and others by the future. Some of the participants in the workshop will say, "I now understand what my life has been about", but others will say "I like this because I can use it tomorrow" and still others will say, "I just like being here and participating".

You can imagine the problems that arise when you try to implement a system of goal-setting or management by objectives into cultures that have a small future orientation. Cultures like France and Venezuela may care less about planning for the future because the future has little or no bearing on the present. In other cultures, the future is very handy. The Spanish invented "manyana" and are very good at it! For the Japanese, experience evolves through time, starting in the distant past and ending in the distant future. Often, they arrange their diagram as concentric circles. Westerners have the idea that experience occurs in a much more discreet manner, in chunks. Another way to represent these extreme perceptions is to note that you can structure time as either SEQUENTIAL or SYN-CHRONIC.

F. *Meaning of nature*

Nature can sound very remote but it is very close in the sense of culture and how it affects business and management at large. Look back at the different ways people have dealt with nature over time. Prior to the Renaissance in 15th century Europe, nature was seen as an organism. Nature was out there; and Talos, the goal of nature, was put there by the supreme designer, God. These pre-Renaissance cultures believed that there was an environment and the environment determined what human beings needed to be doing. Nature was in psychological terms, the locus of external control – it controls us rather than the opposite.

The Renaissance turned this organistic view of nature into a mechanistic one. If you picture nature as a machine (like Leonardo da Vinci), you begin to realise that if you push here you can cause a reaction there. Hence developed the idea that you could control nature. This is the mechanistic view of nature; that the environment is something out there that we can control with

science and technology. The pre-Renaissance view of EXTERNAL control converted to one of INTERNAL control.

Very often Westerners try to put control mechanisms on everything. They have budgetary control to control finances, they have pay-for-performance to control compensation. They have staff appraisals that control, etc.; etc. *They now have in the context of this paper "ethical control"!* This approach does not work in societies that don't believe in control and don't allow control. In eastern societies, the organistic model is still very much there. For example, in American football or boxing, the basic principle is that you have an opposing force, so you hit as hard as you can, and if you hit harder, you will win. In Japanese martial arts like Karate and Aikido, the principle is to take the natural force from the environment and use it to your advantage.

This can help to explain how the Japanese view business. For they are the environment and the environment is theirs. They strive to remain in harmony with their environment. Their business environment includes many customers, and since customers are a natural part of the environment, many Japanese companies take customers onto their boards of directors. Relatively unheard of in the West! Likewise, quality is not such a big issue in Japan. They never talk about it because, you don't talk about things that are so obvious and have become habitual. In their minds, a society may be seriously sick if it constantly talks about quality.

5. Dilemma reconciliation

The future for business ethics should be to continue to examine the relationships between norms and values and what these *mean* to the actors. *Norms* are what is usual and accepted practice whereas *values* are what *you* would prefer. When values and norms are convergent, we have little difficulty. When values and norms conflict, we have a source of disharmony. Ethical debate is rightly placed at the centre of inviting society to reflect on its norms and values and the degree to which these are appropriate. Constructive debate can change peoples' values and hence the norms of their groups – although it is known that people often reluctantly change their behaviour first (norms) because they rarely address the issues and start to change the way they think (values) i.e. the *meaning* they give to things.

The first mistake is to ignore these differences and maintain one's own norms in different societies and cultures. This is a "win–lose" relationship and your own ethical principles may alienate your adversary. A second easy mistake to make is to adopt *the "when in Rome, do as Romans do"* paradigm. Here, for the sake of harmony (?), or more likely to close a sale(!), we may think that by abandoning our (norms) behaviours and adopting the norms of the destination culture, we can "fit in" and be accepted. In practice, the tension caused by trying to act out an unfamiliar role and abandon one's own ethical code or principles, is likely to fail as your adversary quickly begins to mistrust you. This will be a lose–win strategy. Compromise at best is only a lose–lose strategy and still requires you to abandon some of your position.

Attempts have been made to produce a universal international code of ethics (cf. Donaldson and Dunfee, 1994; Hosmer, 1995; Caux Round Table, 1996). The writers of the Caux code suggest that this code be based on trying to include two extreme ethical ideals – *kyosei* and human dignity. *Kyosei* is said to mean living and working together for the common good, whereas human dignity is said to mean the sacredness or value of each person. However, this version of the universalism-particularism dilemma ignores the fact that the nationality profile of stakeholders may have changed from the original issue. Thus an American company with American shareholders may now have 50% of its shareholders from the Far East. Its business strategy formulated on the basis of an acceptable ethical code may have been focussed on maximising shareholder *value* whereas it may be more appropriate that the CEO and team now review their strategy formulation on the basis of the changed shareholder *values* (Dickerson, PhD thesis in preparation). The Caux Round Table (1998) web-site does indicate a belief in the reconciliation of values but that their statement is only the start of a process:

As a statement of aspirations, this document aims to express a world standard against which business behaviour can be measured. We seek to begin a process that identifies shared values, reconciles differing values, and thereby develops a shared perspective on business behaviour acceptable to and honoured by all.

Thus, any statement of general principles can only be a starting point. Whereas, studies have shown that cross-cultural training can contribute to: greater feelings of well-being and self-confidence for the manager, improved relationships with host nationals, the development of correct perceptions of host culture members, better adjustment to the new culture, and higher performance (Black and Mendenhall, 1990). In fact, the lack of such training may be the cause of individual and organisational failure; the costs of which are estimated by Black and Mendenhall to be $50–150K for individual failure, and over $2 billion per year to U.S. business as a whole. The ethics of international business relationships are thus considered to be an essential component of training for cultural understanding and sensitivity. As Triandis et al. (1988) pointed out, giving a gift can be an important step to becoming a member of a group, and giving a gift incorrectly could lead to ostracism. This is significant in Japan where gift giving has been considered as an important part of relationship building. It is the interpretation (i.e. *meaning*) of the gift that is the critical factor (Albert, 1986).

Managers must be able to interpret cultural signals often overlooked through selective perception (Albert, 1986), but more than this they need to be aware of inconsistencies in cultural behaviour (Adler and Graham, 1989). Thus learning about another culture is only a first step; one must recognise cultural heterogeneity. Trevino and Nelson (1995) argue that managers should be trained with respect to business ethics beliefs and practices. They can not rely on intuition (Donaldson, 1992) to guide them through the murky waters of dirty tricks, payoffs, and bribes (cf. Adler, 1992). However, these authors all miss the basis point that the only real solution is to recognise then respect and then reconcile these differences (Trompenaars and Hampden-Turner 1998).

Some organisations have developed codes of business conduct with guidelines for dealing with problems (e.g. Caterpillar, Xerox, and General Dynamics) perhaps modified to deal with particular cultural contexts. There may be rewards and sanctions for complying with or breaking company policy. Nevertheless, these approaches are highly ethnocentric in origin, developed without a full and proper understanding of the complexity of *meaning* given to ethical issues in different cultures: nepotism, incompatible values, public expectations, the legitimacy of business and wealth creation. Noble attempts have been made to devise a Transcultural Corporate Ethic (Frederick, 1991) based on respecting national sovereignity, social equity, market integrity, human rights, but such attempts fall short of probing managers beliefs. The danger is that *moral guidelines*, such as drawn up by DeGeorge (1992) may end up being used as the basis for compromise; or Donaldson's (1989) *fundamental international rights* may end up as being overly prescriptive and hence impractical.

To support the work of Trompenaars and Hampden-Turner, Woolliams and Trompenaars (1998) have been concerned to produce self-administered computer based diagnostic tools to help individuals and groups investigate their own orientations and to clarify the *meaning* they give to *meanings*. In this way, both at the level of the individual and through shared exchanges, the whole problem of subjectivity and ethnocentrism can be exposed. Current research is accumulating evidence that it is possible to reconcile different value systems and moreover that this is effective in doing business and managing across cultures. This is the "new approach" that has "added value" over and above "compromise solutions" and produces ethically acceptable outcomes to all parties and is based on a new fundamental model conceived by Trompenaars and Hampden-Turner (1998).

The following is how Hampden-Turner, Trompenaars and Woolliams have now expressed a typical dilemma.

The Letter or the Spirit of the Law?

Six months after the ABC mining company had signed a long-term contract with a foreign buyer to buy bauxite in ten annual instalments, the world price of bauxite collapsed. Instead of paying $4 a tonne below world market price, the buyer now faced the prospect of paying $3 above. The buyer faxed ABC to say it wished to renegotiate the contract. The final words of the fax read: "You cannot expect us as your new partner to carry alone the now ruinous expense of these contract terms." ABC negotiators had a heated discussion about this situation.

Which view do you support?

---

a. A contract is a contract. It means precisely what its terms say. If the world price had risen we would not be crying, nor should they. What partnership are they talking about? We had a deal. We bargained. We won. End of story.
b. A contract symbolises the underlying relationship. It is an honest statement of original intent. However, such rigid terms are too brittle to withstand turbulent environments. Only tacit forms of mutuality have the flexibility to survive.
c. A contract is a function of both the underlying relationship and the legal system covered by it. We should split the difference.
d. A contract symbolises the underlying relationship. It is an honest statement of original intent. Where circumstances transform the mutual spirit of that contract, then terms must be renegotiated to preserve the relationship.
e. A contract is a contract. It means precisely what the terms say. If the world price had risen we would not be crying, nor should they. We would, however, consider a second contract whose terms would help offset their losses.

Option a is clearly the universalistic option (win-lose). *Option b* is the particularistic view (lose-win). *Option c* is the compromise solution (lose-lose).

Both *options d and e* are seeking to reconcile the opposing values. *Option e* starts from an ethical universalistic viewpoint but takes in to account the opposing value and seeks to reconcile and find a unifying solution. *Option d* is the reverse and commences with a particularistic view but still seeks a unified reconciled solution. Both of these are win-win strategies. New evidence reveals that propensity to reconcile is an effective behaviour of high performing global managers. New studies confirm high correlation between such propensity and 360 degree feedback on business and managerial effectiveness (Hampden-Turner, 1998).

6. Trans-cultural competence

This paper demonstrates that a new methodological framework is needed in order that a manager can acquire and develop trans-cultural competence and high performance in the job. High-performing managers consistently exhibit more of this trans-cultural competence than those who give polarised or compromise responses (Trompenaars and Woolliams, 1999). While American managers typically put universalism first, they say, and East Asian managers usually favour particularism, some managers from each region are able to reconcile both approaches. This trans-cultural competence correlates strongly with the extent of their experience with international assignments or working with a diverse workforce, and with ratings by both peers and managers on "suitability for" and "success in" overseas postings and partnerships and/or dealing with diversity. In fact, women in middle management – other than those adopting a male approach in a perceived man's world – tend to have a higher propensity to reconcile opposing values than their male counterparts. Although, when severely challenged and unable to reconcile then these women also show signs of compromise.

Trans-cultural competence is being shown to

be important in wide ranging situations from prospecting for new business through to managing existing projects and day-to-day business. And studies are showing that the propensity to reconcile can be developed through training. The authors are using computer-based models (available on CD-ROM) that enable managers and business professionals to explore their own value systems and to identify their position on various ethical dilemma scales. The resulting self-sufficiency analysis aids the user in understanding and interpreting their relationship and the meaning they ascribe to various published and/or proposed ethical codes. What may emerge are new global business paradigms for dealing with dilemmas of cross-cultural business ethics.

Acknowledgements

Arguments for this paper have been developed through peer review in relation to papers presented at: The First International Conference on Cross Cultural Business Ethics held in Tunis, 10th–11th December, 1998; The Fourth Annual Conference of the U.K. Association of the European Business Ethics Network "Business Ethics for a New Millennium" held at Christ Church, Oxford, 15th–16th April 1999; and The 12th EBEN Annual Conference 1999 "Business Challenging Business Ethics. New instruments for coping with diversity in international business" held at Amsterdam, The Netherlands, 1st–3rd September, 1999.

References

Adler, N.: 1992, *International Dimensions of Organizational Behaviour* (PWS Kent Publishing Co., Boston).

Adler, N. J. and J. L. Graham: 1989, 'Cross-cultural Interaction: The International Comparison Fallacy?', *Journal of International Business Studies* (Fall), 515–537.

Albert, R. D.: 1986, 'Conceptual Framework for the Development and Evaluation of Cross-cultural Orientation Programs', *International Journal of Intercultural Relations* **10**, 197–213.

Al-Refaei, H.: 1998, 'Cultural Transfer of Technology to Gulf GCC Countries', Ph.D. thesis (University of East, London).

Black, J. S. and M. Mendenhall: 1990, 'Cross-cultural Training Effectiveness: A Review and a Theoretical Framework for Future Research', *Academy of Management Review* **15**(1), 113–136.

Carroll, S. J. and M. J. Gannon: 1997, *Ethical Dimensions of International Management*. Sage Series in Business Ethics (Sage Publications, London).

Caux Round Table.: 1996, 'Business Ethics', *The Magazine of Socially Responsible Business* **10**(1), January.

Caux Round Table: 1998, Principles for Business: http://www.cauxroundtable.org.

De George, R.: 1992, 'Ethics and Worse', *Financial Times*, July 3, p. 12.

De George, R.: 1985, *Competing with Integrity in International Business* (Oxford University Press, New York).

Donaldson, T.: 1985, 'Multinational Decision-making Reconciling International Norms', *Journal of Business Ethics* **4**, 357–366.

Donaldson, T.: 1989, *The Ethics of International Business* (Oxford University Press, New York).

Donaldson, T.: 1992, 'When in Rome, Do . . . What? International Business and Cultural Relativism', in P. M. Minus (ed.), *The Ethics of Business in a Global Economy* (Kluwer, Boston), pp. 67–78.

Donaldson, T. and T. W. Dunfee: 1994, 'Toward a Unified Conception of Business Ethics: Integrative Social Contracts Theory', *Academy of Management Review* **19**, 252–284.

Frederick, W. C.: 1991, 'The Moral Authority of Transnational Codes', *Journal of Business Ethics* **10**, 165–177.

Hosmer, L. T.: 1995, 'Trust: The Connecting Link between Organizational Theory and Philosophical Ethics', *Academy of Management Review* **20**, 379–403.

Lewin, K.: 1936, *Some Socio-psychological differences between the US and Germany, Principles of Topological Psychology* (Wiley Inc., U.S.A).

Linthicum, D. O.: 1994, The Nature and Extent of Cultural Values to an Organisations' Culture, DEd Thesis, Temple University, U.S.A.

Stouffer, S. A. and J. Toby: 1951, 'Role Conflict and Personality', *American Journal of Sociology* **LUI-5**, 395–406.

Tayeb, M. H.: 1996, *The Management of a Multicultural Workforce. Chichester* (John Wiley, U.K.).

Trevino, L. K. and K. A. Nelson: 1995, *Managing Business Ethics. Straight Talk About How To Do It Right* (John Wiley and Sons, Inc., NY).

Triandis, H. C., R. Brislin and C. H. Hui: 1988, 'Cross-cultural Training Across the Individualism-collectivism Divide', *International Journal of Intercultural Relations* **12**, 269–289.

Trompenaars, F.: 1993, *Riding the Waves of Culture* (Economist Books, U.K.).

Trompenaars, F. and C. Hampden-Turner: 1998, *Understanding Cultural Diversity in Business* (Irwin, U.K.).

Trompenaars, F. and P. Woolliams: 1999, Trans-Cultural Competence, People Management, U.K., 22nd April.

Woolliams, P. and C. J. Moon: 1999, 'Towards Culture Free Business Ethics', *Business Ethics Discussion Paper* **1**(7), Earlybrave Publications Ltd., U.K.

Woolliams, P. and F. Trompenaars: 1998, *The Meaning of Meaning*, Research Monograph (Earlybrave Publications Ltd., U.K.), pp. 1–41.

Chris J. Moon
Arthur Andersen.
1 Surrey Street,
London WC2R 2PS,
United Kingdom
E-mail: chris.moon@uk.arthurandersen.com

Peter Woolliams
Anglia Business School,
Anglia Polytechnic University,
Danbury Park,
Essex CM3 4AT,
United Kingdom
E-mail: peterwoolliams@aol.com

International Enterprises and Trade Unions

Mari Meel
Maksim Saat

ABSTRACT. A "shipping war" has broken out between two friendly neighbouring countries: Estonia (a rather poor land; liberated of Soviet occupation in 1991), and Finland (a wealthy one; independent since 1918). Led by their trade union the Finnish dockers boycott Estonian ships demanding for Estonian sailors the salary in the same range as that is in wealthy West-European countries. Estonian Sailors' Union finds that such a war is not for their better work-conditions but against their working possibilities: the cheap labour force is the only possibility for a poor country to entice foreign investments in it.

No matter how the "shipping war" will be solved – the problem will remain. This is the problem of two opposites – cheap labour force of poor countries and expensive one of wealthy countries –, and international enterprises standing between them. Could such an enterprise survive without using the cheap labour force? And if it could, how could the poor countries survive then? Could there be found a clear unambiguous ethical solution? What ought to be the role of trade unions in such international business conflicts?

KEY WORDS: global competition, modern humanisation of work, multinational enterprise, trade unions, work ethics, working life quality, work of nations

A "shipping war" has broken out between two friendly neighbouring countries: Estonia (a rather poor land; liberated of Soviet occupation in 1991), and Finland (a wealthy one; independent since 1918). Led by their trade union the Finnish

dockers boycott Estonian ships demanding for Estonian sailors the salary in the same range as that is in wealthy West-European countries. Estonian Sailors' Union finds that such a war is not for their better work-conditions but against their working possibilities: the cheap labour force is the only possibility for a poor country to entice foreign investments in it.

No matter how the "shipping war" will be solved – the problem will remain. This is the problem of two opposites – cheap labour force of poor countries and expensive one of wealthy countries –, and international enterprises standing between them. Could such an enterprise survive without using the cheap labour force? And if it could, how could the poor countries survive then? Could there be found a clear unambiguous ethical solution? What ought to be the role of trade unions in such international business conflicts?

Nowadays we are used to think that an international enterprise, which is operating in the conditions of hard global competition and is therefore forced to innovate its production continuously, keeping the price thereby at a minimum level, tries to organize its work according to modern principles of management. This idea is contradictory to the previous predominant understanding (valid since the beginning of the 20th century till the 1950s–1960s) that the best way for organizing work place is the assembly line where division of labour is applied to its maximum.

The ethicity of modern views on organizing work place and the unethicity of previous ones is perhaps most perfectly grounded by E. F. Schumacher. Proceeding from the Buddhist point of view he argued that a human being is not

Maksim Saat is Professor of Business Administration, and Mari Meel is Assistant Professor of Business Ethics, at the Tallinn Technical University, Ehitajate tee 5, Tallinn, Estonia. Both are members of EBEN.

Journal of Business Ethics **27**: 117–123, 2000.
© 2000 *Kluwer Academic Publishers. Printed in the Netherlands.*

incarnated for plainly vegetating but for development and perfection. Therefore "to organize work in such a manner that it becomes meaningless, boring, stultifying or nerveracking for the worker would be little short of criminal; it would indicate a creater concern with goods than with people, an evil lack of compassion and a soul-destroying degree attachment to the most primitive side of this worldly existence" (Schumacher, 1973, pp. 53–57).

From this viewpoint mechanization and automation are justified only if they enhance man's skill and power, otherwise they are unethical turning the work of man into the work of slave.

As an example of society's and entrepreneur's aspiration towards organising work in more creative manner Paul Kennedy presents Japanese way of automation. Due to chronical shortage of work force and tradition of life-long employment, the entrepreneurs are interested in full automation and use of industrial robots. The number of industrial robots in Japan exceeds 3.7 times that of West Europe and 5.3 times that of the U.S.A. Applying industrial robots enables the Japanese entrepreneurs to free workers from the assembly-line; to retrain them and to use them for more creative work (Kennedy, 1994, pp. 102–106).

And so, the modern management theory tends to see in organising work in a routine way (as for example using assembly lines) something that is quite out of date and unethical; exploitation of workers in order to maximize the owners' profits. But if we look back at the beginning of the 20th century, when Henry Ford founded his Ford Motor Co and started to introduce his assembly line idea – dividing the car-producing process into "the atoms of work process" – then scarcely he saw in it cruel exploitation of workers. The aim of H. Ford was to create the welfare society (Ford, 1938). And the extreme division of labour, where 43% of jobs could be learned in one day and 36% in 1 to 8 days enabled uneducated people earn a worthy income.

Ford proceeded Adam Smith who did see in the division of labour a possibility to increase the productivity of labour and to move from a starving society to a wealthy one. So, from one side we see in H. Ford's assembly line extremely dull and routine work but from the other side such work led to so high productivity that for the first time in history the uneducated people "just from the street" could earn enough to support their families so that there was no need more to force their children to work. It was namely the routine work in the watch factories and car industries that carried the U.S.A. to welfare society. However, as to the problem of dullness of work was not seen as a serious problem then there. As it is said in the Bible: ". . . cursed is the ground for thy sake; in sorrow shalt thou eat of it all the days of thy life. . . . Thorns also and thistles shall it bring forth to thee. . . . In the sweat of thy face shalt thou eat bread, till thou return unto the ground . . ." (The Holy Bible, Genesis, 3, 17–19).

Thus in our Judeo-Christian morale and cultural tradition work must not be a source of happiness and satisfaction but rather a punishment for sin. The social demand for creativity of work (and for avoiding dullness) has developed in the period of welfare society (from about 1960s): firstly the conditions had to ripen in a shape of relatively educated and well-paid work force, who whishes something more than only dull work. Secondly, the social democratic and trade union movement had contributed to it. And thirdly, which is not less important, the entrepreneurs theirselves had started to notice that doing a dull work, the employees are using their capabilities only like automatons: "There is tremendous unused potential in our people," said Percy Barnevik, Former CEO, ABB, "our organisations are constructed so that most of our employees are asked to use 5–10% of their creative capacity at work. It is only when these same individuals go home that they can engage the other 90–95% – to run their households, lead Boy Scout troop or build a summer home. We have to be able to recognise and employ that untapped ability that each individual brings to work every day" (Drivdal, 1998).

Now it is time to ask in what kind of world an international enterprise is located today? Does it lie in the modern world? That is only partially so. In reality it is compact neither in the spatial allocation nor in the character of organising its work (e.g. work-place and work conditions). From the spatial aspect the enterprise is forced to allocate its units following the network-principle all around the world, in order to minimize costs. It is forced to do it because if it does not, some of its competitors would and thus push it out of competition with its cheaper product.

Such global network allocation will simultaneously locate the enterprise into historically different development phases: to learn how children work in Pakistan to support their families one need not read some Pakistani travelogue – reading Jack London or Martin Andersen Nexo will give the same picture. We can understand how the rather merciless and sometimes even criminal primary accumulation of capital occured in the Wild West following the developments in Estonia today. In Malaisia Japanese industrial parks exist side by side with prehistoric slash and burn farming and hunters-gatherers who live on what they can find in the jungle. So we can say that the modern world is a mixture of all epochs and there is no wonder that an enterprise facing global competition, whom difficulties have taught to be flexible, will organise its work in accordance with the development level of the country involved: if in some far away place of the world it will be cheaper to arrange work following Ford's principles, that is what will be done.

Is such organisation of work unethical? In some cases there seems to be no doubt about it: we would probably all agree that namely children should not be forced to do dull work as such a work is especially detrimental to the developing brain and may result in mental retardation of the child. It is indispensable for children to attend school. And not only for children but also for poor countries where child work tends to be a norm: what will they do with the future generation ruined by dull work and having no education? On the other hand, however, a questionnaire arranged with such children (documentaries broadcast by BBC) showed a repeating motif: we would like to go to school more but without this work we would starve. . . .

As from utilitarian aspect we have a dilemma here: in case of such work the developing

organism will be damaged by routinity and dullness; in case of losing the work, the developing organism would suffer from malnutrition, maybe even death due to starvation. Which of the two damages is worse? Likewise we have here a conflict of two deontological requirements: it is unethical to force a person, especially a young one to perform dull work; on the other hand, the rights to work and to minimum means of living are among basic human rights.

What we want to say with this example? – that even in such a seemingly "simple" case of ethical discussion as of using children work, we cannot say that this is something "absolutely bad", and that the best way for solving this case would be a "surgical intervention" – e.g. a complete boycott of the commodities produced by using children labour. Apparently it would be better to use some kind of flexible transition-method. For example if in countries where children-labour is the cultural tradition, the duration of work day would be legally restricted and compulsory education really forced.

Of course most of international enterprises do not use children work. But even in innovative enterprises in the units allocated in underdeveloped countries with cheap work force, work is organised by the principle of assembly line. Though there the assembly line does not occur in its extreme manner (where an operation is divided into its sub-parts) still the work is rather routinuous and highly intense thereby.

One of the most innovative enterprises of Europe could certainly be taken Elcoteq Network (Finnish origin). Elcoteq Network is a company providing electronics manufacturing services (EMS). It was founded in 1991, in the year of deep economic depression for Finland (the depression took place due to collapse of the Soviet Union, the most important trade partner of Finland). In the first year the average personell was only 204 persons and net sales 76.4 MFIM. By 1997 net sales reached 1669.0 MFIM and the average personell 2593 (Elcoteq Network, 1997). By the way, it is in the electronical industry where the world-wide competition is the tightest (The reasons for Elcoteq success we have analysed more thoroughly in one of our previous papers, here we will only deal with the diversities of work organisation in mother-land units and in subsidiary of a developing country (Estonia).

Elcoteq is organised as a network of its subsidiaries according to their production practices in back-, front- and in-factories. A back-factory specializes in producing large series cost effectively; a front-factory manufactures small and medium-size series providing also other value-adding services; an in-factory is a direct extension to the customer's operations.

Five ot the Elcoteq's six enterprises are located in Finland where the living standards and accordingly labour costs are high. One of these five is a back-factory but there mass-production is fully automated. The sixth factory is in Tallinn, in the capital of Estonia, where all the so-called "routine work", mass and large-series production which requires cheap manual work is concentrated: in 1997 from all 2,593 employees of Elcoteq 1,654 (that is 64%) were engaged in Tallinn factory (Elcoteq Network, 1997, p. 10).

The majority of the workers of the Tallinn factory are Russian-speaking women who do not know Estonian, the official language of the country, or any other languages: this is the segment of the population among which unemployment is the highest. The training in the training classes of the factory takes about 3 weeks; piece wage and time labour contracts are applied; there is no trade union. Hence it is relatively easy to increase or decrease the number of employees. For example in 1995 the factory employed 700 to 1,000 persons, depending upon project needs (Elcoteq Network, 1995, pp. 8–9). The work is carried on in 3 shifts and if it is necessary for the terms of order, then on weekends and as well holidays. The average wages are about 6 times smaller than those in Finnish factories: a worker in Elcoteq Lohja factory earns at an average 7,500–8,000 FIM per month; one in Tallinn factory 1,300 FIM (R. Meri, 1998). Nevertheless we cannot say that under Estonians conditions this means hard exploitation of workers: 1,300 FIM (that is 3,500 Estonian kroons) is an average salary for Estonia, besides a woman knowing only one language and having been trained only for 3 weeks can earn such a salary nowhere else. Besides the work is clean and if there is any possibility to be in

contact with toxic substances (for example by soldering) then safeguards and compulsory ventilation are applied. Although the work is very intensive, it continues no longer than 7.5 hours. In addition the working day is interrupted by rest pauses. Workers' satisfaction could be expressed by the fact that only two or three workers resign factory per year.

Also the location of the rooms illustrates the moral policy of the enterprise. If to compare it in Tallinn and Lohja factories, then in the latter both the production rooms and the rooms for management are on one plane and are separated only with light partitions. The purpose is to inspire the employees that the factory is an integral whole, where the atmosphere of collaboration must prevail; also is as possibly "plain" the structure of the organisation; work is organised by teams and creativity is encouraged. In the Tallinn factory the rooms for top management are separated from the others.

What conclusions can we draw from the example of Elcoteq? It seems that nowadays even an innovative enterprise stands by one foot in the modern principles of work organisation but by the other foot it stays in Fordism: mass production that needs inexpensive manual work is located in an underdeveloped country, of course provided that labour force is sufficiently disciplined and cheap there.

Would it be right to judge such a double-faced behaviour from the ethical viewpoint? It would be senseless since without such a behaviour the enterprise evidently could not survive. Besides, these two "feet" do not stand still at all: firstly, if there is sufficiently educated labour force in the underdeveloped country the corresponding work-places could be located there. For example by Danish management consultant Kim Moller Scandinavian companies with subsidiaries all over world prefer to locate their accounting offices not in Scandinavia but in New Delhi, where it is said to be very good and very cheap accountants (Moller, 1998). Also the top management of Elcoteq Tallinn has consisted of Estonians since its founding in 1993: in addition to the special education they have good command of Estonian, Finnish, English and of course Russian. The last gives them an essential advantage as compared with Finns in communicating with the workers of the factory.

Secondly, if the living standards in the under-developed country rose (and hence the wages of the workers), the cheap manual work would move on to the next country: so Elcoteq is establishing its new plant in St. Petersburg (Russia). In the Tallinn factory equipment enabling automatic control of details stands waiting: at the moment control is carried out by women as so it comes cheaper. Obviously in such an effectively and flexibly working enterprise the equipment is not meant to stay idle for long. Of course the local women would lose their jobs if automation would really proceed; however this would happen only if the factory were forced to rise wages, which would show that the women would have a possibility to find more profitable job as the living standards in the country have risen.

However, reaching this new level may be impeded by a peculiar phenomenon: the labour force of such a rapidly developing country has terrifying competitiveness. Namely, to reach a new level in its development, the country has inevitably to pass a phase of relative poverty and scarcity of capital (investments) and therefore its labour force, including the highly skilled labour, is extremely cheap as compared with countries of high living standards.

If there was no such intermediate phase, it would not be possible to reach a new level, as in that case there would not be technological and managerial skills necessary for building up a new statehood. This is frightening for the expensive labour force of countries with high living standards: to a certain extent people in the mother country have got used to and put up with the fact that for mass production cheap labour of poor countries is needed (if mass production cannot be fully automated); however, if they suddenly notice that the poor country is able to arrange shipping, aviation, medical care, telecommunications, banking etc. considerably less expensively as the poor country already has specialists with sufficiently high qualifications yet much cheaper, the wealthier country senses danger to its employment and living standards.

Such a situation has led to a kind of "shipping war" between Estonia and Finland, which may expand into other spheres as well. The "war" started in December 1998 when the international trade union association of transportation workers and the Union of Finnish Sailors demanded that the trade union of the Estonian Shipping Company should conclude a collective agreement fixing the monthly wages of a common sailor as US$ 2600 (34,000 Estonian kroons). Led by unions the dockers in Helsinki put two Estonian ships – Rakvere and Calibur – under a boycott refusing to load and unload goods (ÄP No. 226, 19 Dec. 1998, p. 2). Dockers from Århus in Denmark and Antwerp in Belgium are supporting the demand on Finnish sailor's union, boycotting the merchant ship Fiina Timber of the Estonian Shipping Company (ÄP No. 12 (1377), 20 Jan. 1999, p. 2).

The Estonian Shipping Company regards such a demand by the union of a foreign country as absurd: the wages should be bargained in accordance with the demand and supply of labour following the rules of the free market. The Estonian sailors have not been discontented with their present income (about US$ 750 a month). Besides the monthly salary of Estonian highly paid MPs is presently about US$ 1000 and the monthly pay of neither the ministers nor the president reaches US$ 2400. The net salaries of middle managers of the sectors with the highest incomes (banking, aviation, dairy industry) are not over US$ 1000 ("Võti tulevikku", 1999). Besides, one should bear in mind that the relationship of Estonian and Finnish sailors' wages to the average wages of the relevant country is approximately the same. In Estonia the average monthly wages make up US$ 321 and the average wages of a common sailor of a liner US$ 472, thus the ratio is about 2.3. In Finland the average monthly wages are US$ 894 and a common sailor of a liner gets US$ 1795 a month, the ratio is thus 2.0 (ÄP No 226 (1359), 16 Dec. 1998).

The Estonian Sailors' Union brought an action against the Finnish union, demanding that an end be put to the boycott and compensation be paid for damages. The Finnish district court found that Finnish dockers acted correctly since Estonians provided unfair competition. The

Estonian Sailors' Union appealed the decision of the Helsinki court.

Meanwhile the war is threatening to expand outside shipping: the Estonian public regards the action of Finnish union as unfair competition since the Finnish union is making use of its monopolistic status (influence, impunity) towards the government and using such an absurd demand they are pushing Estonian sailors out of competition (Elcoteq's CEO Antti Piippo said in an interview that Estonia's advantage is absence of trade unions). However, now unorganised workers find it impossible to fight the European "sacred cow".

Some important facts might help explain the legal background of this conflict. First, Århus and Helsinki or two ship lines serving the Nordic countries are involved. Their demand is based on an agreement made in 1995 in Athens, according to which sailors on ships on the same line must get equal wages based on the higher wages. Secondly, the Estonian Shipping Company is Estonian only as to its name – the Estonian government owns 30%, the remaining 70% is owned by a Norwegian shipping company. Thirdly, Finland subsidises the wages of its sailors, paying about 40% of these (These facts were presented in ÄP No. 226, 16 Dec. 1998, p. 31). The Estonian government does not support the Estonian Shipping Company. Besides, in Finland the ship owner is not liable to pay social tax for a sailor who is away from land over 180 days a year. In Estonia no such exemption is used and this is a disadvantage to an Estonian ship (ÄP No. 229 (1362), 21 Dec. 1998, p. 2).

These facts demonstrate that the problem does not involve only trade unions and ship owners but also the government's role in entrepreneurship and the behaviour of an international company in states that do not belong to the so-called first world and the role an international company plays in a small country.

Finding a legal solution will obviously be complicated and time consuming since there are several agreements not just one that have to be considered. A solution to this war will be found by the court – this is apparently not our problem. We are interested in the ethical aspect of the problem. We can hardly say that some of

the parties has something else besides its own interest in mind. Finnish sailors are afraid that Estonian sailors will push their wages down; the Estonian Shipping Company is afraid of going bankrupt due to the boycott; and so do Estonian sailors. If the boycott continues the Norwegian partner may lose interest in the company, may take its investments out of Estonia and Estonian sailors would lose their jobs. For Estonian shipping the war may end so that Estonia will be declared a country of the flag of convenience, which among other things would mean that ship owners would not be obliged to hire Estonian seamen and Estonia would lose its national merchant marine. The Estonian economy is in recession anyhow due to the economic crisis in Russia, international exchange market crisis and hard summer for agriculture. Therefore the boycott as well as the possible expansion of the war is of great concern for Estonia. The rapid progress of Estonia seen as a rival is making Finnish public as concerned.

In the world economy in principle two policies of market economy are applied: liberal and social. The Estonian government and economy are following the principles of extremely free market economy like the U.S.A. and Southeast Asia, characterised by minimum interference of the state in the economy. According to these principles free market relationships are followed in entrepreneurship, labour market as well as international trade. Thus, according to the liberal economic policy of the Estonian government the low wages of the Estonian Shipping Company are not a sign of unfair competition, on the contrary, it is fair competition.

West European and especially Scandinavian countries behave in the labour market following principles of social democracy with the government playing an important role in entrepreneurship and in defending the interests of the employees. From their standpoint we have unfair competition since on a ship line between two Nordic countries (Finland and Denmark) where the employees' wages are guaranteed by agreements and supported by subsidies there appears a competitor using the labour force of a country with low wages, who is pushing down transportation costs and threatening to leave the sailors of these two Nordic countries jobless.

However, if we look for a solution best for a wide public, then high wages are one of the most serious problems in North and West Europe as these weaken the competitiveness of their labour force and products, besides extensive strikes organised by unions destabilise their economy and cause large damage. For example, the strike of French lorry drivers caused much damage to both Estonian and Finnish transportation firms and their employees. Hence we might argue that for Europe as a whole it would probably not be bad at all if the low-paid but rather highly qualified labour from the Baltic countries brought a breath of free market to the European labour market? Besides, it would be advantageous to the ecological situation on the Earth if the living standards in the welfare states fell a little. So much from the utilitarian point of view.

However, from the deontological aspect we may argue that such a skilfully arranged attack from the trade union of a rich country jeopardises two basic human rights of the citizens of the poor country: their right to work and to minimum means of livelihood.

What is especially interesting here, and the point of this story: the traditional social-democratic idea about international solidarity of the working class, inherited from Marx, does not seem to function today. For a rapidly developing poor country the workers of a wealty country may be enemies wishing to suffocate them

whereas the enterprises that import them dull work help them, although involuntarily, towards a welfare society.

References

Drivdal, A.: 1998, *Value Management*. AIESEC International Conference for B.E. in Estonia, March 30–31.

Elcoteq Network Annual Report: 1995, Frenckellin Kirjapaino Oy.

Elcoteq Network Annual Report: 1997, Frenckellin Kirjapaino Oy.

Ford, H.: 1938, *Minu elu ja töö* (*My Life and Work*) (Tartu, Loodus), 261 p.

The Holy Bible.

Kennedy, P.: 1994, *Uuden Vuosituhannen Haasteet* (Preparing for the 21 Century) (Otava), 448 p.

Meri, R.: 1998, *Elcoteq teeb Tallinna tuntuks* (Õhtuleht), Jan. 5, p. 8.

Moller, K.: 1998, *Social Responsibility of Business and Social Audit*. AIESEC International Conference for B.E. in Estonia, March 30–31.

Schumacher, E. F.: 1973, *Small Is Beautiful* (Harper, New York), 241 p.

Võti Tulevikku: 1999, Infokataloog.

ÄRIPÄEV: 1998, Dec. 16, No. 226 (1359), p. 2.

ÄRIPÄEV: 1998, Dec. 19, No. 227 (1360), p. 2.

ÄRIPÄEV: 1998, Dec. 21, No. 229 (1362), p. 2.

ÄRIPÄEV: 1998, Jan. 20, No. 12 (1377), p. 2.

Tallinn Technical University,
Tallinn, Estonia
E-mail: msaat@tv.ttu.ee

An Ethics of Care or an Ethics of Justice

Warren French
Alexander Weis

ABSTRACT. A conflict within the community of those investigating business ethics is whether decision makers are motivated by an ethics of justice or an ethics of caring. The proposition put forward in this paper is that ethical orientations are strongly related to cultural backgrounds. Specifically, Hofstede's cultural stereotyping using his masculine-feminine dimension may well match a culture's reliance on justice or caring when decisions are made. A study of college graduates from six countries showed that Hofstede's dimension was remarkably accurate in predicating a justice or caring orientation for decision makers from five of the six countries.

KEY WORDS: business ethics, caring, feminine, Hofstede, justice, masculine

The survival of mankind will depend to a large extent on the ability to act together. International collaboration presupposes some understanding of where others' thinking differs from ours. Exploring the way in which nationality predisposes our thinking is therefore not an intellectual luxury.

Warren French is the I.W. Cousins Professor of Business Ethics – Terry College of Business, University of Georgia. He teaches an MBA course in business ethics both on-site as well as by the Internet. He also has served as a visiting faculty member at the University of Lyon III in France where he taught business ethics. His research area is conflict resolution through discourse ethics.

Alexander Weiss earned his undergraduate degree from the Friedrich-Alexander Universität Erlangen-Nürnberg and his MBA from the Terry College of Business, University of Georgia. He has served as a consultant for Gulfstream Aerospace.

The preceding quote comes from the opening lines of Hofstede's (1980) text on culture and work related values. His study of business people's values in 40 countries revealed four dimensions on which cultures differed. One of those four dimensions he labeled masculinity-femininity. His description of femininity as nuturance parallels the description given by Gilligan (1982) in her call for an approach to ethics based on caring.

Ethical conflicts in business are unlikely to diminish as transactions become more globalized. Understanding cultural values that underlie these conflicts is a precondition for resolving them (Habermas, 1990). Is an appeal to nurturing or caring the way to approach members of some cultures? There are those who would answer no to that question. They question the rigor of the research upon which Gilligan advances the notion of an ethics of care (Rest, 1986). Using the writings of Plato, Kant, Rawls and Kohlberg as grounding they claim that an ethics of justice provides an adequate basis for evaluating moral decisions.

An ethics of justice

An ethics of care focuses on character traits such as sympathy, compassion, and friendship. These are social virtues. An ethics of justice, in contrast, places a premium on individual autonomous choice and equality. Variations of this theory, i.e., distributive justice, libertarian justice, encompass notions of balancing rights and responsibilities. A more social variation of an ethics of justice is offered by Walzer (1983). He believes the principles of justice are the product of particular cultures. It follows from his observations that some cultures may stress individualistic approaches to justice while others would take a more community focused approach.

Apart from the individualistic vs. community dimension of justice a second dimension is worth noting. Ethics of justice theories appear to take one of three perspectives, focusing on principles, purposes or results. These perspectives align respectively with deontological, teleological and consequentialist ethics. Some authors stress moral principles in the form of obligations (deontos). The work of Rawls (1971) dealing with procedure exemplifies this approach. Other authors look at the purpose (telos) of and intentions behind an act. They are less concerned with procedures and more interested in the consequences of an act – the surrogate measure of fulfilled intentions. The principle behind most Western theories of justice appears to be that of equity (a characteristic of Hofstede's masculinity dimension) which, in turn, is driven by merit not by care or nuturance. The exception is the pure egalitarian theory which is driven by people's needs, usually economic needs. The pure egalitarian theory as well as the communitarian approach to justice which stresses societal virtues are more akin to an ethics of care than to a distributive ethics of justice.

An ethics of caring

Tronto (1993) argues that care can serve as both a moral value and the basis of societal achievement. She finds fault with Kant's disengaged approach to morality. Community harmony is the goal she attributes to morality – a goal attained by a care ethic. Lyons (1988) postulates that those who view the self as separated from others (a partial description of Hofstede's masculinity dimension) are likely to advocate a morality based on justice. In contrast, she claims that those who see the self connected to others are likely to advocate a morality based on care.

Waithe (1989) traces an ethics of caring back to the writings of Aristotle and notes that an ethics of justice has been the prevailing Western approach for only the last several centuries (Baier, 1987). MacIntyre (1984), in turn, with his

interest in virtue and concern for others, strongly embraces an ethics of care.

If the ethics of care has one major benefit for those confronted with ethical problems in business, that benefit is its flexibility. Reitner (1996) points out that contrasted with an ethics of justice, an ethics of care allows for creative resolution of ethical conflicts. Following rules is secondary to preserving relationships.

Gilligan's break from an ethics of justice was explained in her text entitled *In a Different Voice*. As Seigfried (1989) points out that "different voice" is not necessarily confined to women. An ethics of caring or nuturance extends to men as well and is influenced by social, political and economic contexts. Her claim meshes well with Hofstede's findings that an emphasis on care for others rather than concentration on our autonomous self (to which Lyons has attributed an ethics of justice) marks the societal cultures which he has labeled as feminine.

Hofstede's findings, though, do not mesh with the conclusions drawn by Rest (1986) when reporting the intercultural applications of his text on moral reasoning. His results, plus other metaanalytic research findings (Thoma, 1984), support the view that the prevailing grounding for moral judgments is that of an ethics of justice. Yet, Rest does not rule out the possibility that some concept other than justice can provide a strong basis for explaining cross cultural ethical decisions.

Cultural considerations

If one takes the position that ethical questions arise because of conflicts of interests (Baier, 1965) and that the goal of moral discussion should be to resolve those conflicts (Habermas, 1990) then cultural approaches to moral discussion should be considered in tandem with cultural predispositions toward justice or caring. Hall (1981, 1990) notes that the context in which communications are delivered varies significantly between countries. He uses the designation's high-context (HC) and low-context (LC) communication cultures.

What makes these HC-LC distinctions important is Habermas' admonition that moral discussion can't be successful without an understanding of underlying cultural values. This may be an obstacle when a LC party negotiates with a less than forthcoming HC party. Since "HC actions are by definition rooted in the past, slow to change, and highly stable" Hall (1989, p. 93), the LC party had best make the effort to discover the HC party's value structure. The HC person appears to be less rule driven allowing for some bending of the rules to reconcile the problem. This effort to understand the other party's reasoning and the particulars of the situation lead one to believe that an ethics of caring may be more typical than a pure deontological form of an ethics of justice in HC cultures.

The investigation

There is, however, an alternative position to the one taken by Hofstede on different cultural values and by Gilligan and Rest on an ethics of caring versus an ethics of justice. It is one put forward by Ohmae (1990). This alternative position is a pragmatic one. Simply stated, it is that all countries seriously engaged in international commerce will move toward a similar set of business values. If this is true, traditional value differences between negotiators from different countries will be superceded by the desire to resolve conflicts. This implies that business people from these countries, especially younger people, will suppress traditional deontological values and take a teleological or consequentialist approach to resolving ethical conflicts. This is one of the assumptions that is investigated in the following sections.

To focus the investigation on the issues raised in the previous paragraphs, the following propositions were posed:

Proposition 1: Negotiators from countries whose cultures were labeled as feminine as contrasted with negotiators whose cultures were labeled as masculine in the Hofstede classification scheme will express values more in line with an ethics of caring than with an ethics of meritarian justice.

Proposition 2: Negotiators from high communication context cultures as contrasted with negotiators from low communication context cultures, when negotiating ethical issues with a party from a low communication context culture, will make a greater effort than the opposing party to understand the other party's moral stance.

By analyzing the discourse of negotiators from different cultures which embody Hofstede's and Hall's distinctions of masculinity-femininity and high-low communications contexts evidence can be brought forward to support these propositions. What is needed, then, are moral issues which produce conflict and can be the subject of negotiation.

Research method

The moral issues that were chosen for negotiation were selected from a set of six issues which Kurtines (1989) had created for the purpose of encouraging moral discourse. He labeled those issues: "Fair Day's Pay," "You Broke It – You Bought It," "Lying," "Breaking a Promise," "Stealing," and "Punishment." The subjects who were paired to negotiate resolutions to these issues had chosen conflicting positions on two issues. Each pair of subjects negotiated those two issues.

Each negotiating pair came from different countries. The countries represented by the 60 subjects were France, Germany, Turkey, India, China and the U.S.A. (Hofstede had classified three – Germany, India and the U.S.A. as being high on his masculine dimension. Hall, in turn, had depicted only Germany and the U.S.A. as low communication context cultures. A synopsis of the values endemic to each of those countries is presented at the end of this section.) None of the subjects had knowledge of either contextual communications theory or the procedures of discourse ethics. All, though, had some training in negotiation techniques. Each of the subjects possessed a university degree and, after experience in the workplace, had returned to a university setting for graduate training in business.

The high communication context subjects were classified according to Hall's cultural descriptions and Hofstede's national identifications. Hofstede's masculine-feminine cultural classification system was also used to identify subjects' predispositions toward an ethics of justice versus an ethics of caring. Americans were paired with representatives from each of the other five countries. There were six representatives from each of those other countries. Each pair of negotiators were provided an audio tape and tape recorder. They were instructed to try and resolve the two issues over which they expressed conflicting views. A minor reward was offered to the negotiators for their participation, based on the sincerity of their efforts rather than on the success of their conflict resolution.

To assess the merit of the second research proposition, an extension of the Kurtines and Pollard (1989) moral discourse classification scheme was used. See Exhibit 1. Each negotiator's comment, following or preceding the other negotiator's comments became the unit of analysis. Two judges, each from a different low communications context-masculine culture, evaluated the negotiators' comments using Kurtines' taxonomy. Discrepant evaluations by the judges were resolved after a joint reanalysis of the data. The negotiators' comments that relate to the first research proposition will be presented as synthesized comments.

The two research propositions, although logically deduced from the literature are advanced with some trepidation. Change is endemic to all cultures, although some faster than others. There is emerging evidence that Hofstede's masculine-feminine dimension of culture and its demonstration in justice versus caring may be blending in some countries, especially among younger business people. If this is true, Habermas' worries about cultural value misunderstandings become moot and the potential for a common platform for intercultural business ethics gets closer to reality. That change, as it applies to the countries represented by the negotiators acting as subjects in this research, is summarized below.

France

To point out the uniqueness of the French national character, the following observation has been advanced. In France everything is permitted, even that which is forbidden (Hofstede, 1980). This observation underlines the pragmatic attitude the French people have toward life and the principles that guide it.

In his survey of European values and norms

EXHIBIT 1
Stages of sociomoral discussions

Non-productive Discussion – Statements not relative to the negotiations
Ordinary Communicative Action 1 – Statement of position
Ordinary Communicative Action 2 – Statement of interests/reasons
Ordinary Communicative Action 3 – Statement of moral values
*Reflective Communicative Action 0 – Elicitation of the other's stance
*Reflective Communicative Action 1 – Restatement of the other's position
*Reflective Communicative Action 2 – Restatement of the other's interests/reasons
*Reflective Communicative Action 3 – Restatement of the other's moral values
Integrative Communicative Action 0 – Elicitation of a new stance
Integrative Communicative Action 1 – Statement of a new position
Integrative Communicative Action 2 – Statement of a new position based on original interests/reasons
Integrative Communicative Action 3 – Statement of new interests/reasons for a new position
Integrative Communicative Action 4 – Statement of a new position based on original values
Integrative Communicative Action 5 – Statement of a new position based on new values

---

* Indicates statements pertinent to research proposition 2.

Meulemann (1995) found that only 57% of the respondents (the lowest portion among Europeans) mentioned that traditional moral institutions were of importance to them. Underlining this research finding is the fact that the traditional institutions, like church, political parties, workers' unions, have lost their coordination function in society (Les Coordinations) which they held for a long time as intermediaries between state and citizens, thus leading to the highly conflictual nature of social relations in France today (Corbett, 1994).

Yet, 50% of the French people belong to an association of one kind or another, potentially making the solidarite' trait a powerful force in French society. One may be led to conclude then that the French are collectivist in nature rather than being motivated by individualism or the idea of justice. In truth, France is a nation that has a very multifaceted national character. Hofstede sees France as a "feminine" or caring society accepting authority, ". . . but only insofar as it allows them to be individualistic and buffers them from life's uncertainty so that a high equality of life can be maintained" (Gannon, 1994, p. 95).

When it comes to a choice between justice vs. caring, it seems that the French and their actions are motivated by both: an ethics of caring, especially when it comes to the idea of solidarite, and an ethics of justice when individual claims are addressed.

Germany

Current discussion of values that guide the behavior of Germans reveals the phrases "Wertewandel" (change of values) and "Werteverfall" (decay of values), which depict the impact the individualization of society has on the commonly held value patterns. For example, Doenhoff (1998) warns that support for guiding principles such as law, morality, and honesty is in the process of decay.

Darendorf (1997) disagrees claiming that the values of personal and institutional freedom will prevail if only to assure competitive viability within a global business environment. Still, . . . "Germans are like many other peoples who

manifest inconsistent and contradictory values . . ." (Gannon, 1994). Beck (1998) proposes the term "Wertekonflikt" (conflict of values), to describe the present situation of the Germany society. Perhaps, this conflict is embodied in recent research (Wuthnow, 1998) which reveals that the present generation is attempting to balance social responsibility with individual well being.

While Germans of today still seem to be guided primarily by individualistic rather than by communitarian values, traditional institutions and values seem to have lost their impact on the majority of the society. Still, rules and the importance of order are strong motivators of behavior and conformity is expected. Justice and especially institutional justice have not lost their importance in supporting ideas of self-actualization, but altruistic motives also beginning to play an increasing role in everyday life.

Turkey

Turkey represents a blending of old and new, East and West. Inherent in this blending for the "patriotic Turk" is the Kemalistic notion of modernity, which strives to "transform the nation culturally while at the same time retaining its distinctiveness" (Kadioglu, 1996). In this transformation, encounters between East and West result not in reciprocal exchanges but in the decline of the weaker, typified in the Middle East by the decline of the Islamic identity (Goele, 1997).

This approach toward modernization aimed at Western orientation has been criticized by groups that are tolerant toward religious images and ideas founded in Islam, while the "secular Westernists are (. . .) becoming more and more hostile to religious images by relying on and commodifying the image of Mustafa Atatuerk" (Kadioglu, 1996).

Tradition, and especially traditional institutions like family and religion still play an important role in today's Turkey. "In Turkey, one belongs to a few groups, but group affiliation is very important. A Turk's identity is largely determined by the group, such as the family, school group or work group (. . .)." This group affiliation displays itself in the subordination of the individual's goals to those of the group. "There is a reliance on, trust of, and sharing among the members of the group but mistrust of outsiders (Dindi et al., 1989)." This tendency reflects an ethics of caring more than it does an ethics of justice. To care for the well-being of the affiliated "others" is not only expected, but is also the responsibility of every Turk.

India

As in the case with other countries, moral values in Indian businesses appear to be in a state of flux. Gupta (1994) claims that India is second to none when it comes to an erosion of cultural values. Narasimhan (1994) concurs and notes that within India there is a strong perception of widespread corruption.

Bhatia (1997) notes that in Hindu morality the concept of dharma (values for righteous conduct) embodies the goal of maintaining social order. But, is social order attained through caring or justice? Chakrobarty (1991) lists caring but not justice as a prime virtue. Dasgupta (1965) counters that justice must be present, for it is necessary for stability and social order.

England et al. (1974) claims that Indian managers are moralistically oriented. Moralists are defined as those who have a "bureaucratic humanism" orientation versus the economic orientation of pragmatists. This translates to an institutionalized ethics of caring. However, the more successful managers in India tend to be pragmatists not moralists.

Chakrobarty reports that Indian managers feel pressure to adapt to conditions that are often not under their control. In contrast to the Western cultures where individual hard work prevails, in India family and authority values hold sway. Individual autonomy may be prized as a value but it has proven difficult to implement. That implies pragmatic ethics of expediency where the success of the task allows for many means. In moral terms this is a form of consequentialism.

China

Given the strong influence of political philosophy on the cultural and educational spheres of Chinese life, the link with China's past ethical values is weaker than one might imagine (De Mente, 1989). But at least two values have survived and are evident in the behavior of Chinese business people. Those values are harmony and obligation.

Harmony as a motivating goal may emanate from past experiences with a less than tolerant justice system. Preference has been to reconcile problems individually rather than relying on formal justice channels. Obligations, in turn, can be classified as either natural or acquired. Stemming from the Confucian virtue of filial piety, there are natural obligations to family and relatives. Acquired obligations are acknowledged toward friends and a network of associates who have been built and nurtured over time. Metzger (1981) notes that obligations even take precedence over personal integrity. When obligations are not lived up to, shame, self-perceived as well as directed by one's social network, accrues to an individual. That shame and the anticipated public embarrassment which results from an unfulfilled obligation are considered worse than physical punishment.

China is collectivist, but selectively collectivist. An ethics of caring, a Confucian demonstration of *jen* or beneficence (Ma, 1988), is present in Chinese behavior but limited to familial and social networks. Justice, in turn, is also present but in an equalitarian form directed toward the pragmatic end of harmony. It, too, is most evident in the context of living up to obligations incurred within that same familial and social network.

United States

American values are in a state of change. This change is apparent in the work of Josephson (1995) as he shortened his previous list of prime values from ten to six. Among the six which he advances are both justice and caring.

The United States is a relatively young nation,

populated primarily by immigrants. The majority of those immigrants trace their ethnic roots to Europe. As immigrants they brought the values of their native countries with them. The diversity of values evidenced within the U.S. business environment bears witness to the fact that ethnic cultural values persist even when cultures are geographically transplanted.

There is one value, though, that appears to mark Americans' character. The value that arises most frequently in Americans' discussion of ethical disputes in business is that of freedom or individual autonomy, seemingly grounded in an ethics of justice. This value exists in concert with the operating philosophy of pragmatism, the telic mindset of focusing on the accomplishment of tasks. Cavannagh (1976) states that Americans are pragmatic to the point of being anti-intellectual. He claims that the effectiveness of business is not grounded on any consideration of whether business values are praiseworthy or consistent with those of society. Like other nations American values are in transition with societal concerns taking a more prominent position. But, as Cavannagh points to the future of American values, it is no accident that he lists the "Central role of the person" first and "Consideration for others" ninth (Cavannagh, 1976, p. 188).

Results

Exhibit 2 contains the values offered by the negotiators to justify their respective positions on the moral issues. These subjects' countries are listed in Exhibit 2 from top to bottom in increasing order of their scores on Hofstede's masculinity dimension. The results of the analysis of the subjects' stated values give partial support to research *Proposition 1*. Negotiators from cultures labeled as feminine did express values more in line with an ethics of caring than with an ethics of meritarian justice. But, so did negotiators from one of the three cultures Hofstede labeled as masculine. (It was possible for both parties to use either meritarian justice or caring arguments to back up each of the opposing positions for all of the ethical issues.) A summary of the negotiations is presented below.

France

The French scored the lowest on Hofstede's masculinity dimension, and our results bear this out. In each of the twelve negotiations in which the French subjects took part, they exhibited values matching an ethics of caring. Most of the thrust of their negotiations centered on an act's consequences for other people rather than on moral principles. When pressed for the moral reasoning behind their decisions two obligations stood out – obligations to friends and obligations to family. Formal notions of meritarian justice took a lower priority than was given to these two obligations.

China

The majority of the Chinese negotiators exhibited consequentialist reasoning as did the French. In contrast to the French, they were not reticent to expound quietly, if somewhat rigidly, on their moral reasoning. The principles behind that reasoning were helping or not hurting people close to them. In ten of their twelve negotiations, their expressed values embodied an ethics of caring rather than an ethics of justice. One Chinese took an ethics of justice approach on both of his moral issues, and he did so within a mixed deontological framework.

Turkey

The Turks were last of the groups analyzed that fell under Hofstede's classification as feminine in cultural values. Seven of their twelve negotiations were built on an ethics of caring foundation. The values constituting that foundation could be found in the arguments of both the French and the Chinese negotiators. The Turks, though, were decidedly less consequentialist in their orientation than were the French and Chinese. The only negotiator, other than one of the 30 Americans, to ground his arguments on deontogical religious beliefs was one of the six Turks.

EXHIBIT 2
Ethical values by country

Focus on justice	Focus on caring
France	*France*
–	Friendship: entails mutual help
	Beneficence: to friends in need
	Filial Piety: outweighs equal compensation
	Compassion: outweighs justice
	Utility: to society
China	*China*
Honesty: as an obligation	Nonmaleficence: in not adding to friend's pain
Equity: based on order and equal responsibility	Beneficence: in helping friends in time of pain
	Filial Piety: as a prime responsibility
Turkey	*Turkey*
Honesty: as a reciprocal obligation/right	Friendship: entails reciprocity
	Beneficence: to friends in need
	Nonmaleficence: in not adding to friends' pain
	Filial Piety: as a prime responsibility
India	*India*
Honesty: as a reciprocal obligation/right	Beneficence: to friends in need
Equity: based on responsibility for one's own actions	Nonmaleficence: in not hurting a friend
Equity: as a basis for social order	Nonmaleficence: for societal well-being
Trust: is the basis of friendship	Utility: to society
U.S.A.	*U.S.A.*
Equity: based on reciprocity	Beneficence: to friends in need
Equity: based on responsibility for one's own actions	Nonmaleficence: in not hurting friends
Honesty: as an obligation	Friendship: entails mutual help
Autonomy: as a personal right	Utility: for societal well-being
Nondiscrimination: in business decisions	Utility: as an economic calculation
	Utility: in good vs. pain
Germany	*Germany*
Equity: based on responsibility for one's own actions	Harmony: for society
Honesty: as a reciprocal obligation/right	Filial Piety: as a prime responsibility
Justice: in egalitarian form	Friendship: entails mutual help
	Nonmaleficence: in not endangering friends
	Beneficence: to friend in need

India

According to our interpretation and application of Hofstede's classification scheme, the Indian negotiators, coming from what had been identified as a masculine culture, should have argued from a meritarian justice basis. That was the case

in seven of the twelve negotiations. The Indians relied more on a deontogical approach to ethics than did any of the negotiators from feminine cultures. Three particular values marked their negotiations – the obligation to be truthful and the related obligation of helping and/or not hurting friends.

U.S.A.

It is interesting to note that the Americans negotiating with the Indian subjects also relied on justice rather than caring in seven of their 12 negotiations. In total, the Americans used values related to an ethics of justice in 46 of these 60 negotiations verifying their masculine classification by Hofstede. They, more than any of the six cultures, relied on meritarian justice as the grounding for their ethical arguments. Underlying many of their deontological arguments was the concept of an individual decision maker's freedom, a freedom that they considered more important than the consequences of an act.

Germany

According to Hofstede's data, the German negotiators should have demonstrated the most masculine approach to the ethical issues. One interpretation of that approach is that they should have been the greatest advocates of an ethics of meritarian justice. This was not the case.

Representatives from the other five cultures offered ethical rationales as one would predict from Hofstede's classification scheme. In addition, the comparative degree to which they offered those justifications was exactly as would have been predicted from Hofstede's classification data. Only in six of their 12 negotiations did the Germans rely on an ethics of justice. The other half of their negotiations reflected an ethics of care. Our prediction, based on the results from the other intercultural negotiations would have been 10 out of 12 arguments grounded on meritarian justice values. Whether the Germans adopted an ethics of justice or caring approach to their negotiations was of relatively little practical significance in the results of those negotiations. As can be seen in Exhibit 3, the Germans were the most successful of the cultures in resolving the ethical conflicts.

Exhibit 3 portrays the negotiation statements as they relate to *Proposition 2*. That proposition states that negotiators from high communications context (HC) cultures will make a greater effort to understand the opposing negotiator's moral stance than will low communications context

EXHIBITION 3

Percentage of reflective negotiation statements and successful conflict resolutions

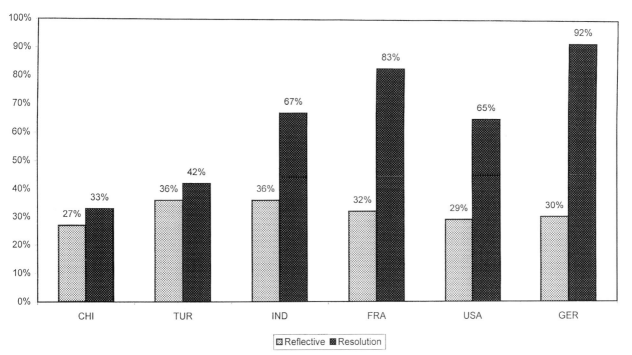

(LC) negotiators. The rationale for the proposition is that HC negotiators need more information about the situation, including the views of the opposing negotiator (the statements classified as reflective (R) in the coding scheme described in Exhibit 1), before attempting a resolution to the ethical conflict. The percentages in Exhibit 3 were obtained by taking each negotiator's number of reflective statements and dividing by that individual's total of reflective, ordinary and NPD statements. The average of the six R percentages for each country's negotiators is what is presented in the exhibit. The countries are arranged in the exhibit from left to right to signify a range from HC to LC. As can be seen from that data, there was less than a 10% difference between the highest and lowest percentages. Thus, *Proposition 2* could not be supported. Also, there was no evidence to suggest that the use of reflective statements correlated with conflict resolution. It is interesting to note, though, that China, whose negotiators were expected to have the highest R percentage, had the lowest. They also were the least successful of the negotiators.

Discussion

It has been over 20 years since both Hofstede and Hall gathered the information for their works on cultural values and communication. Our research subjects (in their 20s and 30s) would be the age of the children of Hofstede's sampled IBM employees. Have values and communication orientations as they relate to moral discussions changed since the 1970s?

As pointed out in an earlier section, scholars in the field of cultural values seem to believe that change is occurring. Based on reports of these changes, buttressed by the findings reported in Exhibit 2, we believe that Rest's dismissal of an ethics of caring is dated. Even in the U.S.A. where an ethics of meritarian justice receives strong support, it does not provide the sole rationale for ethical decisions. Perhaps, the thought attributed to Thomas Acquinas that justice without mercy is meaningless is slowly penetrating the younger business people from the cultures represented by our sample. The only way

to conclude that an ethics of justice holds sway is to broaden the definition to include egalitarian justice. That broadening, de facto, would subsume an ethics of caring under the term justice.

In effect, the nuturance component of Hofstede's femininity dimension is both noticeable and operational in countries such as Germany and the U.S.A. which he labeled as masculine. This seems to be particularly true among the younger businesspeople from Germany in our sample albeit a sample of limited size. There does, indeed, appear to be a "Wertewandel" and, as pointed out earlier, "caring" motives are showing themselves in ethical decisions.

Other than the justice versus caring equilibrium in Germany, the most surprising results came from the Chinese negotiators. Pan et al. (1994) offer insights into the character of young Chinese businesspeople which may partially explain our results. China is an evolving culture which is influenced by three major forces – tradition, Marxism and, now, Western values. How these three forces are balanced in an ethical decision is difficult to predict. What can be said is that the China which Hall observed over a quarter century ago has definitely changed, especially the behavior of young business people. Is this evolution in China and in our other sampled cultures leading to Ohmae's prediction of a pragmatic drive to resolve ethical conflict by referring to an internationally accepted set of business values? Our reaction is "not yet." The ethics of care as applied in *Proposition 1* expressed by our sample should not be projected onto all of their decisions about moral conflict. Our subjects, for the most part, used it selectively by confining it to the social network of the decision maker.

Setting social networks and cultural values aside, what proved more difficult to understand were the results relating to *Proposition 2*. It might be assumed that an ideal ethical discourse in a Habermasian sense would contain a balance of Reflective and Ordinary statements as they are described in Exhibit 1. However, the effort of negotiators from different cultures to express understanding of each other's moral stances fell far from the balance one might have hoped for.

Even more disappointing in this study was while reflective statements were used in just over 30% of the discussions prior to considering alternative moral resolutions, grounding for those resolutions in the form of Integrative Communicative Action Statements (see Exhibit 1) was extremely low. None of the 60 negotiators paid reference to mutually shared values that could underlie resolution of the conflicts. In just 7 of the negotiations was there mention of any value which could provide backing for possible resolutions. Even more surprising was that only 1% of the 60 subjects tested potential resolutions against personal (non-value laden) interests. This matches the findings of Van Es (1996) with respect to Dutch negotiators – that resolution of conflict through discourse should not be expected to be based on values as opposed to mutual interests. Our results cast some doubt on the viability of Habermas' discourse thesis. To believe that discourse among intelligent, educated business people will naturally result in a different ethical position grounded on newly revealed mutually shared values may be somewhat naive. Practically speaking, can only guided discourse (French and Mühlfriedel, 1996) be expected to arrive at conflict resolution based on new mutually shared values?

In summary, if discourse ethics as a field of practical application is to be pursued further, its limitations as pointed out by Van Es must be recognized and then adjusted for. In turn, we can not expect the underlying values searched for in discourse ethics to be confined to an ethics of justice. That thinking may be at the core of Habermas' theory, but it is too narrow. In more recent literature, the ethical decision maker is viewed as one whose cognitive, analytical skills are tempered by contextual and human influences. The moral discussion of the negotiators in our study calls for this broadened approach.

Reference

Baier, A. C.: 1987, 'Hume, The Women's Moral Theorist', in E. J. Kittay and D. T. Meyers (eds.), *Women and Moral Theory* (Rowman and Littlefield, Totowa, NJ).

Baier, K.: 1965, *The Moral Point of View* (Random House, New York).

Beck, U.: 1998, 'Kinder der Freiheit: Wider das Lamento über den Werteverfall', in Ulrich Beck (eds.), *Kinder der Freiheit* (Suhrkamp Verlag, Frankfurt am Main).

Bhatia, S.: 1997, 'Arjuna's Dilemma: Can Voices of Justice Speak to Hindu Morality?', *AME Conference*, Emory University, Atlanta.

Cavannagh, G. F.: 1976, *American Business Values in Transition* (Prentice-Hall, Englewood Cliffs, NJ).

Chakrobarty, S. K.: 1991, *Management by Values* (Oxford University Press, Delhi).

Dasgupta, S.: 1965, *Development of Moral Philosophy in India* (Frederick Ungar Publishing, New York).

Darendorf, R.: 1997, *After 1989* (St. Martin's Press, New York).

DeMente, B.: 1989, *Chinese Etiquette and Ethics in Business* (NTC Business Books, Lincolnwood, IL).

Dini, H.: *Turkish Culture for Americans* (International Concepts, Boulder).

Doenhoff, M. Graefin: 1998, *Die neue Mittwochsgesellschaft – Gespraeche über Probleme von Buerger und Staat* (Deutsche Verlags – Anstalt, Stuttgart).

England, G. W., O. P. Dhingra and C. A. Naresh: 1974, *The Manager and the Man* (Kent University Press, Ohio).

French, W. and B. Mühlfriedel: 1996, 'Discourse Instead of Recourse: Is It Worth Using a Guided Approach to Negotiation When Working Across Cultures?', in H. Lange, A. Löhr and H. Steinmann (eds.), *Working Across Cultures* (Kluwer Academic Publishers, Dordrecht).

Gannon, M. J.: 1994, *Understanding Global Cultures: Metaphorical Journeys Through 17 Countries* (Sage, Thousand Oaks, CA).

Gilligan, C.: 1982, *In a Different Voice: Psychological Theory and Women's Development* (Harvard University Press, Cambridge MA).

Goele, N.: 1997, 'The Quest for the Islamic Self within the Context of Modernity', in Sibel Bozdogan and Resat Kasaba (eds.), *Rethinking Modernity and National Identity in Turkey* (University of Washington Press, Seattle).

Gupta, S. K.: 1994, 'Ethics and Industry', in T. A. Mathias (ed.), *Corporate Ethics* (Allied Publishers, New Delhi), pp. 123–126.

Habermas, J.: 1990, *Moral Consciousness and Communicative Action*, translated by Christian Lenhardt and Shierry Weber Nicholsen (The MIT Press, Cambridge, MA).

Hall, E. T.: 1981, *Beyond Culture* (Anchor-Doubleday, New York).

Hall, E. T. and M. R. Hall: 1990, *Understanding Cultural Differences* (Intercultural Press, Yarmouth, ME).

Hofstede, G.: 1980, *Cultural Consequences* (Sage, Beverly Hills).

Hume, D.: 1978, *A Treatise of Human Nature*, 2nd edn. (Oxford University Press, Oxford).

Josephson, M.: 1995, *Ethics*, Issue 29, p. 50.

Kadioglu, A.: 1996, 'The Paradox of Turkish Nationalism and the Construction of Official Identity', in Sylvia Kedourie (ed.), *Turkey: Identity, Democracy, Politics* (Frank Cass, Portland, OR).

Kurtines, W. M.: 1989, *The Communicative Functioning Scale: Moral Dilemmas*, Unpublished Manuscript (Florida International University Department of Psychology, Miami).

Kurtines, W. M. and S. R. Pollard: 1984, *The Communicative Competence Scale – Critical Discussion Manual*, Unpublished Paper (Florida International University Department of Psychology, Miami).

Lyons, N.: 1988, 'Two Perspectives: On Self, Relationships, and Morality', in Carol Gilligan, Janie Victoria Ward and Jill McLean Taylor, with Betty Bardige (eds.), *Mapping the Moral Domain: A Contribution of Women's Thinking to Psychology and Education* (Harvard University Graduate School of Education, Cambridge), pp. 21–48.

Ma, H. K.: 1998, 'The Chinese Perspectives on Moral Judgment Development', *International Journal of Psychology* **23**, 201–227.

MacIntyre, A.: 1984, *After Virtue: A Study in Moral Theory*, 2nd edn. (University of Notre Dame Press, Notre Dame, IN).

Metzger, T. A.: 1981, 'The Question of Moral Development and the Concept of Culture', in Richard W. Wilson, Sidney L. Greenblatt and Amy A. Wilson (eds.), *Moral Behavior in Chinese Society* (Praeger, New York), pp. ix–xxv.

Meulemann, H.: 1996, *Werte und Wertewandel* (Juventa-Verlag, Muenchen).

Narasimhan, R. 1994, 'A Practical View of Business Ethics', in T. A. Mathias (ed.), *Corporate Ethics* (Allied Publishers, New Delhi), pp. 128–132.

Ohmae, K.: 1990, *The Borderless World: Power and Strategy in the Interlinked Economy* (Harper Business, New York).

Pan, Z., S. H. Chaffee, G. C. Chu and Y. Ju: 1994, *To See Ourselves* (Westview Press, Boulder, CO).

Rawls, J.: 1971, *A Theory of Justice* (Harvard University Press, Cambridge, MA).

Reiter, S. A.: 1996, 'The Koblberg-Gilligan Controversy: Lessons For Accounting Ethics Education', *Critical Perspectives on Accounting* **7**(1), 33–54.

Rest, James R. 1983, 'Morality', in P. Mussen (ed.), *Carmichael's Manual of Child Psychology*, Vol. 3: *Cognitive Development* (John Wiley and Sons, New York), pp. 556–629.

Rest, J. R.: 1986, *Moral Development: Advances in Research and Theory* (Praeger, New York).

Siegfried, C. Haddock 1989, 'Pragmatism, Feminism, and Sensitivity to Context', in Mary M. Brabeck (ed.), Who Cares? (Praeger, New York).

Thoma, S. J.: 1984, *Estimating Gender Differences in the Comprehension and Preference of Moral Issues*, Unpublished Manuscript (University of Minnesota, Minneapolis, MN).

Tronto, J. C.: 1993, *Moral Boundaries* (Routledge, New York).

Van Es, R. 1996, *Negotiating Ethics* (Eburon, Delft).

Worthe, M. E.: 1989, 'Twenty-three Hundred Years of Women Philosophers: Toward a Gender Undifferentiated Moral Theory', in Mary M. Brabeck (ed.), *Who Cares?* (Praeger, New York), pp. 3–18.

Walzer, M.: 1983, *Spheres of Justice: A Defense of Pluralism and Equality* (Basic Books, New York).

Brucks Hall – University of Georgia,
Athens, GA 30602,
U.S.A.
E-mail: wfrench@terry.uga.edu

The Limits of Shareholder Value

Peter Koslowski

ABSTRACT. Shareholder value orientation has been introduced as a means to improve the performance of the corporation. The paper investigates the theoretical justification for the claim that increasing shareholder value is the purpose of corporate governance. It demonstrates that shareholder value is the control principle, not the purpose of the firm. The idea that shareholder value is the only goal of the corporation is a mistaken transfer from the financial to the industrial firm. The paper also questions that the merger of manager interests and owner interests introduced by the remuneration of managers by stock options improves the management performance. The self-apportioning of stock options by the management is in danger of becoming a form of insider trading.

KEY WORDS: corporate governance, holding structure, shareholder value, stock options

Globalization increases the chances to realize a higher shareholder value in financial investments since the investment opportunities increase in a globalized market. The owner of capital is confronted with more opportunities to invest her capital and undergoes higher opportunity costs if the capital is not properly invested. These developments move the criterion of maximizing shareholder value to the centre of the debate. The orientation on shareholder value is a means to increase the allocation efficiency of investments in the world market, an effect that should be welcomed. The shareholder value principle is also an instrument to prevent the shirking of managers and the shirking of whole firms. Managers and firms might have developed slack which can be reduced by a stronger emphasis on the residual profit and the increase of shareholder value.

I. Shareholder value as a means of controlling the firm

The profit of the firm is the means to prevent shirking in the operations of all members of a firm. In Alchian's and Demsetz's theory,[1] the owner functions as the one who prevents the shirking of the firm's members, and the firm's profit is the means to prevent the owner from shirking in his duty to prevent the shirking of the other members of the firm. The idea is that if the owner does not fulfill her monitoring function the residual profit will decrease, and she will be punished by decreased profits or even losses and thereby be kept to her function to prevent shirking in her firm.

The shareholder value principle with its emphasis on future cash flows changes the perspective on profit as residual profit. Profit is not measured any more as a figure of the past but as an *expected* future residual. The firm must maximize the future profit measured in dividends and the increase of the value of shares in the stock exchange. The management has to see that the future residual profit after reduction of all costs is maximized. This orientation on a future residual profit with all the problems of forecasting a future return on investment does not change the basic nature of profit.

Peter Koslowski is director of the Center for Ethical Economy and Business Culture, the Hannover Institute of Philosophical Research, Hannover, Germany. His book Principles of Ethical Economy *(in German) of 1988 has been translated into Chinese, French, and Russian, and will be published in English this year by Kluwer.*

Profit and shareholder value, seen from the point of the firm, are not the final purpose of the firm, but an instrumental end. Profit and shareholder value are the means to prevent shirking and to make sure that all members of the firm deliver their contractual contributions to the firm in an optimal way as agreed upon in the contract.

Among all the members of the different groups of the firm, it is true only for the group of the shareholders that the profit and the value of the shares are also their individual goal. For all the other groups this goal is only interesting as a means to secure the success of the firm as a whole, not as a final end that they could make their own purpose.

This implies that the shareholder value can be considered to be the purpose of the firm only in a very mediated way. It is first of all the purpose of one group of the firm, the shareholders, and its prominence amongst the goals of the other groups of the firm is only justified by its function of preventing the shirking of the owners who in turn prevent the shirking of all other members of the firm. From the point of view of all other members of the firm shareholder value, however, cannot be considered to be *the* purpose of the firm. It is only one criterion of the firm's success. As the future residual it can be considered to be a control variable for the other goals and purposes of the firm and for its success. The fact that shareholder value is a residual and remains so even if it is projected into the future cannot mean that it is the first principle or the first purpose of the firm. A residual control principle remains what it is: a control principle, and not the final end of an organization.

II. The purpose of the firm

The debate on shareholder value belongs to the discussion of the purposes or goals of the firm in the theory of business administration. What is interesting of the partly scholastic distinctions of the many goals of a firm for the problem of shareholder value is that the idea that the firm be a one-purpose-institution is untenable. Every

firm has many purposes. The various groups of a firm have their own purposes which they try to realize in the firm. Labour expects high wages from the firm, customers expect optimal goods from the firm, shareholders expect maximum returns on their investment, the community expects high taxes and public benefit payments from the firm and so on. Some of these goals are conflicting, like the goal of maximum wages and maximum profits; some are complementary.

If one wants to distinguish one of these purposes as the first purpose or final teleology of the firm, it is clear that the goal of none of the particular groups constituting the firm can be the only purpose of the firm since the other groups also have the right to the pursuit of their purpose in the firm. If there is one major purpose of the firm, it must be a purpose that could be consented to by all groups of the firm. This means that it must be useful to all members of the firm and to the public. Since all members of the firm and all members of society are consumers in some way, either in the direct way of being consumers of the product of the firm in question or by being consumer of the goods for which the product of the firm is an imput, one must conclude that the most general purpose of the firm is to provide for consumers' satisfaction by its products.

All members of the firm are consumers and therefore interested in the maximum productivity of the firm leading to the optimal products of the firm. Not all members of the firm are, however, shareholders. The shareholders' purpose can, therefore, not be the purpose of all the firm members. It can be deduced from this that the purpose of the firm is the production of optimal products or of optimal inputs for other products under the constraints that the goals of the major groups in the firm or touched by the firm's operation are taken care of, i.e. under the condition that the goals of paying adequate wages, adequate dividends, and adequate prices to the suppliers are fulfilled.

The necessary condition for the existence of the firm and the main purpose for which firms come into being is the production of products, not the production of profits or shareholder values. This main purpose of the firm may only be realized if sufficient returns on investment are earned, and in this sense, the realization of shareholder value is a condition for the realization of the main purpose of the firm, it is however not the first condition. The main purpose of the firm, the production of best products, implies that the firm must be productive and efficient. How this productivity and efficiency is reached is a secondary question. Since it is the purpose and task of the business firm to provide the public with the best products produced at the lowest opportunity cost, also those conditions are obligatory that best secure the realization of this purpose of the firm. The means of securing the purpose of the firm are, however, not the primary purpose of the firm. If the purpose of the firm, the production of optimal products, can best be achieved by market efficiency and shareholder value maximization, they are the best means to achieve this goal. If it can be achieved by other means or be achieved by other means even better, these means must be chosen. Productivity is an obligation of the firm independent of market efficiency.[2]

It is an old principle of the Aristotelian natural law tradition, also dominant in Catholic social thought, that the obligation arises from the nature of the matter: *obligatio oritur a natura rei*.[3] This principle is also central in Radbruch's philosophy of law. The idea of law and of legal obligation is derived, according to Radbruch, from

- the purpose of the institutional realm a law is to rule,
- the principle of equal right, and
- the principle of legal security or secure expectations as to the content and the enforcement of the law.[4]

Applied to the theory of the firm, the principle that the obligation is derived from the nature and purpose of the matter or institution in question requires that the main ethical and legal obligation of the firm must be deduced from its first purpose, and not from the conditions which secure the realization of its purpose. This first purpose of the firm is, however, not the maximization of the residual profit and of the share value in the stock market but the production of optimal products under the condition of the realization of the secondary goals of its member groups or stakeholders.

It is the virtue of the stakeholder approach that it brings back to the theory of the firm the idea that the firm is a multi-purpose-organization and not a single-purpose-organization institutionalized only for the purpose of the shareholders' wealth as it is assumed in the financial theory of the firm. The stakeholder approach, however, cannot give an integration of the several goals of the stakeholders but leaves them to be on equal level. The principle of the integration of the different stakeholders' goals with the overriding productivity goal of the firm is not developed in the stakeholder theory introduced by R. E. Freeman.[5]

The stakeholders' goals are subordinate to the total purpose of the firm which implies that their claims to the total income of the firm are not only limited by the strategic power they can exert in the firm in the contest with the claims of the other stakeholder groups, but that they are limited by the claims the firm as such and its persistence in time as an institution have on all its member groups. The continuing production of first class goods is the disciplining force in the strategic negotiations between the different stakeholder groups beside the disciplining force of the residual or of the principle of shareholder value maximization. Productivity as an obligation and as the purpose of the firm defines the main goal of the firm and renders the other goals to be subordinate purposes. It also renders the shareholder value maximization to be only one goal amongst others and a goal that is subordinate to the productivity goal although it might, as the residual, exert dominance amongst the several goals of the stakeholders. The stakeholders' stakes are ranked in the firm's hierarchy of goals below the productivity goal. The purpose of the firm is the production of its product or products, the rendering of its specific service to the market and public.

III. Shareholder value as the product and main purpose of firms: the financial institutions

There is one group of firms in which the production goal of the firm coincides with the goal of maximizing shareholder value, the financial institutions in which the firm's product is the maximization of shareholder value, however the maximization of its customers' shareholder value. In the financial institutions, like investment banks, investment funds, life insurance companies, and pension funds, shareholder value is not only the residual measuring the performance of the firm but the very product for which these firms have come into existence. These institutions have come into being to render to their customers the product or service of securing the maximum return on their investment, the maximum shareholder value for them. In the financial institutions, shareholder value is the main purpose of the firm, and the performance of the firm can be measured by its performance in maximizing its clients' shareholder value.

A person that gives her savings to an investment fund purchases from this firm the product of maximizing her shareholder value. The investment fund in turn maximizes its purpose and optimally fulfills its obligation if it maximizes the customers' shareholder value – but not its own shareholders' shareholder value. In the financial institutions and financial services industry the shareholder value is not only the residual condition for the optimal working of the firm but the very product of the firm and therefore gains a particular importance unlike in other firms.

IV. Spill-over effects from the financial institutions to the industrial firm: predominance of the shareholder value orientation and the holding structure

The Western economies are presently characterized by a transfer from the institutional conditions of the financial institutions to industrial institutions which, in turn, renders shareholder value to be the only purpose of the firm. Since in the financial institutions the costumers' shareholder value is the product these institutions sell, shareholder value is the central and pivotal criterion for their business operations and business success. In the financial institutions, shareholder value is the purpose and the criterion or instrumental control variable of this industry.

The special conditions of the financial services industries have been transferred to all the industrial firms assuming that in them also shareholder value is not only the control variable but also the main purpose of the firm's operations. This spill-over from the financial firms to the industrial firms has caused an inversion of the shareholder value principle from being the control principle to being the purpose of the firm. Since in the financial institutions the control principle is at the same time the purpose of the institution – although in the first case it is defined as the shareholder value of the firm's owners whereas in the second case it is defined as the shareholder value of the firm's customers – one has been tempted to think that the unity of the shareholder value principle as the control principle and as the purpose of the firm applies also to the industrial institutions.

In the radical version of the shareholder value approach as defended by Jensen and Meckling[6] and others the inversion of the firm's purpose and of the firm's control principle takes place. The radical shareholder value approach takes the residual and the book-keeping of the firm's success for the firm's final purpose. The shareholder value realized is the book-keeping for the firm's success but it is not its final purpose.

The spill-over from the financial institutions to the industrial firms is particularly visible in the career of the holding firm, a trend which, interestingly enough, has been reversed recently in spite of the dominance of the shareholder value principle.

In the transformation of the industrial firm into a conglomerate and a holding firm which only serves as the monitoring for the firms' investment funds in its different divisions, the firm's headquarters is considered to be the financial service institution for itself that ensures that all its divisions yield the maximum shareholder value for the holding. The holding's head-quarters does not give for that purpose much consideration to the material purpose and product of the divisions themselves.

For the holding firm, the shareholder value has become the purpose and the product of the firm just like for an investment fund maximizing shareholder value is its original business and product. For the holding firm, the products of the divisions have become only a means to secure the shareholder value of the holding head-quarters.

The holding firm is a particularly good example the inversion of means and ends. It implies that the end of the firm, the product of the divisions, becomes a means for the share-holder value of the holding although the share-holder value was originally the means for controlling and making sure that the firm produces good products.

It is revealing that the newest economic devel-opments demonstrate that the holding structure is much less advantageous than it appeared to be several years ago. Industrial firms are returning and find it to be most profitable to return to their original strength and main task, the production of the products of their core competence. They no longer envisage themselves as investment funds for their own capital and do not take their divisions only to be investment opportunities for the funds of the holding's equity.

Understanding shareholder value to be the control principle of the firm makes sure that the holding firm considers shareholder value not to be its main purpose and, thereby, fails to secure its optimal performance. Rather, understanding the shareholder value principle rightly as a control principle grants that the firm realizes the optimality of its product and, by it, the optimality of its financial performance. The large corpora-tion can only maximize its shareholder value if it considers shareholder value not to be the purpose but only the control principle of its operations.

It seems to be the virtue of the shareholder value principle as a control principle that it is self-fulfilling and self-enforcing inasmuch as it makes sure that it does not become the main purpose of the firm, since it does not realize the

maximum shareholder value if it is taken for the purpose of the firm. There is no built-in tendency in the shareholder value principle to cause by itself the inversion of means and ends and to turn itself from the means of the firm to its end or purpose.

V. Effects of the inversion of the means and ends of the firm on corporate governance: speculation instead of production

The inversion of the purpose of the firm from the product being the first purpose to maxi-mizing shareholder value being the first purpose turns the management's production task into a speculation task, as the example of the holding firm demonstrates. The idea that, by the invis-ible hand of the labor market and by the con-tracts of the firm, the overall orientation on shareholder value necessarily also realizes the common good of the firm does not hold. It is true that the industrial firm can only maximize shareholder value if it produces some useful goods and keeps the implicit contracts with its employees and customers in some way. It realizes this common good of the firm, however, only "somehow" and "on the back" of the shareholder value maximization since the new overall purpose of the firm, i.e. maximizing shareholder value, is increasingly realized by mere speculation.

Since the price of shares in the stock market does not just reflect the real value of the firm's productivity and performance but is also subject to mere speculation, the management has an interest in becoming involved in speculative manipulations of the value of the firm's shares and therefore of its shareholder value. This dis-traction of the management's attention and inten-tion from the main purpose of the firm, its product or products, to the secondary goal of the firm, maximizing shareholder value, results in two detrimental effects:

First it creates perverse incentives for the man-agement to take more interest in speculation than in production or at least to become interested too much in speculation instead of concentrating on production. It results secondly in a certain short-termism in managing the firm, in looking at the shareholder value and returns on investment for every quarterly report. The "terror of the quarterly report" is increased.

Incentives are central for any economic order, and it is one of the main arguments for the shareholder value principle that it creates efficient incentives for the management to maximize the overall value of the firm. Incentives can however also create perverse incentives, can distract the intention to activities that are not in the interest of the firm. If shareholder value becomes the overall purpose of the firm, the managers have strong incentives to invest their attention and their time in finding ways and means to manipulate the price of shares in the stock market and in means that are not in the interest of those members of the firm that are not shareholders. The possible perverse incentives the shareholder value principle exerts on the management, if it is considered to be the only purpose of the firm, are considerable. They direct the resources of the management to unproductive instead of productive action.

The second effect, the short-termism of an exaggerated attention to the short-term share price in the stock market, is also not in the long-run interest of the firm if profitable long-run strategies are hindered by it. It is important to note, however, that short-termism is not by itself an economically and ethically negative phenomenon. It might be necessary and ethically legitimate to liquidate an investment after a very short time if one has found out that it was the wrong decision or subjected to sudden adverse developments.[7] The time structure of the management's decision-making and of that of the shareholders can, however, be shortened unduly by the shareholder value maximization.

The inversion of the principle of shareholder value maximization from a control principle to the main purpose of the firm treats the members of the organization of the firm as means for the end of maximizing shareholder value. This using the members of the organization as a means for an end is not objectionable in itself. The Kantian formulation of the categorical imperative is that one should act in such a way that one never treats

the other as a means *only*, not that one should never use another person as a means for a legitimate purpose. The firm that makes shareholder value maximization its first purpose may not treat its members as means only for this purpose but it will be in danger of doing so and it will give its members the impression that they are means for this end only and not also ends in themselves for the firm.

The stakeholder principle, in turn, makes sure that all stakeholders and member groups of the firm will have their interest respected but it does not provide the firm with a principle of ranking the stakes of the stakeholders in the negotiation process of the firm. In the end, the stakeholder approach leaves the stakeholders with an open battle for power and rewards in the firm. Whereas the shareholder approach seems to acknowledge only one interest of one stakeholder group, the shareholders, the stakeholder approach acknowledges the many interests but it gives no principle of justice for the process of mediation between the interests. It remains a principle of strategic bargaining.

This becomes evident from the fact that in the bargaining process the different stakeholder groups must refer in the justification of their claims to the firm to a principle of justice. The principle of justice in the economy and the firm is that the payments and rewards for services rendered should be determined according to the value of the contribution rendered to the purpose of the organization or firm.[8] This is the content of Thomas Aquinas' principle: *Suum cuique tribuere*, give to each what is owed to him or her. Everyone should receive what she contributes to the common purpose of the organization. This principle was also the deeper justification of the theory of income in the theory of marginal productivity. Its normative content is that the factors of production should be compensated according to their marginal product.

The principle that all members of the organization should be paid according to their contribution to the goal of the firm is different from the shareholder value principle which tends to imply that it is the task of the firm to concentrate, in its consideration of the principle that persons should be rewarded according to their contributions, on the return payments to share-holders only.

The idea that the residual profit belongs only to the entrepreneur and/or the capital owner has been questioned on the ground that the dispositive factor may not be the only one responsible for the dispositive success of the firm since there might also be dispositive elements in labour's contribution to the success of the firm. Since however labour is usually not ready to share also into the residual loss, the imputation of the residual profit primarily to the owners is justified.

That the residual profit is imputed to only one group makes it necessary to strive for a stronger participation of the workers in the formation of capital and therefore in their sharing in the residual profit and shareholder value. The call for more workers' participation in the ownership of the means of production is a corollary of the new emphasis on shareholder value maximization. If the shareholder value moves to the centre of the goals of the firm, it should also be the case that labour as owner of shares has a higher share in the shareholder value created by the firm.

There is a sequence of disciplining principles in the firm and a sequence of controls that step in when one of them fails: The shareholders prevent the firm members' shirking; the stake-holders discipline the shareholders and their claim to returns on capital and prevent them from believing that their goal is the only goal of the firm; the purpose of the firm, the product, and the principle of justice that any member of the firm should be compensated according to this person's contribution to the firm discipline the stakeholders. The shareholder value principle and the shareholders discipline the firm; the stake-holder value principle and the stakeholders dis-cipline and limit the shareholders; the purpose of the firm disciplines and limits both, the share-holders and the stakeholders.

VI. The emphasis on shareholder value and the managers' interests: merger between shareholder and manager interests?

The shareholder value principle cannot be inter-preted only as an increased control on the per-formance of the managers. Rather the firm's overemphasis on shareholder value may also lead to a strategic alliance between shareholders and managers against the other stakeholders. If the shareholders and the managers form one stake-holder group with shared interests, the managers are tempted to decide in their own and their shareholders' interest to realize a higher share value at the cost of the firm and of the other stakeholders.

The development of income of the managers of the British state owned companies that have been privatized and turnt into joint-stock com-panies is an indicator for this process. The most striking effect of the privatization of these firms has been the multiplication of the managers' income.

Shareholder value maximization creates incen-tives for the managers to look more after profits from speculative gains than after profit from superior productivity and products. These incen-tives can become perverse incentives since the value of the shares in the stock market is not only the result of the management's or firm's real per-formance but also of its perceived performance. Its share price is influenced as well by the mere speculation of others in these shares.

The speculative element in the price of shares and in the shareholder value renders it problem-atic to link the managers' salary to the develop-ment of the market value of the firm's shares. If the firm's shares increase their value and price due to mere speculation in the stock market and if the management receives higher additional income from stock options and the like, the managers' attention is attracted more to the movement of share prices than to the operations of their firms.

A case study for this problem is the law suit against a stock option plan of DaimlerChrysler for its managers. One of the shareholders of the firm, Ekkehard Wenger, a professor of business administration, has brought the law suit against the firm that this plan violates the interests of the shareholders. Wenger argues that a conversion of stock options into real DaimlerChrysler shares after three years under the condition that the share price had risen by 15 percent during the period of three years is not acceptable since, at a rate of increase of value of 5 percent p.a., there is no extraordinary performance of the management if the average rate of increase in the stock market is just the same. A special remuneration being dependent on the success of the firm could only be justified if the rate of increase in the price of the firm's share were higher than the average rate of increase of share value in the stock market.

The court at Stuttgart, Germany, dismissed this action with the statement that "judging the managerial content of such a stock option scheme is not the task of the court."[9] Even after this court decision, however, the question as to the managerial appropriateness of the scheme remains open to discussion. Whether an *average* increase of the value of a firm's shares justifies an additional income of its management in stock options and whether such schemes may not induce an exaggerated concentration of the managers on the price of the firm's shares and thereby create perverse incentives is an open question.

It can even be asked whether the overemphasis on share options and the like in the remunerations of managers does not include an element of insider trading. If the management decides on the firm's share option plans and is, at the same time, in control of the firm's policy – and therefore also of its share price policy – it first of all decides itself about its remuneration and secondly is able to maniplate the share price by its management policy. The CEO of Porsche, Wendelin Wiedeking, described this kind of share option plans introduced by the management's own decision as a case of insider trading.[10] He suggests that managers, because of the danger that they conduct insider trading, should not own any stock of the companies they are employed at.

Another argument against the overemphasis on stock options in the income of managers is that the ability of the firm to raise equity in the capital market is reduced if the possible investors or shareholders must have the impression that the management has already appropriated in advance the main proportion of the future shareholder value to itself by the stock option plans favoring the management.

Shareholder value as the control instrument and disciplining method is particularly important in making sure that the firm makes profit in every period and in regulating the time structure and time preference of investment. Rappaport[11] demonstrates this effect of the shareholder value principle which might be considered to be the main advantageous effect of the shareholder value principle on the firm's performance and on dividend policy. The shareholder value criterion forces the firm to make sure in every year that investment in the firm is profitable in every year which implies that a dividend is paid every year.

Rappaport's argument is that, theoretically, it would be useful not to pay any dividend at all if the returns on capital from the firm in the coming years are positive and above market interest rate. In this case all profits should be kept in the firm since they will render even higher profits in the future if they are accumulated within the firm and not paid off as dividends.

Against this idea of keeping the profits in the firm for self-financing and the formation of equity the argument of the shareholder value theory is very simple: If the firm does not pay dividend the shareholders leave it. Behind this apparent unfaithfulness of the shareholders is a deeper wisdom: The shareholders cannot be sure that what the management says about future profits and dividends kept within the firm and not paid off is true. They can secondly not be sure about the future since the whole economic situation might change in the next three years and the profits kept in the firm for three years will be lost in the fourth year. In this case the shareholder will not gain anything from waiting.[12]

The emphasis of the shareholder value approach on shareholder value in every year corresponds to the shorter time horizon in rendering investments profitable in capitalist democratic societies. This shorter time horizon seems to be desirable also from an ethical perspective. It is not obvious at the first glance that it can be efficient to favor the short term although decision makers are usually leaning towards short-termism and everything that supports long-term investment seems to have a higher ethical value. It is, nevertheless, reasonable to insist on paying-off investment in every period. The example of undemocratic, non-capitalist societies demonstrates that in these societies the population has very often been cheated by justifying present sacrifices in welfare by promising increased wealth in the future. Stalin, for example, had engineers decaptivated that told him that certain projects of large investment in the North of Russia or Sibiria would never be profitable. Since he disliked this forecast he had its conveyors killed.

Beyond the cruel demanding and enforcing of sacrifices for the future by terror, this case is interesting for the time perspective on investments, for the sacrifices that one is expected to make for one's investment and for the ethical relevance of this question. In a democratic capitalist society the population and the investors expect a return on their investment within a comparably short time period. An investment that cannot secure its profitability in the short run will not be made. This recommendation supported by the shareholder value criterion is not only economically efficient but also ethically legitimate for wealthy societies. Whether it holds equally true for developing economies is another question that cannot be answered here.

The other side effect of this compulsion to pay dividend in every year induced by the shareholder value criterion is that the formation of a monopoly or market controlling position in the market is rendered more difficult. If the shareholders can force the managers to pay dividends and not to keep profits within the company to form reserves or equity and if the shareholders use the profits for consumption and not for reinvestment in shares in the same company, it will be more difficult for the firm to grow and to dominate and control its market.

VII. Shareholder value as indirect intention

One of the difficulties of the shareholder value approach is that it makes profit maximization or shareholder value maximization a goal that is ethically not questioned anymore. From the point of view of business ethics, however, the pursuit of profit is only legitimate, as is the pursuit of any finite goal, under ethical constraints and in the order of goals the human person adopts for herself. Not every pursuit and formation of profit is accepted by the law as well as by ethics. Profits from insider trading, e.g., are a form of profit formation that might even be efficient from the point of view of allocation in the economist's judgement. Profits from insider trading are, however, prohibited by the law since they contradict central principles of law, particularly the principle of equality before the law. There are also other forms of profit and kinds of profit formation that are neither legally nor ethically acceptable, like all forms of profit that arise from corruption. It is, therefore, obvious that shareholder value maximization is illegitimate where bribery or other forms of corruption are used to achieve it.

The constraints on kinds of profit maximization do not only concern the law, although the legal restrictions are the most essential. They concern also the ethical norms since there are always lags in the development of the law. Usually ethical norms lead the formation of legal norms. As an example insider trading in the stock exchange was declared to be unethical before it had become illegal and sanctioned by penal law. It was declared unethical by the informal rules of the ethics of the professions, of the stock market brokers' and bankers' professions.

The discussion about the purpose of the firm and the right relationship of means and ends is a methodological approach typical to the natural right tradition. The idea that the firm has something like a "natural" purpose and that this purpose ought not to be made a means for another end will be subject to criticism from theories of subjective value that claim that the human is free to set her purposes and that there is nothing like a natural purpose and, therefore, also not anything like a "natural" purpose of the firm.

There is some justification in this argument insofar as a person that is not interested in the purpose of the firm per se, but only interested in maximizing her shareholder value, might be more successful and do more good than a person that is very much striving for the purpose of the firm and not interested in profit but in the end does not achieve fulfilling the purpose of the firm, producing a good product, and the purpose of high shareholder value, whereas the other person might have intended to maximize the shareholder value as her goal only, but realizes the "social good" of the good product as well.

At this point, two distinctions are useful: the distinction between individual and social ethics and the distinction between one-purpose motivation and multi-purpose motivation.

Social ethics cannot compel economic agents to accept its concept of the order of purposes and to make it their own order of purposes but it can show that for the social institutions and the ethical foundations of the institutions it is better if the right order of goals is followed although the economic agents within these socio-ethical institutions cannot be denied the freedom to reverse their order of goals. The natural right tradition does not force everyone to have the same order of goals but it can justify and give good reasons what the right order of purposes should be and why the institutions should adopt and propagate this order of goals.

The fact that better results are sometimes achieved by bad motives and bad results are sometimes achieved instead of good motives does not discredit the nexus between desirable motives and desirable results. It may be better in single cases to achieve good results by bad motives than to achieve bad results by good motives. For the justification of social norms, motives, and expectations of results, for the theory of social ethics, this fact does not change the observation that it is even better to achieve good consequences with good motives. Although it might sometimes be better to realize good results with bad motives than bad results with good motives, the best state, seen from the point of view of social ethics, is

still the one in which good results are realized by good motives.

The idea that the maximum efficiency and common good of society is reached if the individuals in the economy follow only their abstract concept of maximizing their own profit and shareholder value is linked to the Protestant idea of the incapability of the sinner to do the good. It is thereby also linked to the concept of original sin. The Protestant idea of social coordination is that since the human is so much distorted by original sin he or she cannot intend the common good as such. The common good can, therefore, only be reached by the invisible hand using the individuals' inevitably selfish intentions and needs for its good. The idea is particularly strong in Lutheran thought where the human is considered to be so fallen that his or her will is a slave's will, being the slave of the human's own selfishness.[13] Nothing good can be expected from the direct intention of the human will. Society must be instituted in such a way that it arranges by its institutions that the common good is intended only as the indirect purpose or *dolus eventualis* or even as an effect not intended at all but only realized as the side effect in the pursuit of another selfish goal which is all that the fallen human is capable of.

If shareholder value maximization is made the first purpose of the firm, the firm's common good, the good product and the fulfillment of the stakeholders' stakes in the firm, is made the side effect of the direct intention or *dolus directus* to the realization of the private good, to shareholder value maximization.

In Protestant thinking, this is considered to be the best solution possible. Catholic social thought considers this situation to be the second best solution, second best even under conditions of original sin which makes the human selfish and being interested in profit maximization only and not in the purpose of the firm itself. Catholic social thought considers this situation still to be a *second* best situation. It is only the second best solution since the best solution is possible even under conditions of original sin. Although the human is affected by original sin and, therefore, selfish and lazy, human action is still capable of the direct intention to the good. In contrast to the Lutheran concept of original sin which takes the human to be incapable of doing the good by intention, the Catholic understanding of original sin holds that the human is able to do the good intentionally even under conditions of original sin. In the case of the purpose of the firm, this implies that the human individual is still able to adopt the purpose of the common good of this community, the purpose of the firm, in addition to his or her intention to maximize self-interest or shareholder value.

Catholic thought suggests that the human person is a sinner but that this sinner is still able to do the good although the institutional framework, in the case at hand, the firm, must take into account the sinful human nature. Sharholder value maximization being the second best solution implies that the owners of the firm must pursue the purpose of the firm and their own purpose of shareholder value maximization at the same time and that they should consider the first purpose of the firm to be the good it produces.

The distinction between a one-purpose and a multipurpose motivation comes in here. Shareholder value as a control principle of the firm should not imply that the owner of the firm knows only one purpose, the maximization of shareholder value, but that he or she pursues the purpose of the firm and his or her own purpose of shareholder value maximization at the same time.

The motivational structure of the entrepreneur and manager can be described by the concept of the "overdetermination of action", a concept that is also close to the understanding of the structure of human motivation in common good thinking. The concept of the overdetermination of action, of the *Überdeterminiertheit der Handlung*, was originally introduced by Sigmund Freud.[14] Freud developed this idea in his interpretation of dreams: Our dreams are over-determined by several motives overlying and overlapping each other. Not only our dreams but also our actions and even our economic actions are overdetermined by several motives.

The concept of the overdetermination and of overlapping determinants of economic action is more suitable for describing the firm's and the shareholder's purpose than the concept of the

inversion of intentions and purposes and of making the purpose of the firm to be only the means for shareholder value maximization. Good shareholder value should be the side-effect of a good product and firm, rather than a good product and a good firm being the side-effect of shareholder value maximization.

Notes

[1] A. A. Alchian and H. Demsetz: 1977, 'Production, Information Costs, and Economic Organization', in A. A. Alchian, *Economic Forces at Work* (Liberty Press, Indianapolis), pp. 73–110.

[2] This point is also stressed in Lee A. Tavis: 'The Moral Issue in Allocating Corporate Resources. Shareholders Versus Stakeholders', in M. Naughton (ed.), *The Nature and Purpose of the Business Organization within Catholic Social Thought*, forthcoming.

[3] Luis de Molina: 1602, *De iustitia et iure* (Madrid). – Cf. P. Koslowski: 1982, 6th ed. 1998, *Ethik des Kapitalismus* (Mohr Siebeck, Tübingen). English translation: 1996, *Ethics of Capitalism and Critique of Sociobiology. Two Essays* with a Comment by James M. Buchanan (Springer, Berlin, New York, Tokyo).

[4] Gustav Radbruch: 8th ed. 1973, *Rechtsphilosophie* (Philosophy of Right) (Koehler, Stuttgart), p. 114.

[5] R. E. Freeman: 1984, *Strategic Management: A Stakeholder Approach* (Pitman, Boston), and R. E. Freeman: 1994, 'The Politics of Stakeholder Theory: Some Future Directions', *Business Ethics Quaterly* **4**, 413ff. – Compare also David W. Lutz: 1998, 'Kritik des Shareholder-Ansatzes und des Stakeholder-Ansatzes' (Critique of the Shareholder Approach and of the Stakeholder Approach), in P. Koslowski (ed.), *Shareholder Value und die Kriterien des Unternehmenserfolgs* (Shareholder Value and the Criteria of the Success of the Firm) (Physica, Heidelberg), pp. 187–200.

[6] M. C. Jensen and W. H. Meckling: 1979, 'The Theory of the Firm: Managerial Behavior, Agency Costs, and Ownership Structure', in K. Brunner (ed.), *Economics and Social Institutions* (Martinus Nijhoff, Boston), pp. 163–231.

[7] Cf. P. Koslowski: 1997, *Ethik der Banken und der Börse* (The Ethics of Banking and the Stock Exchange) (Mohr Siebeck, Tübingen). Abridged English version: P. Koslowski: 1995, 'The Ethics of Banking', in A. Argandoña (ed.), *The Ethical Dimension of Financial Institutions and Markets* (Springer, Berlin, New York, Tokyo).

[8] Cf. for this principle G. Schmoller: 1881, 'Die Gerechtigkeit in der Volkswirthschaft' (Justice in the Economy), *Jahrbücher für Gesetzgebung, Verwaltung und Volkswirthschaft im Deutschen Reich* **5**, 19–54. – Cf. for the Historical School of economics P. Koslowski: 1991, *Gesellschaftliche Koordination. Eine Theorie der Marktwirtschaft* (Societal Coordination. A Theory of the Market Economy) (Mohr Siebeck, Tübingen); P. Koslowski (ed.): 1995, reprinted 1997, *The Theory of Ethical Economy in the Historical School. Wilhelm Roscher, Lorenz von Stein, Gustav Schmoller, Wilhelm Dilthey and Contemporary Theory* (Springer, Berlin, New York, Tokyo); and P. Koslowski (ed.): 1997, *Methodology of the Social Sciences, Ethics, and Economics in the Newer Historical School. From Max Weber and Rickert to Sombart and Rothacker* (Springer, Berlin, New York, Tokyo).

[9] Cf. 'Niederlage für Daimler-Kritiker Wenger' (Defeat for Daimler's critic Wenger), in *Süddeutsche Zeitung* **185**, 13 August 1998, p. 17, as well as 'Wenger unterliegt Daimler' and comment by Mathias Philip: 'Aktienoptionen' (Share Options), in *Hannoversche Allgemeine Zeitung*, Hannover, **188**, 13 August 1998, p. 9. The comment takes position for Wenger against Daimler-Benz. See also *Frankfurter Allgemeine Zeitung* of the same day.

[10] Cf. "Ich besitze keine einzige Porsche-Aktie' Der Manager hält wenig von Aktienoptionen zur Steigerung des Firmenwertes' ('I do not own a single Porsche share' The manager does not believe in share options as a means to increase the firm's value), in *Süddeutsche Zeitung*, München, **41**, 20 February 2000, p. 28.

[11] A. Rappaport: 1986, *Creating Shareholder Value. The New Standard for Business Performance* (The Free Press, New York), pp. 25ff.

[12] Cf. Günter H. Roth: 1988, 'Shareholder Value und Dividendenausschüttung' (Shareholder Value and Paying-off Dividends), in P. Koslowski (ed.), *Shareholder Value und die Kriterien des Unternehmenserfolgs*, op. cit.

[13] Cf. Martin Luther, *De servo arbitrio*.

[14] S. Freud: 1900, *Die Traumdeutung* (The Interpretation of Dreams) (S. Fischer, Frankfurt am Main) 1982.

Forschungsinstitut für Philosophie Hannover,
Gerberstrasse 26,
D-30169 Hannover.
E-mail: peter.koslowski@t-online.de

Ethical Business and Investment: A Model for Business and Society

Rodger Spiller

ABSTRACT. Two key questions lie at the heart of the business challenge for business ethics: is it possible for business and investors to do well while doing good; and if so, how can this be achieved? This paper adopts an international investment perspective to address these questions. It demonstrates that it is possible for business and investors to achieve a triple bottom line of environmental, social and financial performance.

A new integrated model of Ethical Business including an Ethical Scorecard performance measurement technology is presented based on international ethical investment criteria and case studies of businesses rated highly by ethical investors. Ethical Performance Scores are presented for these businesses and New Zealand business. Examples from New Zealand are presented to illustrate the Ethical Scorecard and ethical business practice. The model and scoring system provide a basis for international benchmarking of ethical business to assist investors, managers and researchers.

Rodger Spiller is Director of the New Zealand Centre for Business Ethics, which works with the Auckland University of Technology, Auckland University, Manukau Institute of Technology and private sector support to encourage business ethics research, education and practice. Rodger is Managing Director of the personal investment advisory and financial planning firm, Money Matters (NZ) Ltd, a Certified Financial Planner and Chartered Accountant. Rodger's PhD is in business ethics and investment. He has researched ethical business practices in Australasia, the US and Europe. He is Executive Director of New Zealand Businesses for Social Responsibility and a Director of Transparency International (NZ).

In search of ethical business

Ethical Business (EB) philosophy emphasises "doing well while doing good" and redefines the meaning of corporate responsibility: "Only if business learns that to do well it has to do good can we hope to tackle the major social challenges facing developed societies today" (Drucker, 1984, p. 55). Within EB, business is urged to take "responsibility for the whole". Harman (1990) explains why this is necessary:

> Business has become, in this last half-century, the most powerful institution on the planet. The dominant institution in any society needs to take responsibility for the whole. This is a new role for business, not yet well understood and accepted. (Harman, 1990, p. 12)

In 1991 Kanter developed this theme by posing some challenging "root questions" about what guides business decisions:

> Is wealth production really the goal of business, as some economists say, or is wealth a by-product, an incentive en route to other ends? When a corporate mission statement contains only one goal – to create shareholder value – has an essential ingredient been lost? (Kanter, 1991, p. 10)

Her conclusion reflects the essence of EB:

> Money should never be separated from mission. It is an instrument, not an end. Detached from values, it may indeed be the root of all evil. Linked effectively to social purpose, it can be the root of opportunity. (Kanter, 1991, p. 10)

Similar questions and the concomitant search for models of EB prompted the establishment in

 Journal of Business Ethics **27**: 149–160, 2000.
© 2000 *Kluwer Academic Publishers. Printed in the Netherlands.*

1990 of The Business Enterprise Trust, whose US Trustees included the Board Chairs of businesses including Johnson and Johnson, IBM and Hewlett Packard, and such noted academics as Peter Drucker and Robert Reich. The Trust placed advertisements in the *New York Times* and *Wall Street Journal*, asking readers to "Tell us about the business decision you most admire":

> It's one of the great untold stories in business – the success of individuals and companies who know there's more to good business than next quarter's bottom line:
>
> - Employees who aren't afraid to show moral courage and act on principle.
> - Entrepreneurs willing to take risks for a socially visionary product or service.
> - Managers who have pioneered enlightened business practices.
> - Investors and executives with a long-term perspective and commitment to the commonweal.
>
> If you have encountered such acts of courage, integrity or social vision in business we invite you to nominate them for one of the 1990 Business Enterprise Awards. . . . These stories become models for all of us – and for the next generation of business leaders. They help shape the future of American business. (Hanson, 1990, p. 1)

This paper responds to the call from leading business people and academics such as those involved with the Business Enterprise Trust for more research defining and illustrating EB. This is done through adopting an international investment perspective and linking this with management and business ethics. A particular focus is ethical investment (EI) in which investors are constantly judging the environmental, social, and financial performance of business and considering this triple bottom line in their investment decision making. Indeed, EI researchers make an award similar to that of the Business Enterprise Award whenever they assess a business as having satisfied their investment criteria.

The EI community has identified a similar need to that articulated by the Business Enterprise Trust. United States socially responsible investment (the US term for EI) researcher Steven Lydenberg (1996) called for

. . . more work by the socially responsible investment community on the important question of how to define more explicitly what we all instinctively recognise as a socially responsible company. This daunting task of putting all the pieces together into a cohesive whole still lies ahead for those who would reimagine and redefine the relationship between corporations and society. (Lyndenberg, 1996, p. 76)

This paper tackles this "daunting task" by integrating and expanding the management and EI approaches. To date there have been minimal connections between these two worlds, which is unfortunate because the EI perspective has the potential to make a significant contribution in assisting management theorists and practitioners. The model and examples presented here can provide a framework for recognising, understanding, implementing and evaluating EB, thereby increasing the quality and quantity of EB. Before presenting some findings from my search for EB I firstly address the financial objection that prevents many business practitioners and investors from seriously considering EB.

Ethical rewards and the triple bottom line

Many investors believe that EB provides superior financial performance. Benefits that a company might experience include: increasing productivity and loyalty of employees; improving customer sales and loyalty; growing supplier commitment; improving environmental quality; and reducing legislative demands with strengthening community and government relations. Management quality can increase and when combined with enhanced relationships with stakeholders, can improve financial performance for shareholders.

Despite these potential benefits critics argue that EI and EB must involve a reduction in financial return and/or an increase in risk. Many business practitioners and investors who believe that environmental and social responsibility are a distraction from the business of business, which they see as being solely the task of making profits, share this view. The belief has led to a tendency for EI and EB to be dismissed. The EI experience provides valuable insights to address this objection.

The most comprehensive and ongoing guide to the performance of EI in the US is the Domini Social Index (DSI) created by leading EI research organisation Kinder, Lydenberg, Domini and Co., Inc. (KLD). The DSI comprises 400 companies and is designed to represent the market of stocks that most ethical investors buy from, thereby acting as a standard by which the performance of ethically screened portfolios can be measured. It can be compared with the S&P 500, which represents the market of large capitalisation stocks most investors buy from. The performance of the DSI has demonstrated that there is no cost to EI (KLD, 1996; Luck and Pillote, 1993). This conclusion is consistent with those of Hamilton, Jo and Statman (1993) in the US and Mallin, Saadouni and Briston (1995) in the UK who found no significant difference between the performance of ethical funds and that of conventional funds.

Providing financial support for the view that EB outperforms conventional business, Herremans, Akathaporn and McInnes (1993) found that UK socially responsible companies have higher stock market returns, and the authors suggested that ethical investing strategies are fundamentally sound since their selection criteria help to effectively lower investment risk. More recently, Russo and Fouts (1997) found that environmental performance and economic performance were positively correlated in the US, with environmentally conscious portfolios achieving *better* returns compared both with the S&P 500 index and those companies considered to be not environmentally conscious. My own analysis of the performance of the NZSE 40 (the index of the 40 largest companies listed on the New Zealand Stock Exchange) and an ethical portfolio screened for the conventional "sin" stocks of alcohol, gambling, and tobacco showed that there was no significant difference between the two portfolios for the five years to 31 March 1998.

The international experience suggests that there need not be a cost to investing ethically. Accordingly, it can be concluded that it is possible for investors to "do well while doing good", achieving a triple bottom line of environmental, social, and financial wealth creation. The major financial objection to EI and EB has therefore been resolved.

The "Four P's of ethical business"

Having shown that business can do well while doing good the next question is how can this be achieved? My approach to this question was two-pronged: on the one hand to research companies internationally rated most highly by EI researchers, and, on the other, to review a wide range of literature from texts on ethics through to accountancy. My findings are summarised in what I refer to as "the Four P's of ethical business": *purpose, principles, practices, and performance measurement*. This model is illustrated in Figure 1 below.

The purpose of EB is to create environmental, social, and financial wealth, thereby making a positive contribution to the environment and society in a financially responsible manner. The principles that guide the EB include fairness, caring, honesty, and courage. EB practices address stakeholder concerns – such stakeholders include the community, the environment, employees, customers, suppliers, and shareholders. EB performance measurement involves accounting for environmental and social as well as financial performance. This involves qualitative as well as quantitative measures and utilising both stakeholder perceptions and company data to determine performance in terms of the triple bottom line.

Purpose

The EB aim to create environmental and social as well as financial wealth occurs most explicitly in those businesses that respond to the challenge made by Drucker (1984) for business to identify and respond to environmental and social needs by transforming these problems into opportunities.

The approach recommended by Drucker (1984) goes beyond the views that business should "do well in order to do good" or that

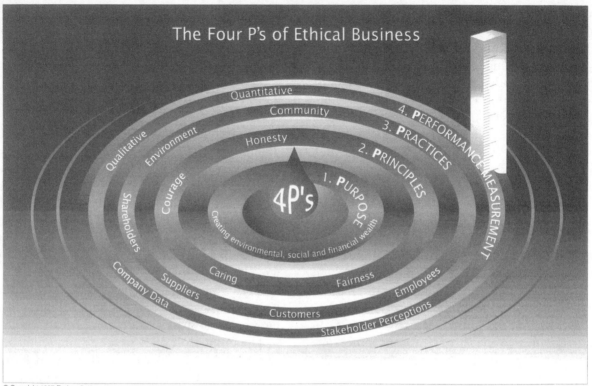

Figure 1.

business social responsibility can be achieved through simply donating money. For him, social responsibility extends from the goods and services created through to the way in which these are produced, and beyond. A key challenge here is to recognise the relationship between the business and the environmental and social problems that the business could assist in addressing. Mitroff, Mason and Pearson (1994) describe this as a spiritual activity and encourage business to pursue "world service and spirituality". They maintain that the essence of spirituality in organisations is

> to encourage and allow everyone involved with an organisation to draw his or her own unique spiritual connections between the resources of that organisation and an important social or environmental problem that those resources could help alleviate. (Mitroff, Mason and Pearson, 1994, p. 81)

EB practitioners and ethical investors argue that profit is a means to an end rather than an end in itself. O'Toole (1985) noted that "profits are like

breathing. You must breathe to live: but you don't live to breathe." In other words, focusing solely on profit maximisation fails to provide a sufficiently meaningful purpose for business and investors to commit to, and fails to recognise a wish to assist other people and the planet.

Principles

The principles that ethical investors want to see reflected in the businesses in which they invest can be deduced from an analysis of Aristotelian virtues. While there is room for debate about which virtues to select and what they should be called, the selection that follows provides a sketch of what a plausible list might look like.

- *Honesty* lies at the heart of the functioning of business, which is built on a free-enterprise model of individual choice and liberty. Informed choice and a properly functioning market each require honesty. A lack of honesty impacts not just on the participants who have been deceived in a transaction but also on the business system that relies on an ability to make mutually beneficial agreements (Solomon, 1992).

- The virtue of *fairness* or justice implies that a company has a sense of value, being willing to exchange value for value in a market that is inherently subjective (Solomon, 1992). It also involves a company being concerned to have fairness characterise all of its relationships, including those with society and the environment. Justice was considered by both Aristotle and Plato to be the basic virtue. As "fairness", it is the essential element in keeping the members of an organisation and everyone concerned with it (in other words all the stakeholders) committed to and supportive of the enterprise. Without this commitment and support business cannot function effectively.

- *Caring* is a fundamental attitude within the model EB. It involves a genuine concern and attention to the well-being of others and the environment. Solomon (1992) describes caring as the "glue" of organisational life – an attitude that provides employees and all other stakeholders with a real sense of connection to, and support from, the business. This in turn provides a strong bond with the business and a reason for "sticking with it" and also caring about its well-being (Solomon, 1992, p. 226).

- *Courage* was the first virtue listed by Aristotle. This meant courage in combat, which can be equated to the courage displayed by EB practitioners who refuse to accept that the only social responsibility of investors and business is profit maximisation. Describing courage as the essence of greatness, O'Toole (1985) maintains that this virtue not only serves business and society but is also critical for the survival of capitalism.

Practices

It is at the level of business practices that the true test of EB occurs as practices reflect the applica-

tion of purpose and principles. While it is relatively easy for a business to produce a statement of purpose and principles, it is far more challenging to implement it.

To guide implementation, I have identified ten key business practices for each of the six main stakeholder groups: community; environment; employees; customers; suppliers, and shareholders. By necessity many of these practices summarise various facets, for example "Fulfilling work" includes "employee work/life balance". These practices are drawn from applying the EI perspective to an evaluation of EB case studies and business literature. As would be expected in an emerging field, the list of 60 practices summarised below is neither exhaustive, nor uncontroversial. However, it does provide a starting point, a menu from which companies can choose, preferably in conjunction with their stakeholders, the areas on which to focus.

1. Community
1.1. Generous financial donations
1.2. Innovative giving
1.3. Support for education and job training programmes
1.4. Direct involvement in community projects and affairs
1.5. Community volunteer programmes
1.6. Support for the local community
1.7. Campaigning for environmental and social change
1.8. An employee-led approach to philanthropy
1.9. Efficient and effective community activity
1.10. Disclosure of environmental and social performance

2. Environment
2.1. Environmental policies, organisation and management
2.2. Materials policy of reduction, reuse and recycling
2.3. Monitoring, minimising and taking responsibility for releases to the environment
2.4. Waste management
2.5. Energy conservation
2.6. Effective emergency response

2.7. Public dialogue and disclosure
2.8. Product stewardship
2.9. Environmental requirements for suppliers
2.10. Environmental audits

3.   Employees
3.1. Fair remuneration
3.2. Effective communication
3.3. Learning and development opportunities
3.4. Fulfilling work
3.5. A healthy and safe work environment
3.6. Equal employment opportunities
3.7. Job security
3.8. Competent leadership
3.9. Community spirit
3.10. Social mission integration

4.   Customers
4.1. Industry-leading quality programme
4.2. Value for money
4.3. Truthful promotion
4.4. Full product disclosure
4.5. Leadership in research and development
4.6. Minimal packaging
4.7. Rapid and respectful responses to customer comments, complaints and concerns
4.8. Customer dialogue
4.9. Safe products
4.10. Environmentally and socially responsible production and product composition

5.   Suppliers
5.1. Develop and maintain long-term purchasing relationships
5.2. Clear expectations
5.3. Pay fair prices and bills according to terms agreed upon
5.4. Fair and competent handling of conflicts and disputes
5.5. Reliable anticipated purchasing requirements
5.6. Encouragement to provide innovative suggestions
5.7. Assist suppliers to improve their environmental and social performance
5.8. Utilise local suppliers
5.9. Sourcing from minority-owned suppliers
5.10. Inclusion of an environmental and social element in the selection of suppliers

6.   Shareholders
6.1. Good rate of long-term return to shareholders
6.2. Disseminate comprehensive and clear information
6.3. Encourage staff ownership of shares
6.4. Develop and build relationships with shareholders
6.5. Clear dividend policy and payment of appropriate dividends
6.6. Corporate governance issues are well managed
6.7. Access to company's directors and senior managers
6.8. Annual report and accounts provide a comprehensive picture of the company's overall performance
6.9. Clear long-term business strategy
6.10. Open communication with the financial community

Performance measurement

Internationally there is a growing demand from stakeholders for businesses to report on their performance in terms of those issues that have an impact on the stakeholders. This can be seen in the development of ethical accounting and the work of the Institute of Social and Ethical AccountAbility.

Ethical accounting requires company participation however many companies are reluctant to publish such reports. This presents a problem for the EI community, which needs to understand and provide investors with a picture of a company's ethical performance. This problem can be addressed using my concept of an Ethical Scorecard. The Ethical Scorecard can be a transition step for a company prior to the publication of a full ethical accounting statement or where such accounting exists the Scorecard can be used either by the company or EI researchers to present this information to investors.

The concept of a "Scorecard" has been popularised by Kaplan and Norton (1996) authors of *The Balanced Scorecard*. The Balanced Scorecard seeks to provide managers with the information they require by translating the company's mission and strategy into performance objectives and measures, along with targets and initiatives in terms of what Kaplan and Norton describe as four balanced perspectives: financial, customers, internal business processes, and learning and growth.

The Ethical Scorecard extends the Balanced Scorecard focus on satisfying shareholders and customers to take account of the other primary stakeholders in terms of employees, suppliers, community, and the environment. While the Balanced Scorecard focuses on how the company appears to its shareholders and customers, the Ethical Scorecard incorporates the perceptions of all stakeholders.

The company's purpose and vision is central to and the starting point for The Ethical Scorecard. Purpose is considered in terms of creating wealth through achieving a triple bottom line of environmental, social and financial performance.

Ethical principles are highlighted within The Ethical Scorecard. These principles can be derived from a company's Code of Ethics and where this does not exist can be created, preferably through a process of dialogue with stakeholders. Ethical principles provide an important navigational tool to guide action.

The primary focus of The Ethical Scorecard is the company's practices. These can be categorised in terms of the six main stakeholder groups and considered in terms of the inventory of 60 best practices that I created based on international case studies and investment analysis and which are presented above.

The Ethical Scorecard can be prepared at varying levels of depth. It can simply be an account of publicly available information regarding quantitative measures, from the level of donations disclosed in the company's accounts to its financial results, and qualitative assessments such as stakeholder perceptions of company performance included in media reports. Additional research with stakeholders can strengthen this data.

Company involvement is preferable. This can range from the provision of information to external researchers, through to a complete embracing of the Ethical Scorecard and ethical

accounting technology and the utilisation of this as a management tool. The greater the involvement of the company, the greater the potential for it to obtain the benefits offered from measuring performance in terms of the triple bottom line. The Ethical Scorecard offers a diagnostic tool and strategy for integrating various management technologies aimed at improving the company's performance from quality management through to employee satisfaction tools.

The Ethical Scorecard includes assessments of the significance of company performance relative to other companies. This benchmarking concept was applied by Kirk Hanson of the Stanford Business School in his "Social Evaluation" of The Body Shop. Introducing the report, he noted that:

> The company requested an examination of its social performance on those dimensions addressed in its Mission Statement and Trading Charter, but authorised me to include any other dimensions which I felt were critical to an assessment of its social impact and the fulfilment of its mission. . . . I sought to evaluate The Body Shop against comparable companies, against the company's own values and goals, against the practices of the most outstanding companies ("best practice"), and against the company's claims regarding its social performance. (Hanson, 1995, pp. 1, 3)

The terminology used in the Ethical Scorecard is similar to that applied by Boston based investment research firm Kinder, Lydenberg and Domini in its rating of "strengths and concerns". I have assigned numeric ratings to assess each of the sixty practices to obtain an overall quantitative Ethical Performance Score (EPS) that summarises the Ethical Scorecard. A major strength is recorded as 2, a strength as 1, no strengths or concerns, or equal strengths and concerns, or no information as 0, a concern as −1 and a major concern as −2. The perfect EPS is 120 where each of the sixty practices is a major strength. Conversely the worst EPS is −120 where each of the sixty practices is a major concern. A neutral score is 0.

The model practices represent the ideal company from an EI perspective and what the EB case study companies, particularly The Body

Shop and Ben & Jerry's state that they aspire to achieve. These companies are not perfect nor do they claim to be. Perfection is not a realistic expectation. What ethical investors do expect is a positive score and continuous improvement. In some cases information about these practices was not available from the reports provided by the EB companies. This highlights a shortfall between the EI reporting requirements and existing EB reporting. The Ethical Scorecard addresses this shortcoming by integrating the EI perspective with EB.

EPS ratings for each of the international case study companies are presented in Table I. These ratings are not presented as a definitive statement of the ethical performance of the companies, but simply report the findings based on the practices information on which this research is based.

The EPS results reflect the pioneering work of The Body Shop and Ben & Jerry's. The similarity in their scores may be partly attributed to their sharing ideas and insights regarding NPB initiatives. The EPS results for Blackmores and Lend Lease indicate a solid basis for the positive regard in which ethical investors hold these companies.

The Ethical Scorecard can be used as a tool for identifying companies whose practices are exemplary. This process is reflected in business ethics awards, which have an important role to play in creating improved business practice, by recognising leading companies whose practices provide examples for others to learn from. It is being used in the New Zealand Business Ethics Awards, which are being modelled on The Business Enterprise Trust.

Ultimately, the Ethical Scorecard has the ability not only to assist investors but also to provide a major contribution to company management wishing to improve business environmental, social, and financial performance. It provides a valuable tool for operationalising ethics and value-based leadership.

Ethical business in New Zealand

This section presents the EPS for the NZSE 40 index of the largest 40 companies on the New Zealand sharemarket and provides examples of one practice from each stakeholder grouping from the Ethical Scorecard of the NZSE 40. This analysis is based on an extensive search of a range of information sources including companies, media and special interest groups. The focus was the 1996 reporting year supplemented by information from the recent history prior to 1996 of the NZSE 40 companies.

The EPS for the NZSE 40 was 5. In percentage terms this equates to 52%. While there is substantial room for improvement the NZSE 40 EPS and Ethical Scorecard, examples from which are presented below, reflects a wide range of positive practices. The highest ranked company was Fisher & Paykel which at an EPS of 32 or 63% was clearly in first position. This performance is similar to the international case study companies. The examples below illustrate some of the Fisher & Paykel practices along with other best practices from the NZSE 40.

TABLE I
Ethical performance scores

Company	Stakeholder group ethical performance scores						Total EPS
	Community	Environment	Employees	Customers	Suppliers	Shareholders	
The Body Shop	13	11	11	3	6	0	44
Ben & Jerry's	14	10	7	8	3	1	43
Blackmores	5	7	7	9	1	4	33
Lend Lease	7	6	8	3	1	5	30

Community – innovative giving

- Carter Holt Harvey co-sponsored "Habitat for Humanity New Zealand", an interest-free home ownership scheme launched in South Auckland for low-income families. Habitat for Humanity was sponsored to build 10 homes in Otara which were to be sold for about $70 000 each and will also build a further 20 homes throughout the country. Habitat for Humanity New Zealand purchased the land and the sponsoring companies supplied materials and labour. Social agents welcomed the initiative, saying market rentals had made state homes unaffordable (*New Zealand Herald*, 22 June 1995).
- St Lukes Group supported the Courageous Kids Awards promotion. Developed by the company's Plaza Pakuranga in partnership with the local newspaper, *Howick and Pakuranga Times*, it involved nomination by the community of children who have overcome great odds, or faced a difficult challenge. All children were presented with certificates and awards. This project has attracted nation-wide media attention (St Lukes Group, 1996, p. 13).
- Ports of Auckland is a major supporter of youth development through its ongoing commitment to the Spirit of Adventure Trust and sailing programmes based at Westhaven Marina, including an ongoing commitment to sailing for the visually impaired (Ports of Auckland, 1996, p. 20).

Environment – recycling

- Fisher & Paykel has a recycling plant for its old appliances, separating out the reusable and recyclable components. Established in 1993 in conjunction with a major retailer, the operation involves selling the recyclable raw materials and disposing of the rest in keeping with an agreement with the regional authority. It currently strips around 45 appliances daily using trade-ins from retailers and in-house factory rejects. The plastics salvaged from refrigerators and freezers are now reused as vacuum-formed bases for packaging new appliances (*Consumer*, 1995, p. 31; *The Independent*, 11 June 1993).
- Through Milburn's oil recovery programme, used oil, historically land-filled, illegally dumped or burned in an uncontrollable manner, is being used as a partial replacement for coal (a non-renewable resource) for fuelling the company's Westport Works cement kilns. The result is disposal of used oil in an environmentally sound manner and extraction of the full energy value (Milburn New Zealand, 1996, p. 6; *The New Zealand Herald*, 15 September 1994; *The Merchant*, August 1995; *The New Zealand Manufacturer*, March 1996).

Employees – learning and development opportunities

- Fisher & Paykel's focus on training has assured it a high percentage of long-serving employees. Each task is analysed and the training required specified (*The Sunday Star*, 15 August 1993). Company policy encourages staff to become skilled in a range of tasks such as problem solving, leadership, and quality improvement. This is also part of the composite agreement between Fisher & Paykel and the 11 unions, which rewards employees for their occupational skills, the number of different jobs they can do and their involvement in improvement activities (*New Zealand Business*, July 1992).
- Fisher & Paykel's training is mainly carried out on-the-job, two hours' training per week allocated to each employee (*Export News*, 1994, 1995). All employees are reviewed at least once a year and some more often (*The Sunday Star*, 15 August 1993). Near each processing line are team meeting areas with whiteboards which list members and details the skills they have attained or would like to attain.
- The Warehouse was given "a big tick for its commitment to staff training' by the

union (*Metro*, 1996, p. 79). The Warehouse induction programme consists of six modules that are completed in 10 hours over three months. Each Warehouse store has an in-store trainer responsible for on-the-job coaching and operational training. An area trainer – responsible for in-house training – supervises this position. The training programme includes units on customer service, loss prevention, security, health and safety, a two-stage management development component and area management development (*The Merchant*, December 1995).

Customers – environmentally and socially responsible production and product composition

- Fisher & Paykel's research and development expertise has responded to the environmental challenge of replacing chlorofluorocarbons (CFCs) traditionally used in refrigerators and considered to be a significant offender in atmospheric ozone breakdown. CFCs are used to make the polyurethane foam that insulates fridges and also serve as the liquid refrigerant which performs the cooling. In August 1994, Fisher & Paykel succeeded in eliminating CFC insulating foam and coolants from its fridges. It now uses a natural hydrocarbon called pentane, and the coolant R134a, both of which are non-ozone-damaging. Fisher & Paykel said that it is continuing to research and introduce ways to reduce energy use (*Consumer*, 1995, p. 31).
- St Lukes WestCity shopping centre is seeking to address public demands for environmentally friendly practices. The eco-initiative at the company's newly developed centre is a joint effort between the Waitakere City Council, the Ministry for the Environment and the St Lukes Group. Clean Retail is a scheme that aims to implement environmental practices with retailers in Waitakere City, using WestCity as a leader in encouraging other businesses to

take part. Based around the three Rs of environmental policy – reduce, reuse and recycle – Clean Retail includes such practices as reducing waste, energy and water use. Retailers are encouraged to use less packaging, recycle all waste, carry out environmental audits, set achievable goals, and monitor procedures on a regular basis (*New Zealand Hardware*, 1997). St Lukes has also demonstrated social responsibility by adopting a policy phasing out smoking in public areas in its seven shopping centres (*The New Zealand Herald*, 8 April 1994).

Suppliers – inclusion of an environmental and social element in the selection of suppliers

- Fisher & Paykel and The Warehouse are two New Zealand examples of companies that have publicly stated commitments in this area. Fisher & Paykel says that it only deals with suppliers that avoid "unnecessary harm to the environment" (*Consumer*, 1995, p. 31) and The Warehouse announced in 1995 that the company would buy no more French products until the nuclear issue had been resolved (*The Dominion*, 9 August 1995).

Shareholders – corporate governance issues are well managed

- Carter Holt Harvey discusses corporate governance issues in the company's 1996 Annual Report, with regard to the board of directors and the board audit committee, finance committee and management development and compensation committee. The report notes that the board of directors comprises nine non-executive directors (including the chairman) and one executive director (the chief executive officer and managing director) and that it normally meets eight times per year. The report states that the board is committed to a high standard of corporate governance. It also notes that policy areas such as health and safety, staff training and development, environment, ethical conduct and regulatory compliance are regarded as important (Carter Holt Harvey, 1996, p. 68).

- The St Lukes Group board of directors has nine members, eight of whom are non-executives. The Chairman is a non-executive director as required by company policy. The report notes that the board seeks to appoint directors with complementary experience and knowledge who will, at all times, act in accordance with the highest ethical standards and will contribute in a positive and constructive manner to the board discussions and debate (St Lukes Group, 1996, p. 29).

Conclusion

The international evidence shows that there need not be any cost to investing ethically and this has also been shown to be true in New Zealand. It can therefore be said that business and investors can do well while doing good.

The experience of EB coupled with the EI perspective provides guidance for achieving this. The "Four P's of Ethical Business" model provides a holistic and explicit account of ethical business, an Ethical Scorecard system, ethical inventory of ten best practices for each of the six main stakeholder groups and an ethical performance scoring system. This provide a basis for international benchmarking of ethical business performance to assist investors, managers and researchers to recognise, understand, implement and evaluate EB, thereby increasing the quality and quantity of EB.

Actual examples of EB, such as those provided from New Zealand business, provide illustrations and guidance for others. Key questions for every business in terms of ethical performance are: Where are we now? Where do we want to be? How will we get there? There can be little doubt that sustainable wealth creation for business and investors will increasingly rely upon a solid ethical foundation.

References

Carter Holt Harvey: 1996, *Annual Report* (Auckland).

Consumer: 1995, 'The Green Green Grass of Home' (May).

The Dominion: 1995, 'Major Retail Group Says "Non" to Goods' (August).

Drucker, P.: 1984, 'The New Meaning of Corporate Social Responsibility', *California Management Review* **262**, 53–62.

Export News: 1994, 'Communication Key in Relations Policy' (22 August).

Export News: 1995, 'Leadership Stresses Innovation at F&P' (5 May).

Hamilton, S., H. Jo and M. Statman: 1993, 'Doing Well While Doing Good', *Financial Analysts Journal* (November/December), 62–66.

Hanson, K.: 1990, *Tell Us About the Business Decision You Most Admire* (The Business Enterprise Trust Stanford, CA).

Hanson, K.: 1995, *Social Evaluation of the Body Shop International 1995* (The Body Shop International West Sussex, U.K.).

Harman, W.: 1990, *Why a World Business Academy?* (World Business Academy Burlingame, CA).

Herremans, I., P. Akathaporn and M. McInnes: 1993, 'An Investigation of Corporate Social Responsibility Reputation and Economic Performance', *Accounting, Organisations and Society* **18**(7, 8), 587–604.

The Independent: 1993, 'F&P Keeps One Jump Ahead of Design Pirates' (11 June).

Kanter, R. M.: 1991, 'Money is the Root . . .', *Harvard Business Review* (May/June), 9–10.

Kaplan, R. S. and D. P. Norton: 1996, *The Balanced Scorecard* (Harvard Business School Press, Boston, MA).

Kinder, P., S. D. Lydenberg and A. L. Domini (eds.): 1992, *The Social Investment Almanac* (Henry Holt and Company, New York).

Kinder, Lydenberg, Domini and Company: 1996, 'Press Release' (February 19).

KLD – see Kinder, Lydenberg (Domini and Company).

Lydenberg, S. D.: 1996, 'Companies with a Social Vision', *Business and Society Review* **97**, 75–76.

Luck, C. and N. Pilotte: 1993, 'Domini Social Index Performance', *The Journal of Investin* (Fall), 60–62.

Mallin, C. A., B. Saadouni and R. J. Briston: 1995, 'The Financial Performance of Ethical Investment Funds', *Journal of Business Finance and Accounting* **22**, 483.

The Merchant: 1995, 'Oil Recovery Programme' (1 August).

The Merchant: 1995, 'Education and Training: Keys to Professionalism' (December).

Metro: 1996, 'Is This Man a Saint?' (December).

Milburn New Zealand: 1996, *Annual Report* (Christchurch).

Mitroff, I. I., R. O. Mason and C. M. Pearson: 1994, *Frame Break: The Radical Redesign of American Business* (Jossey-Bass Publishers, San Francisco).

New Zealand Business: 1992, 'How to Measure Your Team's Performance' (July).

New Zealand Hardware: 1997, 'West City – New Zealand's First Eco Shopping Centre' (July).

The New Zealand Herald: 1994, 'Shopping Centres to Ban Smoking' (8 April).

The New Zealand Herald: 1994, 'Milburn Idea Used for Oil' (15 September).

The New Zealand Herald: 1995, 'Interest-free Home Plan' (22 June).

The New Zealand Manufacturer: 1996, 'Insulate your Pallet' (3 March).

New Zealand Refining: 1996, *Annual Report* (Whangarei).

O'Toole, J.: 1985, *Vanguard Management* (Doubleday, New York).

Ports of Auckland: 1996, *Annual Report* (Auckland).

Russo, M. V. and P. A. Fouts: 1997, 'A Resource-based Perspective on Corporate Environmental Performance and Profitability', *Academy of Management Journal* **40**(3), 534–559.

Solomon, R. C.: 1992, *Ethics and Excellence* (Oxford University Press, Oxford).

St Lukes Group: 1996, *Annual Report* (Auckland).

The Sunday Star: 1993, 'Rhetoric and Reality' (15 August).

New Zealand Centre for Business Ethics,
P.O. Box 250,
Auckland 1,
New Zealand
E-mail: rodger@moneymatters.co.nz

Reasons To Be Ethical: Self-Interest and Ethical Business

John Kaler

ABSTRACT. This paper examines the self-interested reasons that businesses can have for ethical behaviour. It distinguishes between economic and non-economic reasons and, among the latter, notes those connected with the self-esteem of managers. It offers a detailed typology of prudential reasons for ethical behaviour, laying particular stress on those to do with avoiding punishment by society for wrongdoing and, more particularly still, stresses the role of campaigning pressure groups within that particular category of reasons. It goes on to suggest that because of their occupation of the moral high ground, campaigning groups are well placed to damage the self-esteem of managers and that this is why those groups seem able to exert an influence that goes beyond their somewhat limited capacity to inflict economic damage upon businesses. The paper concludes with the suggestion that we may be witnessing a "virtuous spiral" whereby rising public expectations of morality in business lead to ever increasing moral commitments by business that then cause those expectations to rise still further.

KEY WORDS: ethical business, ethical consumerism, ethical investment, pressure groups, prudential reasons, public opinion, virtuous spiral

1. Introduction

There is a narrowly analytic and, as far as possible (see section 2), not very theoretical focus to this paper. It is not attempting to answer that

John Kaler is a Senior Lecturer in the University of Plymouth Business School, teaching business ethics, cultural issues in business, and jurisprudence. He is the co-author (with G. Chryssides) of An Introduction to Business Ethics *(Chapman & Hall, 1993; ITP, 1996 second edition forthcoming 2000) and of* Essentials of Business Ethics *(McGraw-Hill, 1996).*

perennial question "why be ethical?" (e.g., Singer, 1979, pp. 201–220). It is also not investigating the nature of reasons and their role in ethics (e.g., Smith, 1994).[1] What it *is* doing is attempting to explore the relationship between self-interest and ethical business practices through an examination of different sorts of prudential reasons for behaving ethically.[2]

What, given this focus on the particular, is not being investigated is that very general prudential reason for behaving ethically provided by what might be called the "instrumental" view of business ethics: the "good ethics is good business", "ethics pays" contention (Chryssides and Kaler, 1993, p. 27). Such a view is not necessarily false, but its investigation is a whole research programme in itself; one which has continued over the years and continues to be added to (see Price, 1997, pp. 261–263, for a survey of results from 1972 to 1997). Accordingly, it is not an issue which can be gone into here in addition to the more specific matters being investigated. Moreover, the investigation of these more specific matters is not even being presented as evidence for the truth of the instrumental view. It is no doubt correct that the various kinds of prudential reasons being investigated contribute to a situation in which it "pays to be ethical". But it is not, except perhaps in passing, the aim of this paper to investigate these reasons in order to assess the weight of their individual or collective contributions to that eventual end. Again, this would be a research programme in its own right; one to which this paper is merely helping lay the groundwork. If the paper has any aim beyond this ground laying, it is to suggest that prudential reasons, and in particular what I shall classify as the "negative external"

 Journal of Business Ethics **27**: 161–173, 2000.
© 2000 *Kluwer Academic Publishers. Printed in the Netherlands.*

variety (section 5.2), contribute to an unfolding process that is likely to increase the overall pressure on business to behave ethically (section 6). Such an increase will, of course, make it that much more true that "ethics pays". But what is being made more true is, I will assume, at best a strictly qualified version of the instrumental view: one which says that while it is possible and even probable that ethics pays for businesses in general over the long term, it will not for individual businesses on particular occasions (Chryssides and Kaler, 1993, pp 31–32). So not only is any support I might tentatively offer to the instrumental view strictly incidental, it is also support for a strictly qualified version of that viewpoint.

2. Self interest and morality

On what is hopefully just a terminological point, it should also be noted that I do not see any compelling grounds for withholding the description "ethical" from behaviour motivated by self-interested as opposed to altruistic reasons. To claim otherwise is to subscribe to some more or less Kantian approach that equates moral actions with moral motives. I certainly do not want to deny the importance of motives to morality: of, in short, doing the right thing for the right reasons. Notions of moral credit depend upon this conjunction (Chryssides and Kaler, 1993, p. 30). Its presence is, moreover, some sort of guarantee of consistency. Those who do the right thing for the right reason can be relied upon to do that thing even at some cost to themselves. In contrast, those who act from ulterior motives will cease to do the right thing when it no longer accords with that self-serving reason. None the less, while bearing these important qualifications in mind, it remains possible, as every lawyer knows, to distinguish the morality of the act from the morality of the actor: the goodness or badness of the result from the goodness or badness of the intention behind it (Clarkson and Keating, 1994, pp. 135–158). Apart from anything else, there is the apparently undeniable fact that behaviour is invariably a mixture of prudential and altruistic reasons. So to insist on altruism alone is to leave

very little behaviour that counts as "moral". More tellingly perhaps, in so far as it is defined by a notion of the "common good", the prudential would seem to be an essential component of the moral; albeit that it is a collective rather than merely individual or sectional self-interest that is involved (Chryssides and Kaler, 1993, pp. 27–28). Once more, only the sort of Kant-like insistence on purity of motive that I have already rejected will do the gainsaying. I will, therefore, accept that in distinguishing moral behaviour from prudential reasons for its performance, I am not speaking of any absolute distinction between prudence and morality. Rather, the point of the distinction is to allude to circumstances in which self-interest of a personal or merely sectional sort is the sole or predominating reason for the behaviour (Chryssides and Kaler, 1993, p. 31). Only then, I will assume, is there enough of a separation between morality and self-interest for it to necessarily follow that a prudential reason is a non-moral reason – and then only to the extent of any predominating. However, though this assumption is certainly subscribed to, its articulation is more by way of background clarification than anything else. Nothing I wish to go on to say fundamentally depends upon that assumption or even upon the general viewpoint which it embodies. Anyone taking what I have identified as the Kantian line would simply need to insist that where I contrast moral behaviour with prudential reasons, the slightest degree of self-interest will establish the contrast rather than just a predominating degree. This is, however, simply a variation on the conditions establishing the contrast, not a rejection of the contrast itself.[3] So as nothing I want to say in relation to this contrast depends upon the degree of self-interest necessary to establishing it, nothing I want to go on to say depends upon agreement regarding that degree. Likewise, and whatever the degree of self-interest necessary for making reasons prudential rather than moral, nothing I want to say hinges upon whether the resultant behaviours can be properly described as "ethical" or not. As I have indicated, I see no compelling grounds for inhibitions on this scope. However, anyone that does have such inhibitions can simply translate my talk of non-moral prudential reasons for "*ethical* behaviour" to "ethical-*like* behaviour." (Either way, it will be the same behaviour.) In a similar fashion, anyone objecting to my description of an approach insisting upon purity of motive as "Kantian", can alter it to "*allegedly* Kantian". (Either way, it is the same approach.)

Somewhat elaborated to allow for gradations, this suggested but not required view of the dividing line between self-interest and morality can be summarized as follows. (Note that the prudential might convert from "non-moral" to "immoral" to the extent that, through omission or commission, it involves harm to others as well as benefit to the prudentially motivated. Note too that malevolent harm would be an added dimension of immorality. Conversely, note that while altruism is distinguished from the "ordinarily moral" by the absence of self-interest, for self-interest to be not just absent but damaged constitutes the added dimension of self-sacrifice.)

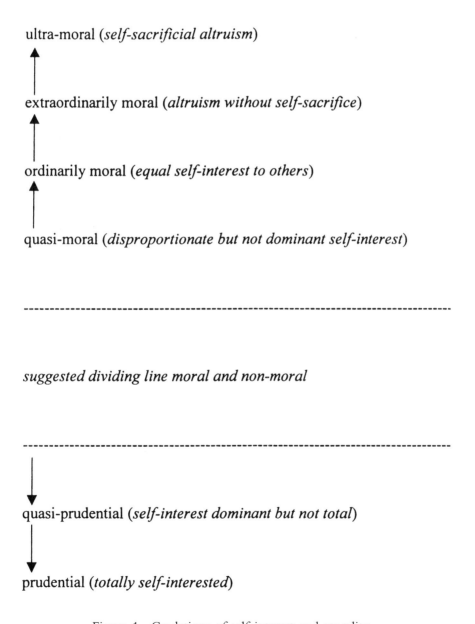

Figure 1. Gradations of self-interest and morality.

3. Understanding business self-interest

Business self-interest is most readily thought of in terms of commercial success and, more particularly, profit. This leads naturally on to the notion of businesses as profit maximizers. However, as almost any economics or management textbook tells us, this notion is very questionable (Griffiths and Wall, 1995, pp. 51–67; Thompson, 1993, pp. 131–134). According to various "theories of the firm", in practice businesses will, to varying degrees and sometimes simultaneously, follow several different objectives of which profit maximization is just one. Prominent among these other objectives are apparently equally commercial ones such as increased sales revenue and growth ("commercial" because at least indirectly linked to profit). However, a very great complication here is the separation of ownership and control: the separation, typical of public companies, of owners (usually shareholders) from a separate class of professional managers. Because of this it becomes plausible to suggest, as in fact some theories of the firm do, that for managers some of these apparently commercial objectives are pursued for reasons that are not strictly, or narrowly, economic. So, for example, we find it suggested that increased sales revenue and growth are pursued to increase the status and power of managers rather than, or as well as, any economic benefit that might come to those managers by way of pay increases (Griffiths and Wall, 1995, pp. 51–54).

This notion of non-economic gratification playing a part in business activity can be extended. In principle, there is no reason why owners should not be similarly gratified along with managers. They too might desire benefits that are more than just pecuniary. In particular cases at least, status and power could be just as much, and as little, a motivating factor for them as for managers: the status and power that comes with owning, or partly owning, the market leader for instance. Also, neither for manager nor owners need profit itself be thought of as a narrowly pecuniary benefit. For either of them, it might be the accompanying status and power rather than the profit itself that is the object of

desire. In fact, unless they suffer from the pathological condition of miserliness, this almost certainly is the case; for almost no one, it can be presumed, desires money for its own sake but nearly always for the benefits which its possession brings. Moreover, beyond what is necessary for survival, those resultant benefits can be regarded as, to a large extent at least, forms of psychological gratification. This is most obviously true in so far as the possession of money permits the pleasures of consumption and display. But it is to at least some extent true of the non-economic objectives of status and power talked about in relation to businesses by theorists of the firm. These things too are presumably objects of desire for managers and (I have suggested) owners for reasons that connect with the satisfying of emotions.

With this last observation it becomes rather obvious that specifying just what "self-interest" means in relation to business is rather more complicated than it might at first seem. We can glibly talk of it as an "economic" self-interest, but clearly this is only half the story. There is first of all the complication that with regard to an important category of business, two at least potentially different sets of interests are involved: those of managers as opposed to owners. Secondly, for managers in particular but also perhaps to some extent for owners, those interests are more than just narrowly economic but are tied up with what was described as "psychological gratifications". It follows, therefore, that unless some sort of sense is made of these two complications it is difficult to be clear about business self-interest and, with that, difficult to be clear about just what it means for business to follow ethical practices for prudential reasons.

For reasons of space only a crude but hopefully effective demarcation can be attempted here. What I would suggest is that despite the complications it remains broadly true that business self-interest is at least primarily economic in the sense that it is the pursuit of profit, or factors relating to profit, that, directly or indirectly, constitute the core of that self-interest. Those objectives other than profit proposed by some theorists of the firm such as sales and growth are, we can presume, at least related to profit and so in some more or less pecuniary sense can be described as "economic". Likewise, even if what is conceived of as an economic self-interest must be ultimately reduced to psychological gratifications, those gratifications are arrived at *through* the pursuit of economic self-interest and so to that extent remain describable as "economic".

Where, even for crude effectiveness, complications cannot be glossed over is with regard to managers. Given that the profits of a business do not belong to them, they clearly have a rather more indirect relationship to the economic self-interest of businesses than owners. Profit defines the economic self-interest of managers only to the extent their remuneration relates to profit or to profit-related factors such as dividends, share price, market share, or whatever. Moreover, the question of psychological gratification is less easily glossed over in their case. Very arguably, their pride and self-esteem is more closely related to the economic performance of the business than is the case with owners. Managers are, after all, responsible for that performance; investors need merely sit in judgement upon it. So for managers in particular, it is not simply that a successful economic performance brings psychological gratification through pecuniary rewards. There is also the likelihood that such success is *itself* a source of psychological gratification quite apart from that supplied through any attendant pecuniary rewards. The very success can be gratifying and not just by means of the money it brings.

This possibility presents a very clear exception to the rule that business self-interest can be spoken of as "economic" in some more or less pecuniary sense. Money is involved but it is being valued neither for itself nor for what it can buy, but rather for what it signifies by way of achievement. Thus, to the extent that economic success is pursued for something like the pleasure of achievement it is not for so straightforwardly a self-interested reason as when pecuniary considerations are uppermost. Then we are presented, with a paradigm of the self-interested reason: money and what it can buy. With a sense of achievement, on the other hand, it is not at all obvious that we are even in the realm of self-interested reasons.

Nonetheless, I would want to classify reasons relating to a specifically managerial sense of achievement as "self-interested." The grounds for this are, at least in broad outline, fairly obvious. It amounts to no more than the commonplace contention that acting for reasons of self-gratification can be no less an instance of doing the right thing for the wrong reason than acting for reasons of pecuniary gain. Take, for instance, the making of charitable donations in order to gain public esteem. Although not putting it in the same league as acting for pecuniary benefit, we quite rightly do not regard this as altruism. Mix it sufficiently with pride and vanity, or such like emotions, and we will probably regard it as not just non-altruistic but the very converse of altruistic: as much an action done for a self-interested reason as any done for pecuniary gain. (To mark this distinction is not, of course, to go as far as psychological egoism and label every act "self-interested" on the grounds that every act involves the satisfying of a predominant desire. Rather, it is a question of distinguishing between desires and labelling *some* "self-interested".)

Though not wishing to speculate on the extent, it is, I think, plausible to suggest that in so far as managers pursue economic success for non-pecuniary reasons, these reasons are very often sufficiently mixed with emotions such as pride and vanity to be labelled "self-interested". Accordingly, though I shall primarily think of business self-interest as economic in a pecuniary sense, I shall allow that in the case of managers at least, business self-interest can take a non-pecuniary turn. (In their capacity as managers, owner-managers will, of course, share in this feature.)

What I shall not allow is that businesses have a self-interest of their own over and above that of their owners and/or managers. To do so is to accept some notion of businesses as moral actors in their own right over and above the people connected with them. On the grounds of simplicity as well as very familiar theoretical objections (Chryssides and Kaler, 1993, pp. 238–240), this is not a claim I wish to make. For me, talk of "business self-interest" is shorthand for the self-interest of owners and/or managers.

4. A typology of prudential reasons

4.1. *Positive and negative reasons*

Prudential reasons for ethical behaviour by businesses fall into two main categories. They are either positive or negative. The positive are all about obtaining rewards. They concern opportunities and so necessarily demand a proactive stance. The negative, on the other hand, are all about avoiding punishment. They concern threats rather than opportunities. So while a proactive stance towards them is certainly possible, it does not necessarily follow. Equally possible, and perhaps in practice more usual, is a reactive stance.

It must, of course, be noted that what is being characterized are reasons for behaviour and not the behaviour itself. For example, while the reason a business adopts equal opportunity practices can well be on the strictly negative grounds of reacting to a threat of industrial action, this is obviously not the only way of looking at equal opportunity practices. Their implementation might equally well be viewed as an opportunity to be seized. The thinking could be that equality of opportunity serves the commercial self-interest of a business in that it widens the pool of talent that is drawn upon and, in this way, improves the quality of the staff that gets employed by the business (Straw, 1989, p. 12). In short, "negative" and "positive" (and all subsequent contrasts) are being presented as the distinguishing marks of reasons alone. Which particular category of prudential reason can be used to justify which particular category of moral behaviour is an additional issue that must be approached on a case by case basis. It depends on assessing the plausibility of arguments linking a particular category of behaviour to a particular reason – something that cannot be attempted here. (In practice, of course, any behaviour might be linked to any reason however ill-founded the arguments.)

4.2. *Internal and external reasons*

A further division concerns the nature of the factor being taken into consideration by a positive or negative reason. It is the issue of whether that factor is "internal" in the sense of being a constituent part of the business or, conversely, "external" in the sense of being something outside the business. For example, reasons that speak of employee approval are internal (and positive), those that speak of public disapproval are external (and negative).

As the example illustrates, "internal" and "external" are most easily understood in terms of people. What this reflects is the fact that prudential reasons for ethical behaviour by businesses will be invariably couched in terms of the attitudes and reactions of people. The only obvious exception concerns environmental considerations and the opportunities or threats that they present: cost savings through energy efficiency, the avoidance of resource depletion through recycling, and so on. However, this very large exception and, I suspect, possibly any other that might be thought of, will clearly belong to the external side of the internal *v.* external divide. As far as the internal side is concerned, the factor involved in any prudential reason is, I take it, always going to be a human grouping and will, moreover, be one of a trio consisting of employees, owners and, in so far as they are distinct from the other two, managers. The same exclusively human focus is admittedly not the case for external prudential reasons in that there is at least one notable exception in environmental considerations. However, while acknowledging this exception and allowing the possibility of others, for ease of exposition I shall presume a relation to human groupings when looking at external reasons. Note though, that even with this restriction, because external reasons relate to factors outside the business and this covers the whole of the wider society, there is the rather obvious contrast with internal reasons of an indefinite number of human groupings that might relate to external reasons.

4.3. *Governmental and non-governmental*

A third subdivision concerns whether the (human) factor invoked has governmental or non-governmental status: for example, the pressure to be ethical exerted by state regulatory bodies as opposed to the pressure that might be exerted by a self-regulatory body such as a trade association.

As reasons classifiable as "internal" relate to constituent parts of a business, such reasons cannot be classifiable as anything but "non-governmental". Consequently, this third subdivision is only useful in distinguishing between reasons classifiable as "external". In relation to those reasons it is, to some extent, a subdivision which applies to both the positive and negative varieties. For instance, co-operation with either a state regulatory body or a self-regulatory body could be viewed as either an opportunity to be seized or a threat to be countered. There could even be rewards in the form of financial inducements for that co-operation. (An illustration of this would be the U.K. government's "New Deal" programme with its offer of subsidies to employers taking on the young unemployed.) However, where this division into governmental and non-governmental sources most usually and perhaps most usefully belongs is in distinguishing between reasons that are not just external but also negative. This follows because while gov-

ernmental agencies might, as pointed out, be involved in providing opportunities for reward, they are probably mostly concerned with threats of punishment.[4] Moreover, while opportunities for reward are perhaps rather more present on the non-governmental side, there is probably a bias towards the negative even here – most obviously in the almost entirely threatening role of campaigning pressure groups (section 5.2). Accordingly, I shall, at least for the purposes of exposition, locate the division between the governmental and non-governmental on the negative side of the schema so far outlined.

5. The reasons in practice

5.1. *Positive prudential reasons and business case arguments*

Positive prudential reasons for ethical behaviour are very often invoked in defence of the instrumental view of business ethics. At their most general, they are claims about being rewarded for ethical behaviour through the goodwill it engenders among consumers, the general public, employees, and other businesses (Chryssides and Kaler, 1993, pp. 23–26).[5] More specifically, positive prudential reasons tend to get invoked in "business case" arguments for particular forms of ethical behaviour.

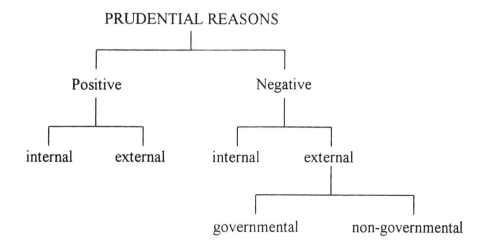

Figure 2. Classification of prudential reasons for ethical behaviour by businesses.

An example already cited (section 4.1), is the business case argument for equal opportunity policies on the very positive grounds that they widen the pool of available talent. Another is the business case argument for community involvement mounted by the U.K. organization, Business in the Community (BITC, 1992). It lists the positive prudential reasons for community involvement programmes as "building reputations" (through increased brand awareness, networking, and public approval), "building people" (through enhancement of the skills, experience, and commitment of staff), and "building markets" (through the economic regeneration of communities). As the second set of reasons look inwards to the firm's employees while the first and third look outwards to the wider society, this example again illustrates the way positive reasons can be either internal or external (section 4.2).

What the example also illustrates is that the way prudential reasons for ethical behaviour can be preferred over strictly moral ones. This could spring from a belief that this is tactically the best approach (Straw, 1989, p. 12). But, arguably, it would also reflect a tendency among business people to see moral reasons as embarrassingly unbusinesslike (Chryssides and Kaler, 1993, p. 32). Likewise, a preference for the positive variety of prudential reasons in mounting business case arguments could arguably reflect the related feeling that to be businesslike is to be positive. For though the positive does perhaps tend to get emphasized in the mounting of such arguments, they can, of course, also be based upon strictly negative prudential reasons; as when, for example, business case arguments for equality of opportunity include reference to avoiding the costs of litigation (Echiejile, 1995). More generally, business case arguments and, along with them, the entire instrumental view of business ethics, can be justified for strictly negative prudential reasons to do with the disapproval and loss of goodwill that can come with unethical behaviour. That is to say, for the sort of reasons discussed next.

5.2. *Negative prudential reasons: the dominance of external pressures*

As we saw above, positive prudential reasons for ethical behaviour by businesses can just as effectively be internal in character as they can be external. That is to say, the human grouping figuring within a positive reason can as easily be drawn from the internal trio of employees, owners, and managers, as it can from any of an indefinite number of groupings drawn from the wider society outside the business (section 4.2). With negative prudential reasons, however, the situation is somewhat different. In terms of providing negative grounds for ethical behaviour by businesses, the role of employees, owners, and managers seems rather limited and even somewhat problematic.

The *most* problematic of the trio are managers. It is easy enough to see why. The point about what I am labelling negative prudential reasons is in so far as, along with prudential reasons in general (section 4.2), they relate to human groupings, then the threat which negative reasons present comes down to the pressure that a particular grouping can exert upon a business by way of an adverse attitude or reaction in the event of unethical behaviour by that business. This being so, and given also that managers control businesses, it follows that negative prudential reasons will, in practice, be about pressure exerted on *managers*; for it is only by influencing those in control that the behaviour of the business can be influenced. Consequently, managers cannot, at least with regard to the business they manage, be a credible source of threats constituting negative prudential reasons for ethical behaviour simply because this would require them to be exerting pressure on *themselves*: to be, in effect, threatening themselves; something which, if not impossible, hardly amounts to much of a threat. (Managers can, of course, exert pressure on themselves by way of the workings of their conscience, but this would give rise to moral as distinct from prudential reasons, and only the latter are at issue here. They can also pressure managers in businesses *other than* those they manage. But then, of course, the negative prudential reasons produced are of an external sort rather than of the internal variety at issue here.)

In contrast, nothing in principle rules out the employees and owners of a business from exerting pressure for ethical behaviour by that business. In practice though, and be it from indifference or inability it is difficult to say, neither seems to be very much of a source of such pressure. By and large, what pressure they do exert on the businesses they work for or own is mostly directed at furthering their self-interest through improvements in working conditions and wages or the enhancement of financial returns respectively. Consequently, it is mostly only in so far as the furtherance of those interests constitutes an advance in the ethical behaviour of those businesses through an overlapping of the moral and the prudential (section 2) that employees and owners are much of a force for improving the ethical performance of businesses. Arguably, because of a relatively disadvantaged position in relation to the businesses they work for, such a coinciding is perhaps more likely to be true of employees than owners. For example, improvements in working conditions and wages might coincide with a more equitable distribution of resources. Conversely, pressure by owners for an enhanced financial return can be seen as pressure furthering a moral advance only if those owners are somehow being deprived of what is rightfully theirs through the knavery or incompetence of managers. Any coinciding of morality and the self-interest of owners beyond this probably demands adherence to a stockholder view of businesses in which, as in Friedman's agency argument, the enhancement of owner value is seen as a *moral* imperative on managers. Accordingly, it is only from such a viewpoint that the phenomenon of "shareholder activism" can be construed as pressure for enhanced moral behaviour by business. (Granted that it concerns campaigning for increased shareholder value rather than campaigning against specific instances of knavery or incompetence by managers.)

In making this point about shareholder activism I am, of course, distinguishing it from the very different phenomenon of "ethical investment" (Sparkes, 1998, pp. 141–143); something which although not entirely separate from share-

holder activism is, I think, best thought of as belonging to specifically *external* negative reasons as part of the more general phenomenon of "ethical consumerism" (see below).

Turning now to external negative reasons, we are, as noted (section 4.2), confronted with a wide variety of groupings from which pressure for ethical behaviour by businesses could originate. Given the limitations just indicated with regard to internal groupings, these many external groupings are also very clearly the more effective of the two kinds of sources for such pressure. Moreover, given two very plausible possibilities, it could even be claimed that this same specifically external pressure is the source of the most effective reasons of *any* kind for ethical behaviour by business.

The two very plausible possibilities in question relate to behaviour in general and not just that of businesses. They are that in terms of ensuring ethical behaviour, (i) prudential reasons are more effective than specifically moral ones, and that among prudential reasons, (ii) negative reasons are more effective than positive ones. So as it is clearly the case that among negative prudential reasons for ethical behaviour by businesses, the internal are less effective than the external, it would follow, given assumptions (i) and (ii), that negative prudential reasons of a specifically external sort constitute the most effective reasons of any kind for ethical behaviour by businesses. (It need hardly be added that the plausibility of assumptions (i) and (ii) is much more a matter of the prevalence of human weakness than of human viciousness.)

Whether or not this large claim for external negative reasons is conceded, it must certainly be allowed that these reasons relate to groupings capable of exerting very considerable pressure upon businesses. This is most clearly the case where the pressure is governmental as distinct from non-governmental in source (section 4.3). Most obviously, the law and the various regulatory bodies established by law can exert that huge pressure that comes from the power to inflict legal punishment. But there is also the very substantial influence that governments and governmental bodies can have through policy decisions of various kinds (fiscal measures, administrative procedures, purchasing strategies, etc.), as well as, in the case of governments, through the threat of legislation (a factor behind a lot of self-regulation by businesses).

With regard to the non-governmental pressures involved in negative external reasons, the most powerful pressure is that exerted by the public in general and consumers in particular when the behaviour of businesses meets with their disapproval rather than, as featured in 5.1, their approval. In terms of the disapproval I have distinguished as "public", the resultant pressure is indirect. It is exercised through influencing governments to act, or threaten to act, in response to behaviour that meets with public disapproval. (An example is the threat to legislate over "fat cat" executive pay in the U.K. See Martinson, 1999.) In terms of a consumer disapproval, the pressure is direct. It is the public in their role as customers rather than as citizens, threatening not to buy the products of businesses meeting with their disapproval.

A particularly pronounced and explicitly moral manifestation of pressure exercised through consumer opinion is the much discussed phenomenon of "green" and/or "ethical" consumerism. As indicated above, I would include within this category the equally much discussed phenomenon of the "ethical investor" as a specifically *financial* form of ethical consumerism. The justification for this inclusion is that ethical investment is mostly a combination of a negative policy of not buying shares in companies that are disapproved of along with a perhaps less practised positive policy of buying shares in companies that are approved of (Cowton, 1994, pp. 217–222). To that extent, it is all about consumer purchases and so differs from ethical consuming in general only in the nature of the product avoided or favoured when purchasing.

Ethical investment can go beyond ethical purchasing only in so far as it involves a specifically *ethical* form of shareholder activism (Chryssides and Kaler, 1996, pp. 108–112). That is to say, instead of shareholder activism in that usual sense noted above of the pursuit of shareholder value, there is an activism that is additionally or exclusively directed at serving moral rather than self-interested ends. Such an approach would arguably

do more to improve the ethical performance of businesses than merely buying and not buying their shares – something which, unless there is a shortage of potential purchasers, can largely pass them by. In particular, a specifically ethical shareholder activism could mean that rather than avoiding shares in companies that are disapproved of, their shares would be bought in order to be in a position to exert pressure for moral improvement (Chryssides and Kaler, 1996, p. 112).

With this move towards activism, two things happen to ethical investment. Firstly, to the extent it is moving away from a strictly consumerist stance it is ceasing to be an external form of pressure. In acting through "voice" (Hirschman, 1990), it becomes an internal form; no different from conventional shareholder activism except in its specifically moral orientation. Secondly, it begins to overlap with that emphatically negative and external source of pressure for improving the moral performance of business constituted by campaigning groups such as Greenpeace, Friends of the Earth, World Development Movement, etc. This second consequence follows because, as with campaigning groups, an activist form of ethical investment is exerting pressure upon businesses in the furtherance of specifically moral objectives; the difference lies in the fact that an activist form of ethical investment will exert that pressure exclusively through shareholding, while for campaigning groups shareholding, of a strictly nominal sort (Barrie, 1997), is only one campaigning tactic among many rather than its defining aspect.

It is this fundamentally moral orientation that distinguishes what I am calling "campaigning groups" from other sorts of NGO's such as trade unions or trade associations that might also constitute external sources of pressure for improving the moral performance of business (Willetts, 1998). Though not necessarily devoid of a moral orientation, these other NGO's are vehicles for the promotion of a sectional self-interest which, as noted in relation to employees and shareholders (section 5.1), need be only coincidentally connected to moral outcomes. With campaigning groups, on the other hand, those outcomes are expressly sought.

It is also, I would suggest, this more or less single minded pursuit of moral outcomes that, in relation to their size and resources, makes campaigning groups by far the most potent of the non-governmental sources of pressure for improving the ethical performance of businesses. This is not to suggest that other factors such as the spirit of the times (Cohen, 1998) or the opportunities opened up by the Internet (Reed, 1999) do not play a part. But their strong moral focus does, I think, go some way to explaining why, at least in terms of the attention businesses are now giving to them (Bray, 1997), they seem to be exerting an influence that goes beyond any capacity they might have to inflict direct economic damage on businesses through the organizing of consumer boycotts. It does not, for example, seem to have been sales reductions through boycotts that led to Shell's Brent Spar surrender (Lascelles et al., 1995; Bray, 1997, p. 20). Nor, in general, does the achievement of the aims of a boycott seem to necessarily depend upon significantly reducing sales (Smith, 1990). Arguably then, the power of campaigning groups lies not so much in their capacity to influence consumer choices as in their ability to sway public opinion and, through that, lead governments to act. (This certainly seems to have been the case with Shell and Brent Spar. See Bray, 1997, p. 20.) This ability is, however, very much linked to the very moralistic orientation of campaigning groups. To agree with such groups is, it would appear, to be on the side of the angels. So unless what campaigning groups are proposing involves some cost to them, the public are likely, all things being equal, to go along with it. Conversely, for businesses to oppose these proposals is for them to be then cast into the role of villains. And here we come to a third factor over and above that of any capacity to influence consumer choices or pressure governments into acting. It is the ability of campaigning groups to damage the self-esteem of (senior) managers by spreading a view of them as moral miscreants: people who have led the businesses they control into wrongdoing. With this third factor, therefore, there is the involvement of that strictly managerial and non-economic dimension to business self-interest constituted by managers'

sense of achievement in the success of the businesses they manage (section 3). Clearly, for managers and the businesses they manage to be objects of moral scorn is something that is counter to business self-interest in this very specific sense. Thus, even when campaigning groups are not able to influence consumers or governments, they can still, through their occupation of the moral high ground, damage business self-interest and, thereby, exert pressure upon businesses with regard to their ethical behaviour.

Taken together the possibilities of not only influencing consumers and governments but damaging the self-esteem of managers represents quite a considerable capacity on the part of campaigning groups to exert pressure beyond their size and resources. It is no wonder, therefore, that at least some businesses seem to be increasingly seeking to co-operate with, rather than confront campaigning groups (Wagstyl and Corzine, 1997). As one Shell executive put it to me, campaigning groups have an expertise in tapping into public opinion that businesses do not have. As I put it to him, it is an expertise in relating to people as moral agents rather than as simply the consumers they seem to be for businesses.

6. Conclusion: a virtuous spiral?

I have emphasised the negative and external in assessing prudential reasons for ethical behaviour by businesses and have identified governments, public/consumer opinion, and campaigning groups as the principal sources of such appropriately negative and external pressures. Arguably, it is in the dynamic interaction of these three elements with businesses that what might be called a "virtuous spiral" is emerging. What is arguably happening is that, with the encouragement of campaigning groups (and it might not be too immodest to add, business ethicists), there are rising expectations on the part of the public regarding the ethical performance of business. (Opinion polls in the U.K. certainly seem to indicate this. See Brown, 1999.) Faced with a public disapproval that campaigning groups might exploit and governments be forced to act on, business responds with efforts to appear more socially responsible. (Witness the growth of ethical auditing and reporting. See Zadek et al., 1997.) This response, however, merely raises the expectations of the public and increases their disapproval when, as will inevitably happen, businesses fail to meet the standards they have set for themselves. Businesses respond with yet higher standards which raise public expectations higher . . . and so it goes on. That, anyway, is one possibility.

Notes

[1] Given this exclusion, I shall not bother to distinguish between reasons as explanations, justifications or, though it shall be my primary focus, motivating forces – distinctions explored in Smith.

[2] I shall use "prudential" in its derivative and pejorative sense of self-interested rather than in its primary and virtuous sense of "judicious".

[3] Among ethical theories, only perhaps ethical egoism rejects any distinction between the moral and the self-interested.

[4] As Bentham famously observed,

> By punishment alone it seems not impossible but that the whole business of government be carried on: though certainly not so well carried on as by a mixture of that and reward together. But by reward alone it is most certain that no material part of that business could ever be carried on for half an hour (Bentham, 1970, p. 135).

[5] With regard to consumers, rewards for ethical behaviour can be actively pursued through a marketing strategy directed at the ethical and green consumer or the ethical investor. As, however, these phenomena are as much, if not more, about punishment for *unethical* behaviour, for expository economy they will be discussed in relation to negative prudential reasons (section 5.2).

References

Barrie, C.: 1997, 'Campaigning Shareholders Attack BAe Arms Sales', *Guardian,* May 1, p. 26.
Bentham, J.: 1970, *Of Laws in General*, ed. H.L.A. Hart (Athlone Press, London).
Bray, J. (ed.): 1997, *No Hiding Place* (Control Risks Group, London).
Brown, K.: 1999, 'Approval of Business in Britain at 30-Year Low', *Financial Times,* February 22, p. 18.
Business in the Community: 1992, *Annual Review* (BITC, London).
Chryssides, G. and J. Kaler: 1993, *An Introduction to Business Ethics* (International Thomson Business Press, London).
Chryssides, G. and J. Kaler: 1996, *Essentials of Business Ethics* (McGraw-Hill, London).
Clarkson, C. M. V. and H. M. Keating: 1994, *Criminal Law: Text and Materials* (Sweet & Maxwell, London).
Cohen, M.: 1998, 'Evidence of a New Environmental Ethic: Assessing the Trend Towards Investor and Consumer Activism', in I. Jones and M. G. Pollit (eds.), *The Role of Business Ethics in Economic Performance* (Macmillan, London), pp. 111–140.
Cowton, C. J.: 1994, 'The Development of Ethical Investment Products', in A. R. Prindl and B. Prodam (eds.), *Ethical Conflicts in Finance* (Blackwell, Oxford), pp. 213–232.
Echiejile, I.: 1995, 'The Business Case for Diversity', *Professional Manager* (July), 8–11.
Griffiths, A. and S. Wall (eds.): 1995, *Applied Economics* (Longman, London).
Hirschman, A. O.: 1970, *Exit, Voice, and Loyalty* (Harvard University Press, Cambridge, Mass.).
Lascelles, D. et al.: 1995, 'Brent Spar Dents Oil Giant's Pride Rather Than its Profits', *Financial Times,* June 10, p. 13.
Martinson, J.: 1999, 'Byers Warns Over Executive Pay', *Financial Times,* March 24, p. 10.
Price, A.: 1997, 'In Search of Legitimisation – Payback and Practice', in G. Moore (ed.), *Business Ethics: Principle and Practice* (Business Education Publishers, Sunderland).
Reed, M.: 1999, 'Wide Open to the Web Warriors', on http://www.marketing.haynet.com (from *Market-ing,* February 4).
Singer, P.: 1979, *Practical Ethics* (Cambridge University Press, Cambridge).
Smith, M.: 1994, *The Moral Problem* (Blackwell, Oxford).
Smith, N. C.: 1990, *Morality and the Market* (Routledge, London).
Sparkes, R.: 1998, 'The Challenge of Ethical Investment: Activism, Assets and Analysis', in I. Jones and M. Pollitt (eds.), *The Role of Ethics in Economic Performance* (Macmillan, London).
Straw, J.: 1989, *Equal Opportunities: The Way Ahead* (Institute of Personnel Management, London).

Thompson, J. L.: 1993, *Strategic Management: Awareness and Change* (Chapman & Hall, London).

Wagstyl, S. and R. Corzine: 1997, 'Rights and Wrongs', *Financial Times,* March 18, p. 24.

Willetts, P.: 1998, 'Political Globalization and the Impact of NGOs Upon Transnational Companies', in J. V. Mitchell (ed.), *Companies in a World of Conflict: NGOs, Sanctions and Corporate Responsibility* (Earthscan, London).

Zadek, S. et al.: 1997, *Building Corporate Accountability* (Earthscan, London).

Business School,
University of Plymouth,
Drake Circus,
Plymouth,
Devon PL4 8AA,
United Kingdom
E-mail: j.kaler@pbs.plym.ac

The Spanish Code for Good Corporate Governance (Olivencia Report): An Ethical Analysis

J. Félix Lozano

ABSTRACT. The aim of this article is to analyse the "Report on good corporate governance" (Olivencia Report) from an ethical point of view. This report was drawn up by a group of experts at the request of the National Commission of the Spanish Stock Exchange Commission (Comisión Nacional del Mercado de Valores), in winter 1998, and began to be implemented over late 1998.

This paper is the result of several sessions of discussions with businessmen and managers about the role that can be played by the Olivencia Report, its virtues and weaknesses.

Our general criticism is that this Report sets out from a concept of the company as Shareholder and not as Stakeholder. This approach affects three concrete aspects of the report that we analyse in greater detail:

- The affirmation as to the company's ultimate objective.
- The role of the independent non-executive consultant.
- The role of the vice president.

We believe that this code could be very important and useful for guiding future trends in companies' governing bodies, but we think that these weaknesses in its approach represent a lack of ethical sensibility and that it does not match the moral level of a modern society.

KEY WORDS: code, company boards, corporate governance, ethics, responsability, stakeholders approach

J. Félix Lozano. *Philosophy graduate, with further studies at Erlangen-Nürnberg University (Germany). Assistant Director of the ÉTNOR Foundation. Assistant lecturer of Business Ethics and Professional Deontology at Valencia Polytechnic University.*

1. Introduction

In mid-March 1997, a group of experts was requested by the Commission of the Spanish Stock Exchange (CNMV) to draw up a report in order to improve the governance of quoted companies.

This request had already been made public in January 1997[1] when, given the difficulties involved in the reform of "Ley de Sociedades Anónimas" (Company Law), the President of the Commission of the Spanish Stock Exchange proposed the drawing-up of an 'ethical code for good corporate governance'.

The Special Commission for the study of an ethical code for Company Boards presented their report and recommendations in February 1998.[2] Some of the most important Spanish companies had already made public during that same year their will to adopt the code of good governance. Among the most notable are Tabacalera, Telefónica, and Repsol (companies which are in the process of privatization) and Banco Popular.[3]

This report, commonly named the 'Olivencia report' presented a series of recommendations for quoted companies. Although the report is not legally binding, companies are required to provide information regarding the degree of attention they pay to it (whether or not it is being implemented and to what extent).

Given the importance of the document and its relation with the field of ethics, Fundación Etnor decided it was necessary to dedicate some time to a detailed analysis of the report.

In November 1998 we were honoured with the presence of Mr Manuel Olivencia, president of the report commission. He presented his work and encouraged us to analyse it in depth and improve it with criticism and comments if necessary.

Our analysis focused on various aspects, which we have criticised as much from a functional point of view as from a fundamentally ethical point of view.

Our major interest has aimed at the concept of the company that appears to inform the Olivencia report, in which there is an implicit perception of the company as *Shareholder* rather than as *Stakeholder*.

This fact affects three particular aspects of the report, which we analysed in detail:

- The shareholder is considered the only recipient of this report. As a result the perception of partner and the perception of company as a project where a plurality of internal and external interests are present both disappear.
- The role of the vice president, seen as independent, as a controller of the executive president.
- The report transmits an idea of the board of directors as a place of great pressures, where a serious struggle for power takes place and where different forces have to be appropriately balanced (problems relating to responsibility).

2. The report on good governance[4]

As has been mentioned above, the report on good governance was drawn up by a group of experts at the request of the National Commission of the Spanish Stock Exchange. Their work was carried out over a period of nearly one year, and was published at the beginning of 1998. During that year it caused a great impact and interest in the business and economic world.

The report comprises three major parts: the first part is an introduction, the second part is a report on the board of directors and the third is the code of good governance where 4 general and 23 specific considerations are set out.

a) In the introduction, apart from the composition of the commission, the double task of the commission is stated. "The drawing-up of a report on the problems of boards of directors of companies that have an influence on the financial markets" (1). And the drawing-up *of an ethical code* of good governance to be voluntarily adopted by these companies[5] (2). The authors acknowledge that there had been many calls for this report from professionals, the market, and the government. We cannot underestimate the importance of notorious corruption cases in the governance of several important Spanish companies in recent years. The report also was also influenced by a series of reforms and documents that were being carried out in other European countries. The Caldbury report is particularly important. The introduction goes on to insist that these reforms should not be imposed through legal channels. On the contrary, companies should adopt them "of their own free will and under a regime of self-regulation"

b) The second part, 'the report on the board of directors' is the longest. Some of the aspects that are analysed in detail will be later presented as conclusions. This section starts by mentioning the fundamental mission of the board of directors and goes on to deal with more specific aspects relating to the composition of the board (section 2) and its structure (section 3). It also analyses the board's conduct as well as procedures for the appointment and dismissal of board members (section 4 and 5). It devotes three specific sections to the role of the board member; to his/her powers of information (section 6), his/her remuneration (section 7) and his/her loyalties (section 8). The next section focuses on the relationship between the board member and the shareholders (section 9) and goes on in the next two sections to analyse the relationship with the markets (section 10) and the auditors (section 11). This second parts ends with a reminder of the fact that the code is voluntary and of the need for public information with regard to the degree of its implementation.[6]

c) The code of good governance itself comprises 4 general and 23 specific recommendations that deal with particular aspects of the composition and functions of the board of directors.

3. Ethical aspects of the code

We believe that ethical aspects are not treated appropriately in this document. Although it is true that Mr Olivencia has stated that 'this is not an ethical code',[7] it is evident that ethics plays a very important part in good governance, and that ethical aspects are dealt with in the text in an indirect and not very clear way.

We must bear in mind that the National Commission of the Spanish Stock Exchange asked explicitly for an 'ethical code' and that furthermore the commission of the report was in part a response to the famous cases of corruption mentioned earlier.[8]

To start with, as regards conceptual aspects, we must point out that it is not as ethically rigorous as one might expect. The members of the commission recognize the difficulty of the concept of *ethics* and state: "the word ethics has to be understood in the widest sense, as referring to the rules, principles and models of behaviour that correspond to criteria of correctness and rationality. Given the most usual connotation of the word ethics (as referring to 'permanent moral values'), which is misleading here, the commission prefers to use the term *code of good governance*".

As it can be drawn from this statement, even though the ethical aspect had been emphasised in the initial request of the National Commission of the Stock Exchange, it has been reduced here to series of rules for good performance (efficient performance to maximise the shareholders' profit).

One of the most important aspects is the reference to the purpose of the company. The report's authors state that: 'the good governance of companies requires a clear definition of the purposes that the company administration must

aim for' (II, 1.3) We agree on this, since the purpose of a company, together with the means it uses to achieve this purpose is what gives social legitimacy to an institution of such importance in our society.

However we clearly disagree with the sentences that follow: "The commission is convinced that the so-called 'financial solution' is the most adequate if there is to be an effective and precise exercise of the principle of responsibility, as well as being the solution that best meets the expectations of the shareholders, to whom after all the management of the company has to answer. We therefore recommend the establishment of the maximising of the company's value or 'the creation of value for the shareholder' (a term commonly used in the world of finance) as the ultimate objective of the company and consequently as the criterion which should inform the actions of the Board" (II, 1.3).

The choice of this criterion as the basic referent of good corporate governance defines and limits the entire report.[9] We believe it is important to comment on the concept of the company that informs this report.

– After a thorough reading of the report we can conclude that it is based around the Stockholder model.[10] The authors themselves recognise this to be "the most adequate" model for corporate governance because of its efficacy and accuracy. Following this model they define as the main task of the board of directors "the supervision and control of the company"[11] and as the basic objective 'the creation of value for the shareholder'. The report focuses on the design of an organ and a series of functions that will avoid clashes of interests between the shareholders, possible abuses of power by major shareholders with respect to minor shareholders, and problems of representation.

They state marginally that other perspectives, such as those that refer to social interest, are ambiguous. But they insist that regarding the maximising of profit as the key parameter "does not mean (. . .) the shareholders' interests should be pursued at any price'. The report states that the limits to the maximising of profit "will have to be developed with due attention to the demands of the law (for instance, fiscal and environmental laws), fulfilling the explicit and implicit contractual commitments engaged in with other interested parties (employees, suppliers, creditors, customers) and *in general, observing those ethical duties that are reasonably appropriate for the responsible management of businesses*".[12] We believe that the purpose of the company should be to contribute effectively to the society in which it carries out its activity by applying moral values that are characteristic of a post-conventional level of the moral conscience of developed societies. Even though we admit this statement is difficult to put into practice we consider it should be borne in mind as a regulatory guideline.[13]

It can be appreciated that the vagueness with respect to ethics needs emphasising. We can state that the concept of ethics on which the report is based is insufficiently developed. It possesses two distinctive features:

A) It is based on an insufficiently developed ethics of conviction. The report leads one to understand that there are some fundamental ethical principles, that do not necessarily work against profit, but which can on occasions, *if not completely reasonable*, work against business.

B) Another defining feature of the ethics presented in the report is the conventional level on which it is located. As can be seen from the previous statement, only the law and contractual commitments can limit the search for greater profit.

– The other aspect we must emphasise is the perception of the Board of Directors as a place of tension and permanent confrontation where as many procedures as possible must be developed to avoid the control of power by certain groups; either major shareholders or as a result of problems of representation. From this point of view one can understand the role of the vice chairman as the chairman's *watchman* "a co-ordinating vice-chair with subsidiary powers to call Board meetings, include new items in the agenda, transfer information to the shareholders and, in general, transmit their worries" (II, 3.3).

– One of the most original aspects of the report is the recommendation of bringing independent members onto the Board of Directors. These counsellors have the task of "defending the interests of floating capital on the Board of Directors" (II, 2.1). The Olivencia report understands as independent as "those counsellors who are not linked either to the management team or the control shareholding cores which have an influence on this team". This board member needs to be experienced, competent and have professional prestige.

We have two fundamental objections to this figure:

1. We do not agree on the fact that they are only considered to represent floating capital: the interests of other groups that are also involved in the company are not represented.

2. Secondly, the report recommends limiting their presence to a maximum of eight years. We believe this implies an unjustified lack of confidence in the freedom and independence of these members. In our opinion for an independent counsellor to be truly independent he should not be relieved from his/her duties unless the terms for this position have fundamentally changed.

4. Conclusions

Our general appraisal of the report is positive. First of all, we think it is a necessary document to improve the governance of Spanish companies and we believe it will make them more competitive in the international market.

Furthermore it is worth emphasising that it does not use the law to impose a series of guidelines, and that it has dealt effectively with some of the most common problems of corporate governance.

After mentioning these positive aspects, we believe we should make a series of criticisms from an ethical point of view. In our opinion, a good opportunity to incorporate ethical aspects into corporate governance and contribute to the opening of the company to society has been missed.

We can sum up our criticisms in five points:

1. The following statement from the report is, in our opinion, unfortunate: "the ultimate objective of a company is the maximising of the company's value". We believe that if this statement had included the words "in the medium or long-term" it would have increased the ethical value of the report. We think the regulating time factor and an attention to the survival of the company are both fundamental factors for good corporate governance.
2. The report lacks a fully developed concept of ethics. As far as we are concerned, in order to avoid ambiguity or misunderstanding, the report avoids ethical considerations and has been reduced to a series of functional recommendations for the good-efficient-functioning of the Board of Directors.
3. The lack of a more considered concept of ethics is also evident in the section that refers to the role of the board members. This section only mentions the term ethics with reference to the board members' personal behaviour, thus implicitly denying the possibility of an organisational ethics, in this case of the Board, that goes beyond personal honesty.
4. We consider it a mistake that more attention has not been paid to the social responsibility of the company, as this theory is nowadays becoming generally accepted. The need for a social legitimacy for the institutions that make up our society is an economic necessity and an ethical demand appropriate to a pluralistic society with a postconventional moral conscience.
5. The report does not consider the Stake-

holder model as a possible guide to criteria for good corporate governance. In our opinion, this lack of attention to this model is an anachronism that could still, even if all the other recommendations in the Olivencia report are followed, threaten the survival of the company.

Notes

[1] Cf. EXPANSIÓN 30th January 1999.
[2] The commission members are: Manuel Olivencia (president), Luis Ramallo (vice president), Pedro Ballvé, Eduardo Bueno, J. María López de Letona, Cándido Paz-Ares, Víctor Pérez, Enrique Piñel, Jesús Platero and Antonio J. Alonso (secretary). It is worth noting that none of the commission members are researchers or ethics teachers, even though there are well-known training and research centres in Spain, both public and private, that have been working in the field of business ethics for years.
[3] Cf. EXPANSIÓN 21st May 1998.
[4] An English version can be found at www.cnmv.es.
[5] Our italics.
[6] This would appear to be a contradiction. The Olivencia report trusts in the markets to reward the adoption of the good governance code. That is why, while it is not legally binding, the degree of implementation must be reported to the National Commission of the Spanish Stock Exchange.
[7] Olivencia, M. (1998), *El código del buen gobierno de la empresa*, Documento ÉTNOR no. 4.
[8] We are referring in particular to the KIO and BANESTO cases. Regarding the Banesto case, reference can be made to the study of Ernesto Ekaizer (1997), *El farol*, Madrid, Temas de hoy.
[9] Several criticisms have been made of this statement. For instance A. Caldbury's words in EXPANSION, 11, July 1998, "the Olivencia report creates value for the shareholder. It is an effective report". In another article in EXPANSION, 11, November 1998, it is stated: "the British expert commented that even though creating value for the shareholder is important for any company, it is also necessary to serve other collectives that also have an influence in the company. We can not forget the employees, suppliers and the social environment of the company when creating value".
[10] Cf. T. Garicano Rojas (1998), "Different models and attitudes in corporate governance: Stockholders and Stakeholders", ACTUALIDAD COMERCIAL ESPAÑOLA, 1998/no. 769, pp. 23–34.

[11] Caldbury himself has criticized these views. Cf. EXPANSIÓN 11, November 98, "The Board of Directors should not only be a controlling body as the Olivencia report suggests, but should also assume the role of leader of the company."

[12] Our italics.

[13] A. Cortina (1994), *Etica de la empresa*, Madrid Trotta. Especially chapter 4. Although this statement may seem rather abstract, not only academics, but also businessmen such as R. Mohn – President of Bertelsmann – have made similar statements. Cf. R. Mohn (1996).

Literature

Comisión especial para el estudio de un código ético de los consejos de administración de las sociedades: 1998, *El gobierno de las sociedades*. ACTUALIDAD COMERCIAL ESPAÑOLA, 1998/no. 769, pp. 113–142.

Cortina, A.: 1994, *Ética de la empresa* (Trotta, Madrid).

Ekaizer, E.: 1997, *El farol* (Temas de hoy, Madrid).

EXPANSIÓN, 30 enero 1999.

EXPANSIÓN, 21 mayo 1998.

EXPANSIÓN, 11 julio de 98.

EXPANSIÓN, 11 noviembre 1998.

Garicano Rojas, T.: 1998, 'Los distintos modelos y actitudes ante el gobierno de la empresa: Stockholders y Stakeholders', ACTUALIDAD COMERCIAL ESPAÑOLA, 1998/no. 769, pp. 23–34.

Garralda, J.: 1998, 'Reflexiones éticas sobre el Consejo de Administración', ACTUALIDAD COMERCIAL ESPAÑOLA, 1998/no. 769, pp. 41–47.

Melé, D. (coord): 1996, *Ética en el gobierno de la empresa* (ediciones de la Universidad de Navarra, Pamplona).

Mohn, R.: 1996, *Al éxito por la cooperación* (Plaza y Janés, Barcelona).

www.cnmv.es.

Adjunto Dirección,
FUNDACIÓN ÉTNOR,
C/Navarro Reverter, 10, 8,
46004 Valencia – Spain
E-mail: jflozano@etnor.org www.etnor.org

The Cultural Dimension of Codes of Corporate Governance: A Focus on the Olivencia Report

Alejo José G. Sison

ABSTRACT. The article deals with the sociocultural and historical background of the Olivencia Report and relates this to the document's content, particularly, to its recommendations for Spanish Boards. A discussion of the distinctively Spanish understandings of loyalty, due diligence and transparency is included. The work ends with insights into parallelisms between corporate governance and political government, specifically on the role of culture, democratic representation and accountability, the distribution of power, the protection of property rights and equality.

KEY WORDS: corporate culture, corporate governance, European corporate culture, Olivencia Report, Spanish corporate culture, Spain

ABBREVIATIONS: *Banco Bilbao Vizcaya* (BBV), *Banco Santander Central Hispano* (BSCH), European Community (EC), European Union (EU), New York Stock Exchange (NYSE), National Association of Corporate Directors (NACD), Olivencia Report (OR), Securities and Exchange Commission (SEC), *Yacimientos Petrolíferos Fiscales* (YPF)

Alejo José G. Sison holds a doctorate in Philosophy from the University of Navarre (1990) with a dissertation in Ancient Greek Ethics. From 1990 to 1994, he taught at the Philosophy Department and at the International Graduate School of Management (IESE) of the University of Navarre. Since 1994 he has been Associate Professor of Business Ethics and Socioeconomics at the University of Asia & the Pacific (Manila). He spent the school year 1997–1998 as a Fulbright Senior Research Scholar and Visiting Fellow at Harvard University. At present, he is back at the University of Navarre and is the Executive Secretary of its Institute for Enterprise and Humanism.

I. Introduction

Hofstede (1993, pp. 1–5) has done us an invaluable service with a definition of culture – a people's "acquired pattern of thinking, feeling and acting" – readily accepted in management. He explains culture by way of a computer metaphor, as the "collective programming of the mind which distinguishes one category of people from another", the "software" that is invisible in itself but visible in its consequences. In this sense, "culture" is useful in identifying both a corporation and a nation-state.

"Corporate culture" relates to "national culture" through the shared values of their members and citizens, respectively. These values consist of semi-conscious feelings about good and evil acquired in early childhood and difficult to change once adulthood has been reached. In Aristotelian terminology, such values correspond to *ethos* ("character"), which depends on a person's habits, actions and inclinations (Nicomachean Ethics, 1103a 17–18). Both values and *ethos* are operative judgments about good and evil; they form the core of culture.

Hofstede identifies four dimensions through which culture may be analyzed: individualism ↔ collectivism, large power distance ↔ small power distance, strong uncertainty-avoidance ↔ weak uncertainty avoidance and masculinity ↔ femininity. The tendency towards either pole in each dimension is a constant in the behavior of a person or group.

Initially, Spanish culture looks masculine, risk-averse and hierarchical. What is difficult to determine is whether Spaniards are individualists or collectivists. Spaniards have strong family ties and regional identities, which would make them individualists. Yet large bureaucracies in government and corporations make Spaniards appear like collectivists. The connections among these different dimensions demand careful interpretation. In theory, risk-aversion fits well with collectivism and bureaucracy, but 15th century Spaniards were brave and enterprising enough to lead the conquest and settlement of the New World. . . .

In recent years, Spanish multinationals have been quick to take advantage of the liberalization of Latin American economies, acquiring enormous stakes (Biurrun et al., 1999). The Spanish telecom, *Telefónica* has a larger share of its business in foreign markets, controlling 67.77% of *Telesp* Brazil since 1998 and 35% of *Telefónica del Perú* since 1994 (The Economist, 1998b). In the first semester of 1999, *Repsol*, with its $13.5B purchase of *Yacimientos Petrolíferos Fiscales* (*YPF*) of Argentina, became the 10th largest oil and gas company in the world (Ralea, 1999). This was the biggest takeover by a Spanish firm to date. Also in 1999, *Banco Santander Central Hispano* (*BSCH*) became the prime financial group in Latin America, managing 15 banks in 11 different countries, while the energy firm, *Endesa*, bought 64% of *Enersis* Chile.

Instead of putting aside Hofstede's analytical tools, one should simply acknowledge their limitations. They were never meant to be strict and fast rules. They were devised to provide a basis of comparison in the study of elusive realities. Therefore, rather than analyze Spanish corporate culture through each of these dimensions, it may be better to focus on its predominant values, endeavoring to understand them within context.

This is how I propose to study the Olivencia Report on corporate governance, a document representing contemporary Spanish organizational and national culture. The comparisons with other documents would serve mainly as contrast with the particular values espoused by top Spanish management (Alvarez et al., 1999).

On February 28, 1997, the Spanish Council of Ministers agreed to create a special Commission for the formulation of a Code of Ethics for Directors of Publicly-Listed Companies (*sociedades cotizadas*). On March 24,

1997 a Commission headed by Manuel Olivencia, a Business Law professor, was constituted. This initiative was in response to structural changes in the Spanish business environment, particularly privatization (Olivencia Report, hence, OR, 1998, I.1).

Firstly, as privatization marked the transfer of ownership, it also increased the number of stockholders. Aside from property interests, the new owners earned a stake in governance. Secondly, the recourse to capital markets emphasized the separation between ownership and management. The gains in scale (number of stockholders and equity) could be threatened by conflicts of interest among the different owners. Conflicts could arise from the divergent interests of controlling investors, majority-but-not-controlling investors, institutional investors and individual, private investors. As the highest governing body, boards face gargantuan challenges in trying to achieve balance, harmony, transparency and accountability, without sacrificing profitability. The Report was meant to serve as guidance in these issues (OR, 1998, I.2).

Aside from privatization, there were other developments which pressed for reforms. Foremost was the trend towards integration within the European Union and the global community. For example, the EU Fifth Directive on the harmonization of Company Law could require firms with over 500 employees to adopt two-tier supervisory and management boards. Having a unitary board composed of executive management directors and supervisory non-executive directors would be insufficient. Moreover, as a corporation ventures into the global context, it goes beyond the reach of any single government. Thence come demands for improved self-regulation among firms, either individually or in associations.

The Commission followed a simple procedure to fulfill its mandate (OR, 1998, I.3). First, it studied the British and American pioneering experiences in Codes of Corporate Governance. Secondly, it carried out mandatory consultations with public and private organizations, in Spain and abroad. Thirdly, it analyzed the stockholder structure and board composition of publicly-traded companies, particularly the Ibex-35.

Finally, the Commission spent approximately 200 hours throughout 42 sessions in drafting the Report.

The result was a 68-page document with 3 main parts. The first explains the origin of the Commission, its objectives and procedures, followed by a description of Spain's economic environment. Next comes an account of the *status quo* of Spanish boards, a discussion of their structural weaknesses, the causes of these and remedies. It ends with a "Code of Good Governance" (*Código de Buen Gobierno*) – a 23-point list of "best practices".

Upon whose initiative did this Code of Corporate Governance arise? The short response is that it is a public-sector initiative, carried out by the executive branch of Spanish national government. We have the corresponding decrees from the Council of Ministers as proof. Yet these same documents mention a reform movement arising from the grassroots of Spanish society itself. We could then say that the Report arose in answer to a "public" demand (OR, 1998, I.5).

This seems to indicate that in Spanish society, it is difficult for an initiative to gel, unless taken under wing by government. This project could not have prospered as a private initiative, exclusively. It would have stalled, victim of partisan interests. There is always a need for the Spanish state to intervene – often in the lead role – in socioeconomic reforms.

On the other hand, it is surprising that adhesion to the Olivencia guidelines be voluntary (OR, 1998, II.12.1). The Report insists that it has no desire to regulate the composition and functioning of boards, let alone, to typify certain acts as illegal. The Commission would like to rely on a sense of personal or professional responsibility and "moral persuasion". The Commission also wishes to leave a margin for the autonomy and uniqueness of each firm. Even the concrete measures recommended, as the incorporation of independent directors, the limits in the number of board members, the creation of operating committees, etc., should be applied on a case to case basis. There is a bias for the spirit rather than the letter of the principles.

What kind of corporate document is the Olivencia Report? Some portions read as a "Mission Statement" for boards, others, as an account of how boards have evolved in Spain. However, the whole Report is geared towards the elaboration of a "Code of Good Governance" (*Código de Buen Gobierno*). How different is this from the conventional "Codes of Ethics/Conduct" for directors?

Firstly, it is not a "code" in the legal sense (OR, 1998, I.4). It is not a body of norms that gives rise to obligations, nor does it contain penalties. There is no authority that looks after its enforcement. It is more of an "integrity-based" rather than a "compliance-based" code (Paine, 1996).

Secondly, the Report avoids the use of "ethics" due to some connotations among Spanish-speakers. "Ethics" in Spanish refers to the controversial set of "moral values" to which individual agents freely but privately subscribe. In a modern and secular society, supposedly, it is not the competence of any Commission to pass judgment over private values. Instead of "ethics", the expression "Good Governance" is employed, signifying "rules, principles and models of conduct in accord with criteria of correction and rationality" (OR, 1998, I,4). Inadvertently, the problem posed by the use of "ethics" resurfaces, for the standards of "correction" and "rationality", even in the limited sphere of Spanish society, are far from settled.

What are the underlying macroeconomic principles in the Olivencia Report? The Report favors economic deregulation, liberalization and privatization. There is an earnest attempt for Spain to abandon its collectivist, centralized and statist past (The Economist, 1996c).

This drift of events may be interpreted in several ways, but it certainly signals the obsolescence of the nation-state as main reference for the economy. As Spain moves toward full integration within the euro-zone, in exchange for currency stability, expanded markets and streamlined business opportunities, it gives up more than just the peseta and independent monetary policy. Tax, employment and other socioeconomic policies are invariably affected. The "multi-lateral partnership" model for the European Union notwithstanding, in the end, policies would be decided in accordance with either the federal archetype of Germany or the centralized system of France. At the same time, regional autonomies – such as Catalonia or the Basque Country – could take advantage of the disintegration of the nation-state to vindicate their identities and aspirations towards increased "sovereignty", counterbalancing Brussel's centripetal moves.

In light of these tendencies, the Olivencia report seeks to provide a sounder basis for investor (local and foreign) confidence through some form of "democratization". What sets apart publicly-listed Spanish firms is the great concentration of shares in a majority stockholder, usually a bank or a family (Cuervo-Cazurra, 1998). Although corporations with free-float stocks accounting for more than 75% of their shares are a minority, these account for almost half of the stockmarket capitalization (OR, 1998, I.3).

What "theory of the firm" serves as backdrop for the Olivencia report? The elaboration of "Ethical Codes" or "Codes of Conduct" becomes a concern when a "stakeholder" rather than a "stockholder" mindset is operational. According to the stakeholder theory, a business is a societal institution for the purpose of creating "value" in products or services, employment and profits. The interests of all parties with a "stake" in the business, as customers, employees, suppliers, contractors, competitors, the community, government, the environment and even international bodies have to be considered, albeit in varying degrees (Goodpaster, 1991). Whereas the stockholder mentality emphasizes return on equity, productivity, innovative technology and competition, the stakeholder mindset underscores wages, job security, environmental safety and social cooperation (The Economist, 1996a).

The Olivencia report spells out the responsibilities and rights of directors playing a dual role as management and owners. The interests of investors occupy the first place: "The Commission has reached the conviction that the so-called 'financial' solution is the most adequate one for an effective and precise exercise of the principle of responsibility, the one which best responds to the expectations of investors to whom in the end, management would have to render an account. For this reason, we recommend that the maximization of value for the firm, or the creation of value for the investor, to follow a phrase in financial environments, be established as the ultimate objective of the corporation and the criterion that presides over the decisions of the Board" (OR, 1998, II.1.3).

However, the Report seems oblivious to the ambiguity of "value creation", the content and measures of which are unsettled: For the long or the short term? For whom? In terms of sales, profits or stock price? How about shareholder dividend? What do we value more, increased market share or innovative products and services?, and so on.

The "social interest" is rejected for it fails to provide clear, practical criteria for the Board, the Report claims. Moreover, the "social interest" does not favor capital formation or efficiency. Neither does it accommodate organizational structure to the incentives and risks of parties. Beneath the "stakeholder" skin, the Olivencia report is very much "stockholder" in substance.

II. Structure and content, recommendations and rationales

Mission, composition, structure and meetings protocol of the board

The first four points deal with the mission, composition, structure and meetings protocol of Boards. These discussions give rise to items 1 to 10 in the Code of Good Governance.

The Report proposes the oversight of management as the mission of Boards (OR, 1998, II.1.1). The Report lists five tasks belonging to the exclusive competence of the Board (OR, 1998, II.1.2): 1) the approval of general strategies, 2) the appointment, compensation and termination of top executives, 3) the control of senior management, 4) the identification of major corporate risks and the implantation of internal control systems, and 5) the setting of communication policies. This does not mean, however, that the Board may not solicit help from other bodies.

The Report cites two frequent errors in

understanding a Board's mission. One is the Board's acting as shadow management, the other, its playing an ornamental or ceremonial role.

Regarding the composition of the Board (OR, 1998, II.2), the Report advocates (1) the introduction of "independent directors", (2) that there be more external directors than internal ones, and (3) that the number of directors range between 5 to 15. Internal directors are those who come from management, while external directors are nominated by outstanding stockholders. An "independent director" is an external director representing the interests of free-float stocks. She may or may not own stocks herself: although in the former case, her interests would align themselves better with free-float capital. The reason behind the majority of external directors is to avoid the concentration of powers in a closed group. Other stakeholder groups, such as employees, suppliers, customers or clients are not represented in Spanish boards.

The major problems Spanish firms face in the composition of its Boards are: (1) the absence of independent directors, (2) the excessive number of members, and (3) that some directors are chosen for other than professional reasons.

With regard to structure (OR, 1998, II.3), the crucial issue is whether or not the C.E.O. should be the Chair. In the former, there would clearly be a strong leader in the firm. Yet the concentration of power may pave the way for abuse, as well as cause confusion between managing the firm and presiding over its Board. Since in the majority of Spanish corporations, the C.E.O. and Chair are the same person, precautions against "presidentialism" (*presidencialismo*) are necessary. The powers of the C.E.O. may be held in check by the Board Secretary, the Executive Committee, and the Operating Committees. The Board Secretary is an independent and stable figure who looks after the legality of proceedings. The Executive Committee should mirror the diversity and balance of the Board *en banc*. The Report mentions four Operating Committees – Audit, Nominations, Compensations, Compliance – and suggests that these be headed by external directors.

The Report suggests that Board Meetings be held regularly (OR, 1998, II.4), with a meeting-per-month minimum and a hundred hours-per-year maximum. Members should receive precise, adequate and timely information regarding the agenda, to facilitate participation in deliberations. The recourse to proxies is discouraged. Proceedings should be carefully recorded. Once a year, the Board should evaluate its work in a special session.

Operating committees

The remaining points concern the activities of the Operating Committees: the Nominations Committee (OR, 1998, II.5 and recommendations 11–13), the Compensations Committee (OR, 1998, II. 7 and recommendation 15), the Compliance Committee (OR, 1998, II.6, II.8 and recommendations 14, 16, 17) and the Audit Committee (OR, 1998, II.9 through II.12 and recommendations 18–23).

The Nominations Committee (OR, 1998, II.5) plays an important role in the presentation of Board candidates. A formal and transparent procedure must be followed in the recruitment of independent directors. Variety and pluralism in their backgrounds are desirable, while interlocking directorships should be avoided. This is to safeguard a director's independence, which could be jeopardized by family, business and other relations. Although independent directors are encouraged to hold stocks in the firm, their investment should be limited, as befits free-float capital. Rules should describe situations when directors must tender their resignations or automatically be terminated. Age limits for internal directors (between 65 to 70 yrs. of age) and reelection limits for independent directors (just 1 term) are suggested.

The Compensations Committee (OR, 1998, II.7) ensures that the remuneration of directors and top management is linked to individual and corporate performance. Remuneration is reasonable if it approximates the market value of comparable work by a person with similar qualifications. The Compensations Committee examines the items on the remuneration package, taking into account Corporate and Tax Laws: salaries, allowances, bonuses, and benefits (insurance, pension, etc.). The publication of the remuneration packages of directors and top management is preferable to merely citing these as percentage of profits.

The Compliance Committee (OR, 1998, II.6, II.8) oversees the rights of directors to obtain information and to seek advice. So as not to interfere with operations, requests for information should be coursed through the Board Chair or Secretary. Notice should be served if the matter of consultation with an outside expert is confidential.

The director has the duty to inform about herself, family, friends and pursuits for governance purposes. Of particular importance are the guidelines concerning conflicts of interest (a director should abstain from deliberations when she is party, as in sessions concerning reelection or termination, for example), the confidentiality of information (discretion and passivity or the prohibition of "insider trading"), the exploitation of business opportunities in or through the company (for which a corporate director should first seek board approval), and the use of company resources (where the limit of private use lies). The Report believes that these guidelines should be extended to owners of outstanding shares. It may be wise for the Board to reserve for itself decisions over the transactions of such investors.

The Audit Committee (OR, 1998, II.9 through II.12) supervises the flow of information, specially financial data. It makes sure that data are truthful, clear, accurate, timely, prompt, regular and dependable. The "market" includes institutional investors (mutual funds, pension funds, insurance companies, etc. which comprise around 25% of the Spanish stockmarket), regulators, external auditors and the general public. Significant changes in shareholder groups, management, the business environment, or any other factor that could alter stock price should be relayed. The Audit Committee should diligently prepare the General Stockholders' Meeting, the normal venue for such information.

Extra care has to be taken in choosing external auditors. The Report suggests that a firm not represent more than 10% of the auditor's business, to safeguard independence. Aside from conforming to the "generally accepted accounting principles", externally audited reports should be comparable with other reports, avoiding reservations and misleading information. Unfortunately, around 27% of the Annual Reports of Spanish firms contain "limiting clauses and conditions". Annual Reports should assess a firm's compliance with the principles of corporate governance. Finally, the Audit Committee should also evaluate the effectiveness of control systems.

III. Comparative study of ethical–cultural values

The bases for our comparative study are the Cadbury Report from the United Kingdom, the Vienot Report from France, the Report of the Belgian Commission on Corporate Governance and the directives from the National Association of Corporate Directors (NACD) of the United States (Charkham, 1995).

Each of these documents pursues a different purpose (Rodríguez-Llauder, 1995). The Cadbury Report and the Belgian Report seek enhanced credibility for the firm by increasing available information. The Vienot Report was written in reaction to abuses and was meant to control these. Hence, a greater emphasis on the "social interest" of the firm. The NACD directives wish to augment the sense of professionalism among board members. The Olivencia Report was elaborated primarily, though not exclusively, for the privatization of firms.

Another source of differences would be shareholder structures. The concentration of shares in Continental Europe is greater than in the United Kingdom or the United States. The largest single investor in continental countries controls an average of 30% of the votes (up to 50% in Germany and Italy), whereas in Britain and in America, it would be 10% and less than 5%, respectively (The Economist, 1999).

In southern European countries, including Spain, France, Italy and Greece, shares are normally held by banks and family fortunes.

In France, interlocking directorships among *Enarques* are widespread in the CAC 40 firms (The Economist, 1997). In Spain, aside from the concentration in ownership, the shares traded tend to be the same: the top 5 firms of the Ibex-35 account for 65% of the daily exchange, thus distorting the index (Sánchez, 1999). Continental Europe adopts a manager-friendly capitalism, sensitive to job security and the protection of national champions, while Anglo-Saxon countries adhere to a more shareholder-friendly business philosophy.

Corporate and Tax Laws also have a great impact on the behavior of directors. French Laws establish that internal directors comprise at most 1/3 of the board. German firms have two boards: a supervisory, non-executive one (*Aufsichtsrat*) and a management one (*Vorstand*). An increasing number of American boards are dominated by external directors. Stock options and pension benefits, common forms of compensation for American directors, are quite rare and even frowned upon – as with executive compensation disclosure – in some European national corporate cultures. Although French firms make use of share options, they do so to avoid high rates of personal income tax; German firms have been slow to adopt share options due to high capital gains taxes. Furthermore, the pay difference between top executives and regular employees is much greater in the United States than in Europe.

Recently, *Banco Popular*, a major Spanish bank experimented with giving direct compensation only to directors occupying executive posts, to retirees and to academics (Brines, 1999a). But the most controversial development has been the approximately 30,000M pesetas worth of stock options that top *Telefónica* executives stand to earn (Canales, 1999). Although 40% of the Ibex 35 firms offer stock options, these are limited to the Executive Committee and senior executives. *Jazztel*, a new telecom operator is an exception in offering stock options to its 180 employees. This situation is very different from the U.S., where 10% of the employees, specially in the technology sector, have stock options. The uproar over the gains of *Telefónica* executives has triggered modifications in Spanish Tax Laws, such that tax exemptions are to be whittled down from 30% to 2.5%.

Lastly, an outstanding characteristic of Spanish Boards is its youth. According to the Spencer Stuart European Board Index Survey of 1999, the average age of the Spanish director is 55.3 years, more than 6 years younger than her Dutch counterpart. Spanish Boards are also among the least international, with foreigners comprising 8.7%, compared to Swiss Boards which are 29.7% foreign (Lafont, 1999b).

There are three common values that stand out across reports on corporate governance and national corporate cultures: loyalty, due diligence and transparency. We shall now turn to these, and see how they apply to Spain.

Loyalty

Presumably, loyalty is the remedy to the myriad of "conflicts of interest" that beset directors. Yet this misses the fact that loyalty could be "misplaced" or "excessive"; rather than the cure, it could be the cause of "conflicts of interest". Besides, could we really expect loyalty from individuals elected because of their "independence" of thought, from people known to be "value or (self-)interest maximizers"?

To say that loyalty defeats "conflicts of interest" because it induces the director to defend what is best for the firm as a whole is vacuous. Not only does it overlook the difficulty of ascertaining what is best for the firm as a whole. It also forgets that "conflicts of interest" are unavoidable in business. Boards were formed precisely to make sure that conflicts are resolved not through force, but through reason and dialogue.

Loyalty becomes a problem when one considers the title by which a person forms part of the Board. There are different entry criteria, and each indicates to whom loyalty is owed: to management, if one is an internal director, to whoever owns a significant packet of stocks, in the case of external directors, and to the owners of free-float capital, for independent directors. Reinforcing layers of loyalty come through family ties, friendship, and long-term professional association (retirees). In Spain, family ties carry more weight than in other national corporate settings. When one represents institutional investors, such as insurance and pension funds, most likely, she will not be motivated by a desire to gain management control or to influence strategy, but to guarantee the return and the liquidity of investments. Spanish banks have been known to exercise a lot of power as stockholders and creditors. For this reason, it would be preferable to source credit from several banks.

The consequences of the merger between *Banco Santander* and *Banco Central-Hispanoamericano* on the career of Ana Patricia Botín, makes an interesting case for the conflict between corporate and family loyalty (Zamarro, 1999; Brines, 1999b). Previous to the merger, Ana Patricia Botín, daughter of the *Banco Santander* president, was considered the most powerful woman in Spanish finance, being a member of *Banco Santander*'s executive committee, a director, the manager of its wholesale banking business and the chief architect of its overseas expansion. She was the bank's "crown princess". Then came the merger announcement of *Banco Santander* with *Banco Central-Hispanoamericano* on January 15, 1999. It was supposed to be a merger among equals, resulting in a bank with its own personality, culture and values. Among these new corporate values, professionalism and team-work were given special importance. Emilio Botín of *Santander* and José María Amusátegui of *Central-Hispanoamericano* would continue as co-presidents, but it was agreed that Angel Corcóstegui, from *Central-Hispanoamericano*, would be the C.E.O. and Senior Vice-President.

A month after, declarations by sources close to Ana Patricia Botín expressing yearnings for a lost "family business" culture were leaked. This provoked forceful complaints on the part of Corcóstegui who found the new bank's professional culture imperiled. Finally, Corcóstegui prevailed and Emilio Botín had to accept his daughter's resignation from her executive functions in the *Banco Santander Central-Hispano* (BSCH).

Given the dynamics of human relations, it is possible for loyalties to shift – and betrayals to occur – once directors have been confirmed. No

doubt they owe their board seats to whoever sponsored them; but once in, should they still take instructions from sponsors? Or should they use their independent judgment, although this may run counter to the interests of their sponsor? There is an absence in the Spanish document of any concrete directive, unlike in the French Report, where the primacy of the firm's "social interest" is maintained. The Spanish director has greater freedom than her French counterpart. In the Vienot Report, it's as if the director, once elected to the board, severs her ties with the sponsor and acquires an exclusive commitment to the firm's "social interest".

The demand for loyalty countervenes the "independence" required of directors as counselors. This is true not only for the representatives of "free float" capital or "independents", but for other directors as well. "Independence" means being "unattached" or not having loyalties, so as to be fair and impartial. Yet this condition could not be met: directors are there primarily to protect the property interests of owners. Not even in the case of independent directors could this condition be satisfied, for these are often encouraged to make investments to align their stakes with those of the corporation. It is indeed rare to find an independent director whose only input lies with her professional expertise, devoid of ownership interests. And finally, how could directors exercise independence of judgment in their compensations and dividends? This is impossible in for-profit firms.

In mid-1999, the EU Telecoms Commissioner, Martin Bangemann announced that he was accepting a directorship and consultancy post at *Telefónica*. He was reported to receive 1M euros a year for this new job, more than the 870,000 euros a year pension due him as EU Commissioner. Lawyers maintained that there were no violations involved, despite protests from several quarters, including the EU government itself, which threatened to strip Bangemann of pension rights. Bangemann promised not to reveal any confidential information about the telecoms market. Just the same, the EU Commission, to save its already badly tarnished image, decided to include a corresponding restriction in the code of conduct for future commissioners (European Voice, 1999; Segovia, 1999).

There is consensus regarding practices which constitute a "lack of loyalty": insider trading, the (ab-)use of corporate assets for strictly personal purposes, the use of confidential information for private business. . . . It is difficult, however, to defend the "intrinsic malice" of these acts. Such operations tread on the gray areas of the law and are subject to reproach on the basis of the intentions of the agent and other circumstances: e.g. wanting to "milk" the corporation by oneself, without leaving "enough and as good" for the rest. The contention is not that of earning a profit, but one of depriving others of the same opportunity, as fairness requires. Not only a "lack of loyalty" and "greed", but also "envy" on the part of the aggrieved would have to be considered.

Due diligence

A second value for corporate directors is "due diligence". It was formerly held that boards, having selected senior management and created compensation schemes, should simply step back and watch the organization prosper. Only in exceptional circumstances, as a succession problem, threatened insolvency or an MBO, should the board be ready to advise the C.E.O. Such a view is erroneous, for it ignores the responsibility of the board to monitor senior management in an informed way.

In Spanish corporations, "due diligence" means, negatively, that the board is not a social club (Griego, 1984). Given the origin of most corporations in family businesses, it is common that boards be set only to comply with legal conditions. In fact, all the power resides exclusively in the owner-founder and family patriarch. Directors are to behave like rubber stamps and their suggestions are never binding (de Urquijo, 1998).

Another obstacle could arise from the cross-directorships prevalent among major Spanish financial-industrial groups (Lafont, 1999a). Thus, the Ybarras, Zubirías, Icazas, Zabálburus, López-

Dórigas, Oriols, Urrutias and their representatives claim the lion's share of directorships in the *Banco Bilbao Vizcaya* (*BBV*), in the *Iberdrola* power company, in the *Continente* retail chain, and in the *Acerinox* metallurgical concern, for example. Similar arrangements could be found in the *Agbar, Gas Natural, Acesa* and *Hidrocantábrico* group dominated by the Fainé and Brufau families or in the *Corporación Financiera Alba, Banca March, Pryca* and *ACS* group, controlled by the March family. It is impossible to monitor so many fronts equally.

Positively, "due diligence" encompasses good faith, prudence and professionalism. Acting on good faith signifies moral rectitude, the desire to do the corporation no harm, and the intention to act always in the firm's interests. Prudence means discharging duties with care, as a prudent person in similar conditions would. "Due diligence" means, above all, "professionalism". "Professionalism" stands for regular attendance in meetings, adequate information-gathering, the study of issues, financial literacy and legal competence. Being a professional includes the right to rely on the professionalism of others, the confidence in the other members of the team.

Transparency

Transparency means the free flow of information and the disclosure of reasons or motives behind decisions. It is not the exclusive concern of the Audit or Compliance Committees, but of every member of the board. Transparency does not contradict discretion: not all stakeholders have the right to know as much as a director does. There is a judgment-call on the amount, detail and timing of information considered "reasonable" for each category of stakeholder.

Spain comes last in transparency in the 1999 Heidrick and Struggles Report on European Corporate Boards (Polo, 1999). Ibex 35 companies hardly give information regarding the age, tenure, executive responsibilities and cross directorships of its Board; and less than half indicate share ownership.

Information does not only mean power and control, but profit opportunities as well. That is why corporate boards – Spanish ones, too – are very secretive. Such behavior is supposed to shield people from having to explain or justify themselves to prying, and not always benevolent judges. Nonetheless, transparency is our best guard against corruption, for illegal activities thrive when shielded from public view.

In this connection, some basic but effective tests have been devised (Driscoll and Hoffman, 1994). The first is called the "skunk test": directors are supposed to ask themselves, "Does this course of conduct smell?" To find something offensive to the moral sense of smell could be the first indicator of it being wrong, although one may not be able say exactly why. Secondly, there is the "child test": "Would I advise my child to do this?" Knowing the affection and sense of responsibility that a parent has towards her child, behavior that does not pass this test would not be worth carrying out. A variation is "What if my child were to find out?" Such test plays on how much a parent values her child's esteem. Finally, it is recommended that one take the "newspaper test": "Would I like my board to read about this in the papers?" This test concerns not only one's family circle or colleagues, but also the general public, with its affinities and prejudices. Whatever withstands this would, in principle, withstand scrutiny by courts. Probably the most crucial item on which to apply this test would be executive pay (The Greenbury Code, 1995). On the average, directors of Ibex 35 companies receive 16M pesetas a year, although the majority earns only between 5 to 15M pesetas a year.

Although external auditors give a big boost to transparency, present accounting rules and auditing principles require some scrutiny. Not only are standards disparate among firms and countries, but they also encourage "short-termism", an obsession with quarterly earnings figures. After all, the bonuses managers receive are based on short-term performance measures, so they have strong incentives to window-dress financial reports (The Economist, 1998b).

Democratization of the firm or its "Americanization"?

A closer analysis of the reasons motivating reforms indicates a common thrust towards increased stakeholder participation or democratization. Just like liberal thought challenges absolutist power, good corporate governance challenges the concentration of power due to ownership, credit or expertise. Whoever invokes authority or exercises power should be ready to account for it. She should not be intimidated by audits. The democratization of the firm eliminates privileges because all stakeholders are endowed – in theory – with a voice and vote.

These concerns, however, are difficult to balance with bureaucracy and property rights. The dominant economic system places a premium on the stakes of capitalists, rather than on labor. However, certain initiatives to increase employee participation in corporate governance through direct representation, as in German boards, or through employee share-option schemes, as in some British and American companies, have been put into practice.

Once democratization is accomplished, the firm has other hurdles to overcome. First is the possible "tyranny by the majority", where the only right of dissident minorities is that of exit. Second is the dilemma of representation, where the agent is in a quandary whether she should limit herself to her commission or exercise her own discretion, even in ways different from her mandate.

Some quarters suggest that what corporate governance reform seeks is the "Americanization" of firms (Valdmanis, 1999; The Economist, 1996b; Albert, 1993). We would then find ourselves before another version of the shareholder ↔ stakeholder dilemma, clothed in national colors. Spaniards, like their continental European kin, are inclined towards a stakeholder approach, while Anglo-Saxon culture, represented by the British and the Americans, defend the shareholder view. There is no agreement among theorists on which model is superior; and some look for explanations not in the model, but in the unsynchronized business cycles. It is however true that European firms increasingly behave like their American counterparts, not only in corporate governance reform and shareholder activism (The Shareholder Online Handbook, 1999), but also in mergers and (hostile) acquisitions, the setting of profit targets, reengineering, the use of stock options and share buy-backs. A recent study reveals that 9 out of the top 10 firms by market capitalization in Spain are theoretically prey to takeovers (Lafont and Biurrun, 1999). Nonetheless, there are powerful defense measures in place, as golden shares and a 10% statutory limit to voting rights. However, if NYSE listings are a reliable criterion, the handful of Spanish firms (*Banco Bilbao Vizcaya Argentaria, Banco Santander Central Hispano, Endesa, Repsol* and *Telefónica*) indicates that these have been slow in embracing American ways.

Reform measures have focused almost exclusively on "formal" conditions and have neglected "material" ones. The aims of corporate governance reform could not be guaranteed by formalities such as codes of ethics, the separation of powers and the distribution of functions among committees alone (Zurutza, 1999). Studies contesting the positive impact of codes on corporate performance come as no surprise (Buckland and Doble, 1998). Simultaneously, there have been observations that corporate governance reform has been half-hearted (Institute of Chartered Accountants in England and Wales, 1999). Of equal or even greater importance than formalities is a change in the minds and hearts of directors, the renewal and reform of their character. But this would open up an entirely different host of issues that we would have to address separately. . . .

References

Albert, M.: 1993, *Capitalism Against Capitalism* (Whurr, London).

Alvarez, J. L. et al.: 1999, *Prácticas de Gobierno en España* (Estudios y Ediciones IESE, Barcelona).

Aristotle, *Nicomachean Ethics*, 1103 a 17–18.

Biurrun, P. et al.: 1999, 'La gran ofensiva en Latinoamérica', *Actualidad Económica* (May 24–30), 42–43.

Bourse de Bruxelles: 1998, *Rapport de la Commission Belge du Corporate Governance* (Brussels, Belgium).

Brines, J.: 1999a, 'Quién es quién en el consejo del Popular', *Actualidad Económica* (March 1–7), 34–37; 1999b, 'Por qué se va Ana Patricia Botín', *Actualidad Económica* (March 8–14), 80–83.

Buckland, R. and M. Doble: 1998, 'Corporate Governance and the Impact of Cadbury', http://www.summa.org.uk/finalsumma/eaa/eaa95/abstrac ts/232.htm.

Cadbury Committee on Corporate Governance: 1992, 'Code of Best Practice' (The Cadbury Report), London, U.K. (In 1995, a Committee chaired by Sir Ronald Hampel was formed to evaluate the impact of the Report and to revise it.)

Canales, M.: 1999, 'El futuro de las stock options', *El Mundo Nueva Economía* (November 28), 37.

Charkham, J.: 1995, *Keeping Good Company: A Study of Corporate Governance in Five Countries* (Oxford University Press, Oxford/New York).

Comisión Especial para el estudio de un Código Etico de los Consejos de Administración de las Sociedades: 1998, 'El Gobierno de las Sociedades Cotizadas (The Olivencia Report)', Madrid, Spain.

Conseil National du Patronal Française et l'Association Française des Entreprisees Privées: 1995, 'Le Conseil d'Administration des Sociétés Cotées' (The Viènot Report), Paris, France.

Cuervo-Cazurra, A.: 1998, 'La reforma del consejo de administración en España: límites a la aplicación de los modelos anglosajones', *Información Comercial Española. Revista de Economía* (769), 9–21.

de Urquijo, J.: 1998, *El Consejo de Administración. Funciones y Responsabilidad Financiera de los Consejos* (Ediciones Deusto, Bilbao).

Driscoll, D.-M. and W. M. Hoffman: 1994, 'Doing the Right Thing: Business Ethics and Boards of Directors', *Director's Monthly* **XVIII**(11), 1–7.

The Economist: 1996a, 'Shareholder Values', February 10; 1996b, '*Le Defi Americain*, Again', July 13; 1996c, 'A Survey of Spain: In Transit', December 14; 1997, '*Vive le governance*', January 11; 1998a, 'Financial Misstatements', January 17; 1998b, 'Telephones from Toledo to Tierra del Fuego', December 12; 1999, 'The Price of Friendliness', February 27.

European Voice, 1999, 'Bangeman Faces Threat to Pension, Martin Won't Dial Up Any Secrets', July 8–14.

Fletcher, G. P.: 1993, *Loyalty. An Essay on the Morality of Relationships* (Oxford University Press, Oxford/New York).

Goodpaster, K.: 1991, 'Business Ethics and Stakeholder Analysis', *Business Ethics Quarterly* **I**(1), 53–73.

Greenbury, R.: 1995, 'The Greenbury Report on Executive Pay', London, U.K.

Griego, J.: 1984, 'Cómo hacer eficaz al Consejo de Administración', *Nota de Investigación* (0-385-001/DGN-303), IESE, Barcelona/Madrid, Spain.

Hofstede, G.: 1993, 'Europe: Intercultural Conflict and Synergy in Europe', in D. J. Hickson (ed.), *Management in Western Europe. Society, Culture and Organization in Twelve Nations* (Walter de Gruyter, Berlin), pp. 1–5.

Institute of Chartered Accountants in England and Wales: 1999, 'Adding Value in the Boardroom. Building on Cadbury's Success', http://www.icaew.co.uk/depts/td/hampel/cover.htm.

Lafont, I.: 1999a, 'Los mejores y peores consejos de administración', *Actualidad Económica* (May 17–23), 16–30; 1999b, 'Así son los consejos de las empresas europeas', *Actualidad Económica* (November 1–7), 38–46.

Lafont, I. and P Biurrun: 1999, '¿Son opables las grandes empresas españolas?', *Actualidad Económica* (July 26–August 1), 20–25.

National Association of Corporate Directors: 1994, 'NACD Blue Ribbon Commission Report on Performance, Evaluation of CEOs, Boards and Directors', Washington, DC, U.S.A.

(The Olivencia Report: See "*Comisión Especial para el estudio de un Código Etico de los Consejos de Administración de las Sociedades*").

Paine, L. S.: 1996, 'Venturing Beyond Compliance', in K. A. Edelman (ed.), *The Evolving Role of Ethics in Business* (The Conference Board, New York, NY), pp. 13–16.

Polo, A.: 1999, 'España ocupa el último lugar europeo en transparencia', *Expansión* (May 31), 10.

Ralea, F.: 1999, 'Inversiones con rechazo', *El País Negocios* (May 9), 1999, 5.

Rodríguez-LLauder, M. D.: 1995, 'Los Consejos de Administración Vistos desde el Ambito Americano, Inglés y Francés', *Nota Técnica* (0-396-007/DGN-517), IESE, Barcelona/Madrid, Spain.

Sánchez, C.: 1999, 'La CNMV propone que se cree un índice alternativo al Ibex 35', *El Mundo* (June 4), 46.

Segovia, C.: 1999, 'Los juristas de la UE no aprecian 'falta grave' de Bangemann', *El Mundo* (July 8), 33.

The Shareholder Online Handbook: 1999, http://www.bath.ac.uk/Centres/Ethical/Share/3nonex.htm.

Valdmanis, T.: 1999, 'Europe Catches Merger Fever', *USA Today* (March 10).

Zamarro, P.: 1999, 'Botín apuesta por un BSCH profesional', *Dinero* **780** (March 4).

Zurutza, E.: 1999, 'No se cumplen las recomendaciones para el buen gobierno de las empresas', *Expansión* (September 3), 46–47.

Institute for Enterprise and Humanism,
University of Navarre,
31080 Pamplona, Spain
E-mail: ajsison@unav.es or agsison@hotmail.com

Innovation and Ethics
Ethical Considerations in
the Innovation Business*

Yves Fassin

ABSTRACT. In our global economy knowledge-based industry is taking more importance. Recent years have seen the success of an increasing number of start-up companies, most technology-based enterprises financed by private persons or companies, or through venture capital funds and public offering. In many years, those companies are faced at certain critical moments with matters involving intellectual property rights, insider information and raising money. These facts all have an ethical dimension. There is an increasing need for ethical behaviour from all parties involved. A code of conduct of all parties should be applied. This paper describes the growth process of a company and the valuation of an innovation project. It will overview a number of ethical issues, at different stages in the innovation business, and in the lifetime of a start-up company, such as the problems of intellectual property, the confidentiality of information, the negotiation process between the entrepreneur and the financier, the marketing of raising funds and of an IPO, and finally the information and insider trading. The paper concludes with a plea for increased ethical behaviour and the need for rules of best practice for all parties: the inventor, the entrepreneur, the financial investor, and other stakeholders.

Yves Fassin combines a career as an entrepreneur with an academic activity. He is a partner of the Vlerick Leuven Gent Management School and taught technological innvoation at the FUCAM, University of Mons. His research interests include innovation, technology transfer, entrepreneurship, venture capital and IPOs, and business ethical issues in these fields.

In our global economy knowledge-based industry is taking more importance. Recent years have seen the success of an increasing number of start-up companies, most technology-based enterprises financed by private persons or companies, or through venture capital funds and public offering on the stock markets.

Business Ethics covers the very complex relation between ethics and economics and management (Bowie, 1982; Sen, 1987). Applications of ethics in business have concentrated on the relation between ethics and marketing, on the relationship between the firm and its employees, on the relationship of the firm towards their customers and other stakeholders (Garrett and Klonoski, 1986). Recent research in ethics and finance (De George, 1987; Keasey et al., 1997) and in corporate governance have covered the particular problems related to the high growth and public offerings of companies (Fassin, 1993; Wright et al., 1997). On the other hand engineering ethics studies the ethical aspects of production and engineering, with special attention towards product reliability, safety and environmental aspects of new technology. New developments in science have created a new discussion on the ethical aspects in science (Drenth, 1994; Toulouse, 1998) with special attention towards the university-industry collaboration (Comerford, 1987; Kenney, 1987; Fassin, 1991).

The innovation business combines the concerns of both business and engineering ethics. The high-tech growing companies add the sensitive issues of ethics and finance, and ethics and science.

Journal of Business Ethics **27**: 193–203, 2000.
© 2000 *Kluwer Academic Publishers. Printed in the Netherlands.*

The company's growth process

In the old days, innovation was mainly the result of some bright inventor working by himself on technical problems to find a solution on new problems. If he had some entrepreneurial spirit, he invested some of his own savings to set up a company to exploit his invention. When he needed more money he would ask some relatives or friends to participate in his venture. The further development of the company was financed with bank loans and mainly reservations of profits. Years later when the company grew bigger and needed additional capital, some companies could go for an initial public offering on the stock market.

Nowadays things have changed dramatically in the high tech business. It is not possible for a single individual to combine all the intellectual know-how and to finance by himself the development of new ideas.

In most cases new inventions lean on the existing know how developed in laboratories at the universities and in industrial labs. Innovation is not the result of the development of a new idea of a single individual, but needs an interaction of many specialists from different disciplines. This multidisciplinary approach needs teamwork and interaction from market and production. There has been an increasing impact from science in the innovation process.

The other main difference lays in the means: multidisciplinary high tech development needs very specialised equipment and necessitates tremendous financial means, from the early phases on. Except from some big multinationals, or some governmental agencies, it is not possible anymore to find the financial means to launch a new technology-based enterprise by individuals. New forms of financing have risen in the last decades: venture capital companies are active private investors who invest in emerging companies and in start-ups.

Innovation is important for the industry (Lattès, 1988). Business' aim is to create wealth. Innovation leads to new products, new markets and to commercial and financial success. It is worth to analyse the different steps in the evolution from idea to commercial success, and also to study the multiple hurdles to reach this success. As nowadays high technology innovation often leads towards university spin-off companies, special attention will be spent on the specific problems of the university-industry collaboration (Bullock, 1983; Segal Quine, 1985; Van Dierdonck, 1988).

The stages in the innovation process

Most successful innovations derive from some basic idea. An inventor has an idea, and works to develop his idea in some practical realisation, in his garage or in his company. With the increasing importance of science in technology, some bright ideas nowadays also emerge in scientific laboratories, from the researchers' mind. Starting from the new idea, the inventor or researcher wants to test it, and wants to develop his idea towards a first practical application, to the first positive results. Further work leads towards a prototype, the first realisation that can bring the new idea into working. But the work is not finished. The prototype seldom can give satisfaction. The work has to be refined, further study has to be undertaken to overcome some technical problems. This phase is generally called the development phase. The final result is a pre-industrial product. This product can satisfy the technical needs, but further engineering is necessary to reduce the production price in order to meet satisfactory cost price for the product. This is generally done in the phase of upscaling. Once the technical problems resolved and when the production cost arrives at an acceptable cost price level, and when the marketing research gives a positive signal, the product is launched on the market.

Steps in the innovation process

Idea or scientific discovery
Test – research
Prototype
Development
Production – industrialisation
Upscaling
Marketing
Commercial success

The costs and the valuation of an innovation project

The innovation process follows roughly this same schematic sequence, but with a lot of interactions and feedback loops. At each step the cost of the process increases, and so increases the value of the project, or at least the potential value of the potential innovation. The costs increase quiet more than normally expected, in each phase. Even when the first test for the idea can be executed with a reasonable budget, as many innovations that started in a garage, the next phase to a prototype generally are a factor bigger then the first costs. To come to a pre-industrial product requires additional budgets, a few times bigger then previously. Upscaling again requires budgets with a higher magnitude. And to launch a product successfully on a market requires even more important budgets.

It is important to see this evolution in costs related to the stages of the project over time. The costs are rising exponentially. And so is the potential value of the project.

But the success of the launch is not yet guaranteed. The literature on innovation has proven that many new products are not always transformed in successful commercial successes, even if they are technically nice developments. The key to the commercial success is the market. Many reasons can lead to non-success.

The value is function of stage of development and time, and the probability of success. Time reflects the uncertainty. The further in the development, the lower the uncertainty factor, but higher the assessment of the probability factor. This means certainty in case of non-success; in case of success, it will increase the probability factor. It also means that the value of an innovation project is never assured until the final step has been reached successfully. At that time the project value has also increased exponentially, or has decreased towards zero because of rejection from the market.

Value of innovation project =
f (time, probability of success)

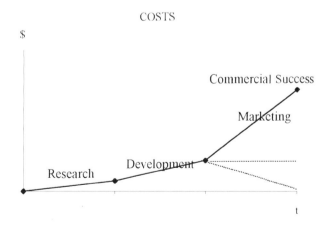

The graph does also show that it takes a lot of time to go through the whole process; the time from idea to commercial success should not be underestimated. Experience has shown that especially in the biotechnology sector it takes more than ten years to develop a product from a scientific discovery and to bring it to the market.

The role of the inventor or researcher

These graphs illustrate that putting a value on an innovative idea is a hazardous operation. It also proves that the brightest idea, without the appropriate technical development and the marketing has little or no chance of success.

While in some case in the past, some inventors could combine the qualities of creativity with marketing and management skills, and built a business by themselves, nowadays this is exceptional. For the researcher or inventor, the graphs should demonstrate that even if they were at the birth of the innovation, without other efforts and complementary competencies, it would be difficult to put their bright idea into a successful product. Some inventors sometimes have difficulties in accepting this fact. Even if their initial idea is the most important step in the whole process, the final success will depend from many other factors. And with the technological evolution and the increasing interdependence of sciences, only exceptions are able to realise the different phases themselves.

It is sometimes difficult to accept for inventors and especially for academicians, that even if they are bright in their field, that technical development and marketing can better be left to specialists, of course with their assistance and support. It is therefor also difficult for an inventor to accept that all the credit and the biggest financial rewards are not returning to him. The industrialisation phase and the marketing need so big financial efforts that no individuals can assume. The same financial logic applies for the university's know how and spin-offs.

The value of the project increases but so do the required resources. A practical consequence is that the valorisation of the know-how will increase if the development of the project is further evolved. The individual inventor has limited resources. So has the university. Its first mission is not to develop a project towards a commercial product, neither to commercialise it. This means that the technology transfer from the university will more often be during the pre-development and prototyping phase. This implies that the value at that stage is lower then the potential value.

The need for complementary resources

The previous description of the first phases in the development of a project means that in order to develop the inventor or researcher needs external help; advice and input from different complementary management disciplines: marketing, finance, law and management expertise. He needs to surround himself with other people to form a team to develop his innovation process into a business. He needs commercial and marketing people to sell his product. He needs financial experts to write a business plan and to raise money. He needs lawyers and accountants as experts. Other consultants and headhunters can help him to find people to form his teams.

The innovation process at the university labs appeal to specific mechanism for transfer (Thomas, 1989; Stipp, 1990; Wade, 1984; Fassin, 1991). For the special case of the university professor, the industrial liaison office of the university will advice for the best solution for technology transfer and provide assistance in the search for industrial or financial partners. Their role is also to try to obtain the best conditions for this transfer. As the value is lower than at a later stage, the risks are higher. It will not be easy to obtain an important down payment. The university liaison office can help in negotiating the best deal. In many cases it will be a risk-sharing agreement with a royalty on future sales. Convincing the professor that a realistic agreement is acceptable will also be the internal advice role of the liaison office.

In some cases and depending from the resources and the evolution in the entrepreneurial spirit of the university, it will be possible to take a higher risk and to participate to the spin-off company. The liaison office can take the initiative and help in writing the business plan.

The need for links with the market

However, another important lesson from the literature on innovation is that the successful product will be the one that meets the customer's need. An innovative success will depend from both the technological advantages and the market's needs. Therefore it is good to have the close interaction between market and technology in the early phase, as feedback from the market will lead to adaptation and increase the chances for success. Both the engineer's and the academic's tendency is often to continue too long in their laboratory. The other frequent error of the engineer and academics is to continue too long to improve the prototype and to look for a perfect technical solution. Again financial imperatives have to be considered. The advantage of an innovation is also an advantage in time. Because also the competition is active. Continuing to improve the prototype will delay the launch, will diminish the time lead and increase the risk that the competitor comes first. And the innovation does not stop with the launch. Continuous improvements will lead to upgrade from the product and a new time advantage to the competitors.

The selection process in the innovation business

But innovation is always a risky business, with a lot of hurdles and only a limited chance for success. As described, the process has several steps. At each step the costs increase, while the rate of success eliminates many projects. Researchers all over the companies and universities in the world have thousands of ideas every day. So do individual inventors. Only a portion them overcome the technical aspects of the idea to bring the idea to a first prototype. Only a portion of these survives the next step of upscaling or industrialisation, to reach an acceptable production cost price. Finally a happy few come to the stage of a product. And there the marketing can transform this product in a commercial success.

This difficult path to success is represented in the figure, with two triangles, the one with the base on top, the other one with the base down. The first represent the funnel shaped inverse triangle illustrates the laborious way from idea to innovative success: on thousand ideas, only one hundred come to a prototype; only ten survive to the technical and industrialisation phase to become a product ready to be launched. Only one becomes a commercial success. The factor ten reflects more an order of magnitude and will depend from the sector.

THE INNOVATION PROCESS

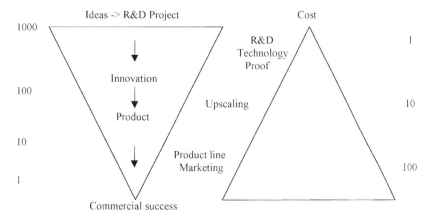

The triangle on the right represents the increase of cost during the successive stages. Development and industrialisation already tenfold the original research costs. Marketing tenfold this again. This also gives the explanation of the low rate of success. In all companies and organisations no matter how big they are, there are limits to the budgets for R&D, so for marketing. This means choices have to be made. A selection of projects, with go and no go decisions are inevitable. Only a selected number of projects can pass the various hurdles. They also need the internal product champion who is fighting to obtain the funds to continue. And probably some projects are killed in this process and never reach the stage of product neither commercial success. On the other hands, this also often creates opportunities for new smaller high technology based companies to work out special products in specific niche markets.

The same selection process applies for those start-up companies: on the hundreds of new-technology based companies not all will succeed; some will die, some will survive, a few one will be success-stories. Growing companies, and especially high technology based firms, need a lot of cash during their expansion phase. Several promising companies did not survive because a lack of finance at some crucial stage in their development.

And only a few exceptions will be exceptional: the Apple, Microsoft, Cisco, PGS.

The principle of venture capital is precisely based on this spread of risk and potential rate of success. On ten investments three may go into bankruptcy, four will survive, two can be a success and will be sold at three to ten times the original investment sum, while one real big success will make ten to hundred times when going public or when sold to a big company.

Some of these companies will be acquired by other technological companies or by bigger multinationals. They will have done their part of the job in the development phase, while the bigger company will be able to integrate this new project in their product-line, with their world-wide marketing and organisation.

Venture capital managers will stress the impor-

tance of a team working together to achieve the firm's objectives. The success of the company will depend from a few key people with preferably different background and viewpoints. The main concern of the CEO is to motivate his team through turbulent times. The case of the industry-university collaboration in innovation is even more difficult. There is a double challenge: it is working with people, and it is working in the difficult discipline of innovation. As all collaboration work between people, it has trials, successes but also failures. Although the recognised advantages of collaboration, some barriers still exist that will prevent a fluent co-operation. Innovation research found three types of barriers: cultural barriers (e.g. mutual incomprehension), institutional (unpadded norms and policies) and operational barriers (problems arising during the project for some rules, norms, etc.) (Van Dierdonck, 1988). Those barriers can occur on both the industrial and university side. One should be aware of these problems when starting some collaboration.

The strategies for valorisation

The implication of the value of the project is important for the strategy of the inventor. The alternatives are either to continue to invest in development and to control the project financially, or to sell the project for a lump sum or with a royalty agreement. The third way is to form a partnership with complementary resources. For both the university project and the individual entrepreneur, a trade off has to be made between risk and rewards. This strategy will lead to different types of collaboration. In the first case, the entrepreneur will invest himself. It will probably take longer to develop his business but he will keep control and the total rewards if he succeeds, he will loose everything in case of failure. The second strategy will transfer the risk to the commercial entity in exchange for a smaller but assured financial reward. The third way leads to sharing the risks and rewards. In case of success, the inventor will receive a small part of a bigger reward.

Strategies for valorisation of the know-how

Traditional strategy	Individual investment	Total success or total failure
Safe strategy	Transfer with license	Risk-free but low rewards
Alternative: partnership	Risk-sharing	Increased chance for expansion

The choice of a strategy will greatly depend on the entrepreneur's objectives and motivation. Traditionally, entrepreneurs chose for the first strategy, universities chose for the second approach. Thanks to the increased availability of venture capital, the third alternative way offers a good alternative to share the risks and to give the necessary financial means for a quicker expansion. For the university the third alternative offers new possibilities to participate in the further development of their projects with increased chances for higher rewards while reducing the risks.

Ethical aspects in the innovation business

Technology based companies have the ethical problems of every production and engineering company concerning safety, product reliability and environmental issues. Some technologies as biotechnology and life sciences do also have the moral dilemmas.

These ethical aspects of the technology itself have received a lot of attention in literature and are beyond the scope of our article.

In addition, many of those technology based growing companies are faced at certain critical moments with matters involving another ethical dimension: intellectual property rights, insider information and raising money. At different stages in the innovation business, and in the lifetime of a start-up company, ethical problems can occur such as:

- intellectual property – origin of the knowledge or know how, external funding
- confidentiality of information
- the negotiation process between the entrepreneur and the financier
- the marketing of raising funds and the IPO
- insider trading

1. *Problems of intellectual property*

In a world where knowledge and know how take an increasing importance, problems of intellectual property arise more often than in the past. The inventor nowadays does not work by himself anymore. Many new inventions are based on teamwork and capitalise on previous foundlings from different disciplines.

The innovation from university laboratories has even more complex problems because of the different status of people working in the labs: from professors with a full employee or governmental citizen status, over their laboratory assistants, doctoral students and student.

The origin of the funding can also affect the ownership of the invention. As in many excellent laboratories, researchers are working on different projects funded by different sources: governmental funds, regional funds, international funding, private companies funding, grants, research contracts, consultancy agreements, etc. Rights-of-first-refusal must be respected.

2. *The confidentiality of information*

In the same way, confidentiality agreements should be respected. While the classical academic rule forces to publish results, working with private companies implies confidentiality of information. The confidentiality problem also occurs for scientific experts working in governmental bodies and in international commissions where they have access to information. In the same way, the venture capitalist companies have access to business plans of many companies in the same sector. They should treat this information confidential.

3. *The negotiation process*

A major issue related to business ethics is the negotiation process at different stages in the life of the company: at the start-up, when raising the start-up capital, during the different rounds of capital increase with venture capital companies, investors, and accountants before going public. The graph illustrating the increasing potential value of an innovation business shows the importance of good timing in the financing rounds. Cash flow forecasts can give another approach for the valuation of the company.

The structuring of a deal is the result of a negotiation process. The exchange is a percentage of the equity of the company against new capital (Higgins, 1998). Entrepreneurs in search of finance are sometimes in a very weak negotiation position because they desperately need the money to grow or even to survive. The deal structure is important for later stages were the entrepreneur's part could be diluted, because he does not have additional private funds for capital increase.

In most cases, the entrepreneur will receive a premium for the achieved work in the past and for the first risk-taking. As he is the key person and the one who will make the success of the company, the venture fund will give him a serious incentive. He has to be the first beneficiary in case of success. In some badly structured deals too large a part of the financial result has been drained towards the venture fund, so that the entrepreneur felt betrayed. This has lead to the term of "vulture" capitalist in the United States. Venture capitalists are seen as people who play with other people's money to make benefits on the back of the hard working entrepreneurs. They are perceived as not taking risks while benefiting from the successes. Their attitude has been criticised as too opportunistic (Amit, 1990; The Economist, 5th October 1991).

Especially for the high tech based companies, one should acknowledge the efforts of the various partners involved in the idea and prototype development. The inventor, the university professor in case of a university spin-off, the university as an institution and the financiers of the project, all deserve their fair share in the new company or a fair compensation for their contribution.

A similar problem of valuation occurs at every stage of capital increase, syndication with other financial partners or trade sale to other companies. The importance of a good timing should be emphasised. In difficult times the entrepreneur is in a weak position against the financiers as venture capitalists or bankers.

4. *The marketing of raising funds and the IPO*

Raising funds is a difficult exercise for every entrepreneur or inventor and even more for an academician. It is a marketing exercise. The inventor has to sell his idea, to prove that he can change his bright invention in a successful commercial venture and to run a business. The entrepreneur has to sell his project, his business plan. Particularly in the high-tech business where big investments have to be made before a possible return in a few years time.

Most problems have been caused by the exit mechanisms of venture capital funds. In order to realise the capital gain – the ultimate objective of the venture manager that does not always correspond to the entrepreneur's objective – the venture funds equity part has to be sold. To maximise their gain, they will try to sell it at the highest price, defined by a new negotiation. Again the position of the venture fund manager is stronger because he has more internal information. The venture capitalist is confronted to the classical problem of insider trading.

The royal road for exit is the initial public offering, the introduction on the stock exchange. Again, in an opportunistic way, and as good financiers, the venture fund and the entrepreneur will choose the timing. Every initial public offering needs a careful preparation and a marketing communication program, with special PR advisors. The IPO is launched with information packages, publicity and press campaign. To have an interesting IPO the investment bankers have to tell a story. They sell the bright future of the company with a brilliant business plan, anticipating in their price-setting the future cash-flows.

5. *The information and insider trading*

We have already mentioned the problem of insider trading in raising funds with venture capital and of going public. Once the company is public, it is subject as all listed company to give information on its result, performance and forecasts. It is then confronted with the classical problem of insider trading. But as high tech stocks and the Nasdaq stock exchange are very volatile, which ask for an additional careful treatment of information. The same problems related to insider information also apply to the staff of the company and to the researchers. The stock options plans have increased the danger of insider (The Economist, August 7th, 1999) trading.

Cases of unethical behaviour

Here again, some short term opportunistic cases have caused great damage to the reputation of the venture capital industry and high tech business. The problem with those successful IPOs is the difficulty in achieving the high result of the forecast. The introduction of some dubious companies on stock exchanges, followed by poor results and decline has created enormous distrust in the stock markets and in the venture capital profession. In some cases the analysts have been too optimistic in the chances of technological breakthrough, or in the huge increases of sales. One should always bear in mind that the innovation business is a risky enterprise, as explained.

Of course there are also cases of unethical behaviour. Although they are the exception, as in most professions. But due to the large publicity and press attention, and also due to the large amount of money involved, they have caused enormous damages.

In some cases, the scientific base of the story was not fully proven, or misleading. In some cases there have been patent fights after the IPO. In some other cases, the key people involved in the start-up of a company left the company short after the introduction. In a few recent cases of insider trading company directors have manipulated the stock prices, and sold their shares before bad news was made public. In some cases, the banks may have a dubious role with conflicts of interests; the IPO of a high-tech company was delayed by the bank for a few months, in the meantime, the shortage of cash was solved with a very profitable mezzanine financing; in another case a bank had been too far engaged with loans to a company, by bringing the company public it solved its own problem. Another conflict of interest appears when CEO of innovative companies are on the Board of investment funds.

Analysts and journalists have a huge power, because their comments or advice will be followed by thousands of individuals. One can question the actual tendency when acknowledging that most analysts are very young and have a finance background, with low technological insight and no experience on running a company.

In another recent case some analyst attacked a public company on the quality of its research. Press articles or Internet messages based on interview without serious scientific value can cause big damages to a firm's stock price.

Conclusion

We have discussed the different steps in the innovation process, with the valuation of projects and the selection process in innovation. The innovation business has created lots of new technology based companies. At different critical moments all these innovative companies are faced with matters involving ethical aspects. The different aspects of ethical components in the innovation business are gathered in the following table with their relative importance during the successive stages of the innovation business.

	Research	Development	Growth	IPO	Post-IPO
Intellectual Property	***	*	*		
Confidentiality of information	***	**	**		
Negotiation	*	**	***	**	
Marketing			**	***	**
Insider Trading				**	***

Innovation is very complex. The Innovation Business combines different disciplines. Ethics and innovation is at the crossroad between ethics and technology, ethics and science, ethics and marketing, and ethics and finance, and ethics and people.

ETHICS AND INNOVATION

The impact of the different domains results in an increased impact of people, from different disciplines that all intervene in the innovation business. The only right answer to the ethical problems is an increased ethical behaviour from all parties. All participants of the innovation process should follow some rules of best practice. All parties: the inventor, the entrepreneur and his team, the financial investor, the venture capitalist, the investment banker, the lawyers and accountants, analysts and journalists should subscribe to the general rules of business ethics and comply to the corporate governance rules.

Note

* Paper presented at the 12th European Business Ethics Network Conference in Amsterdam, October 2nd, 1999.

Bibliography

Amit, R., L. Glosten and E. Muller: 1990, 'Does Venture Capital Foster the Most Promising Entrepreneurial Firms?', *California Management Review* (Spring), 102–111.

Andrews, K. R.: 1989, 'Ethics in Practice', *Harvard Business Review*.

Bowie, N. E.: 1982, *Business Ethics*.

Bullock, M.: 1983, *Academic Enterprise, Industrial Innovation and the Development of High Technology Financing in the United States* (Brand Brothers and Co, London).

Comerford, K. A.: 1987, 'Intellectual Property Rights and the Transfer of Technology from University to Industry', *Industry & Higher Education* (September).

'Conflict of interest on the American Campus': 1982, *The Economist* (May 22). *The Economist 1991* (5th October).

De George, R. T.: 1987, 'Ethics and the Financial Community, An Overview', in O. F. Williams, F. K. Rilly and J. W. Houck (eds.), *The Common Good and U.S. Capitalism* (Washington).

Drenth, P.: 1994, 'La responsabilité sociale et scientifique du chercheur', Premier Congrès de l'Académie turque des Sciences', Ankara, 26 mai, *In Toulouse,* op. cit.

Fassin, Y.: 1991, 'Academic Ethos versus Business Ethics', *The International Journal of Technology Management* (5/6), 533–546.

Fassin, Y.: 1993, 'Ethics and Venture Capital', *Business Ethics* **2**(3) (July).

Flynn, D.: 1991, 'The Critical Relations between Venture Capitalists and Entrepreneurs', *Small Business Economics* **3**(3).

Garrett, T. M. and R. J. Klonoski: 1986, *Business Ethics*, 2nd Edition (Prentice-Hall).

Higgins, R.: 1998, *Analysis for Financial Management*, 5th Edition, Chapter 9 (Irwin McGrew-Hill).

Keasey, K., S. Thompson and M. Wright: 1997,

Corporate Governance – Economic, Management and Financial Issues (Oxford University Press).

Kenney, M.: 1987, 'The Ethical Dilemmas of University-Industry Collaborations', *Journal of Business Ethics* **6**, 127–135.

Lattes, R.: 1988, *L'Apprenti et le Sorcier – Les défis de l'Innovation* (Plon, Paris).

Neave, G.: 1984, 'On the Road to Silicon Valley? The Changing Relationship between Higher Education and Government in Western Europe', *European Journal of Education* **19**(2).

Sen, A.: 1987, *On Ethics and Economics* (Oxford).

Stipp, D.: 1990, 'Academia Seeks to Keep Research "Clean"', *The Wall Street Journal* (March 16).

'The Cambridge Phenomenon': 1985, *Segal Quince & Partners* (Cambridge).

'The trouble with stock options': 1999, *The Economist*(August 7th).

Thomas, D.: 1989, 'Intellectual Property Rights and Wrongs: A University View', *Industry and Higher Education* (March).

Toulouse, G.: 1998, *Regards sur l'Ethique des Sciences* (Hachette Littératures).

Van Dierdonck, R., K. Debackere and P. Desiere: 1988, 'Samenwerking universiteit-industrie: een onderzoek naar de houding van het academisch milieu', *Vlerick School voor Management* (Rijksuniversiteit Gent).

Wade, N.: 1984, *The Science Business, Report on the Twentieth Century Fund Task Force on the Commercialization of Scientific Research* (Priority Press, New York).

Wright, M., S. Thompson and K. Robbie: 1997, 'Venture Capitalists, Buy-outs, and Corporate Governance', in KEASEY et al., op. cit.

Vlerick Leuven Gent Management School,
Bellevue 6,
B-9050 GENT
E-mail: fassin@online.be

Human Rights and Business Ethics: Fashioning a New Social Contract[1]

Wesley Cragg

ABSTRACT. This paper argues that widely accepted understanding of the respective responsibilities of business and government in the post war industrialized world can be traced back to a tacit "social contract" that emerged following the second world war. The effect of this contract was to assign responsibility for generating wealth to business and responsibility for ensuring the equitable sharing of wealth to governments. Without question, this arrangement has resulted in substantial improvements in the quality of life in the industrialized world in the intervening period. I argue that with advance of economic globalization and the growing power and influence of multi national corporations, this division of responsibilities is not longer viable or defensible. What is needed, fifty years after the United Nations Declaration of Human Rights, is a new social contract that shares responsibilities for human rights and related ethical responsibilities in a manner more in keeping with the vision captured by the post war Declaration. I conclude by suggesting some reasons for thinking that a new social contract may be emerging.

KEY WORDS: corporate social responsibility, ethics, globalization, government, human rights, social contract, U.N. Declaraton of Human Rights

Wesley Cragg is the Gardiner Professor of Business Ethics at the Schulich School of Business, York University (Canada) with a cross appointment to the philosophy department. He is responsible for encouraging and coordinating research and curriculum development on the ethical dimensions of public, para-public, not-for-profit and private sector management in the business school. He has published widely in applied ethics, philosophy of law and punishment, philosophy of education and moral, social, political and legal theory. His current research includes issues in business and occupational ethics, environmental ethics, and the use and effectiveness of voluntary codes to regulate international business transactions.

In 1948, the United Nations Declaration of Human Rights was adopted by the United Nations. In the intervening fifty years, it has been formally endorsed by most of the countries of the world. The Declaration itself was a response to human rights abuses that preceded and accompanied the second world war, a global war that created a global moral crisis to which the United Nations Declaration was a collective and global response.

The Universal Declaration began:

Whereas recognition of the inherent dignity and of the equal and inalienable rights of all members of the human family is the foundation of freedom, justice and peace in the world, and

Whereas disregard and contempt for human rights have resulted in barbarous acts which have outraged the conscience of mankind, and, the advent of a world in which human beings shall enjoy freedom of speech and belief, *and freedom from fear and want* has been proclaimed as the highest aspiration of the common people. . . .

The General Assembly:

Proclaims this Universal Declaration of Human Rights as a common standard of achievement of all peoples and all nations, to the end that every individual and *every organ of society* . . . shall strive to . . . secure their universal and effective recognition and observance. . . .

In the years following the proclamation, it came to be widely assumed that the Declaration of Human Rights was addressed principally to governments. In the liberal democracies of the developed world, governments, urged on by their citizens, did proceed to take up the challenge. Human rights were enshrined in constitutions;

the Canadian constitution is an example. Laws designed to protect minorities from discrimination were passed. Provision was made for refugees, though it was not always as generous as it might be. A social safety net was put in place to protect the poor including health insurance, unemployment insurance, old age security and so on. Constitutional guarantees were put in place to restrain governments in the exercise of their powers thus protecting freedom of expression and of the press, freedom of assembly, the right to a fair trial and so on.

One consequence of the assumption that protecting and enhancing human rights was a government responsibility, however, was *a de facto* division of responsibilities between governments and the private sector. The private sector assumed primary responsibility for generating wealth while the public sector accepted responsibility for ensuring respect for human rights including freedom from "fear and want".

Let me describe this arrangement as a tacit social contract. It is this "contract" that I want to examine and evaluate in what follows.

Establishing the existence of a "contract" or a general understanding of respective responsibilities in complex societies or tracing causally its impact is not an exact science. However, I do want to suggest that understanding the division of responsibilities between business and government in the post war industrialized world as forming a tacit social contract is illuminating however difficult it might be to prove its existence. It is illuminating, I want to suggest, because it highlights the striking character of that division of responsibilities and its implications for the way in which much of the private sector perceives its role and responsibilities. Specifically, as generators of wealth, many private sector corporations and business people have been persuaded to the view that their sole social responsibility is simply to maximize profits in lawful ways. As a result, many in the corporate world tend to pay little attention to human rights issues as a corporate responsibility.

The evidence supporting the existence of a tacit understanding of the social responsibilities of the private sector is extensive and multi dimensional. There are for example the theories

of management that emerged in powerfully articulate forms in the sixties and seventies that argued that a corporation's sole obligation is wealth maximization for the benefit of its owners or shareholders whose property it is. As Milton Friedman put it both simply and elegantly, the social responsibility of the modern corporation is simply to maximize profits. To go beyond this objective is a misuse of power that is doomed to fail and in the process impede the exercise on the part of civil authorities of their own proper responsibilities.[2]

One would expect that companies that see profit maximization as their primary obligation to define their social and ethical responsibilities narrowly. They would regard themselves as having a limited number of informal obligations defined by local conventions and culture. These would include obligations owed by the company to employees and the reciprocal obligations of employees to their employer. Other obligations would those be set out in contracts with employees, suppliers, customers, clients and so on. Taken together, these informal and contractual obligations could be anticipated to include: honesty in financial transactions, respect for company property, avoidance of conflict of interest, meeting contractual obligations, respect for the law and respect for basic rules of civility.

One would also expect that when companies with this management orientation went beyond their ethical duties narrowly defined and their legal obligations, it would be for clearly defined public relations purposes governed by enlightened self interest.

In short, as Milton Friedman suggested, where the primary obligation is wealth maximization, obligations to stakeholders can be expected to be defined by the law, prevailing ethical customs and good public relations.

There is a good deal of evidence to suggest that this view has become the dominant view since the second world war. The codes of conduct that have become common features of corporate policy and public relations in the last three or four decades are one rich source of supporting documentation.[3] What they reveal is a focus on "measures designed to protect the firm from wrongful acts by its employees".[4] That is to say, the primary purpose of codes of conduct historically has been the protection of the corporations. Public relations also emerges as a key factor in this regard. Thus, a 1978 U.K. study of advertising codes of ethics around the world found that for example "industry will dedicate resources to code administration only if it expects benefits such as consumer goodwill or the removal of government legislation", a view that studies of Canadian and American codes have echoed.[5]

Further evidence comes directly from the private sector itself. A good example is a statement by François Vincke Secretary General of PetroFina, who says in a recent discussion of the International Chamber of Commerce's campaign against bribery that "until recently, . . . corporate responsibility was dictated by the law, or to put it in even simpler terms: the ethical code of a company was the criminal code".[6] Perhaps even more persuasive is a report to the OECD by a business sector advisory group which states categorically that: "Most industrialized societies recognize that generating long-term economic profit is the corporations primary objective."[7] The authors of the report acknowledge that ethics and ethics codes have a clear place in corporate governance whose goal is profit maximization. However, those ethical values must connect directly or indirectly to enhancing the bottom line. Furthermore, corporations that go beyond these ethical parameters should disclose their social agenda. The implication is clear. Commitment to respect human rights in international commerce even where it is not mandated by law implies a willingness to diverge from the goal of maximizing long term economic profitability.[8] There is no parallel suggestion that companies that propose not to respect international human rights and other ethical standards in their operations disclose this fact as well. Thus, implicit among the assumptions of the report is the tacit understanding that the primary ethical obligation of a modern corporation is to maximize profitability within the constraints of law. This implication is reinforced by the report's suggestion that where important social objectives are at stake, governments will have to assume the leadership position.[9]

This view has come to dominate the thinking not only of business but also of governments and international economic institutions established to deal with the growth of international trade. Its effect has been to separate economics, which in the minds of many means "the science of profit maximization", from any ethical values beyond those required to ensure the achievement of the corporations primary objective, namely profit maximization.

The post war social contract evaluated

The post war period has seen remarkable growth in respect for human rights and economic wealth for industrialized countries. While not everyone has shared equally in the wealth generated, it is unarguable that the economic wealth available to the citizens of the industrialized world today is many times greater than the wealth available to citizens of the same countries either before or after the war. Respect for human rights has also become an entrenched feature of the industrialized world's political and social systems. Once again, not everyone has benefited equally. But it is surely evident that human rights and related moral principles are more widely respected and constitutionally entrenched than was the case fifty years ago. The benefits have been enormous.

We might therefore describe the outcome of the tacit social contract that has guided post war economic development in the developed world as follows: **profit maximization + a free market + the law = economic wealth (development)**.

This formula, though apparently widely endorsed, has none the less come under considerable scrutiny in recently years. Two factors have been particularly influential. First is a series of "moral crises" involving illegal or unethical conduct on the part of employees and senior management acting in what they thought was the best interests of their employers that resulted in significant damage to a number of large and apparently successful corporations. What these crises have revealed is that the mantra of profit maximization can work both for and against corporations and their shareholders by rationalizing unethical and illegal actions. Cutting ethical corners, which many have come to believe is at least sometimes the price that tough minded business people have to pay to compete successfully, can backfire resulting in serious public relations costs and financial penalties.

The Lockheed bribery scandal in the late 1970's was for many the first clear warning sign. Both the actions of Lockheed senior management and subsequent investigations on the part of the U.S. Senate made it painfully clear that respected business leaders were prepared to condone bribery in foreign business transactions if that was what it took to beat the competition. Particularly important for our purposes, however, was the fact that those condoning corruption saw it as justifiable in the international market if it did not involve breaking the laws of the corporation's own country or what were seen as the moral conventions of the country in which it took place. Even more insidious was what appeared to be an implied suggestion that similar conduct might also be justified in the home market if competing successfully demanded it. This conclusion was relatively easily rationalized if law was equated with law enforcement and risks associated with skirting the law were carefully and rationally calculated.

The Bophal disaster further illustrated ambiguities about how the social contract was to be interpreted in international commence. Against what laws and environmental regulations should management be judged, India's or those of the country in which a company was headquartered, in this case the United States? What moral conventions, for example with regard to health and safety standards, should prevail, those of the host country or those of the parent?

Increasingly, companies also have also begun to realize that the mantra of profit maximization can be turned against a corporation when it becomes the frame of reference for individual employees. This knowledge in turn has made it more and more difficult for senior management to accept the idea that "business is business and ethics is ethics" particularly when confronted with employee fraud and other forms of unethical activity,[10] a lesson driven home for many by the collapse of Barrings Bank.

For many, what these developments have stimulated over the past two decades is the growing realization that ethics and business are much more closely connected than the tacit social contract, forged in the post war period, would suggest. The remedy offered has been to develop better articulated and more robust understandings of the role of ethics in leadership and corporate culture. The result has been the growth of interest in corporate codes of conduct that set out acceptable standards of conduct for both corporations and their employees.

What is more, decisions to create codes and build more ethical corporate cultures have had some surprising results. Many corporations have discovered that substantial positive benefits can flow from building a reputation as an ethical company. Employees prefer to work for ethical companies. A reputation for ethical business practices attracts better qualified, better motivated job applicants. Employee morale and public relations benefit. Long term profitability can be enhanced and so on. These discoveries have added additional weight to the view that ethics and business are related and that indeed there is a place for ethics in free market economies.

The difficulty is that the resulting codes are largely self serving. Their primary function, as Craig Forcese points out in his two volume study for the International Centre for Human Rights and Democratic Development (Montreal, Canada), has been to ensure that the corporation and its employees meet their reciprocal obligations to each other and to the law and act in ways that enhance the corporations public image. Hence corporate codes have not been extended, for the most part, to cover issues like respect for human rights.

Of course, human rights are covered in the country in which corporations are headquartered since they are embedded in the legal structures of the industrialized world. Hence, in those contexts explicit reference to human rights values is redundant. However, the laws of industrialized states do not as a rule extend beyond their borders. Hence they do not govern corporate operations abroad, specifically in the developing world. As a result, current interest in ethics codes has not altered in any fundamental way the post war social contract.

The second factor relevant to an evaluation of the post war conception of the social responsibilities of corporations is globalization. Globalization is a complex phenomenon and not easily characterized accurately. What can be said, however, is that it has had dramatic impacts on the legal environment in which corporations, particularly multinational corporations, conduct business. These changes in turn have significant implications for corporations and the post war social contract.

First is the fact of corporate power. The largest transnational corporations have budgets that dwarf those of most of the world's nations. This power has been enhanced by corporate mobility. In today's world, corporations have a great deal of freedom in deciding where to do business. They can choose the countries in which they invest. They can choose their suppliers. And their suppliers can choose with remarkable freedom where in turn they will produce the goods and services they offer. An equally important parallel development has been advances in communications technology that allow the movement of capital virtually instantaneously from one country to another.

The effect of these developments has been to give multinational corporations remarkable freedom to choose the legal systems that will govern their operations. Corporations are now free to seek out those environments in which the laws in place provide the most favourable conditions for maximizing profits. This fact in turn has given corporations a powerful tool for persuading the countries in which they do business to create a favourable legal environment, namely one that puts the fewest possible regulatory constraints on the conduct of business. Thus, various states have made themselves into havens for firms seeking to avoid tax and banking restrictions, corporate disclosure and other regulatory regimes in their home country.

Globalization has also provided nation states with an incentive to engage in "regulatory competition". The temptation to attract investment by promising a legal environment that minimizes labour or environmental standards, for example,

is obvious. The result has been what some have described as a "race to the bottom."[11]

In contrast, while globalization has strengthened the capacity of multinational corporations to choose and shape the regulatory environment in which they operate, it has weakened the capacity of nation states to regulate business activity. Law as we know it is the creation of nation states. The jurisdiction of national legal systems is bounded by the principle of extraterritoriality limiting the capacity of states to project their domestic law abroad. The ability of states to control the legal environment regulating international commerce has been further weakened by free trade agreements such as NAFTA and the WTO.[12] The effect of these factors both apart and in combination has been to put much of the activity of multinationals beyond the effective reach of any one country's legal system.

Parallelling these developments has been the emergence and increasing importance of transnational agencies and institutions, for example the OECD. However, to date, few if any of these agencies and institutions – the European Union is the single obvious, but still limited, exception – have been willing or able to stand proxy for the state, to make regulatory standards effective across national boundaries. Even when they are able to "legislate" (e.g. the ILO) many countries refuse to treat such regulatory standards as legally binding until and unless they are expressly incorporated into domestic law. When they are able to "adjudicate" (e.g. the United Nations or the World Court) they seldom have at their disposal effective regimes of enforcement, and sanctions must still be applied by states.

Nor is globalization the only obstacle to state regulation. The popularity of neo-conservative policies has led many governments in the developed world to reduce state regulation of the economy, taxation and state expenditure thus liberating market forces and, hopefully, stimulating investment, jobs and general prosperity. While the state has by no means disappeared and has even deployed its coercive powers more vigorously in certain fields of social control, for example the bribery of foreign public officials, in many areas, business is being freed from many of the constraints which had been imposed over half a century of interventionist state policies.[13]

The result of these domestic and global shifts is the apparent emergence of what might be called a regulatory vacuum with regard to many aspects of international commerce. It is a vacuum furthermore which many corporations have shown considerable willingness to exploit. Thus, it is now painfully obvious that many business leaders are prepared to ignore some of the most basic norms of human behaviour in the name of profit maximization. It is equally obvious that many of their competitors feel compelled to follow their lead or lose an important competitive advantage.

What are the implications of these developments for an evaluation of what I have described as the economic assumptions underlying the post war social contract, namely that "free markets + profit maximization + the law = economic wealth (development)"? It would appear to be this. Where corporations are able to control the legal environment that governs their activities then "law" drops from the equation. When law is removed from the equation, the formula equates unconstrained profit maximization with the generation of economic wealth and development.

The most appropriate moral characterization of unconstrained profit maximization is greed. It is perhaps unsurprising, therefore, given the account just offered, that we have seen serious efforts over the past two decades, particularly on the part of a few private sector commentators and "cutting edge" business tycoons, to rehabilitate greed. The 1980's, for example, are now widely known in North America as the greed decade. It was a decade in which a few enormously "successful" entrepreneurs toured business schools extolling the virtues of greed. It was also a decade in which an undisciplined pursuit of profits caused a spectrum of disasters from the wide spread collapse of financial institutions (in the United States, for example) to the destruction of fishing stocks that had been the source of livelihood and subsistence for communities for centuries (in Canada's Maritime provinces, for example). And it was a decade that ended in a damaging recession from which many

communities in the industrial world began to recover only after almost another decade steady economic growth.

In 1990's, the collapse of the "tiger" economies and the spread of "the Asian flu" is widely agreed to have involved two factors. The first was the lack of accountability and the apparently irresponsible use of power on the part of Asian financial institutions and conglomerates. But equally important has been the pursuit of profits at any cost on the part of investment mangers and financial institutions in the industrialized democracies.[14]

Hedge funds provide an excellent example of management for profit maximization in a global economy in which legal constraints are minimal. These funds are managed with a view to making as much money as possible in as short a period of time as possible for wealthy investors. Global financial markets are largely unregulated. Hedge funds exploit that fact for the benefit of their managers and shareholders. In the process, they have been known to seriously destabilize financial systems around the world.

The story of Long-Term Capital Management illustrates the phenomenon. This hedge fund was managed by some of the world's most gifted and knowledgeable money managers who used the financial resources of some of the world's largest and most powerful financial institutions and their own talents to gamble on the movement of money markets. The result was the near collapse of the financial systems of the industrialized world, an outcome that was avoided only by the intervention of the American Federal Reserve Board.[15] In reviewing these events, surely the name, Long-term Capital Management, is not without significance. Neither is the fact that two of the managers of the fund at the time of its collapse were Nobel laureates. But perhaps most important is the obvious implication that greed under the guise of profit maximization can have very destructive impacts on a global market economy.

In this environment, ethics that goes beyond the bounds of corporate self interest is seen as not simply irrelevant to economic development but also an impediment forcing corporations to choose between ethics, including respect for human rights, and profits. Equally import, there is no evidence that an economy built simply on unconstrained profit maximization will result in economic development let alone minimally equitable development of the sort that has characterized the post war economies of the industrialized world.

How then are these post war deveopments to be characterized, ethically speaking? As already noted, the unrestrained pursuit of profit maximization is simply another word for greed. And greed has been condemned as personally and socially destructive by all of the world's great religions and by moral leaders at virtually every stage of the development of human civilization. Furthermore, there is today no shortage of evidence confirming that view. What that evidence suggests is that unrestrained profit maximization or greed is the enemy not the driving force of a free market economy.

Building a new social contract

What then are the lessons to be learned from the post war experience? The first, surely, is the need to reexamine the ethical foundations of market economies and the relative responsibilities of the private and public sectors in ensuring that business activity leads to equitable economic development. A second and equally important lesson is that events provoking global crises and changes can provoke the kind of serious rethinking of responsibilities that seems now to be required. The 1948 Declaration of Human Rights stands as a powerful example, coming as it did as a response to the moral crisis provoked by the horrors of the second world war. A second example is the rethinking that many corporations have undergone in the past three decades faced with moral crises caused by ethically questionable state and corporate conduct.[16] Most recently, events in Seattle in response to World Trade Organization meetings designed to facilitate further economic globalization have provoked calls for serious reevaluation of the values driving the new economy. A third lesson, however, must be added to the previous two. As was the case in 1948, events over the past half century have

given rise to resources, insights and experience that are now available to guide the process of reexamination and development of new standards if we choose to use them.

Let me conclude by highlighting some of those resources, insights and experience. Note first that in response to the damaging effects of corruption on economic development, some of the world's most influential international economic institutions (e.g. the World Bank, the International Monetary Fund, the Asian Development Bank) are now beginning slowly to accept that ethics and economics are integrally related. One consequence of this reexamination is the recently concluded Organization for Economic Cooperation and Development convention calling on member countries to criminalize the bribery of foreign public officials. This convention has emerged from the realization on the part of a number of powerful multinational corporations that corruption is inconsistent with the operation of a market economy and is a serious impediment to economic development. Equally important has been the realization that the problem of corruption cannot be solved by individual corporations or the public or private sectors acting alone. Finally, events leading up to the creation of the convention have illustrated the impact that NGOs, Transparency International in this case, can have in bringing about coordinated actions by national governments and international institutions in dealing with this kind of global problem.

The OECD and it nation state members have also developed Corporate Governance Guidelines and Guidelines for Multi National Enterprises. In both cases, there is evidence that the industrialized nations and their international institutions are moving beyond understandings of corporate social responsibilities that have dominated corporate and government thinking since the second world war.

Second, faced with the need to provide principles and codes to guide corporations in the global market place, coalitions of business leaders, religious leaders and members of civil society are forming with a view to articulating model international codes of conduct. Two examples are the *CAUX Round Table Principles for Business* and *An*

Interfaith Declaration by Christians, Muslims and Jews. The Interfaith Declaration builds on the values of justice, mutual respect, stewardship and honesty. The Caux Principles are grounded on two moral concepts, the Japanese concept of "kyosei" which means living and working together for the common good, and the concept of human dignity. Both these statements give a central place to respect for human rights in business activity.

Third, a number of governments have begun to develop codes for the conduct of international business. A good example is the "Standard of Principles for Canadian Business". This code highlights respect for human rights and social justice. The American government has also published a statement on Model Business Principles and has become heavily involved in negotiations with American multinational companies in the apparel industry. And while these efforts cannot be said to have been particularly influential to date, they do indicate a growing awareness that ethics has a serious role to play in the private sector.

Fourth, increasingly, multinational corporations too are recognizing that the old social contract is no longer valid. The best indication of this is the development of corporate codes that explicitly recognize that one of the central ethical obligations of business is to ensure respect for human rights in their own operations. An example is the Code of Conduct for Alcan Aluminum Ltd., a Canadian multinational company in the aluminum business. This code states that "Alcan is guided by principles of non-discrimination and respect for human rights and freedoms". Placer Dome, a Canadian mining company, is a second example of a multinational corporation that has recently made a public commitment to operating world wide in accordance with principles of sustainable development which include respect for the human rights.

What these developments indicate is that segments of the business community are increasingly aware that ethics and economics are closely related. Thus, the Pacific Basin Economic Council Charter on Standards for Transactions Between Business and Government links good

governance and economic growth and calls for honesty, integrity, transparency and accountability in business transactions as a key to building public confidence in business and government.

Fifth, civil society is beginning to play a central role in the growing awareness that respect for human rights is a private sector as well as a public sector responsibility. International coalitions are beginning to create new benchmarks and tools for assessing corporate social performance. AA1000, developed by the Institute for Social and Ethical Accountability,[17] is a first attempt to generate an internationally recognized auditing standard. SA8000 is a performance oriented labour rights standard linking directly to the work of the International Labour Organization. SA8000 is intended to play a role in social accountability similar to the ISO environmental management standards that are now widely used to encourage environmentally responsible business practices. These initiatives are slowly becoming influential factors reshaping public and corporate understandings of the responsibilities of transnational corporations.

Finally, perhaps of most significance is the leadership being offered by a small number of transnational corporations that have committed themselves to competitive business practices consistent with respect for human rights in all aspects of their operations. What is unique about these corporate leaders is their commitment to allowing and encouraging independent evaluation and monitoring of the impact of their codes on the way they do business. An excellent recent example is a decision on the part of Levi Strauss, a large multinational corporation in the apparel industry whose code sets out "Terms of Engagement" for its suppliers that require respect for employee human and labour rights, to obtain an independent evaluation of the effectiveness of its "Terms of Engagement" in its business operations in the Dominican Republic. In pursuit of this objective, Levi Strauss engaged a group of four NGOs including Oxfam (England) to undertake an independent study. That study has now been concluded and its results are publicly available. This private sector/civil society "partnership" model as a way of building ethics back into the global market is now being explored by corporations in manufacturing, resource extraction and retailing around the world.

What then is to be learned from these developments?

1. We need a new social contract to frame business activities in the emerging global market place. The wide spread view in the private sector that the protection of human rights is a government, not a corporate responsibility is not tenable in a global economy. As the Pacific Basin Economic Council points out in its Charter, the purpose of trade liberalization is to promote development that increases living standards. Both traditional wisdom and recent experience demonstrate that domestic or global markets that ignore internationally recognized ethical norms do not promote economic development and improve living standards. What they do promote is the reallocation of existing wealth from those who are already poor to those who are already rich.

2. The new social contract must include recognition on the part of the business community that they have an obligation to operate in all aspects of their operations within the framework of policies and codes that encompass respect for human rights and other values of fundamental human importance, for example environmental protection.

3. The new social contract must acknowledge that building respect for fundamental human values in the private sector requires business and government partnerships. It is clear that national government and international regulation is essential to creating a level economic playing field for the conduct of international commerce. It should be equally clear that government and international regulation is require to protect the market and those it is designed to benefit from the worst vices of an outdated business culture which is prepared to tolerate and even encourage crony, casino and rogue capitalism and where greed is extolled as the driving force of business activity.

4. The new social contract needs to ensure a significant role for civil society in monitoring the adherence of corporations to the codes they adopt. This cooperation should be based on private sector/civil society partnerships whose goal is to work together for benefit of all stakeholders.

5. Finally and perhaps most important, we need to remind ourselves, as Gandhi and others have pointed out, that commerce without conscience is a formula for human exploitation, not human development.

Notes

[1] This research was funded in part by a SSHRC Strategic Funding Grant in support of a York University project entitled "Voluntary Codes: The Regulatory Norms of a Gobalized Society?". The paper was first read to a conference in Bangkok, Thailand on Human Rights and Business Ethics marking the 50th anniversary of the UN Declaration of Human Rights. The Bangkok conference was funded in part by the Canadian International Development Agency. I would like to thank the Social Sciences and Humanities Council and CIDA for their support. For further information about the voluntary codes study, please contact Wesley Cragg.

[2] See for example: "The Social Responsibility of Business is to Increase Profits" in The New York Times Magazine (Sept. 13, 1970).

[3] American surveys indicate that "by the late 1980's as many as 77% of large U.S. corporations had some sort of corporate code of conduct". "A 1981 survey of 125 of the largest Canadian businesses ranked by revenue found that 49% of the 51 responding corporations had 'corporate statements of objectives'" (Forcese, 1997, p. 14).

[4] Ibid., p. 14.

[5] Ibid., p. 12.

[6] Vincke et al., 1999, p. 15.

[7] Ira M. Millstein (Chairman), April 1998.

[8] Ibid., p. 25.

[9] Ibid., p. 70.

[10] Recent studies indicate the dimensions of the problem. A study by a Canadian accounting and consulting firm recently revealed that large Canadian corporations each lost on average $1.3 million (Can.) from fraud in 1997. Similar studies in the United States have revealed that white collar crime may cost the private sector as much as $100 billion (U.S.) each

year. In 1994, a study of over 4000 U.S. employees found that 31% of employees surveyed had observed conduct at work over the course of a year that violated either the law or the policies of the company for which they worked. Further, fewer than half of the 31% reported the misconduct they had observed to their employer.

[11] See, for example, Roy Culpeper and Gail Whiteman's analysis in "The Corporate Stake in Social Responsibility" (Culpeper et al., 1998).

[12] The ongoing dispute over European Union regulations governing the import of bananas and the conflict between Europe and Canada over the export of beef that has been exposed to genetic engineering are obvious cases in point. In both cases, attempts to regulate goods has been struck down by the WTO.

[13] See for example, Arthurs, 1997.

[14] For an interesting discussion of these and other aspects of the Asian economic crisis see Jomo, 1998.

[15] See for example comments attributed to Paul Volcker, former chairman of the U.S. Federal Reserve Board, by Mathew Ingram in *The Globe and Mail*, Monday, Sept. 13, 1999. In an article entitled "The world according to Paul Volcker", he is said to have described the activities of Long Term Capital as completely unregulated and speculative. He is described as saying further that their activities threatened to destabilize a substantial portion of the U.S. financial industry.

[16] I have in mind here examples like South African apartheid, corporate moral crises like the Lockheed, Bophal, Exon Valdez scandals, and the collapse of the "tiger" economies in the 1990's. Most recently, a Canadian Oil Company, Talisman, has been faced with scrutiny on the part of the Canadian and American governments, INGO's in Canada and abroad and a number of Canadian and American pension funds. At issue is its participation in an oil extraction and export project in an oil field in an area of the country wracked by civil war. The controversy has depressed the value of its shares. In response to the criticism, the company has had to examine its operating policies. It continues to defend its investment and involvement in the Sudan but is also beginning to take steps to define its ethical obligations. It has also signed a code of conduct for Canadian companies doing business internationally that recognizes that corporations have obligations to protect and respect human rights in their international operations.

[17] Located in London England.

References

Arthurs, H. W.: 1997, ' "Mechanical Arts and Merchandise": Canadian Public Administration in the New Economy', *McGill Law Journal* **42**(1), 29–61.

Culpeper, Roy and Gail Whitmen: 1998, 'The Corporate Stake in Social Responsibility', *Canadian Corporations and Social Responsibility*, Canadian Development Report 1998 (Reneuf Publishing, Ottawa, Canada), pp. 13–35.

Forcese, Craig: 1997 (No. 1), *Commerce with Conscience: Human Rights and Corporate Codes of Ethics* (International Centre for Human Rights and Democratic Development, Montreal, Canada).

Forcese, Craig: 1997 (No. 2), *Putting Conscience into Commerce: Strategies for Making Human Rights Business as Usual* (International Centre for Human Rights and Democratic Development, Montreal, Canada).

Jomo, K. S.: 1998, *Tigers in Trouble* (Zed Books, London and New York).

Millstein, Ira M. (Chairman): 1998, *Corporate Governance: Improving Competitiveness and Access to Capital in Global Markets*, A Report to the OECD by the Business Advisory Group on Corporate Governance, Organization for Economic Co-operation and Development (OECD, Paris, France).

Vincke, François, Fritz Heiman and Ron Katz: 1999, *Fighting Bribery: A Corporate Manual* (International Chamber of Commerce, Paris, France).

Schulich School of Business,
York University,
4700 Keele St. – 2006-SSB,
Toronto, Canada M3J 1P3
E-mail: wcragg@schulich-yorku.ca

✓

1.3.2
21.1
21.7

0109
011012